1500/1

MANPOWER AND MANAGEMENT SCIENCE

Editors

D. J. Bartholomew
Professor of Statistics, University of Kent

A. R. Smith
Chief Statistician, Civil Service Department

Lexington Books
D.C. Heath and Company
Lexington, Massachusetts
Toronto   London

Foreword

by Sir William Armstrong GCB MVO

President of the Manpower Society

I am delighted to have this opportunity to put on record my gratitude to the authors of the many papers included in this volume for agreeing to their being published in this form for the benefit of the Manpower Society.

The Manpower Society was conceived as a necessary bridge between the many specialisations and organisations which have an interest in manpower management. We view it as an additional facility for members of other Societies and Institutes, and not as a rival to any established institution. It is immensely encouraging therefore to see this tangible evidence of very real cooperation between one of these established institutions, The Institute of Management Sciences, and our own new Manpower Society.

I am pleased, too, to be able to express thanks to Professor Samuel Eilon who, as Chairman of the XVII International Conference of TIMS, so readily agreed that the papers which were originally prepared for his Conference should be published in this way. I look forward to seeing many more examples of fruitful cooperation of this kind.

London
September 1970

Foreword

by Professor Samuel Eilon

Chairman of TIMS Conference

When I started as chairman to plan the programme for the 17th International Conference of TIMS (The Institute of Management Sciences), which was held at Imperial College in London in July 1970, I was very conscious of the increasing interest in recent years in manpower planning and the important role that management scientists are beginning to play in this field. The interest in manpower planning manifests itself at various levels: At the national level, where the problem is of producing men and women with the appropriate skills to match the requirements of the economy; and at the company level where models of aggregate flow in the organisation need to be constructed.

There is also a realisation that in addition to the classical micro models of assignment of manpower to given arrays of tasks (models which are included in standard courses on linear programming), there is a need to study decisions relating to manpower planning on a much longer time-span than the one implied in assignment models: decisions relating to recruitment, to training and to promotion policies, decisions which cannot be made without reference to the corporate planning activity of the enterprise as a whole and whose outcome cannot be subject to instant evaluations. That attention should be devoted to manpower planning at this strategic level is obvious even on economic grounds alone, particularly in firms where the wages and salaries bill constitutes a significant proportion of total expenditure. But the reasons associated with sound planning are even more compelling, since some manpower resources are more scarce and take much longer to acquire and to prepare for the task than other resources.

I therefore decided to include a session on manpower planning in the conference programme. But the stream of high quality papers submitted soon necessitated no less than three sessions (the largest number of sessions devoted to any one topic). These were chaired by Mr. A.R. Smith (of the Civil Service Department), Mr. R.L. Hopps (of the National Westminster Bank Ltd.) and Professor D.J. Bartholomew (of the University of Kent).

The papers attracted a great deal of attention and good audiences, and I was delighted when further initiative was taken to collect some of the papers together. I very much hope that this volume will stimulate management scientists to devote further efforts to the study of the many intricate problems that we have to face in the field of manpower.

Editors' Introduction

There has recently been a remarkable growth of awareness of the need to improve the efficiency of manpower management. One consequence has been the increased interest in the possibilities of applying the concepts and techniques of a wide range of scientific disciplines to manpower problems.

It has come to be realised that manpower planning, manpower utilization, motivation, remuneration systems, career development, organisation of enterprises, selection, education and training and personnel management generally, are all inter-related aspects of manpower management. It is increasingly realized that the problems encountered in the management of a firm, of a military unit, of a university, of a Government department, and of a whole economy have many features in common. These arise from the fact that all these organizations are composed of people — people who have wills of their own which are liable to make them reluctant to be regarded simply as 'factors of production' or resources to be allocated. They have qualities, beliefs and aspirations which those who manage them must take into account. Even so, people in the aggregate tend to conform to patterns of behaviour which are in many respects capable of being measured and codified: in other words, they can be subjected to study by scientific methods and the results can provide a framework within which policy or executive decisions can be taken on a basis of information as opposed to hunch, intuition or sheer prejudice.

The rapid increase in the amount of work done on the development of scientific manpower management is reflected in the large number and wide range of papers which were presented at the 17th International Conference of the Institute of Management Sciences in July 1970. So great was the number of papers offered that it became necessary to increase the number of sessions devoted to manpower from one to three. Even this increase did not allow more than the barest minimum of time for discussing each paper.

Almost all of the papers given at the Conference are included in this volume. The exceptions are a paper by J.M. Keenan (Western Michigan University) which, in deference to the firm which was the subject of study, is not being published and which was presented at the Conference only in outline; a paper by R.M. Oliver (University of California, Berkeley) which, with the agreement of the Editors, has been withdrawn from this volume and is being published instead in a volume of collected papers by that author; and part of the paper by Drinkwater and Kane (Civil Service Department, UK) which is not being published in the volume because of space constraints but which will probably be published elsewhere as a self-contained paper. A paper by Paul Weinstein (Maryland State Executive) which was prepared for the Conference but not in the event presented on that occasion, is nevertheless included in this volume.

The division by subject matter adopted at the Conference is reflected in the ordering of the papers which follow. The first group deals with the behavioural and organizational aspects of manpower management. The way in which manpower is organized and relationships within the organization have a strong influence on efficiency. So also can the organization's ability to adapt to meet changed circumstances. Both of these aspects are covered by the papers in this group. Some contributors like Wilson and Rooney take a broad overall view of organizations and offer a framework for thinking about their nature and mode of operation. Others, represented here by Mingo and Prijatoff, bring the particular techniques of the behavioural sciences to bear on manpower problems.

The potential of the behavioural sciences for increasing the effectiveness of manpower management and planning was recognized from the beginning by the founders of the Manpower Society, and not least by the Editors of this volume who regarded it as important that the statistical contribution to manpower planning should take adequate account of the diversity of human attributes and behaviour. For that reason amongst others they are pleased to be able to include papers by, for example, Wilson and Cherns *et al* which warn against a superficial attitude to quantitative techniques.

The next group of papers deal with the mathematical and statistical aspects of manpower planning. Most of the authors in this group have a background in Operational Research and their work represents a natural extension of techniques which have already proved their worth in other fields of application. Under-lying the work in this area is the concept that people within an organization make up a dynamic system in which recruitment patterns, leaving rates, career opportunities and the structure of the organization are all inter-related. A change of policy in respect of any one of these factors will affect all the others, sooner or later. The typical approach is to construct a mathematical model of the system being studied and then to use it as a basis for prediction, control and optimization. The inherent uncertainty arising from the freedom of individual choice has led many workers to express their models in stochastic terms and this is a conspicuous feature of the present contributions. The basic Markov chain model, whose validity is investigated by Forbes and Mahoney and Milkovich, has proved to be extremely versatile. When combined with the powerful techniques of mathematical programming as illustrated by Charnes *et al* and Gear *et al* it obviously has great potential which has yet to be fully realised.

An important area of work at the macro-level is represented by a group of two papers by Burke and Clough and by Ford. The first proposes a theory to explain certain relationships between employment and the rate of innovation in industry and bears witness to the fruitful possibilities of inter-disciplinary co-operation. Ford's paper on the relationship between profitability and the employment of technological manpower in industry is an example of the pain taking empirical work which is an essential prerequisite for a working theory of the national manpower system.

Educational planners have been in the van of the recent advances in manpower studies. Their work is represented here by the papers of Menges and Elstermann, McReynolds, Clough and Morgan. The focal point of this work is the university system. The Canadian contribution of Clough and McReynolds considers the problems of selecting students when their performance at school is a function not only of academic ability but of ethnic and social factors. Morgan's paper, looking at the output of a particular university department, provides firm empirical evidence in an area where public controversy has often been conducted with scant regard for the facts.

The final group of papers deals with the management of public service manpower. Here, again, the spectrum of interest is a broad one drawing on experience in Canada, the USA and the UK. Morley describes the management development and career planning programme now employed in the Canadian Public Service and D'Avignon discusses the personnel information system on which the programme is based. An American view of the role of planning in public decision making in given by Weinstein. After reviewing existing planning and programming procedures he suggests a type of programming that would both be useful to the decision maker and provide a first step towards the more sophisticated methods which lie in the future. A British view provided by Harris, attempts to introduce comprehensive and systematic planning and priority determination in a loosely structured government organization. The remaining three papers by Rowntree, Drinkwater *et al* and Morgan describe models which are being used for assessing the likely consequences of policy options in the current major re-structuring of the British Civil Service. These papers might equally have been linked with those in the second group concerned with techniques for manpower planning.

It cannot be claimed that the group of papers presented in this volume is a representative sample of current activity in manpower research. The sample was largely self selected. It may be, for example, that the emphasis on the public and educational sectors is a reflection of the reluctance of companies to publish confidential information. However, we welcome the contributions from El Agizy of IBM and Walmsley of ICI and hope that future conferences will see further examples of work done in an industrial context. Nevertheless, in spite of possible imbalances, we think that the range and depth of interest in manpower research shown by the volume augurs well for the future.

Contents

PART I

1

Basic Assumptions in Manpower Planning: Some Trends, Difficulties and Possibilities

A. T. M. Wilson

London Graduate School of Business Studies

Introduction

One of the more obvious problems in this field is the discrepancy between the outlook and assumptions of model-makers on the one hand and organisational executives on the other. For this reason, the paper considers some relevant features of an organisation in a rather "naturalistic" way, particularly the relation of its establishment to its environment – that is, its ecological situation over manpower. The points and comments which follow, when written down, have every appearance of being self-evident; nevertheless, the discussion may not be without value since their existence is not always recognised in manpower model-building and the forward planning associated with it.

The five groups of comments in the first part of the paper have in each case some bearing on the main theme, developed in the second and summarised in a final section – that is, the growing range and significance of situations which point to the necessity for continuous, integrated, manpower planning at the level of the national community, where something resembling a matrix structure can already be seen to exist. Further developments in this direction seem probable. They have a large number of implications.

Part One

First: manpower planning is an essential part of the overall corporate planning of any organisation and cannot be successfully developed as a separate or parallel activity. For one thing, all the components of a corporate plan are of necessity related to the organisation's "mission" and objectives; and all are concerned with the same future environment, although they focus on different aspects of it. Incomplete or inconsistent basic assumptions, made by different contributors to a corporate plan, are well-known sources of disaster – most obviously, perhaps, in the severe difficulties of post-merger situations in the business world. The recent interest of economists and financial specialists in their different views of "intangibles" (Boulding, 1962), and in techniques and conventions for putting "price-tags" on human resources, may help to improve matters (Hekimian and Jones, 1967; Brummet, Flamholtz and Pyle, 1969). The cost of total replacement of the members of a company's establishment is reportedly thought by many senior U.S. executives (Likert, 1967) to be of the order of twice its total payroll. Detailed study of the component costs of labour turnover (York and Dooley, 1970), and experience of the costs of replacing specialists and managers, on the whole supports some approximation of at least this order. Differences in these global estimates often arise from the way in which senior executive time has been used or been costed.

In the past, situations in which machine power was substituted for manpower on grounds of cost would not invariably have been the concern of corporate planners even if they had existed. Nowadays, decisions of this kind are relatively infrequent, economists report (Salter and Reddaway, 1966; Evans, 1971), and a complex group of factors is usually concerned — for example, the probability of a relatively long life cycle for an improvable product; an adequate market potential; and falling prices of the relevant capital equipment. Where decisions of the latter kind are under consideration, they will obviously fall within the field of corporate planning; and the manpower contribution to the discussion will centre, first, on the future availability and cost of employees with the altered pattern of skills required in a modified production method; and, second, on the design of the related process of organisational change, whether or not redundancy is concerned. It is important to recognise in these discussions of mechanisation or automation that manpower costs, including managerial and specialist salaries, have certain differences from other elements, such as product and market characteristics and equipment costs. For the almost world wide "revolution of aspirations", in all categories of employment is fed by powerful processes of social change which are both a cause and a result of higher educational levels; and this particular revolution is likely to be both prolonged and continuous. Salary and wage levels, therefore, have sociological and political aspects and are not purely financial or economic matters. One particularly obvious example of this is the difference in the significance which is attached to "regular overtime" by factory production planners or by anyone concerned with "wages drift" or with struggles to improve productivity and contain inflation.

Second; manpower planning should take into account the changing content and categorisation of jobs, and the related changes in the character of establishments. There is so far little sign that the contemporary rate of change — technological, economic, educational, social, political — is settling down. Analysis and appraisal of opportunities and threats in the environment are the obvious starting points of corporate planning and of its manpower component. Among the more relevant external situations to be considered in manpower planning is the already mentioned "revolution of aspirations", in the sense of a reasonable and hopeful determination, among those entering employment, increasingly to seek an improvable standard of living in economic terms and a higher level of satisfaction in the job itself. There are growing pressures on management to modify the content of almost traditional operative jobs, to replace their simplified and narrow character by the enriched content made possible or even essential by mechanisation and automation, by higher educational levels, by the possibility of more co-operative attitudes in working groups, and, indeed, by the increasing competition for able and flexible people who are disinterested in traditional jobs and both able and willing to accept the challenge of these new possibilities. It is no doubt a little early, on a conservative view, to evaluate recent experiments in Norway intended to increase job satisfaction and diminish alienation at work (Thorsrud and Emery,

1969), or the practical application of such experiments in increasing the responsibility of jobs as those reported by Paul, Robertson and Herzberg (1968). But it can at least be said that while "job-enrichment" of lower levels and job categories may, on one view, produce a temporary phase of "job-impoverishment" in lower middle management, it should in due course lead to changes of great importance in forward planning: an up-grading of management activities at many levels of an executive chain and more concern with longer term problems at the top; helpful pressures for managers at each level to concentrate on the central aspects of their proper work and, with this, a decrease in excessive attention to the work of subordinates. It is certainly true that the increases in job content and responsibility are likely to lead to a rather smaller establishment with increased job-values; but they have not led to the immediate operational chaos so confidently predicted for this type of change in years gone by.

Some points on definition and categorisation of jobs can be made here. There is an obvious and thorny contrast between, on the one hand, systems of occupational classification aiming to be "rational" by excluding the socio-political aspect of occupations and, on the other, those which assume that no practical classification can completely ignore the hard-won demarcation lines between job-categories and occupations which commemorate past struggles between employers and employed. It is difficult to see any absolutely satisfactory solution to this dilemma, for there is no obvious way in which the two approaches can be integrated without an unwieldy complexity and detail; but if comparative research on manpower and establishments is not to be greatly inhibited, there is an urgent need to seek means by which at least some common elements can be introduced into different systems of occupational classification, both at national level and within individual organisations, so that fruitful comparative study is not made impossible. The existence of this particular difficulty is now widely accepted and it is, for example, being tackled by the Institute of Manpower Studies (1970) and the Department of Employment and Productivity. In the background there is a different but related problem, equally awkward, arising from the fact that in manpower planning people, as well as jobs, need to be classified. This is the problem of the confidential nature of certain types of personnel data in a computerised information system. If job contents are in continuous change, as seems likely, then the career and retraining potential, and the adaptability of the individual, will be at least as important as his basic qualifications and skills. An individual's career potential and adaptability may change; and the results of monitoring this process represent one kind of personnel data which is both centrally important for manpower planning and manifestly sensitive from the point of view of confidentiality — at least, that is, until mores, attitudes and opinions on such matters become very different from what they are now.

Third: some comments on the size and structure of organisations. It is possible to have two component categories of an establishment which are of equal size in terms of numbers but very different in their structure. From a sociological standpoint, the same total number of individuals may be members of a single monolithic unit or of a set of relatively autonomous units. (An analogous situation can be seen in the differences between a single small town or a single integrated manufacturing unit and the situation when a group of villages or component units of a company become a single "administrative complex".) For manpower planning these two types of establishment, despite identity of aggregate size, can have very different implications, in terms of the possibilities of internal redeployment, of external recruiting, and of relations with trades unions and professional organisations.

Establishments with large numbers in each category and level have one particular advantage: they make possible the use of advanced statistical procedures which cannot always be used with even intermediate sizes of organizations. An establishment with only thirty categories of employee would be something of a delight to any manpower planner; but even in such a favourable situation, if we assume twelve rather large categories and eighteen of a smaller and more specialised kind, an aggregate establishment of, say, four thousand people could hardly fail to raise problems of size in the specialist groups (arising from the statistical significance of the characteristics being measured); and the same problem might even occur in the larger categories if age grouping had to be taken into account. This particular difficulty has a special signficance in establishments of intermediate size; for in relatively small establishments forward planning can be undertaken — certainly in relation to key positions — in terms of individual jobs or careers, and individual members of the organisation, without an unrealistic amount of time and effort. Units of this intermediate size are likely to form a large part of any social system, and because of the problems just described, the use of probabilistic models may be made impossible; but this, of course, does not rule out the use of other approaches.

In thinking about overall size — in relation, for example, to growth and acquisitions in a business — it is important to recognise that *diseconomies* of scale can arise — for example, through the disproportionately high need for lateral co-ordination of activities with increase in the total size of an organisation (Haire, 1959; Levy and Donhowe, 1962); and where this problem is tackled by breaking down a single large unit into a number of smaller components units, this may do little more than replace an expensive "size-of-establishment" problem by an equally intractable one of inter-unit relations.

With respect to organisational structure, the implications of work such as the comparative studies by Woodward (1965), the analyses reported in "Organisation Choice" (Trist, *et al*, 1963), and the demonstrated possibilities (Rice and Miller, 1967; Goodman, 1970) of alternative forms of work organisation, have not as yet been fully recognised. A paper by Cherns and others (1970) discusses related issues in more general terms of an "aggregative" approach to manpower planning and the need for a complementary "structural" approach, in which "patterned relationships and shared beliefs are central analytical elements".

Fourth: to be of practical use, manpower planning must go beyond the numerical and demographic, particularly in the sensitive areas of providing both key personnel and the conditions needed to attract and retain them. Consideration must be given, for example, to the specifically human and social characteristics of relevant members of an existing and future establishment —

for example, their degree of willingness to accept adaptation and innovation (Burns and Stalker, 1967; Lawrence and Lorsch, 1969). Manpower planning cannot effectively be confined to estimating the probable nature and range of distant requirements; it must take into account the opportunities and constraints which lie between the present situation and the desired state of affairs at a particular point of future time. It is, therefore, best thought of as a regularly revised plan — with both executive and analytic aspects — to foster a complex process of organisational change. A wide and prolonged range of activities will be needed for its successful accomplishment; among them, for example, the building up, within the members of an organisation, of an awareness of its ecological situation and prospects. The reasons for major change will almost invariable originate in the environment (Trist and Emery, 1965) and some knowledge, or at least awareness, of these reasons is almost a prerequisite for acceptance of change by the members of an organisation. Another factor in successful change is the slow development of means to contain a built-in conflict of manpower planning — that between, on the one hand, the changing manpower needs of an organisation with changing structure and career possibilities in its establishment and, on the other, the changing aggregate of skill, experience and career aspirations in its members (Wilson, 1966).

Fifth: points with some connection with the built-in conflict just mentioned, but having a much wider and more general character.

All organisations are pluralist social systems in that they are members of at least three external social systems and have at least three internal sub-systems. Their pluralist character arises from the incomplete interdependence between these three, both externally and internally. First, any organisation is part of an economic system, since it allocates resources to provide some desired form of goods or services. Second, it provides jobs and job sequences — that is, it is part of an occupational and career system. Third, it needs to regulate the power and influence of its internal groups — that is, to have an internal political sub-system concerned with the regulation of conflict between interest-groups and pressure groups, as well as being part of a larger external system of this kind. If, as has been suggested, a manpower plan must deal not only with desirable ends but with essential means of achieving them — if it is thought of as an organisational change process — it can have no serious prospect of success unless there is full consideration of its relation to these internal occupational and political sub-systems; for both are clearly affected by any change in the content of jobs, in the direction and potential of career paths, and by the size, number and influence of important internal groups and key individuals (Wilson, 1970). The history of large corporations shows how often plans to modify an organisation and its establishment have been obstructed, delayed or even abandoned by serious difficulty over factors of these kinds (Chandler, 1962). Discussion of such matters in terms of the "internal political sub-system of an organisation" may seem a little grandiose; but it can be defended by saying that, from the point of view of forward planning of organisational change, it brings into play such helpful concepts of political science as "the constituency", "the mission", "the program", "opinion leaders", "coalitions", "building consensus", "negotiation", "bargaining", and "trade-offs". These ideas are at least a considerable improvement over discussing resistance to change in the myopic terminology of "politicking", that is, of a kind of private black-market in influence, bargains, rewards and punishments. No doubt this can – and does – exist; but in forward planning a high proportion of open "lobbying" and negotiation, if it can be brought into being, is certainly more effective than a high proportion of private plotting.

Part Two

Nowadays, even large organisations seldom build a railway for their own purposes, although many still find it cheaper and more practical to develop their own sources of power. The general character of this decision problem is that of "buy in, or make ourselves"; and one type of related difficulty of buying-in is familiar whenever a production problem or a labour dispute in a supplier shuts down a user company.

Obviously, where railway transport and electric power are bought in, services of this kind are sufficiently important to the general community to guarantee governmental action if they were to be interrupted for any length of time. The more specialised and less generally used the goods or services "bought-in" from outside, the less is this likely to be true; and on this background two types of rather specialised external service should now be considered. One of these is exemplified by the rapidly spreading practice, particularly in highly-automated continuous process manufacturing, of "contracting out" to a service organisation not only specialist maintenance of, for example, pumping equipment or complex electronic devices, but of more central work in maintaining production equipment – that is, heavy maintenance. The practice seems to have grown up on the extremely reasonable basis that in such units production workers are relatively small in number and that advanced technological maintenance requires specialists and equipment for whom it would be almost impossible to provide full time work, since their tasks tend to occur in short bursts of activity even when they are planned on a regular basis. On the other hand, a number of productive units in different companies, needing roughly similar types of maintenance equipment and maintenance personnel, can provide full-time employment for the establishment of a service agency or a co-operative in this field. In manpower planning this trend has obvious implications at the level of the manufacturing unit. It has further implications at national level; and to this point I will return.

For the moment, attention in this paper is concentrated on a second area where the increasing use of external services is likely to have a considerable impact on manpower planning of future establishments, particularly in organisations of small and intermediate size. Within this particular area the most obvious example of this type of external service is time-shared data-processing, usually for large volumes of recurring categories of fairly simple data; but the trend goes beyond the buying of computer time to include "seconding" of personnel from a computer service agency to handle, for example, complex, "one-off" projects such as evaluation of large capital proposals or the replanning of a distribution system. This particular example of temporary, external, supplementary specialist manpower has some relation to a further, and more general, trend.

Where the jobs within a particular category or unit are few in number, highly specialised in character, likely to change greatly, and very near each other in level of responsibility, an establishment of this kind can seldom provide satisfactory life-long full-time careers. The most obvious example of this situation is that of highly specialised scientific and technical staff, who may also want and need to maintain close contact with research or academic units in some particular field while making contributions, over time, to an industrial or commercial organisation of which they are members. Similar in some ways but different in others is the problem of providing careers for research managers as well as for research specialists; and in this instance efforts to resolve the problem by providing dual and parallel career paths have not been universally successful. These two kinds of difficulty seem likely to be increasingly resolved in future by the use of part-time external advisers, or by a converse arrangement in which members of an industrial or commercial organisation become part-time employees of some specialist external unit, academic or independent. Arrangements of this kind can, of course, be made for a limited period of years and in this way provide for changes in specialist staff to match changing organisational needs.

A more general point can be inserted here. Fourastié (1965) and de Jouvenel (1968) have pointed to the kind of problems likely to arise in a future with a working week of, say, thirty hours, and a decreasing number of years as an employee. "Moonlighting" − undisclosed employment in a second, parallel job to maintain a higher standard of income − is likely to be chosen as a pattern of employment by a considerable number of people, even if one leaves on one side, as a special case, the employment of women who continue to run households.

One further development should be mentioned − the growth of "matrix-type" organisations (Mee, 1964), where the familiar functional groups of a manufacturing organisation form one side of the matrix and and act as a horizontal series of manpower "pools" from which a set of parallel project teams are made up to carry some research finding into practical use through phases of development, pilot-models, production models, "de-bugging", and customer service. The basic proposition is that a work organisation of this kind greatly minimises the difficulties and delays which so often occur at each of these functional inter-faces. The concept has a multiple parentage. It was accepted and expanded for urgent research and development work in the high morale situations of the U.S. Space Agency, but it has obvious antecedents in the "organic" type of organisation so clearly defined, with its appropriate ecological situation, by Burns and Stalker (1967). Project teams and "organic" structures are successful wherever the need to handle rapid change has overcome fears of the threat made by these forms of organisation to the need for job security and settled career prospects of people brought up in less flexible units, with a constant fear of unemployment. There is, so far, little information as to the effect of project team experience on the careers or salary progression curves of their members. My own guess is that many of them, rather than return to work in a traditional and relatively rigid hierarchical set-up, would move from project team to project team, even if this meant moving from company to company. On the other hand, the integrative experience and skill of project team managers means that this relatively new type of professional is likely to be regarded as having high potential for the higher levels of any "organic" or matrix type of organisation.

This is only one example of the more general trend − the intensified search for job-satisfaction − which may represent a contributory factor in the growth of the "Temporary Society" of which Bennis and Slater (1969) have written.

Part Three

The Concept of a Matrix-Type Organisation at National Level

If we add, to the trends, difficulties and possibilities outlined earlier, the professionalisation of management, the widening "market" for executives, specialists and skilled employees, and the growing pressure for "moveable" pension rights, it seems likely that organisations will in future contain a higher proportion of short-service or contract members — people who wish to spend only one phase of a mobile professional career with a particular organisation. Beyond this, there is now an increasing possibility of making, usually with retraining, a complete change of occupation — that is, of having a two-phase or multi-phase career. This situation can already be seen in outstandingly able individuals; it looks like becoming a possibility in future for many more people. In manpower planning these phenomena have particular significance. With increased occupational mobility, "buying-in" of new members at mid-career levels is likely to create less dissatisfaction than it now does in subordinates whose promotion prospects are affected by it, for they too can increasingly seek to move or be "bought in" by another organisation. It is important that "buying-in", as contrasted with internal development of existing members of an organisation, can easily become a self-intensifying process if dissatisfaction with career prospects is created. Should it become more acceptable it will make the "acculturation" of new members of an organisation a particularly significant matter.

The growing use of a widening range of contract services will lead to an increasing dependence on the effectiveness of forward planning, and in particular manpower planning, in external service agencies which will not always be in the same industry. These organisations are likely, for some time at least, to be relative small, rather specialised, and geographically scattered to meet the needs of a suitable group of clients.

If these trends continue, the occupational and manpower system at national level will strongly resemble a large, incomplete and rather confused matrix system — that is, it will be made up of a notional series of manpower pools from which members second themselves, for decreasing lengths of time, to become members of particular ogranisations; and they may also be able to move increasingly from one manpower pool to another. The concept of a "labour market" is, of course, related to this situation; but it carries historical overlays — for example, a dominance of competitive cost considerations, an inflexible and unrealistic view of job contents and establishment categories, and — in practice — disjointed and intermittent forward planning. All three of these features are in contrast with the matrix concept in which continuous forward planning, on an integrated basis, is an essential activity; job content and work group structure are flexible; and movement from job to job is obviously associated with job-satisfaction as well as with salary levels.

Something resembling a matrix organisation, with establishment "pools" and project teams, exists at managerial and specialist levels in large governmental agencies and private corporations. With increased mobility of members between these organisations, no single one of them will be able to plan manpower without regard to competition for recruits; forward planning of a continuous kind will become increasingly necessary at the level of the national community, and even, in some highly specialised occupations, on a multi-national basis. Where integrated forward planning of manpower is difficult, or where the lead-time needed to provide fully trained new recruits is long, problems are likely to arise if continuous planning, however difficult, is not initiated at national as well as organisational and industry level; and there are recent examples of this in the academic world and in the traditional professions in the United Kingdom and elsewhere.

It can certainly be said that without sustained efforts to take into account the trends, difficulties and possibilities which have earlier been listed the problems of model builders and organisational planners in the manpower field may in the near future increase rather than diminish (Institute of Manpower Studies, 1970). The need to develop social as well as economic indicators (Bauer, 1966) is likely to support this point; for so long as manpower planning was largely an intermittent check on cost estimation, manning schedules and head-counting, its full significance was obscured. In the newer types of social accountancy manpower emerges not only as a central national resource but also — since market-tested price-tags can be put on members of an establishment — as a main national asset in terms of the formal definitions of accountancy and economics.

References

Bauer, R.H. (ed.) (1966), *Social Indicators*, M.I.T. Press, Cambridge, Massachusetts.

A symposium of papers by Bauer, Biderman, Bertram Gross and others, on problems and possibilities in this field.

Bennis, W. and Slater, P.E. (1968), *The Temporary Society*, Harper and Rowe, New York.

An informed speculative discussion of trends of importance to "scenario-writing" and manpower planning.

Boulding, K. (1962), "Economics and Accounting: the Uncongenial Twins" in *Studies in Accounting Theory* ed. Baxter and Davidson, Sweet and Maxwell, London.

A clear comparative statement, by a leading economist, of the approaches in looking at a firm and for this reason of considerable interest to manpower planners.

Brummet, R.L., Flamholtz, E.G. and Pyle, W.C., (New York 1969), "Human Resource Accounting: A Tool to Increase Managerial Effectiveness", *Management Accounting*, August.

A brief report of of an operational experiment begun in January, 1968, in a firm of 1300 in five locations. The original suggestion stemmed from Rensis Likert's views, expressed in "The Human Organisation: its Management and Value", McGraw-Hill Book Co., New York, 1967.

Burns, T. and Stalker, G.M. (1967), *The Management of Innovation*, Second Edition, Social Science Paperbacks, Tavistock Publications, London.

The introduction to this edition considers the history, since publication, of the original findings, including the contrast between "organic" and "mechanistic" organisations and their ecological properties.

Chandler, A.D. (1962), *Strategy and Structure: Chapters in the History of American Industrial Enterprise*, M.I.T. Press, Cambridge, Massachusetts.

Among the intensive studies of interplay between the two concepts in the title are those of General Motors, Du Pont, Jersey Oil and Sears Roebuck. The conclusions record, inter alia, that the departure of the original entrepreneur was often an essential pre-condition for any improvement in the organisational structure and establishment of large enterprises.

Cherns, A.B. *et al* (1970), "Aggregates and Structures; Two Complementary Paradigms in Manpower Studies", *Manpower and Management Science*, The English Universities Press, London.

The paper briefly discusses the two approaches and exemplifies the "structural" by outlining a group of problems of organisational design in relation to a completely new factory.

Emery, F.E. and Trist, E.L. (1965), "The Causal Texture of Organisation Environments", *Human Relations*, Vol. 18, pp. 21–32.

The environmental contexts of organisations are changing so rapidly that they cannot be described or conceived by use of a single set of concepts, applicable to nearly all situations; they need separate consideration, particularly in studies of organisational change. Early systems theory was concerned with internal relations of parts to the whole of an organisation – closed-system models. The next step was to relate "wholes" to their environment. Exchanges between organisation and environment can be dealt with by open-system models, but the environmental processes which determine these changes are not dealt with. Hence the additional concept of the "causal texture" of the environment, particularly with respect to its degree and type of uncertainty.

Evans, J.B. (1971), *Making Equipment Replacement Decisions*, Gower Press London (in the press).

An informed discussion of the current "state of the art" in this particular area of decision making.

Fourastie, J. (1965), *Les 40 000 Heures* Robert Laffont, Editions Gonthier, Paris.

In a working life of thirty-five years, should the weekly hours fall to thirty, then in a life time of eighty years there will be only forty thousand at work out of the total seven hundred thousand hours of life – that is, 6% of the total life time will be at work. The author of this book, who is closely connected with the projections of the French National Plan, examines the possible consequences of such a change in the future pattern of life. His book has an interesting appendix: "Reflections sur les Conditions de la Prevision".

Goodman, R.A. (1970), "Organizational Preference in Research and Development", *Human Relations*, Vol. 23, No. 4, August, pp. 279-298.

In its own right research and development has brought into being what amounts to a special category of management; but this situation also illustrates, in magnified form, many problems of management in general. In this paper the experience and views of twenty-three general managers and twenty-three project managers – all highly experienced men – were sought on the appropriate type of organisation for research and development work. The differences in point of view of the two groups are clearly described and analysed. In his paper Goodman uses the word "matrix" in a special sense and contrasts three types of organisation for project work: first, line-staff organisation, where projects work is assigned and performance reviewed by the line manager and the "project manager" is in a rather distant planning role. In what Goodman refers to as a matrix organisation work is assigned by a project manager but performance appraisal is still undertaken by a line manager. In what he describes as project organisation, both work assignment and performance appraisal are undertaken by a project manager. In my own paper, the concept of "matrix" organisation refers, in effect, to either or both of these types of organisation. The basic notion is that of "functional" or "specialist" pools for which project teams are made up.

Haire, M. (1959), "Biological Models and Empirical Histories of the Growth of Organizations" in *Modern Organization Theory*, John Wiley and Sons, New York, Chapter 10. (See Levy and Donhowe)

Hekimian, J.S. and Jones, C.H. (1967), "Put People on Your Balance Sheet", *Harvard Business Review*, January/February, pp. 105-113.

Despite the title, this is a serious discussion by two professors of accountancy of the possibility of using replacement costing, or opportunity costing, to make a financial estimate of the value of employees as assets rather than mere resources with no price-tag — except as part of the difference between the "net worth" of a business on its balance sheet and the actual price paid when it is bought or sold.

Institute of Manpower Studies (1970, "Aims, Organisation and Research Project Programme", University of Sussex, Falmer, Brighton. An outline of the work of a new research organisation.

de Jouvenel, B. (1968), *Arcadie: Essais sur le Mieux-Vivre;* S.E.D.E.I.S., (Futuribles), Paris.

This volume continues the line of thought in a previous book, "L'Art de la Conjecture", Editions du Rocher, Monaco, 1964. They provide a particularly wide and well informed background to forward planning.

Lawrence, P. and Lorsch, J. (1969), *Organisation and Environment,* Richard D. Irwin, Homewood, Illinois (available in paperback).

A comparative study, in a small number of firms, in three industries, of organisational characteristics needed to deal effectively with different market and technological conditions.

Levy, S. and Donhowe, G. (1962), "Explorations of a Biological Model of Industrial Organisation", *Journal of Business*, Vol. XXXV, No. 4 pp. 335-342.

Mason Haire's 1959 study spurred these two workers to study in a number of firms the differential growth rate of employees concerned with external relations and with internal activities. They provide evidence that the "square cube law" of the biologists has some relevance to the firm. The paper also provides data on the important relation of research and development to overall growth in the size of the firm.

Likert, R. (1967), *The Human Organisation: its Management and Value,* McGraw-Hill, p. 103.

This volume contains descriptive comments on situations and considerations which lead to its experimentation with human asset accounting reported by Brummet and others (see reference).

Mee, J.F. (1968), "Matrix Organisations" in *Systems, Organisations, Analysis, Management: A Book of Readings*, (eds. Clelland and Kings),McGraw-Hill, New York and London, pp. 23-26.

A brief summary of the concept, with references.

Paul, W.J., Robertson, K.B. and Herzberg, F. (1969). "Job Enrichment Pays Off", *Harvard Business Review*, March/April, pp. 61-78.

This summarising article describes five "experimental" changes in job content, including alterations in budgetary and financial controls. Its particular interest lies in the determined effort to quantify the results — which were positive — and the fact that the work was carried out in U.K. units of I.C.I.

Rice, A.K. and Miller, E. (1967), *Systems of Organisation*, Tavistock Publications, London

This joint work uses a number of extended research-consultancy projects of the authors — some previously unpublished — to develop a general point of view about organisation.

Salter, W.E.G. and Reddaway, W.B. (1966), *Productivity and Technical Change*, Second Edition, Cambridge University Press.

The first edition provided analyses on the nature and complexity of these concepts, with hypotheses on their relativity. In the second edition, Professor Reddaway shows how these ideas have stood up to the test of time.

Thorsrud, E. and Emery, F.E. (1969), *Mot en Ny Bedriftsorganisasjon*, Tanum, Oslo.

Describes four experiments, each in a different factory, with new forms of work organisation.

Trist, E.L. *et al* (1963), *Organisational Choice*, Tavistock Publications, London.

As the title suggests, the research program it describes and discusses showed that alternative modes of work organisation can exist for the same technology. The studies show the feasibility as well as the desirability of bringing into existence cohesive primary work groups committed to holistic tasks — or, more directly, away from the ideology of mass production where jobs are broken down to the maximal extent and the individual is treated as an extension of the technology. Consideration shows this last attitude to be linked to the disbelief that groups can organise themselves; but self-regulating and effective groups of forty-one men were observed in detail over time. There is a relationship between the wider findings, on the reality of group responsibility, to the narrower concept of increasing responsibility within the individual job.

Wilson, A.T.M. (1970, "Considerations Affecting the Design of a New Establishment", in *Aspects of Manpower Planning*, (ed. Bartholomew and Morris), English Universities Press.

As one means of clarifying the issues under discussion this particular chapter considers some twenty considerations grouped under five headings: General Character of the Proposed Organisation; the Environmental Situation and its Impacts; Opportunities and Constraints; Designing an Establishment; Designing a System of Manpower Planning.

Wilson, A.T.M. (1966), "Some Sociological Aspects of Systematic Management Development", *Journal of Management Studies*, Vol. 3, No. 1, February, pp. 1–18.

Discussion of some basic features of a managerial manpower planning system.
York, D. and Dooley, C. (1970), "Checking the Manpower Costs", *Personnel Management*, June, p. 34.

This is a brief report on the subject by a panel of Manpower Society members. It contains an extended check list of nearly one hundred items of identifiable cost almost entirely in headings familiar to accountants. Further work is to be reported in late 1970.

2
Adaptivity and Human Organisation

B. M. Rooney

**Inter-Bank Research
Organisation, London**

Preliminary

This paper is a speculation. It rests on two premises: that the need for individuals and organisations to adapt to a changing environment is an important source of tension in human society; and secondly that the tension can either be resolved in adaptation (which in turn modifies the environment for other organisations, so generating tension elsewhere) or degenerates into conflict. The argument is proposed that for adaptation to take place there must be a degree of redundance in an organisation (or individual), and there must be linguistic (or more properly semiotic) and ethical community between an organisation and its environment.

It will be clear from the title that the subject is formidably wide. It will therefore also be clear that in a paper of this length it is possible only to make a superficial survey, in the hope of suggesting aspects which deserve closer study.

Introduction

It has become a commonplace to point out that the viable organisation, interacting with its environment, must change with the environment. But to admit this does not seem to make change any the more tolerable either to suffer or to think about. Intellectually, the tendency is to treat of organisations as if there was no coupling between them and their environment. Indeed, to imply that the ideal organisation is really only answerable to itself and is in complete control of all factors which influence its structure. At best the coupling is localised and dealt with as a special problem, such as, in industrial organisations, marketing, or recruitment, The tendency is clearly to be seen in the widespread assumption that the problems of change can be resolved mechanistically by, for example, some formulaic redistribution of the profit cake.

It is also a commonplace to observe that for many reasons the rates of change imposed on organisations seem to have been increasing and may well increase even further. It is not easy to test this belief, although, the results from, for example, Project HINDSIGHT[1] may provide base data. But it seems prudent to consider the characteristics of organisations which can come to recognise the extent of their interaction with their environment and which can modify themselves as the environment changes.

A starting-point is to set down some of the tendencies which can be discerned in Western industrial society. Most of these will be familar:-

FROM	TOWARDS
Less time spent in education	More time spent in education
Once-for-all education	Continuous education
Early specialisation	Sequence of specialisations
Single-firm careers	Many-firm careers
Single-skill field of work	Many-skills field of work
Motivation based on negative or hygienic factors	Motivation based on positive factors
Single-objective firms	Multi-objective firms
Specialised organisation structures	Generalised organisational structures
Authority seen as structural and hierarchical	Authority seen as participative and distributed
Geographical nation states	Industrial nation states
National political restraints on firms	Multi-national political restraints on firms
Dependence on naturally occurring cycles and materials	Independence of naturally occurring cycles and materials

At first sight these tendencies may appear to have little in common, but reflection will show that they all depend on an increasing complexity of organisation, and of interactions in organisation/environment systems. Such an increase can be crudely illustrated by considering for example the complexity of the organised activity needed to produce the outputs of neolithic society and making a comparison with organisations. Thus the agricultural processes of neolithic crop-farmers involved perhaps 10^1 direct interactions between the farmer and his physical environment. The Apollo system, with some 15 million parts, probably represents between 10^9 and 10^{10} systematic interactions.

Furthermore while neolithic agriculture was supported by a relatively small number of subordinate interactions — production of clothes, cooking etc — a modern system depends on a great many subordinate interactions which can be heirarchically ordered. The subordinate interactions are sub-sets of the sets of interactions of the subordinate systems, and these sets will include interactions which may have no direct bearing on any particular system served by the subordinate system. The outcome is an operating environment for any system of extreme uncertainty, a situation characterised by Emery and Trist (1965)[2] as a turbulent environment.

If a general tendency is acknowledged towards increased complexity of systematic interaction, matched by an increasing uncertainty of environment, it becomes an act of prudence to consider the preconditions for organisational survival in such a situation: which is to say the preconditions for self-adaptivity.

Past History of Organisational Adaptation

The evolution of organisations may provide some insights into possibilities and conditions for instituting necessary self-adaptivity. Two features in particular seem especially relevant: systematic diversification, and development of the authority and communication structure. These are now considered in turn.

Systematic Diversification

It appears to be a tendency in all successful human systems for the range of objectives of the system to increase. Figure 1 presents a very simplified form of the financial system, regarded as a system for conveying notions of wealth and value. Characteristically, the development of a structure matched to the achievement of a particular function draws attention to the scope for further refinement. Thus the limitations of barter led first to the use of intermediate objects of value which could be exchanged more flexibly: this in turn led to the development of money of fixed incremental value. But money had its own problems of safe storage and portability; leading to the issue of notes by those who stored it, and to the use of these notes as wealth tokens in their own right. The need for a time-delay element was met by the introduction of credit, and so on. In a sense Figure 1 is taxonomic, classifying the demands of commercial activity.

From the point of view of organisational analysis, two aspects of the process stand out: the growth of organisations specialising in satisfying a limited set of demands, and, secondly, the growth in semantic implications of systematic transactions.

It appears that organisations specialising in a limited number of systematic activities become necessary partly because of the limitations of view which characterise their numbers, because of communication problems within the organisation itself, and partly for reasons of technology or efficiency in translating demands into responses. This question will be considered at more length later in the paper.

The growth in semantic implication calls for some elucidation. At the barter level the message communicated was "our mean subjective assessments, now, of the values of each of these things are equal". It was purely local and relativistic, not implying any absolute concept of value or wealth; and it took no account of possible changes of value of wealth over time. This was remedied by the introduction of money, and it is this introduction of time into the process which has been most fruitful of structural development. Borrowing and credit both say, in effect that the borrower will have more disposable wealth in the future than he has now. Secondly, the concept of money implies some acknowledged scale of value against which particular objects could be measured.

More recent developments, such as the introduction of dealing in equity shares, extend the range of objects to which value can be allotted, and notably introduce a time variable quality into notions of wealth.

Developments in Communication and Authority Structure

In very broad terms, three categories of organisation can be distinguished:-*

* For a similar but more elaborate discussion of environments see Emery and Trist (1965)[2]. The first of the three categories can probably only be hypothetical but is nevertheless conceptually useful.

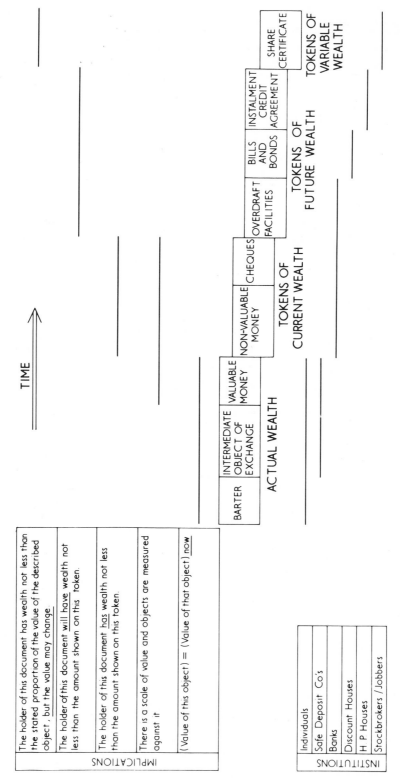

FIG. 1 Organisations, implications and communication mechanisms in the financial system (much simplified).

a. Those which operate in known environments, and in which the communication flow is virtually uni-directional from the centre of authority to those subject to it.

b. Those which, while still operating in environments believed to be known, attempt to take account of changing conditions and thus introduce a form of two-directional information flow. Authority, though, formally vested in the executive is in some degree shared by the advisory element.

c. Those in which the operating environment is only partially known, or even unknown, and information flows in many directions, authority being seen as widely distributed.

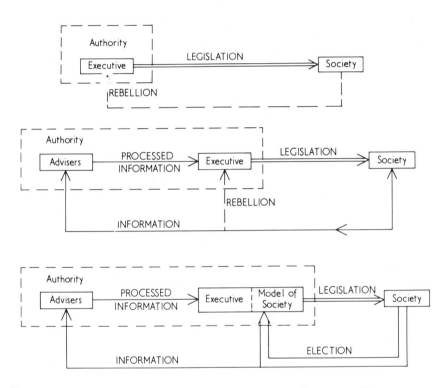

FIG. 2. Structural evolutionary phases of Parliamentary Government System.

Figure 2 gives a very over-simplified presentation of this process for the most complicated organisation in society, namely that of government. At the lowest level this is substantially autocratic, the communication flow being from the executive (the tribal leader or whatever he may have been) to the members of the social unit. The success of the system depends on environmental stability — or at least on the ability of the leader to foresee environmental changes and to persuade or compel the governed into anticipatory action. There is an informal feedback loop to the extent that an unsuccessful leader may find himself deposed, but in general it is true to say that for organisations on this level the implicit assumption is that the executive has sufficiently complete knowledge of the organisation's environment to anticipate demands and so eliminate the need for structural change.

At the second level, the assumption that the environment is intrinsically know-able holds true, but it has become acknowledged that it is probably beyond the powers of an independent individual to achieve sufficient knowledge, both of the environment and of the governed, to eliminate mismatches. Thus an advisory function develops which both represents the views of the governed to the executive and describes more completely the environmental conditions.

One fundamental factor underlies the transition to the second level: size and the associated complexity of interaction both within the organisation and between the organisation and its environment. Although there is an element of indicative forecasting in the advisory process, there is no real suggestion that there is any thing intrinsically unknowable about the relationship between the organisation and its environment.

With increasing size and complexity, the problems of interaction become so great that a need arises for some structural means of bridging the gap between the executive and the governed. Historically, and oversimplifying, the advisory function became differentiated, partly into advisers on the old pattern and partly into a representational model (a parliament) of the governed society. In the clearly differentiated form which has emerged in the United States, there is no functional overlap, but the British version retains vestiges of the earlier state, admittedly somewhat confused by the shift of executive power from the Monarch to the Prime Minister.

The role of Parliament as a model of society is a subject which deserves closer examination than it has perhaps received, especially in the current climate of scepticism about its relevance or effectiveness. For our purpose, however, one may acknowledge that it does have this characteristic, and plays, or is thought to play, a central role in social organisation.

It is an interesting characteristic of this evolutionary process, that the structural elements of the higher forms of organisation are implicit in the lower. At the most primitive level the executive acted as his own adviser, the function becoming differentiated at the next level. Similarly, the model of society exist-ed in the mind of the tribal leader, insofar as his perceptions of his tribe amounted to a model, and this in turn became structurally differentiated.

Conclusions

In considering the whole process, therefore, one may discern a differentiation of systematic objective, an extension of the range of meaning implicit in inter-actions, and a functional differentiation of structure. These historically, seem to have been achieved in response to developments which perhaps served the purpose of drawing attention to the inadequacy of the status quo. But if one is to devise an organisation which in some way is self-adapting, and which does not require periodic upheaval the implications of these evolutionary processes must be worked out. There appear to be three preconditions:

1. The organisation must in some sense know and understand itself: this suggests that there is a need for structural components which both derive
and store this understanding. This may be termed *organisational re-dundancy*.

2. There needs to be some conceptual structure within which possible objectives of the organisation can be assessed: this may be termed an *organisational ethic*.

3. There needs to be a means of communication between the organisation and its environment and also among the structural elements of the organisation: this may be termed an *organisation language*.

These three characteristics are quite clearly interdependent, although the interaction between language and ethic is perhaps particularly close.

Rate of adaptation

It will be useful before going to examine these requirements in more detail to consider the rate at which adaptations can be achieved in organisations. Two broad groups of factors are at first sight influential in the industrial situation: material and human. It goes without saying — and therefore little space will be taken up in saying it — that the periodicities of product development and capital investment cycles are a strong constraint on the rate of practicable adadptivity. But even here human factors tend to dominate, so that Marketing and Personnel Divisions are concerned with penetration rates and learning curves, and Production Divisions with quality control and wastage. Thus it can be suggested that achievable rates for successful adaptation are ultimately conditior. d solely by human factors. It is small comfort to observe that there is little to be said about the rates at which human individuals and groups can tolerate organisational change. Studies such as Project HINDSIGHT[1] may indicate that in the most favourable circumstances major technological advances can occur at roughly thirteen year intervals. But this is open to criticism on the grounds that the foundations for these advances were laid often thirty or more years pre iously; and secondly that there is no satisfactory measure of tolerability or of social cost in adaptation. It might be expected that tolerable rates of change, however described, will be related to time spent in education, time spent in a particular appointment and perhaps to the average length of a generation since early marriage and child-bearing seem frequently to characterise uncertain conditions of life. It can be expected too that the speed and quality of social communication may effect the rate of change. But beyond such general statements there seem little that can be said at this stage of knowledge.

Preconditions for Adaptation

a. *Organisational Redundancy**

The term redundancy is here used in a sense analogous to that in communication theory, as spare capacity or unused possible states of existence.

In adaptive organisations redundancy seems to be necessary both at individual and organisation level.

At individual level it will be observed that the very concept of organisation implies limitation on choice of action — behavioural redundancy. There is evident

* See also Emery (1967).[3]

similarity between this situation and communication, in which for any message to be transmitted the number of possible sequences of signs must be limited. It would appear that any organisation contains inherently the capacity for adapting itself. But this capacity seems frequently — and perhaps necessarily — confounded by the phenomenon of structural identification: the human tendency to identify with the way in which things are done, rather than with what is done. Here again there is a communication analogy, to the extent that as efficient communication requires transmitters and receivers to be matched, efficient human action involving more than one person requires a matching process which is achieved through the storage of experience and training in the human memory. There is thus built up an expectation of what form the communication should take between each of the communicating elements of an organisation. But adaptation necessarily implies de-structuring — a changing of these expected relationships and where only the relationships themselves are perceived by the elements concerned this destructuring appears a falsification of all that has been learnt and stored. Depending on the success of the pre-existing form of the structure, this sense of falsification will be more or less acute.*

Thus while organisation necessarily provides a degree of behavioural redundancy at individual level, efficiency of operation requires of these same individuals that the redundancy should not be devoted to adaptive activity; and this requirement receives conscious or unconscious support from the individuals themselves.

The role of redundancy at organisational level is for this reason primarily to provide a means of channeling individual redundancy into adaptive activity without disrupting the organisation. Insofar as it may appear to limit the efficiency with which certain operations are conducted there are similarities with Stafford Beer's concept of optimal sub-optimality: conceptually it would appear that this is achieved when the minimum necessary degree of redundancy is introduced at all organisational levels.

As it affects individuals, organisational redundancy must take account of expected change rates on the sets of characteristics of each job — and, vice-versa, the abilities of individuals to move from jobs characterised by different sets — these sets being in some degree under the control of the organisation.

In great degree this comes down to identifying the flow rates implicit in the desired rate of structural change and to the degree of training (whether formal or on-the-job) which is necessary to enable individuals to make the transition from one form of job to another. Taken together, these factors will identify the minimum manning levels necessary to operate the organisation.† It will be observed that there is both an operational and a redundancy component in the manning level as suggested here. To this must be added a further element of redundancy which derives from the need to align individual and organisational objectives — which is to say to translate structural to systematic identification.

* Since one is here concerned with perceptions of success at an individual level, there is a risk of some unreality, which, quite evidently, is a potential source of conflict in an adapting situation.

† This approach ignores, at least in the initial stages, the idea that some structural forms might be humanly more acceptable than others.

(Readers may observe a similarity between this concept at the organisational level and the macro-economic suggestions of Professor Paish for national levels of unemployment).

Some evidence of the success of training programmes designed to facilitate the translation of structural into systematic identification is given by studies at Michigan University by Floyd Mann (1957) reported by Trist (1968).[4]

At the organisational level, adaptation calls for a more analytical approach to structural redundancy than has generally characterised most industrial units. In great degree the problems of adaptation arise in large organisations partly because individual members find it difficult or are not encouraged to perceive the organisation as a whole, (especially in its relationship with its environment) and partly because of the time lags of communication between groups within the organisation. The first stage in restructuring, and assuming that all is well at the individual level, is therefore to attempt to reduce the communication time-lags to and order of magnitude very considerably less than the adaptation period. This characteristically leads to some form of matrix organisation in which an amalgamation is attempted between the conventional hierarchy of authority (ranked e.g. by power to spend money, or by the number of individuals or value of assets controlled at each level) and a time hierarchy concerned with possible outputs at different points in the future. The distinguishing features of these two hierarchies are that, whereas the authority hierarchy is essentially functional, with line management supported by personnel and financial staff, the time hierarchy is based on multi-disciplinary groups concerned with periods further and further into the future. Figure 3 gives a very simplified example of this form of matrix organisation; the similarity between this and the second level in the evolutionary process described previously (in Figure 2) will be clear. In organisations of matrix form the redundant element is made up of the group of functions in the time hierarchy, since these are in no sense employed on current tasks and represent spare capacity devoted to establishing both what needs to be adapted to, and the means by which the adaptation is achieved; secondly of the part of top management not concerned with current activity, and finally of the staff functions.

The effectiveness of such organisations is not in question at the present time but it seems doubtful if they will be able to contend with the levels of uncertainty which are implicit in the highly interactive environment postulated. It is implicit in this type of organisation that future environments are, if not definable, at least reducible to a tolerable degree of definition — that they are, so to speak, statistically determinable. This is quite clearly the assumption which underlies the strategies of many large organisations which seemingly attempt to simplify their forecasting problems by constraining their environment. Monopoly is perhaps the most celebrated variant of this strategy, and is popularly considered not to be in the customer's interest: the underlying argument being that the organisation cannot possibly know enough about the future demands of its environment and thus must always be operating, whether wilfully or not, against the true interests of the members of its environment.

This suggests the structural form which may characterise future organisations. Since the objective is to know more of the interactions between the organisation and its environment and since it is impractical usually to test these in real life

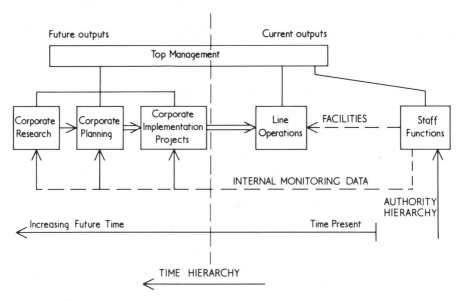

FIG. 3 Functions in Time/Authority matrix organisation

there is an apparent need in the structure for models both of the organisation and of its environment, so that optional strategies can be evaluated.

It is important here to distinguish between two types of model. There is firstly the quantitative model, usually expressed mathematically, which is used to test the possible outcomes of particular decisions. There is growing familiarity with such models and they constitute one element in the advisory activity. But there is a second qualitative type (which might be termed political) which seems to be required in considering relationships between an organisation and its environment, and which is therefore especially relevant to problems of adaptation. The function of these models is to determine — and to update — the bounds of tolerability of the consequences of pursuing particular strategies. In an idealised system the use of such models would permit what control theorists would describe as a bang-bang approach to solving the problems of continuous adaptation, following the line of argument proposed by Pontryagin among others.

A real situation will clearly require both forms of model. A structure incorporating such models corresponds to the third level in the evolutionary process described in Figure 2.*

One may discern in industrial organisations, and more clearly in large industrial groupings, the beginnings of this form of structure. In a real sense, the bargaining organisations representing both employers and employees, Consumers' Associations and so on, are performing for all their inadequacies some parts of the quali-

---

* But one should not seek for too exact an equivalence between Parliamentary government and industrial organisations: the original function of the Parliamentary model was to speed up communication between the executive and society this being achieved by conducting a process of communication between the executive and a model of society and by then enacting legislation jointly. It is perhaps part of Parliament's current problems that it has never progressed beyond this communication function, although there are now welcome signs, in the activities of some Select Committees and in the long-term budgetary forecasts presented to Parliament by the Treasury, that it is beginning to transform itself into a functional model.

tative model role. So too are general meetings of shareholders.

In this context the function of the model is analogous to that of the system model in an adaptive control system; operational policies being tested and the operating consequences evaluated in an interactive sequence of events. In human organisations, the activity is political in the sense that the model provides a means for deciding the range and intensity of response likely to be provoked by a particular strategy, while at the same time it provides a bargaining focus for identifying some strategy which is tolerable to all participants.

Clearly, again, the introduction of a model or set of specialist models contributes itself to organisational redundancy. Moreover models need to be presented with sufficient information on current conditions and future possibilities to work effectively. Thus all of the participating elements in the model will need to work within the framework of the matrix form of organisation already discussed, and the introduction of a model into the structure will extend the pre-existing degree of redundancy.

b. *Systematic community of Language and Ethics*

These two factors are interacting, the significance of this being indicated in the simple diagram, Figure 4, of the relationships between an organisation and its environment expressed in terms of variety of possible states and messages.

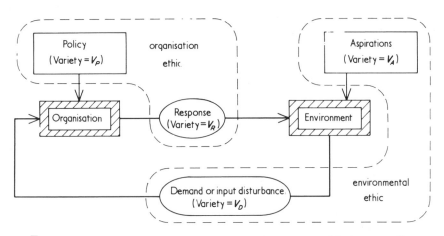

FIG. 4 Basic Communication and Control in Organisation/Environment System.

The input into an organisation is seen, much over-simplified, as being transformed in accordance with some pre-defined policy into a response. By the law of requisite variety,* the varieties, expressed logarithmically, of the input (or disturbance) *minus* that of policy *equals* that of the response.

It is quite clear that in a real organisation one is not dealing only with tangible artefacts but very frequently with perceptions described in more or less linguistic form. Thus an imperfect language will limit the organisation's perception of the input disturbance. Furthermore, policy is expressed in some

* See e.g. Ashby (1964)[5] for a simple exposition.

linguistic form and is limited by it. Finally, each stage of the communication process within the organisation is limited in effectiveness by the semantic potency of the means employed. Thus the transformation which takes place in the organisation is in some degree corrupted by the limitations of its language.

It should be observed that the term language here embraces the complete set of communication techniques employed in a systematic activity: it includes communication by gesture and attitude, indeed the whole set of ritualistic and structural devices for conveying ideas, as well as the more formal verbal languages.

It will be clear, therefore, that the language of an organisation is itself an area of interaction between the organisation and the environment. And, more importantly for adaptation, lack of coincidence in the regions of ideas to which organisational and environmental languages are matched will in time lead to a breakdown of systematic communication. For adaptation to be ensured, therefore, it seems that there must be a community of language between an organisation and its environment.

Mention of the region of ideas leads to the question of the organisational ethic which is seen characteristically as setting a bound to the variety of policy and of response. It will be clear that some form of language is needed to express the organisational ethic. If this expression is only partial or in some other way imperfect, then an artificial ethical constraint operates on the organisation's response to the input disturbance. In passing, it may be observed that the variety of policy is limited partly by language, partly be ethical considerations and partly as a consequence of structural identification and the other limiting factors already discussed.

In considering the effects of the ethical bound, the sequence of events in the adaptive process can, in a very over-simplified form, be set out:

1. The organisation detects an input disturbance, of variety
$V_D = V_A - V_R$. (as defined in Figure 4)

2. This is transformed within the organisation according to current policy, of variety V_P.

3. A response, of variety V_R' is generated.

4. Provided that V_R' does not transgress the ethical limits there is no interruption: the environment accepts the response and generates in time a new disturbance with variety $V_D' = V_A - V_R'$ and the process is repeated.

At some point in the iterative process, however, the bound set by the organisational ethic will be reached; typically the bound is likely to affect first the variety of response. At this stage two things can happen. The more likely is that the policy will be revised through a process of structural adaptation to give a greater V_A. Alternatively ethical bounds are re-set — perhaps by a linguistic re-expression — to tolerate the desired variety of response. But if for any reason one of these alternatives is not chosen, a crisis arises, which characteristically is resolved by the spawning of a new organisation providing the responses which lie outside the original ethical bound. This situation would clearly be a failure of adaptivity in the original organisation.

Examples of type contradictions and conflict situations which result from the application of restrictive organisational ethics are manifold. Two will suffice in illustration.

1. The provision of social welfare benefits, at least for the majority of employees, is deemed to transgress the profitability ethic, and as a result the State has, in most countries, expanded its role to include this function. This suggests, perhaps, a disconcerting paradox that the more rigorously the profitability ethic is applied the more likely it becomes that the range of State activities will increase.

2. The competitive ethic is regarded as creditable in relationships between management of enterprises but wholly disgraceful between leaders of Trades Unions, although both groups are serving very substantially the same social aggregations.

It would appear from the simple model of Figure 4 that such conflicts and contradictions will only be escaped if the responses of the organisation can achieve a variety which stands in some relationship to that of the environment aspirations. These latter are themselves seen to be bounded, together with the variety of demand, by an environment ethic. This suggests that for adaptation there is a need for ethical community throughout the organisational/environment system.

Conclusion

Two apparent implications of this line of argument are proposed by way of conclusion.

It is sometimes suggested that conflict is a fruitful device for promoting adaptivity since it weakens structural identification — indeed in grave cases it is believed to demolish structure and so permit some more suitable reconstruction. Now it is implicit in conflict that an attempt is made to restrict the variety of systematic response, to serve a particular interest. So conflict implies a failure of the ethical community which has been argued for as a condition for adaptation. It would appear therefore that whilst conflict may well weaken structural identification it will not necessarily promote adaptation. Indeed it could be proposed that an ethic which tolerated conflict in support of restricted sets of interactions would lead, if shared by different groups interested in different sets of interactions, to systematic degradation.

The second apparent implication follows to some extent from the first. General tendencies in western industrial society, some of which were listed above, seem often to be used somewhat uncritically in long range planning for society and industry. But if the argument here proposed is valid the extrapolation of these tendencies — however subtle the allowance made for interaction among them — is tantamount to treating symptoms rather than causes. By analogy with medicine, this may achieve short term relief, but ultimate success depends on the viability of the organism. Thinking for the future must therefore, it seems, begin by considering the extent of linguistic and ethical community in a system and the degrees to which these might be altered by possible strategies. Secondly, it is necessary to consider the machinery through which the communities are established and its suitability to conditions which may change. Only then can one extrapolate with any confidence of success.

References

1. Interim Report on Project HINDSIGHT. Dept. of Defence, Washington 1965.

2. Emery F.E. and Trist E.L. (1965): "The Causal Texture of Organisational Environments": *Human Relations* Vol. 18 No. 1 1965. pp. 24–26.

3. Emery F.E. (1967) "The Next 30 Years: Concepts, Methods and Anticipations" *Human Relations* Vol. 20 No. 3 1967. pp. 230.

4. Trist E.L. (1968): Review paper for a symposium on "The Professional Facilitation of Planned Change in Organisations". XVIth International Conference of Applied Psychology; Amsterdam Holland August 1968. (Tavistoch Institute Ref. HRC 79).

5. Ashby W.R. (1964): *An Introduction* to *Cybernetics:* pp. 206 Methuen and Co. Ltd., London 1964.

3

Aggregates and Structures: Two Complementary Paradigms in Manpower Studies

A. B. Cherns

P. A. Clark

T. Wynne Harries

Ruth Sinclair

Loughborough University of Technology (U.K.)

Introduction

Katz and Kahn (1966) argue that the rapidity of change involving organisations is so great that there is a premium on the anticipation and direction of future changes and following through of policy decisions to the "structural implications for the organisation". It is suggested that continuous planning requires both an intelligence function reporting on environmental trends and a policy development function to generate alternative courses of action for anticipated changes in the environment. The aim is to make "prospective generalisations about what organisational behaviour shall be".

Manpower studies are a recent addition to the specialisms on the human-organisational aspects of long term planning. The basic paradigm adopted is that of the supply and demand analysis of micro-economics. Transposed to the study of manpower this paradigm takes individuals and aggregates as the units of analysis. A complementary paradigm of relevance to the formulation of manpower policies is the structural approach in which patterned relationships and shared beliefs are central analytical elements. The structural approach is scrutinised with reference to ongoing work in two projects on organisational design.

The Aggregates Paradigm

Manpower planning is a recent addition to the activities of many firms for although much effort has been expended on the planning of other economic resources, the planning of manpower has largely been neglected. As the size of the wages and salaries bill, in relation to other costs to the firm, has become increasingly critical, the importance of utilising labour resources as effectively as possible has has become more apparent. In many cases manpower planning has developed alongside corporate planning. The use of such techniques within enterprises may be related to such factors as the size of the enterprise, the structure and stability of its market, the nature of its technology. (Pugh *et al*: Lawrence and Lorsch 1969; Woodward 1958, 1965).

The basic paradigm of manpower planning is the reconciliation of estimates of future demand and supply of labour. Basically manpower planners will assess the demand for labour requirements needed to meet the overall objectives of the firm up to a target date; assess the supply of labour resources, and where forecasts of the demand and supply do not tally, suggest ways of reconciling them.

The first step is to define the objectives of the firm and to translate these into forecasts of sales, output, development of new products etc. up to a target date. (Obviously the sophistication of these forecasts will decrease the further ahead the target date, but this does not preclude a firm from having limited objectives which can be continually reassessed for ten years ahead and more detailed objectives for five or one year ahead). Then having reached forecasts for the demand and supply of labour resources, consideration must be given to policies which would reconcile these. In the light of this information the firm may find the best policy is to readjust the original objectives of the enterprise. The development of a manpower plan must be considered as a circular, rather than a linear exercise, and must also be a continuous process capable of taking account of factors which influence the forecasts. Amongst the factors that the planners must consider in making their forecasts of demand and supply are:- changes in productivity; changes in working hours and holidays; estimates of the numbers of workers in each skill level leaving the firms through retirement; voluntary wastage; assessing recruitment levels; training requirements.

When supply and demand equations are used to plan manpower it imposes upon the analysis the use of individuals and aggregates as units. This use of aggregates, while necessary, may obscure some of the structural implications of policy decisions relating to the necessary adjustments for effective manpower use and we therefore suggest a complementary paradigm.

The manpower policy may take various forms as suggested earlier — the overall objectives may be revised; an increase/decrease in recruiting; initiation of train-ing programmes and management development programmes, The forms that manpower policies take may have wide reaching implications. One can think of examples from the military where the manpower policies adopted involved conscription or non-selective recruitment. In Germany, prior to World War II a policy was adopted of conscripting all young men into the armed forces. It was eventually realised that insufficient consideration had been given to the structural implications of this policy for the aircraft industry which also needed young men and the policy of conscription was revised to allow conscripts to fulfil their service by working in the aircraft industry. Another example from the military of a manpower policy with structural implications comes from the selective recruitment for the American Army during the Korean War. In his study of the North Korean prisoner of war camps (1969) Bradbury shows that the much criticised response of the American prisoners of war was related to the system of selective service. The manpower allocation policy meant that the majority of ground forces from which most of the captives were drawn were from the lower socio-economic groups and it is likely that this influenced the American response to captivity.

Chems, Clark, Harries, Sinclair

The Structural Implications of Corporate Policies

Katz and Kahn (1966) argue that the rapidity of change involving enterprise of all kinds is so great that there is a premium on the anticipation and direction of future changes and the following through of policy decisions to the *"structural implications for the organisation"*. It is the recognition of the first part of this argument that has led many organisations to develop some form of manpower planning, but the failure to recognise the "structural implications" of policy decisions can limit the effectiveness of manpower planning.

Looking at this argument in more detail we may consider that the important factor is not the rapidity of change but the close inter-relatedness of various factors, so a change in one aspect of an enterprise or its environment may have immediate repercussions on other aspects. For example, a change in technology, even though it is largely anticipated may have immediate effects on the hierarchical structure of an enterprise, the composition of its labour force, and its system of marketing. In this case it is not the rapidity of the change that is important but the effects of the change — the amount of internal and external organisational space affected by the change.

Looking at this argument another way, one may suggest that it is not the rapidity of change which places a premium on anticipation, but rather through our increased desire and ability to control our environment, by anticipating change, that we in fact create change. This desire to control is more apparent in some enterprises than others. We might hypothesise for example, that it is more prevalent in large scale enterprises with predictable markets with a process technology and professionally oriented management.

Let us consider Katz and Kahn's further argument, "the following through of policy decisions to the structural implications for the enterprise". Let us suppose a policy decision is made to establish a programme of manpower planning. This new activity is likely to take the form of evaluating existing resources within the enterprise, estimating further requirements and taking measures to ensure the right resources are available when necessary. It is possible that in order to make sufficiently accurate forecasts a rigid career structure may be introduced or an existing career structure made more explicit. (We may note the links between manpower planning, management development and performance appraisals in some major enterprises in Britain). When this occurs it has obvious structural implications for the enterprise. It may change the image of a position within the organisation or it may alter the interrelations between individuals or groups of employees. Similarly techniques of achieving the required numbers of workers of each skill level may have structural implications. For example, the blurring of demarcation lines may disturb underlying power positions within the enterprise.

Katz and Kahn further suggest that continuous planning requires both an Intelligence Function, reporting on environmental trends and a Policy Development Function to generate alternative courses of action for anticipated changes in the environment.

An enterprise may have sufficient data available on its manpower requirements to fulfil the intelligence function but this must then be translated into policy decisions to help meet the overall objectives of the enterprise. Similarly, so much emphasis may be laid on planning to meet specific needs that it neglects the intelligence function. One instance of this may be a personnel department which spends time planning recruitment campaigns but which fails to keep useful records on existing staff, promotions prospects etc. etc.

The Structure Paradigm

Members of firms, enterprises and institutions are frequently heard to say that "its the people who matter". Many attempts have been made to make the task of managing the "human aspect" more sophisticated. Recently, there has been a renewed emphasis upon the development of analytical frameworks for the analysis and diagnosis of problems. Management education has been through a range of techniques for achieving this — lectures, group experiences, case studies — but perhaps the most significant developments have come from changes within the Harvard Business School's teaching programme (Zalenick and Moment 1964, Seiler 1966). This development is itself based on the dramatic increase in the volume of research done and published on organisational behaviour. This research has facilitated the development of a specialist knowledge of practical significance, but it has not necessarily resulted in a more worth-while use of behavioural science practitioners.

The analytical frameworks have been moving steadily — much too slowly — from an absorption in the minutiae of the behaviour of the small group to the study of the total organisational structure in relation to its environment. Also the emphasis is switching from regarding the behavioural scientist as the "good guy" who smooths technical and administrative change (eg. Coch and French 1948 and their many successors) to a realisation that it may be possible for the behavioural science practitioner to contribute significantly to the actual design of the future organisation (Miller and Rice 1967). The case study which follows illustrates these developments.

When we are talking about social structures (Blau and Scott 1961) we are referring to the ways in which human conduct becomes socially organised. That is, to the observed regularities in the behaviour of people. Our concern is with regularities which arise from social conditions rather than from the physiological and psychological characteristics of individuals. The two social features which influence the conduct of people are the structure of social relations and the shared beliefs and orientations that unite the members of the collectivity and guide their conduct.

The idea of a structure of relations implies that the component elements stand in some relation to one another. It is argued that a network of social relations transforms an aggregate of individuals into a group and the group is more than the sum of the individuals composing it. The reason for making this assertion is that the structure of social relations is a feature influencing the conduct of individuals.

Social Relations: include the patterns of social interaction; the frequency and duration of contacts between people: the tendency to initiate contacts: the direction of influence between persons and the degree of co-operation. The networks of social relations between the individuals and groups, and the status structure which is defined by them, constitute an essential part of the social structure of an enterprise. The other part is the shared beliefs which serve as standards for human conduct.

34   Cherns, Clark, Harries, Sinclair

When people are in interaction with one another, common ideas arise as to how people *should* behave and what objectives are worthy of prestige. Thus we would expect common values to crystalise and social "norms" to develop. These sociologically sanctioned rules of conduct vary in significance.

The analysis of social relationships in organisations can be thought of in a number of ways. For examples, Woodward in her earlier researches examined the areas of spans of control, levels in the hierarchy, and the ratio of administrative to direct workers in a sample of 100 firms in Essex (Woodward 1958). Her findings indicated that there were profiles for these three dimensions which could be related to the "objectives" of the enterprise. Woodward suggested that firms in mass production were characterised by social relationships which were more formalised and segmented than in process or batch production Similar observations have been made by Blauner who suggests that the extent of employee alienation is connected to the type of technology (Blauner 1964). Finally, Pugh and colleagues have sought to investigate social relationships by considering the structure of the organisation to be identifiable in terms of, for example, centralisation and formalisation (Pugh 1969). The approaches discussed so far lack a dynamic dimension and this may be most readily obtained by examining Crozier's analysis of the French tobacco monopoly (Crozier 1964).

Crozier selected the monopoly because its relations with an external environment were highly stable. The general expectation of what he would find was that the monopoly would represent an ideal example of a bureaucracy. His analysis showed that social relationships were typified by a mass of impersonal rules governing the allocation of work and seniority; the centralising of decisions so that anything not covered by the rules could be passed upward for action; the isolation of the occupational groups from each other so that newcomers were subjected to the pressures of the group they had joined; and finally by the development of "parallel power relationships". This last aspect of the social relationships requires some expansion. Crozier argued that the bargaining power of groups was directly related to the groups ability to control areas of the organisation in which decision making was a matter of personal judgement. (Alternatively, the group might succeed in convincing others that this was the case). This hypothesis related "uncertainty" to power. The implications of this "structural" element for organisational design are obvious. Essentially Crozier has succeeded in taking the ideas about the behaviour of groups in terms of "protest strategies" by Sayles and placed this in the context of an organisational analysis (Sayles 1958).

The second aspect of the structural paradigm is shared beliefs. For the purposes of this paper we shall focus only on the orientations of the employees to their work, to colleagues, the job and the enterprise employing them (Goldthorpe 1967). These beliefs will reflect national characteristics. For example, Crozier argues that the particular form taken by bureaucracy in France reflects the national character, especially with reference to the attitude to face to face relationships (Crozier 1964).

One of the critical issues is the extent to which orientations are formed outside the enterprise and can be regarded as "givens". This is one issue which has been largely neglected, until recently, particularly by industrial sociologists. The tendency has been to examine such aspects as, the formation of group norms and to explain these by reference to the technology and the division of labour. Lupton's (1964) comparative study of two groups possessing quite different shared beliefs about the role of management illustrates the "classical approach". His attempt to break out of this indicates the kinds of problems involved. Cunnison (1966) did in fact follow along lines which were initially similar but were eventually more successful and managed to present a sensitive analysis of the penetration into one factory of orientations generated in the local community.

Goldthorpe would argue that where the orientations of the members of an enterprise are similar then tne most probable explanation is that persons with similar orientations elected to join the same enterprise. In other words, the influencing of managerial strategies on the formation of orientations is relatively low. If this is regarded as a plausible hypothesis then it would suggest that part of the intelligence function of an enterprise should be scanning the environment for data on orientations (Aguilar 1968). This data would then be fed across to the policy development function (Katz and Kahn 1966).

Crozier and Goldthorpe suggest that national (societal) social structures occupy a key role in providing members of society with images of social relationships and with orientations. One of the problems faced by enterprises is that technological innovations are introducing new forms of interpersonal relationships at work. For example, Touraine (1966) attempted to characterise interpersonal relationships in the process industries as "horizontally hierarchised co-operation" If this idea is a useful one, how do enterprises succeed in introducing it? We do not propose to answer this question in the paper but suggest that the matching of the required characteristics of interpersonal relations at work with the actual characteristics of future working populations is a critical issue with considerable implications for enterprises and society.

In this short section, we have attempted to sketch in the outlines of the structural approach. The ᵢext section contains an *illustration* taken from a consultancy project on organisational design.

The Structures Paradigm: Organisational Design at CCE Ltd.

CCE Ltd. is a pseudonym for a large and well-known subsidiary of a major British Company manufacturing consumer products. In the middle 1960's they decided to replace their existing production facilities by building a totally new factory which would contain the latest viable technological developments (Cherns and Clark 1968: Clark and Ford 1970).

Members of the CUSSR became involved in an advisory capacity on "organisational design". In this example which because of its unusual nature helps to highlight the complementary nature of the "aggregates" and "structures" paradigms, we entered a situation in which the established function for manpower planning had already made an overall calculation of the total numbers of persons who would be required. This figure was broken down into departments and functions in a way which enabled the newcomer — ourselves — to see how the totals had been calculated and the kinds of thinking which influenced the calculation. At CCE Ltd. the major concern of the planners was to match the requirements for the next five years against the existing population. Basically, their problems were not of overall shortage, but of changes in the nature of skill requirements for new automated and mechanised technology. We shall focus upon this aspect.

CCE Ltd. had a strong and active interest in the latest ideas about manpower as a human resource (Likert 1967, Gellerman 1964). At the time of stating our activities the thinking about human resources was very largely carried out within the framework of existing ideas and exceptions from these. A close scrutiny of the manpower proposals suggested that the impact of the new technology on the old had been finely calculated to reveal where some jobs would disappear. Then the remainder of the jobs had been examined and it had been noted that there were untidy edges like "fractions of a man" being required to operated widely dispersed machinery. An attempt had then been made to remove these "fractions" by asking the Research and Development executives to redesign the technology to replace them by equipment. There was a strong pressure on the Research and Development executives to provide technological solutions and it was widely accepted that this was the best way of proceeding.

It may be seen from the preceeding account — not yet completed — that the method of tackling the manpower aspect was, at first glance, sensible perhaps even obvious. The analysis of the future requirements in CCE Ltd. was completed by working out the new jobs which would be required to maintain the new technology. The solutions proposed were largely in terms of creating new job categories to be filled by, for example, a "new breed of technician".

Essentially the thinking of CCE Ltd. about the future manpower situation was undertaken in terms of the existing system of job categories which were supplemented by new ones. Each set of jobs was largely examined independently of others and their approach has the characteristics of the "aggregates paradigm". How then can the "structures paradigm" be operated in such a situation?

Behavioural science practitioners face two main problems. The first is in getting their perspective heard at all levels and the second, is in getting decisions to be influenced — not determined — by it. Every manager and specialist has an empathy for people. Few have the detachment and cognitive capabilities to tackle the practical problems, involved in adapting "human resources" approaches to specific problems.

Our first concern was to ensure that the "structures paradigm" could be evaluated by members of CCE Ltd. This was achieved by "trial" in which we worked together with Research and Development, and other specialists from the field of ergonomics, in attempting to carry through a sociotechnical design of part of one of the factory departments. It became quite clear from this exercise that our perspective was different.

The "trial" resulted in a straight confrontation between the "structures" perspective and that of the "aggregates". Put briefly, the job design analysis being utilised in CCE Ltd. failed to consider how the existing social system would inhibit and facilitate the plans for the new factory. One of the categories of worker which we investigated in the existing factory had all the characteristics of a cohesive and active occupational grouping with clear and established norms and boundaries. In the context of the particular department studied the form of decision making actually possessed many of the characteristics which members of the design team regarded as desirable for the new factory. That is to say, they wanted to design an organisation which would embrace a system of management which tended towards "participative" (McGregor 1960; Likert 1961 and 1967, Argyris 1964). Ironically, the major probable impact of the new technology and the manning plans suggested that the future situation would have all the organisational features which the design group did not want at that point. In effect, the whole of that particular department including the subtle systems of organisation which had developed over a number of years would be destroyed ... unless it was possible to redesign both the technical and social systems so that they facilitated the continuance of the traditions which CCE Ltd. valued and encouraged the emergence of responsible involvement in moment-to-moment decision making at the shop floor level.

The "trial" established the general approach of the "structures perspectives". The next stage was to create a series of short life project groups (say four months) which would contain Behavioural Science Practitioners, Research and Development, Production ... and so on, to carry out sociotechnical *analysis* and sociotechnical design on a joint basis. The first group was established and successfully examined one large department in about five months. At the end of the period a number of viable alternative organisational structures had been created, and one in particular recommended as being suitable to that particular department (Cherns and Clark 1968). By this stage it was apparent that the "aggregates" paradigm was being complemented by the "structures" approach. Managers could see ways in which the entire shop floor level and management could be redesigned to take account of the requirements of the technical changes in a way which was consistent with past traditions and the preferences of the work force; which optimised the part played by the human resources, and which fitted the orientations to work of the employees (Goldthorpe *et al* 1967).

The Rabble Hypothesis

In arguing for the application of the Structures Approach and in suggesting some criticisms of the Aggregates Approach we are not necessarily arguing that the latter approach approximates to the Rabble Hypothesis. We had however, recognised that this may be the case in some instances.

The Rabble Hypothesis as outlined by Elton Mayo contained three principal elements. First that society consists of a horde of unorganised individuals. Second, that every individual acts in a manner calculated to secure his self interest. Third, every individual thinks logically to the best of his ability in the service of this aim.

When outlining the Rabble Hypothesis Mayo was anxious to stress that such a viewpoint would inevitably lead to some weakening of the social underpinning of society. He further contended — and here he followed a line of reasoning from a number of French sociologists — that roles in society could be stabilised by attaching an identification of the individual to some known and established grouping. In the case of Mayo, he argued that the principal basis should be the small work group and that the secondary basis should be the industrial organisation. His analysis from experimental studies undertaken over a 20 year period provides apparently irrefutable evidence to support this contention. Indeed, a generation of industrial sociologists tended to focus almost entirely upon events within the

Cherns, Clark Harries, Sinclair

enterprise excluding the wider social structure, the role of the family and similar peer groups and the project of the individual actors. Fortunately this tendency has now been reversed (Goldthorpe *et al* 1967) though it is still hard to believe that we have learned as much about structures, events and processes as we might have done.

In our formulation of the Structures Approach we have no prior commitment to establishing the identification of the individual in either the local community, which may be appropriate in Ireland, or with Trade Unions, which might be appropriate in some sectors of the engineering industry or with any other grouping. The points of identification are, in our approach and in the consultancy work we have undertaken, completely free from these particular biases. Thus we are anxious to disassociate the recommendations of the Structures Approach from the better known arguments of Elton Mayo in his discussion of the Rabble Hypothesis. In practice, the Structures Approach is considerably more demanding both for the consultants and the clients that would be the case in conventional human relations training.

References

Aguilar F.J. (1968) *Scanning the Business Environment*, Macmillan. London.

Argyris C. (1964) *Integrating the Organisation and the Individual*. Wiley New York.

Blau P.M. and Scott W.R. (1961) *Formal Organisations: A Comparative Approach*. Routledge. London.

Blauner R. (1964) *Alienation, Freedom and Technology*. University of Chicago.

Bradbury W.C., Meyers S.M. and Biderman A.D. (1969) *Mass Behaviour in Battle and Captivity*. University of Chicago.

Clark P.A. and Cherns A.B. (1968) "A Role for Social Scientists in Organisational Design". Given to the Behavioural Sciences and OR Conference, London . Published in *Approaches to Organisational Behaviour*, Edited by G. Heald (1970 Tavistock London.

Clark P.A. and Ford J.R. (1970) "Methodological and Theoretical Problems in the Investigation of Planned Organisational Change." *Sociological Review*. Vol. 18, No. 1.

Coch L. and French J.R.P. (1948) "Overcoming Resistance to Change". *Human Relations* 1.

Crozier M. (1964) *The Bureaucratic Phenomenon*. Tavistock London.

Cunnison S. (1966) *Wages and Work Allocation* Tavistock London.

Gellerman (1964) *Motivation and Productivity*. American Management Association.

Goldthorpe J.G. *et al* (1967) *The Affluent Worker*. Oxford University Press London

Katz D. and Kahn R. (1966) *Social Psychology of Organisations*. Wiley. New York.

Lawrence P. and Lorsch J.W. (1967) *Organisation and Environment*. Harvard University Press. Boston.

Likert (1961) *New Patterns of Management*. New York.

Lupton T. (1964) *On the Shop Floor*. Pergamon Press.

Mayo E. (1948) *Human Problems of an Industrial Civilisation*. Routledge.

McGregor D. (1960) *Human Side of Enterprise*. McGraw-Hill

Miller E.J. and Rice A.K. (1967) *Systems of Organisation: The Control of Task and Sentient Boundaries*. Tavistock. London.

Pugh D.S. and colleagues. Reference to articles published in the *Administrative Science Quarterly* between 1963 and 1970.

Sayles L.R. (1958) *Behaviour of Industrial Groups: Prediction and Control.* Columbia University Press.

Seiler J.A. (1966) *Systems Analysis in Organisational Behaviour*. Irwin, Homewood. Illinois.

Touraine A. (1965) *Worker Attidues to Technical Change*. OECD.

Woodward J. (1958) *Management and Technology*. HMSO. London.

Woodward J. (1965) *Industrial Organisations: Theory and Practice*. Oxford University Press.

Zaleznick A. and Moment D. (1964) *Casebook of Interpersonal Behaviour in Organisations*. Wiley. New York.

4

A Study of the 'Cadres Superieurs'* on the Cote D'Azur

V. Brijatoff

Servo, Paris

I — Introduction

1. Aims and Scope of the Study

This is an exposition of the preliminary results of a study of the living conditions of Senior Executives on the Riviera. The preliminary study aims at defining the future plan of a broader investigation. Objectives were:

1.1 validation of the hypothesis that the true mobility of Senior Executives can only be ascertained when studied from the angle of their standard of living, their aspirations, and the satisfaction or non-satisfaction of their needs;

1.2 definition of a methodology for approaching the problem simultaneously from the standpoint of the company, the head of the household and the housewife;

1.3 formulation of the "Executive" characteristics and especially those of the "Senior Executives" not only as seen by themselves but also as seen by the representatives of the company, that is to say by the heads of the personnel;

1.4 and lastly to assess an idea about the Senior Executive's flow: moving outwards from Paris, along the Rhone valley towards Grenoble and then Marseilles; then dividing itself into two streams, one going towards Toulouse, the other towards the Riviera.

The data collected during the course of the preliminary study does not, of course, cover all the points to be studied in the main research.

It is believed that the results to hand are significant enough to warrant publication. It needs to be borne in mind, however, that they are no more than preliminary results unsuitable as a basis for far reaching conclusions. Indeed one cannot stress enough the difficulties of interpretation of results based upon small samples whose inherent bias is magnified by the choice of one single geographical area ie Nice, Cannes and its surrounding region.

---

* The "cadres superieurs" functions are those of Senior Executives in Anglo-Saxon countries. However, unlike the Executives, the "cadres" are a cohesive body with a specific place in the French labour force, making them, in this respect peculiar to the French.

2. Methodology – Highlights

2.1 Framework of the Preliminary Study

2.1.1. Selection of the sample

Bearing in mind the aims of the research, the population has been mainly drawn from the lists of the "Grandes Ecoles" graduates. These sources, however, have two main shortcomings:

- they omit recent graduates (who may be highly mobile); and there are delays in bringing the lists up-to-date,

- they fail, by definition, to cover self-made men.

The graduate lists have therefore been complemented by information collected from telephone directories. But this resulting coverage was still thought unsatisfactory in view of varying ratios of households with telephones. However, telephone directories enabled to some extent the validation of the graduate lists.

It is felt that a valid sample can only be obtained by using information provided by the Executive's employers themselves. But besides the unwillingness of companies to divulge the names of their staff, let alone their addresses, the Executives themselves are touchy about any information obtained through the "official" channel of their own companies. In view of this, such a source of information was disregarded.

However, it was possible to carry out interviews at the place of work because interviews there tended to be regarded less suspiciously by respondents. This approach still possesses limitations. The interviewer cannot appreciate the family environment and the household's standard of living characteristics.

2.1.2. Method of the survey

a) Households

The survey was carried out with the use of both an open ended questionnaire and a closed ended questionnaire. The latter aimed at returning standard information such as household composition, professional characteristics of the head of the household, type of house, housing and leisure equipment, net earned income, as well as such details as the types of leisure and vacations.

The very same questionnaire was filled in, whenever possible, both by the head of the household and by his wife independently, at different times. This had the added advantage of facilitating a comparative analysis of the family standard of living from data obtained from two different sources within the household.

A separate questionnaire was also filled in by the wife only. This was to elicit responses on the household feelings of isolation and neuro-stress. It touched upon perception and description of the leisure facilities for shopping .... (the "centre" – see part 4).

b) The Companies

In order to cross-check the answers to questions on household mobility with a view to relating them to a broader framework, an open ended questionnaire was used in interviews with Heads of Personnel of selected firms established in the district. This questionnaire aimed also at testing some of the results of previous studies on companies' structure and organisation and the mobility of their manpower[1]. The choice of firms was random, the only constraint was that they had to belong to an expanding industrial sector (as defined by the INSEE classification: 10, 22, 27 and 28). They included firms engaged in petrol and hydro-carbons; mechanical engineering; the aircraft industry; and the electrical and electronic industries. The company data is not presented in this paper.

2.2 Nature of the Results

In considering the results one should bear in mind that they are static and represent the situation at a given point in time: they give little information on the history of the household and therefore they provide no explanation as to reasons behind today's situation.

Refusal to participate in the survey was of the order of 20%. From among the participants it is significant that as high a proportion as 60% refused to have their interview taped.

On the whole, the respondents appear to possess a very stable private and family life. Unfortunately it has been impossible to cross-check whether this apparent stability is reflected by a corresponding one:

— at the level of the company (absenteism, late at work, etc ...)

— at the level of the individuals (lack of aggression, of ambition, etc ...) and what are the order and the degree of the probable explanatory variables.

On the problem of mobility, two areas would need further research:

— on the one hand, it would appear necessary to go more deeply into the reasons behind a change of employer. For example one needs to isolate such factors as disagreement with superiors, availability of immediate promotion outside the present company, or the insecurity of employment.

— on the other hand, a number of exogenous factors should be taken into account which create a kind of brake upon potential mobility such as:

— housing shortage

— long-term credit and hire-purchase facilities

— lack of relevant information on available career opportunities etc ...

II – Results of the Survey

1. The "Cadres"

In France, the cadres, however well known have been but little studied as a distinct population in their own right..

Referring to them, some speak of a "new working class", others of "intermediary bodies" existing in the companies and in the Nation, or again words such as professional, elite and technocrat are used to describe them. It is certainly not within the terms of reference of the present research to study any discontent with their role felt by the cadres or again that faced by the boards of a number of companies vis a vis their own cadres. It is however useful to make a note of them as they occurred throughout the study. For it was indeed significant, while conducting the interviews, to see how conscious were the cadres of their own strategic importance within the company's organisation, and to notice their increasing sense of responsibility as regards their own contribution to invention and innovation without which a firm cannot possibly survive.

These tendencies can only gather momentum:

— in view of the numerical growth of the cadres. There is no single satisfactory definition: but they are estimated at some 700 000 on the basis of the subscriptions to specialized pension funds and as many as 3 million when including technicians, artists, the professions, and so on ...

— in view of the growing complexity of their functions. This is the result, not only of the rapid technical transformations taking place in a highly industrialised economy, but also of new functions, not technical in themselves, but born out of changes in the structure of the company, such as management, training and public relations.

1.1 Definition, its difficulties

As too often the case with widely used words, the term "cadres" itself is ambiguous. Parochial to the French, it is difficult to define the "cadres" as a socioprofessional group and they cannot be looked upon as a purely sociological category.

In a study carried out by the French Ministry for Social Affairs[2] the definition used was "the employee classified as cadre by his employer". This is as ambiguous as the alternative "all employees eligible to subscribe to the cadre pension funds".

It is interesting to note that official documents attempting to define both status and salaries of the "cadres" were published in 1945. These sources[3] talk of the "cadres" as having "a commanding function over colleagues performing a great variety of jobs". Therefore they are treated as being distinct from engineers who, according to the same sources, are looked upon as having no such commanding function. These documents have since been used as a basis for much collective bargaining and settlement. In all of them the central idea appears to be that of command. It might be argued that official recognition alone and its influence on collective bargaining might account for the growth of the group "engineer and cadre": but it is insufficient in itself, however, to account for the rapid growth over the last twenty five years, and also to explain the increasing complexity of the functions of the group, especially in the fields of research, production technology and management. In view of this it would appear that appropriate terms of reference are still lacking.... or that on the contrary that they are, today, far too numerous. Indeed, the cadre member can be identified at the same time as being a specialist, a salary-earner and a part of management. In the French industrial company he appears to play what T. Parsons and R.F. Bales have called "boundary role"[4].

1.2 The Definition Adopted

The selected definition was created by the interviewees themselves, when asked to provide their "own definition" for their position. Usually it was related to their status within the hierarchy.

This definition can be summarized and broken down as follows:

- management trainees and beginners (Position 1)
- middle management (Position II, III A and lower section of III B)
- top management (upper section of III B and lower section of III C)
- board of directors (upper section of III C and top posts outside the hierarchy).

An example definition (of Position II and the qualifications of A-B and C) as found in documents of collective bargaining and settlement are given in the annexe.

2. Sample: the Respondents

At first sight and in view of the small number of people interviewed, it may appear out of place to present the results in the form of percentages. However, this method greatly facilitates reading provided, of course, that the temptation to extrapolate is firmly resisted.

2.1 *Age and Household Size*

The survey was concerned with Senior Executives, and some 60% of the respondents were aged between 40 and 44 years old. The average age-differential between husbands and wives was some 3 years only. The spread of the age distribution was between 36 and 54 years old, and that of the length of the marriage was between 7 and 27 years. All the respondents were married with an average of two children per household.

2.2 *Careers*

As a result of bias inherent in the sample, the minimum number of years in the same company was as high as 8 years. The average seniority was of the order of 12 years. These results would indicate that for the population aged 44 and under, representing some 85% of the sample, job-mobility tailed off when the man was in his thirties.

These results were cross-checked by answers to the questionnaires filled in by the respondents. Some 80% considered their propensity to change jobs had come to an end mostly because of:

- the special living conditions of the Riviera,
- such deterrents as housing shortage.

The spread of the distribution of net yearly income was between FF 60 000 and FF 108 000. The average being at some FF 80 400. These results can be compared with those of FAFSID[5] in the case of the graduate engineers.

Percentage breakdown of the net yearly income for graduate engineers in French Francs					
– from 20 000	20 to 40 000	40 to 60 000	60 to 80 000	80 to 100 000	100 000 and over
4%	36%	30%	16.4%	8.6%	5%

Experience abroad, if acquired within the same company, appears to be recognised as warranting higher earnings. For some "young senior executives" with three years experience in the United States net salaries are of the order of FF 84 000 and 96 000 per annum.

3. The Standard of Living on the Riviera

3.1 Housing

Housing shortage has already been mentioned as one of the deterrents to Senior Executive mobility. It is still rare for French companies to be completely responsible for rehousing their senior employees. Removal allowances and certain related expenses only meet the difficulties in part.

Senior Executives interviewed lived mostly in individual houses with gardens. They accounted for some 85%. The remaining 15% made use of the "Residency", the name given to blocks of flats with no more than four storeys.

Whether in houses or flats, the families comprised four to five people, and lived in 6 rooms in addition to kitchen and bathroom.

It is worth mentioning that another reason for the lack of mobility resulting from housing was that all the respondents were house owners and only 10% of them had completed their mortgage repayments on their houses or flats. When required to move, therefore the family has to sell its real estate often hurriedly with all the difficulties that implies.

3.2 Household Equipment

The results of the survey under this heading have been summarized in the following table:

Type of household goods	Equipment %	Notes
TV set	100	often several
Refrigerator	100	often several
Cooker	100	often mixed (gas-electricity)
Polishing machine	20	
Vacuum cleaner	100	
Sewing machine	85	
Dish-washer	20	
Washing machine	90	
Kitchen unit	45	
Telephone	100	
Bicycle or moped	100	often 2 per household
Private car	100	often 2 per household or even 3

It should be noted that the purchasing habits of this particular population are probably peculiar to itself in so far as:

— fridges, TV sets, cookers, polishing machine and so on, were all bought new and for cash;

— the household durables were not the latest models that it to say they were all purchased, on an average, over five years ago (in the case of sewing machines they were 14 years old on average);

— the 45% households with kitchen units indicate that they were ordered as complete sets and that they were paid cash;

— as regards cars, the powerful one (usually that of the husband) was bought new in 90% of the cases and paid for in cash in 55%. The other car was second-hand in 30% of the cases only, and when it was so, it was usually bought on hire-purchase. When a second car is bought new it is again cash payment that is predominant.

3.3 Net Income

Emphasis was placed on whether or not the household was satisfied with its present income. Some 75% were satisfied. In the case of the dissatisfied the study aimed at ascertaining what was the level of income desired.

The 25% of dissatisfied households within the group were those with the lower income. This could have been expected; what is more surprising, however, is that some 40% of the dissatisfied households with an income of FF 60 000 to FF 72 000 per annum would like to earn some 40% more than their present salaries, which appears a significant increase. This is all the more so when it is appreciated that depth study of this sub-group revealed that some 90% of the respondents regarded their mobility as ended.

Income does not appear to create a major problem for this population. Senior Executives on the whole appeared satisfied with the level of earning they have reached. It is worth mentioning however that the level of income stated by the husband is very often *under-quoted* by the wife who gives an estimate of the household income some 10 to 15% lower than the true figure.

Some 46% of the respondents budget their household expenditure systematically. The task is shared: the husband budgeting the heavy commitments (cars, house repairs and improvements, boats, holidays, income tax and so on), while the wife handles the monthly bills for which she often has a fixed budget.

3.4 Leisure and travel

The leisure activities most frequently pursued in order of popularity were:

— hiking
— do-it-yourself (home and garden)
— winter skiing and water skiing
— such sports as tennis, riding, and swimming.

Vacations are often taken twice yearly, in three week and two week periods. It is the family car that is used most frequently as transport both for vacations in France (some 60%) and abroad (some 40%).

Business trips are common:

— to Paris, on average, 6 times a year
— to other parts of Europe, some 4 times a year
— to the USA some twice a year.

Their frequency explains why this type of cadre is away from home at least once a month for from 3 to 5 days at a time.

4. Motivational Aspects

Analysis of the reasons leading to settling on the Riviera are as follows:

- transfer, sometimes initiated by the employer because of relocation as a result of decentralisation: 60%
- change of job or requested transfer inspired by dissatisfaction with living conditions in Paris: 30%
- various causes, including change: 10%.

The reasons given for enjoying living on the Riviera classified by order of popularity, were as follows:

- climate
- environment (sea, hills, green belts, etc ...)
- tempo of life
- better accommodation
- easy access to open-air activities.

In no case was the work quoted as a reason.

Satisfaction is not totally shared by the wives. Because they are not working, except in the house, they have ample free time, but inadequate facilities for enjoying it as they would wish. The rather quiet way of life, with its facilities for open-air activities which are appreciated by their husbands, appears devoid of appeal for their wives, and lacking in social and cultural opportunities.

It would appear that the wife's dissatisfaction, going somtimes as far as real frustration is perhaps the result of:

- recollection of a hectic city life which often carries the impression that "there is always something to do",
- an "isolation complex" — isolation from intellectual and artistic life when away from a major city where cultural activities are located. This is true even for those who would not participate in these pursuits actively.
- the fact that only 30% of those households represented requested transfer. Therefore for most of the households' changes in their living conditions were the results of career developments involving only the head of the household. Therefore, it could appear as if demands of the Senior Executive's careers became more important and took priority over the needs of their own families.
- At home, the Senior Executive relaxes mostly by himself (gardening and do-it-yourself jobs about the house) and his "friends" are mostly professional colleagues.

These findings were cross-checked and confirmed by answers to two specific questions put in one case to the husbands and in the other to the wives.

4.1 Sabbatical Year

It appeared worthwhile to get the Senior Executive's opinion on the value of a sabbatical year of the kind common in US universities for their teaching staff. In the present study it was defined as follows:

"a whole year, every seventh year, during which you could work in a job of your liking, at the end of which you would return to your present occupation".

Of all the respondents 65% were very favourable to the idea providing that *suitable safeguards* were given that at the end of the sabbatical year one was *certain* to get one's job back. Another 20% were no more than favourable, and 15% indifferent.

The Senior Executives "professionalisation" becomes obvious when analysis is made of the use to which this eventual sabbatical year was to be put. In 70% of the cases, it would be used to enhance specialist skills. Among those 70%, only 10% considered achieving these aims by means of a study tour. Of the remaining 30% the sabbatical year was considered as a year away from specialisation and would be used to "broaden one's field of knowledge".

4.2 The Concept of "The Centre"

As the majority of Senior Executives appear to take into account only ways of increasing their special skills, it would seem that a sabbatical would have as a consequence a worsening of the feeling of isolation of their wives. In order to formulate this feeling, a number of questions were asked aiming at defining precisely how the wives viewed themselves both physically and psychologically in relation to the "Centre".

4.2.1 Definition of the Centre

Again the definition was provided by the respondents themselves. Some 60% regarded the "Centre" as a specific street or square, and another 30% looked upon it as a town (Cannes, Nice or even the nearest village). In short it is where:

— there exists a certain degree of anonymity: 100%

— there are shops: 80%

— there are people, traffic and passers-by: 20%

— there is never too much noise: 80%

— and one is not forced into the company of the people one knows: 60%

4.2.2. Its consequences

The most significant response to the concept of Centre is that linking it to potential anonymity. The yearning for intellectual and artistic opportunities has given way to a desire to be alone in the bustle and lost in the crowd and not to be forced to meet friends and acquaintances. The centre is where one escapes, where one loses one's own family stamp. The centre offers a shelter against one's husband's professional activities.

It follows therefore, that the greater the centre is, the better it satisfies those yearnings and one should not forget that whereas professional mobility is regarded as having ended by 80% of the Senior Executives it is considered so by only 55% of their wives.

III — Preliminary Conclusions

The conclusions reached by this preliminary study can be summarized as follows:

1. Definition of the Senior Executive

According to the executives themselves a suitable definition must take into account the following considerations:

— a specific standard of living
— a function of command in professional life
— a hierarchic status in the company
— a decision-making function in professional life
— a professional specialisation capable of applying itself to several fields of business activities.

Salaries per se and formal qualifications such as degrees are but secondary (except from the standpoint of the company's personnel policy — companies are still reluctant to promote self-made men to category III C.)

2. Method

The findings would tend to indicate that the study must be carried out to comprise simultaneously the Senior Executives, their wives, and their firms. This approach yields better results than that of straight forward interviews as it facilitates cross-checking and weighing of the answers obtained from the same household. The preliminary research indicates that the main areas where divergence of opinion between respondents make cross-checking useful are:

— potential mobility
— net income of the household
— reasons behind professional satisfaction
— nature and frequency of travel (leisure or business trips)
— degree of integration in the environment

3. Mobility of Senior Executives

The results of the preliminary study clearly indicate that the degree of mobility is dependent upon a number of elements belonging to the "environment". Indeed we have seen that the majority of Senior Executives interviewed, from among which only 20% voluntarily settled on the Riviera, are completely satisfied with their situation as regards what is called the "objective indices" that is to say: salaries, housing, household equipment etc. It is these indices that are usually retained as significant in all the economic studies. However, our findings appear to indicate that a study of mobility conducted from the narrow standpoint of the Senior Executive's economic standard of living will remain unsatisfactory.

Answers to the problem of mobility seem to lie in a study of the nature of the life followed by Senior Executives and their families.

Providing the answers validate this hypothesis, an increase in the Senior Executive's mobility would be made possible only when he was to be offered a

50   Brijatoff

comparable or even a settlement of the type of life he is leading or by operating influences which are of concern to his wife.

Notes

(1) See V. Brijatoff: "Une approche socio-économique de l'attitude des firmes confrontées aux problèmes de pénurie de main-d'oeuvre" prepared for the OECD and published in *Manpower and Applied Psychology* vol. 3, no. 1 and 2 – The Ergon Press, Cork, 1969.

(2) "Etude spécific sur le recrutement des cadres" – *Fonds national de l'emploi* Juillet 1967 et Mars 1968.

(3) Known also under the title "arretés PARODI".

(4) In *Family, Socialisation and Interaction Process* (Glencoe 1955).

(5) Published in *ID*; Number 34; March 1968; and covering 26 600 people interviewed on their 1967 net earnings.

Annexe: Extracts on Collective Bargainings and Settlements

"Engineers and graduates cadres who start as engineers or sales and management executives are guaranteed automatic advancement based upon seniority during eight years from their 21st birthdays. This is to be so until the time when their training can be regarded as completed and they have thus become eligible for promotion to jobs belonging to categories II and III. The above does not preclude special promotion being granted on merit".

II A – Assistant, often self-made, filling a post graded for engineer or for someone considered equivalent, and for whom a post at this level usually represents the end of a normal career.

II B – Research engineer whose function, as distinct from qualifications, precludes that of command.

II C – Engineer being groomed for potential promotion whenever the company's needs create vacancies, attached to decision-making posts to assist the holders of those posts, but not actually being responsible for decision-making.

Explanatory notes on A: engineer or cadre chosen to fulfil functions necessitating not only a corpus of knowledge equivalent to that implied in achievement of a university degree or professional examination, but also a practical know-how. The exercise of the functions does not, however, imply that he possesses the entire and permanent responsibility for carrying them out. This final responsibility belongs to his superior (who in a small firm may be the managing director). The status of this type of cadre is above that of foreman and skilled worker, as well as being above other cadres and engineers who may be temporarily under his authority and who belong to a lower status.

Explanatory note on B: Engineer or cadre having all the academic and practical knowledge of his functions. His decision-making ability is narrowly restricted to the scope of his function. His place in the hierarchy gives him authority over his own staff which includes engineers and cadres belonging to lower status.

Explanatory note on C: This function is created only when the type of company dictates a high level of technical know-how, or by the size and complexity of the firm requiring coordination between departments. The status of an engineer or cadre in such a position usually gives him command over several engineers or cadres belonging to low status. Such a function carries with it a wide range of responsibilities and opportunities for decision-making.

5
Application of the Q-Sort Method to Manpower Analysis

Kent Mingo
Oklahoma State University

Introduction

This paper develops the Job Aspect Q-Sort as a manpower research tool and applies it within a university work environment in investigating work related need patterns of groups of university teachers, researchers, and administrators. The paper demonstrates the application of the Q-technique in developing and identifying the dimensions of natural work related groupings of professional university employees.

The paper begins with a discussion of the Q-technique as a part of the Q-methodology. Next, the nature of the psychological meaning given to congruency scores, derived from an individual's Self and Ideal-self Q-sorts, is developed within the context of self-psychology as it relates to a work setting. Following this the structure, content, and development of the Job Aspect Q-Sort is detailed. Data results are presented in two segments with the first presenting composite profiles of variously motivated groups of teachers, researchers, and administrators. The second segment of the results presents natural work related groupings, developed by Q-factor analysis, of teachers, researchers, and faculty. Finally, implications and further applications of the use of the Q-technique in manpower settings are developed.

The Q-Method and Q-Technique

Stephenson (1953, p. 1) states that his purpose in developing the Q-method is to develop a methodological approach facilitating the study of single cases or persons. According to Stephenson (1953, p. 1) the Q-method is a set of statistical, psychological, and philosophy of science principles which constitute a research methodology.

The Q-technique is a subset of the Q-method and encompasses the ways by which the Q-method is applied. The Q-technique involves the development of measurement scales, derived from theoretical constructs, for application to the individual as a unit of measurement. The methodological relevance of the Q-method and Q-technique, as developed by Stephenson (1953, p. 31), is shown in Figure 1, which identifies his conceptualization of a genealogical tree of multivariate methodology.

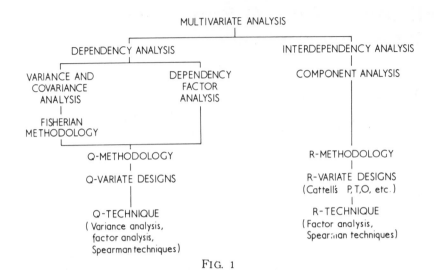

FIG. 1

This chart clarifies how Stephenson (1953, p. 28) differentiates between the Q- and R-methodologies. The Q-methodology involves the joining of two methods of dependency analysis — one encompassing analysis of variance designs and the other a reformulation of factor analysis. In the scheme as a whole, factor analysis is concerned with two different forms of multivariate analyses — interdependency and dependency analysis. Stephenson (1953, p. 28) suggests that interdependency factor analysis might be called "the blind inductive approach" and dependency factor analysis the "open eyed deductive approach".

Interdependency factor analysis is concerned with discovering relationships among data among which no part is regarded as of prior importance over any other. This form of factor analysis produces factors which may or may not have any concrete reality. The dependent form of factor analysis, which embodies the Q-technique, is developed to empirically analyze effects which are formulated prior to analysis. From Stephenson's (1953) view, the importance of the Q-technique lies in the psychological applications which it facilitates, rather than in any one of the statistical devices it employs, and would mean little if it were divorced. from the methodological and psychological matters with which it is associated.

Users of the Q-technique often lose sight of the underlying Q-method. Contributing to this is the confusion between what is meant by the Q- and R-techniques. In the Q-technique one correlates persons over variables instead of variables over persons (R-technique). Using the Q-technique, within the context of dependency factor analysis, the factors which result represent ideal-type of persons analogous to the ideal-traits or factors produced by use of the R-technique. Such ideal types arrived at by Q-factor analysis, are the basis for any taxonomy and may have useful applications within organizational and behavioral contexts. The relationship between the Q-technique and R-technique has been conceptualized by Cattell (1966, p. 69) within the context of a co-variation chart.

The process of Q-sorting is viewed by Block (1961, p. 45) as an "ipsative" procedure, i.e., the variables contained in the Q-sort are ordered or scaled relative to each other, with respect to a specified frame of reference. Focusing upon the process of Q-sorting, Nunnally (1968, p. 546) states that the Q-sort amounts to a comparative rating method rather than an absolute rating method. Nunnally (1968) feels the major reason for using the Q-sort, rather than some other comparative rating method, is that it greatly conserves the time taken to make ratings. Thus the Q-sort is a compromise between two research needs, the need to have precise differentiations made among the stimuli and the need to have comparisons made among the members of large sets of stimuli.

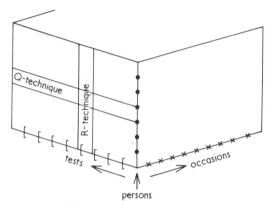

FIG. 2. Co-variation chart

Consistent with Stephenson's (1953) views concerning the Q-method, Cronbach (1953, p. 377) sees a number of advantages in the use of the Q-technique. Cronbach (1953) feels the Q-technique provides a flexible method for obtaining a qualitative description of the individual in a form appropriate for rigorous manipulation. It also permits comparisons of many different persons which co-exist as features of the same individual.. This facilitates manipulation of interpersonal correlations and provides a basis for studying the homogeneity of groups. Cronbach (1953) also considers applying the Q-technique through time allowing patterns of change to be identified upon both interpersonal and intrapersonal levels.

The Q-Technique and Congruency Scores

Conventional techniques of attitude measurement usually do not encompass all of the three components of attitude — cognitive, affective and behavioural. (Fishbein, 1966, p. 203–204). In the Job Aspect Q-Sort the nature of attitudinal constructs assessed are personalized concepts expressed by individuals as self-perceptions of themselves in their current and idealized work roles. The approach is intimately associated with the psychology of the self as developed by Carl Rogers (1954).

The organism, in the self-construct, is conceptualized as functioning so that it reacts as an organized whole to the phenomenal field to satisfy its needs. The major selector mechanism to behaviour is derived from one basic motive, that of actualization, maintenance and enhancement of self. The present research asserts that representations of both Self and Idealself, as derived from the Job

Aspect Q-Sort, are attitude constructs existing in a framework consistent with Rogers (1954). Additionally, self-attitude measurement, as related to the Q-technique, incorporates the three components of attitude into a single instrument. Specifically, the cognitive component is reflected in the pattern in which Q-items are sorted onto a Q-sort board. The affective component is accounted for in the placement of Q-items along a sorting continuum encompassing a positive to negative conceptual span. The behavioural component is reflected in the "ipsative" process of sorting Q-items onto a sorting board.

Intimately related to the measurement of self-referent attitude patterns, with a Q-sort, is the construct of congruency. Congruency concerns the degree of inter-relationship existing between self-referent attitudinal constructs, as measured by a Q-sort. Rogers' (1954) conceptualizes congruency in such a manner to suggest that the Self and Ideal image of a neurotic or poorly integrated person can be represented by two circles in which there is only a slight degree of overlap. This is the condition of incongruency and is reflected in a low correlation coefficient between the Self and Ideal-self Q-sorts of such an individual. After effective therapy such an individual's Self and Ideal-self representations should be represented by two circles with a high degree of overlap. The highly congruent individual represents the end point of a healthy personality adjustment.

Using the Job Aspect Q-Sort high congruency scores are said to be indicative of individuals who are well adjusted in the execution of their work roles and who are deriving fulfillment, to varying degrees, of their self-actualization need within their work context. Individuals with low congruency scores are said to perceive their current work roles as ones in which they are blocked in their ability to derive self-actualization.

The assertion that moderately high congruency scores can be an index of work related self-satisfaction is not without debate. One group, characterized by Rogers (1954) and his associates, takes the position that the discrepancy measure is a direct quantitative indicator of the degree of personal adjustment of an individual. Research by Rogers (1954, p. 191–192), Buttler and Haigh (1954, p. 55–75), Turner and Vanderlippe (1958, p. 202–206), and Nahinsky (1958, p. 360–364; 1963, p. 12–28; 1966, p. 55–64) lend support to the view that the discrepancy or congruency measure, as shown by positive scores, is an index of individual self-satisfaction. On the other hand, a contrasting position argues that the relationship existing between measures of congruence and the degree of personality adjustment are not necessarily linear and thus may not be an indicator of personality adjustment. Research conducted by Block and Thomas (1955, p. 254–259), and Chodorkoff (1954, p. 266–268) lend support to the position that extreme self-satisfaction as well as extreme self-dissatisfaction represent unhealthy personality tendencies.

Congruency scores derived, using the Job Aspect Q-Sort, from work related Self and Ideal-self Q-sorts are interpreted to be a measure of self-in-job actualization. This position is consistent with Hay's (1967, p. 1084–1088) findings, using a Q-sort, of a linear relationship between size of Self-Ideal congruency scores and measures of job performance for a group of engineering managers. Within a university related work context, the meaning of congruency scores derived from the Job Aspect Q-Sort is related more to adjustment to occupational work roles than to personality adjustment in general.

Structure and Content of the Job Aspect Q-Sort

The Job Aspect Q-Sort is an unstructured Q-sort with a forced, symmetrical, unimodal distribution which in shape approximates a normal distribution. The number of categories contained in its sorting continuum is nine. Figure 3 is a representation of the Q-sort board used with the Job Aspect Q-Sort.

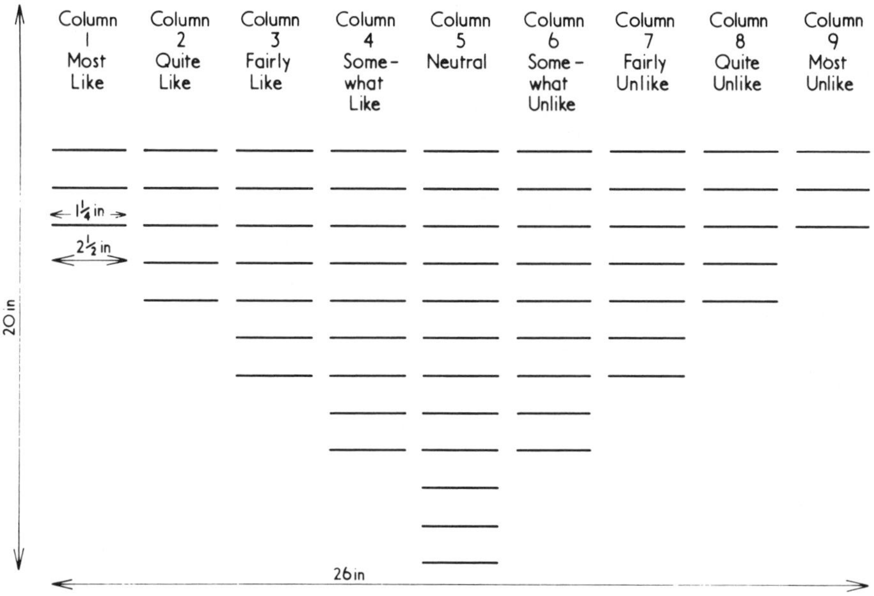

FIG. 3. Representation of Q-sort board

Q-sorts may be structured or unstructured. In a structured Q-sort, Q-items usually are incorporated into an analysis of variance design in two or three dimensions. Block (1961, p. 49) states that the structured Q-sort design has not been widely used and, in practice, definition of its content is an ambiguous task. Unstructured Q-sorts involve identifying an underlying domain or universe encompassing a conceptual problem set and then either intuitively developing Q-items deemed appropriate or operationally specifying a pool of possible Q-items which then can be randomly sampled for inclusion in a Q-sort (Block, 1956, p. 492). In practice, in developing Q-sort content most researchers have adopted "rationalized" variations of the specification procedure which is really a compromise between both methods. Though this is largely a subjective process, it is not without structure and forces the researcher to proceed in pragmatic steps in the development of Q-sort content. Examples of unstructured Q-sorts developed by the "rationalized" specification procedure and their content are provided in research by Morrison (evaluation concepts relative to occupational choice; 1962), Hay (work factor dimensions and managerial effectiveness, 1967), Sommers (product symbolism in differentiating social strata; 1964), Hamm (product symbolism and self-actualization; 1967), and Mingo (work elements and self-actualization; 1968).

The specific job aspects which were selected for use in the Job Aspect Q-Sort were largely drawn from a classification scheme developed by Herzberg

(1957, p. 37–94) and his associates. The eleven classes of job factors contained in the Job Aspect Q-Sort are as follows:

1. *Intrinsic Aspects of Job.* This factor includes all of the many aspects of the work itself. This includes job aspects which tend to be constant for work, regardless of where the job was performed, which lead to job self-actualization.

2. *Supervision.* Those aspects of the job situation which pertain to the relationships of the worker to his immediate supervision.

3. *Working Conditions.* Physical aspects of the working environment, usually a function of a particular organization, which are not necessarily a part of the work.

4. *Wages.* Includes all aspects of the job involving present monetary remuneration for work done..

5. *Opportunity for Advancement.* Includes all job aspects which an individual sees as potential sources of betterment of economic position or organizational status.

6. *Security.* Includes those features of the job situation which lead to assurance for continued employment. This job factor includes the psychological elements related to prospects of continuous work of both work environment related sentiments and sentiments of faith in one's self or company relationships.

7. *Company and Management.* Includes those aspects of an individual's immediate work situation which are a function of organizational administration and policy formulation and implementation.

8. *Social Aspects of Job.* Includes job aspects involved with the relationships of the worker with other employees usually peers.

9. *Communication.* Includes those aspects of the job situation involving the formal spreading of information within the organization.

10. *Security-Based Fringe Benefits.* Includes company provisions which attempt to prepare the worker for emergencies, illness, old age, hospitalization, as well as holidays, leaves, and vacations.

11. *Supportive Work Aspects.* Includes those resources provided by the organization, whether behavioural or instrumental objects, whose purpose is to increase productivity by providing supportive privileges, conditional prerogatives, resources and appropriate organizational structure necessary for facilitating the ability of employees to derive fulfillment of in-job self-actualization needs.

(For a full description of the contents of the Job Aspect Q-Sort, see Appendix I.)
Given the Self and Ideal-self Q-sorts of an individual, using the Job Aspect Q-Sort, it is expected that the degree of congruency which an individual exhibits toward his university work environment will relate to the symbolism contained in the various job aspects as they are perceived in terms of work experience and motivational states. Thus individuals evidencing low congruency, between their Self and Ideal-self Q-sorts, should describe as most like themselves, in their

current university work environment, job aspects concerned with the physical environment, job aspects concerned with the physical environmental context of their work role — i.e., classes of job factors such as Working Conditions, Security-Based Fringe Benefits, and Job Security. Conversely, individuals with high congruency between their Self and Ideal-self Q-sorts should tend to describe those job aspects most like themselves using job aspects concerned with the nature of the work itself — i.e., classes of job factors such as Intrinsic Job Aspects, Opportunity for Advancement, and Supportive Work Aspects. The size of such individual congruency scores, which are rank correlation coefficients adjusted for ties, are used as the basic data units for purposes of analysis.

The developmental process involved in the structuring of the Job Aspect Q-Sort followed criteria set forth in the literature. Specific Q-items were worded, evaluated, and selected following guide lines developed by Block (1956, p. 492; 1961, p. 49, 52–55, and 79), Cronbach (1953, p. 376–388), Goodling and Guthrie (1956, p. 70–72), Kenny (1956, p. 315–318), Rinn (1961), and Wittenborn (1961). The instrument was pre-tested twice, in two stages of development using instructions related to work settings, one upon a group of thirty-two senior business students and in a second instance upon a group of seventeen industrial supervisors. Two separate assessments of reliability were conducted, one with a primary version recording an average reliability correlation of 0.522 for Self-sorts and 0.571 for Ideal-sorts. After item revisions, a second retest produced an average reliability correlation of 0.690 for Self-sorts and 0.748 for Ideal-sorts. The size of the second reliability values compare closely with those reported by Hay in developing a work related Q-sort for application in an engineering management work setting (Hay 1967, p. 1085).

Ninety-six subjects, sixty teachers and researchers, and thirty-six administrators at a large state university, completed Self and Ideal-self sorts of the Job Aspect Q-Sort. Subjects were proportionately selected at random from about 1000 individuals placed in three groups of teachers, researchers, and administrators who had been classified using university records. Each of the subjects was individually approached, given a Q-sort board, and requested to sort a current representation of himself in his current university job environment and a self-representation of his ideal university working environment. Though the Job Aspect Q-Sort in this case is applied within a university work setting with slight modifications it could be used in professional work contexts and with further modification could easily be applied at the level of the first line supervisor.

Results

The data results are developed in two sections with the first section presenting composite group profiles, using average placements of job factor classes, for high and low congruency groups of faculty and administrators. The second segment develops the results of Q-factor analysis of the Self and Ideal-self Q-sorts of selected teachers, researchers, and administrators with the purpose being to show the dimensions of natural work groupings in a university work environment.

Preliminary to the development of composite group profiles, a comparison of the congruency scores of the faculty and administrators tested is presented to demonstrate the differing work related perception patterns of individuals functioning in different university work roles. This evaluation makes use of the rank correlation coefficients, adjusted for ties, for each individual's Self and Ideal-self Q-sorts and involves viewing the rank correlation coefficients as a score for analysis purposes (Block 1961, p. 104).

The range of congruency scores for the sixty faculty (including researchers) was from 0.725 to − 0.452 with a mean value of 0.106. Congruency scores for the thirty-six administrators were from 0.852 to − 0.345 with a mean value of 0.365. Use of the Mann Whitney U test produced a value of 3.27 which is significant at a level greater than 0.001 (Ferguson 1959, p. 359). The high mean congruency scores for administrators suggests they are deriving, in their administrative work roles, significantly higher levels of work related self-satisfaction than are subordinate faculty who function in a non-administrative work context.

Composite Group Profiles

The materials which follow compare composite Self and Ideal-self Q-sorts within work role contexts. Comparisons do not employ factor analysis and are across congruency classifications of low and high and reflect the upper and lower one third of congruency scores of the sixty faculty. The basic data units, used in developing the composite profiles, were the rank scores for individual Q-item placements. The composite profiles show the degree to which low and high congruency faculty groups have common self-referent perceptions of their current and idealized university working environments. Associated with each composite profile are − measures of group consensus, Kendall's (Siegal 1956, p. 229-235) coefficient of concordance W, reflecting the strength of commonness of placement of Q-items for a given group's work related self-perceptions and − the degree of correlation between composite profiles.

Two composite profiles are developed − Composite Self-sorts of Low and High Congruency Faculty and − Composite Ideal-self sorts of Low and High Congruency faculty. These composites are just two examples of the many which could be presented. The purpose served in presenting the two profiles is methodological and demonstrates differences in work related self-perception patterns, given the simple classification of faculty into high and low congruency groups.

Composite-Self-sorts of Low and High Congruency Faculty

Figure 4 presents the composite job factor placements for the Self-sorts of high and low congruency faculty, within the faculty work role setting. Using the average placement of the sixty Q-items as data units, the degree of correlation between these composites is 0.449 (t = 3.86, d.f. = 58, p > 0.001). The degree of correlation is moderately low and suggests that high and low congruency groups of faculty perceive their current job environment in moderately different frames of references.

The motivational differences existing between the faculty groups are shown by their use of job aspects relating to Security and Working Conditions. The Low Congruence faculty used these classifications as most descriptive of self in their current work environment. In contrast, the high congruency group of faculty described those facets of their current job, most like themselves, using job aspects related to Intrinsic and Supervisory job aspects. The coefficient of concordance of 0.234 for the low congruency group of faculty is interpreted as reflecting a negative consensus towards their work environment, while the W of 0.217 for the high congruence faculty suggests a consensus of positive sentiments. The sizes of the concordance scores, for both groups, are low and point to a diversity of consensus.

LOW CONGRUENCY FACULTY

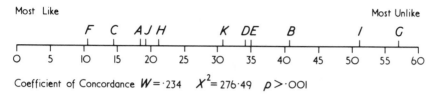

Coefficient of Concordance $W = .234$ $X^2 = 276.49$ $p > .001$

HIGH CONGRUENCY FACULTY

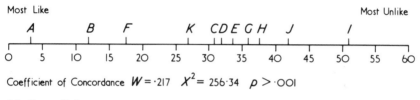

Coefficient of Concordance $W = .217$ $X^2 = 256.34$ $p > .001$

Job Factor Code

A = Intrinsic	E = Opportunity for Advancement	I = Communications
B = Supervisory		J = Security Based Fringe Benefits
C = Working Conditions	F = Security	
	G = Company and Management	K = Supportive Work Aspects
D = Wages	H = Social	

FIG. 4. Relative placement of job factor classes for composite self-sorts of low and high congruency faculty

Of the twenty faculty members contained in the low congruency group six have left the university, in the two and one-half years following the study, while none of the high congruency faculty have departed. This is an important fact as it points to the utility of the congruency measure in predicting personnel turnover. Further evidence of the predictive ability of the congruency measure is demonstrated in that of twelve low congruency administrators, six have left the university while only one of the twelve high congruency administrators has resigned.

Composite Ideal-Self sorts of Low and High Congruency Faculty

Shown in Figure 5 are the composite job factor placements for the Ideal-self sorts of the low and high congruency groups of faculty. The degree of correlation between the composites is 0.769 (t = 9.15, d.f. = 58, p > 0.001). Both coefficients of concordance are taken to reflect positive sentiments and are close in size. The increased correlation between these two groups reflects changes in the higher self-descriptive placement of job aspects related to Intrinsic and

Supervision job aspects for the low congruency faculty in their ideal work environment. In other words, it appears that the dissatisfied faculty group desires an ideal job environment quite similar to the ideal job context of the satisfied faculty members. Such a finding may provide a revealing insight to administrators as one of the major job classification shifts relates to the quantity and quality of interpersonal supervisory activity present in the work setting.

The presentation of composite profiles for variously motivated groups of faculty has demonstrated the Q-method's ability to distinguish between varying patterns of work perceptions. As previously noted, the content of Q-sorts used in work related applications is quite flexible and may be adapted to suit a particular research problem. Neither is the range of comparisons of Q-sort applications constrained as stated by Block (1961, p. 95):

> We can compare "good" and "mediocre" officers, chess-players and dice-throwers, cheerleaders and accountants, psychotherapists and neurologists, the children of elderly parents and children of young parents ... the possible comparisons require only some imagination.

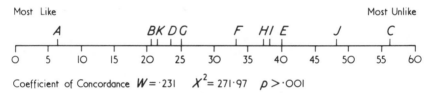

LOW CONGRUENCY FACULTY

Coefficient of Concordance $W = .231$ $X^2 = 271.97$ $p > .001$

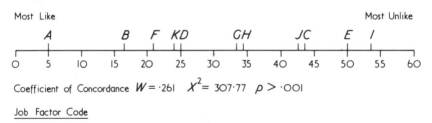

HIGH CONGRUENCY FACULTY

Coefficient of Concordance $W = .261$ $X^2 = 307.77$ $p > .001$

Job Factor Code

A = Intrinsic
B = Supervisory
C = Working Conditions
D = Wages

E = Opportunity for Advancement
F = Security
G = Company and Management
H = Social

I = Communications
J = Security – Based Fringe Benefits
K = Supportive Work Aspects

FIG. 5. Relative placement of job factor classes for composite ideal-self sorts of low and high congruency faculty

Q-Factor Analysis

This section presents two examples of the application of Q-factor analysis to the Self and Ideal-self Q-sort data of eighty faculty and administrators. A reduction in sample size, accomplished by random procedures, was necessary due to computer space limitations in accomodating an 80 × 80 matrix of persons. The first application of Q-factor analysis demonstrates the separation of faculty and administrators into two natural work role related groups and describes the characteristics of these groups by developing composite profiles of classes of job factors. The second application shows, in a more micro focus, the individual makeup of a group established by Q-factor analysis and presents the factor scores for specific Q-items which were most relevant in the establishment of the group.

Composite Profiles Established by Q-Factor Analysis

The data units used in the Q-factor analysis are the specific Q-item placements of eighty separate current job related Q-sorts (Current × Current matrix). It is also possible to develop Ideal × Ideal or Current × Ideal Q-factor analyses. In a Current × Current Q-factor analysis, the result of orthogonal factor rotations produces a series of factors with eighty individuals as the variables contained in the factor. Each person, as a variable, is assigned a factor loading which measures the degree to which the individual is involved in the factor pattern. Factor loadings can be interpreted like correlation coefficients of variables, in this case people, on the factor pattern. This is done by squaring the factor loading and multiplying by 100. The factors described are orthogonally rotated which means that the amount of correlation existing between factors, extracted from the same factor analysis, is zero.

Figure 6 shows the composite profile of one of the orthogonal factors established by factor analyzing the 80 × 80 matrix of Current job perception patterns of university faculty and administrators. Fourteen people whose factor loadings were 0.350 or above were assigned to the factor. The average factor loading value for the individuals grouped in the factor is 0.521. Of the fourteen people, thirteen are faculty, one an administrator, with one faculty member having left the university since the completion of the study. The composite profile shown in Figure 6 was developed using Q-item placements of the fourteen individuals in the same manner as were previous profiles.

Establishing the factor by Q-factor analysis poses no problem; however, interpreting the meaning of a factor is another matter. The labels attached to a factor may be symbolic (symbols without substantive meaning of their own), descriptive (developed from the research's judgment and intuition), and causal (involes reasoning from the pattern to the underlying forces causing them) (Rummel XI, p. 471). Utilizing both descriptive and suspected causal elements the factor is named — FACULTY RESEARCHERS.

Individuals, contained in the factor, work largely in the physical and biological sciences and engineering. As a group, including the administrator who is a known authority in this field, these individuals are productive, mature and economically rational professionals who are scholarly in their academic pursuits. From Figure 6 it is seen that, in their current work environment, these individuals are strongly preoccupied with wages and a mix of physical and supportive work conditions which foster their scientific productivity. Their desire for a productive work environment is associated with a low regard for job aspects associated with policy and structural elements of the higher administration and its communication practices. These researchers tended not to trust the intentions of the administration and held the attitude that if they were administratively harrassed in their ability to obtain task or project work satisfaction they would exercise their high mobility and leave the university.

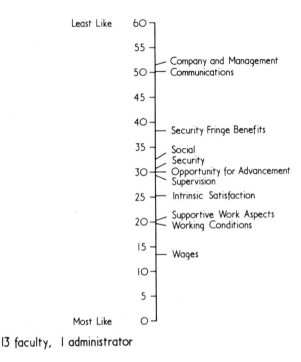

13 faculty, 1 administrator

Fig. 6. Composite self-sorts for a Q-factor named — Faculty Researchers

Still in the current work context, Figure 7 presents the composite profile of the orthogonally defined factor for eighteen faculty and administrators. The average factor loading for the factor is 0.458 with a minimum factor loading of 0.350. Of the eighteen people in the factor thirteen are administrators and five are faculty with none of the group having left the university. Again employing the researcher's prerogative, the factor is named — HARD WORKING ADMINISTRATORS.

The administrators contained in the group tend to be solid and effective individuals in their bureaucratic work roles. They also are individuals who, for the most part, have firmly made the transition into the administrative ranks having foregone their competence in their areas of professional training. They are highly self-actualized men who tend to place much value in on going interaction patterns with their supervisors (shown by the high placement of Supervisory job aspects). These individuals also seem to derive comfort from their attained job security.

The five faculty members contained in the factor perceive their current work setting in an administrative frame of reference. The inner mechanisms of promotion into administrative ranks is not clearly defined; however it well could be that administratively orientated faculty somehow gravitate, omitting administratively orientated cues, into the perceptual fields of administrators who are responsible for selection processes. Whether such an administrative selection process produces dynamic and innovative administrative practices is a topic of some debate, but the process may tend to perpetuate the breed.

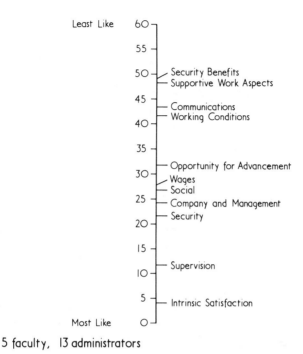

5 faculty, 13 administrators

FIG. 7. Composite self-sorts for a Q-factor named — Hard working administrators

Factor Scores and Q-Factor Interpretation

Figure 8, shows, using scores for analysis purposes, a micro focus of the composition of an orthogonally defined factor, developed in the current work setting, which has been named — PRODUCTIVE AND SELF-ACTUALIZED ADMINISTRATORS AND FACULTY. Factor scores are loadings by which the existence of a pattern for the variables contained in a factor can be determined. The factor score matrix gives a score for each case (60 job aspects) on these patterns. Cases (specific Q-items) will have high or low factor scores as their values are high or low on the variables entering a pattern (Rummell, XI, p. 469). Or in other terms, some of the job aspect placements contained in the Q-sort pattern of an individual are more important in developing a high factor loading for that person than are placements of other job aspects. Factor scores obtained from the BMD–03M computer program are standardized which means they have been scaled to have a mean of zero and about two-thirds of the values lie between +1.00 and –1.00 (Dixon, 1968, p. 169–184). Factor scores greater the ±1.00 are unusually high or low and may point to possible cause and effect relationships among the data. In order to obtain factor scores using the BMD—03M computer program it is necessary to make the assumption of equally appearing intervals for points on the sorting continuum.

Interpreting Figure 8, it is seen that all the individuals contained in the factor have positive factor loadings above 0.400 with an average factor loading of 0.528. This points to common motivational patterns for the individuals grouped in the factor. Positive factor scores relative to job factor classes of Intrinsic job aspects (#2, 3, 5, 6), Supervision (#11), Opportunity for Advancement (#23), and Social Aspects of Work (#43, 44) suggest that these individuals are mature, competent, self-actualized professional administrators and faculty. The positive factor scores for the job aspect enumerated above are related to strong intrinsic motivators and are suggestive of fully integrated personalities as these individuals related to their current university work environment. The job aspects with negative factor scores reinforce this interpretation as they reflect non-motivating job aspects which are not expected to be of importance to self-fulfilled individuals.

Implications

The use of factor scores, in conjunction with Q-factor analysis, has been demonstrated and can be seen to be of value in gaining a greater insight to the relationships existing between groupings of individuals and possible reasons why the patterns exist. The use of Q-factor analysis in developing composite group profiles has been shown to facilitate intensive research activity upon the level of organizational groups. The careful development and use of Q-sorts related to organizational contexts constitute viable research tools which can be applied to behaviourally related organizational problems which previously have been deemed as hopelessly qualitative in character.

In a broader context, group related applications of the Q-method via Q-factor analysis lead to several approaches for research activity. One avenue of research application has been demonstrated in this study in which data generated from Q-sorts were factor analyzed to establish common groupings of individuals. Further definition of the nature of such groups has been shown by the construction of composite arrays of Q-items for individuals contained in a given group.

Additional patterns of research and data development using Q-factor analysis have been suggested by Block (1961, p. 107—113). Given groupings of individuals established by Q-factor analysis, it is possible to relate such groups to outside personal, biographical or demographic variables. This type of data analysis requires that the variables or categories being related to groups established by factor analysis be independent of the Q-data. Another use of Q-factor analysis is to analyse the effect of merging samples of individuals, reflected in a common Q-sort, and then refactor analyzing the data. Such analysis facilitates the evaluation of whether or not certain types of individuals are more likely to be found in a factor pattern than would be expected on the basis of chance. This also allows investigation of whether certain personality types tend to congregate in the various functional parts of the organization, specific types of job patterns or particular occupational identifications.

Upon a more pragmatic level, the apparent ability of the Job Aspect Q-Sort to identify dissatisfied individuals in job settings and predict their higher propensity

DEFINITION OF FACTOR

Individuals contained in the factor

	Discipline	Factor Loading	Status		
1.	Mathematics	0.671		Resigned	
2.	Bio-Chemistry	0.463			
3.	Bio-Chemistry	0.417			
4.	Ag-Economics	0.421			
5.	Ag-Engineering	0.719			
6.	Vo-Tech-Education	0.445	Admin.		
7.	Poultry Science	0.487	Admin.	Resigned	
8.	Education	0.503	Admin.		
9.	Bio-Chemistry	0.538	Admin.		Dean
10.	Veterinary Medicine	0.411	Admin.	Resigned Became Dean	
11.	Educational Psychology	0.500	Admin.	Resigned Became Pres.	
12.	Mechanical Engineering	0.714	Admin.		
13.	Agronomist	0.579	Admin.		Vice-Pres.
	Average Factor Loading	0.528			

RELATED FACTOR SCORES

Job Aspects – (See Appendix)

Positive Factor Scores		Negative Factor Scores	
2. Self-respect	1.29	22. The amount of pay derived from a university position	−1.38
3. Creativity and self-expression	2.03	31. Tenure of job position	−2.26
5. Participation in decisions	1.48	35. The interest of the administration in an individual faculty member	−1.42
6. Pride in accomplishment	1.59		
11. Technical competence and ability of superiors	1.74	49. Provisions made by the university for holidays and vacations	−1.60
13. Geographic location and nature of the community	1.40		
23. Opportunity for professional development	1.60		
43. Competent co-workers	1.74		
44. Pride in belonging to a balanced work group	1.48		

FIG. 8. Productive and self-actualized administrators and faculty

to leave the organization suggests a number of possible managerial uses for Q-sorts. Q-item placements for an individual are indicators of his self-representation. Given a condition of dissatisfaction, and a desire to retain the employee, it may be possible for management to manipulate physical and or behavioural elements in the job environment to aid an individual's re-evaluation of his self-concept with hopefully a resultant increase in his propensity to stay in the organization.

A further possible application of the Q-technique lies with individuals who are leaving the organization. By viewing the departing employee as a potentially unbiased source of information, at least as far as organizationally imposed inhibitions on personal behaviour are concerned, an opportunity exists to obtain information concerning problem areas of a behavioural nature. Other possible areas of organizational application for the Q-technique are found in selection procedures for executives and supervisory personnel, executive and supervisory rating procedures, and in counseling activity related to interpersonal human relations problems.

The Q-technique is not a new method but only one which has been slow in transcending disciplinary boundaries into organizational applications. As a research tool the use of the Q-technique in organizations must be tempered with the realization that its potential may be attained only through careful, deliberate and skeptical applications and research evaluations. The properties of the Q-sort as a measurement tool must also be related to existing measurement techniques used in organizations with time and experience determining its full range of usefulness and application.

References

Block, Jack (1956), "A Comparison of the Forced and Unforced Q-Sorting Procedures", *Educational and Psychological Measurement*, XVI, Winter, p.492.

Block, Jack (1961), *The Q-Sort Method in Personality Assessment and Psychiatric Research*, Charles Thomas, Springfield, Illinois.

Block, Jack and Thomas, Hobart (1955), " Is Satisfaction with Self a Measure of Adjustment?" *Journal of Abnormal and Clinical Psychology*, LI, p. 254–259.

Buttler, J.M. and Haugh, C.U. (1954), "Changes in the Relation Between Self-Concepts and Ideal-Concepts Consequent upon Client Centered Counseling", *Psychotherapy and Personality Changes*, C. Rogers and R. Dymond Editors, University of Chicago Press, Chicago, Illinois..

Cattell, Raymond (1966), "The Data Box", *Handbook of Multivariate Experimental Psychology*, Raymond Cattell Editor, Rand McNally, Chicago, Illinois.

Chodorkoff, Bernard (1954), "Adjustment and the Discrepancy Between the Perceived and Ideal Self", *Journal of Clinical Psychology*, X, p. 266–268.

Cronbach, Lee J. (1953), "Correlation Between Persons as a Research Tool", *Psychotherapy: Theory and Research*, O. Hobart Mowrer, Editor, The Ronald Press, New York.

Dixon, W.J. (1968), *BMD-Biomedical Computer Programs*, University of California Press, Berkeley and Los Angeles.

Ferguson, George (1959), *Statistical Analysis in Psychology and Education*, McGraw-Hill Book Company, New York.

Fishbien, M. (1966), "The Relationship Between Beliefs, Attitudes, and Behaviour", *Cognitive Consistency*, Shel Feldman, Editor, Academic Press, New York.

Goodling, Richard and Guthrie, George (1956), "Some Practical Consideration in Q-Sort Item Selection", *Journal of Counseling Psychology*, III, No. 3, p. 70–72.

Hamm, B. Curtis (1967), "A Study of the Differences Between Self-Actualization Scores and Product Perceptions Among Female Consumers", Unpublished

Doctor's Dissertation, Department of Marketing, University of Texas.

Hay, John E. (1967), "Self-Ideal Congruency Among Engineering Managers", *Personnel and Guidance Journal*, XLV, July, p. 1084–1088.

Herzberg, Frederick; Mausner, Bernard; Peterson, Richard; and Capwell, Dora (1957), *Job Attitudes: Review of Research and Opinions*, Psychological Service of Pittsburgh, Pittsburgh, Pennsylvania.

Hilden, Arnold (1954), *Manual for Q-Sort and Random Sets of Research Concepts*, Arnold H. Hilden, Webster Grove, Missouri (Mimeographed).

Kenny, Douglas T. (1956), "The Influence of Social Desirability on Discrepancy Measures Between Real Self and Ideal Self", *Journal of Consulting Psychology*, XX, No. 4. p. 315–318.

Levy, Leon H. (1956), "The Meaning and Generality of Perceived Actual-Ideal Discrepancies", *Journal of Consulting Psychology*, XX, No. 5, p. 396–398.

Mingo, K. (1968), " A Study of Supportive Work Aspects and Security-Based Fringe Benefits Utilizing the Q-technique", Unpublished doctoral dissertation, Department of Management, University of Colorado.

Morrison, Richard L. (1962), "Self-Concept Implementation in Occupational Choices", *Journal of Counseling Psychology*, IX, No. 3, p. 255–260.

Nahinsky Irwin D. (1965), "The Analysis of Variance of Q-Sort Data", *The Journal of Experimental Education*, XXXIV, No. 1, Fall, p. 66–72.

Nahinsky, Irwin D. (1963), "Q-Sort Approaches in Studying Sex, Socioeconomic Status, and Psychopathological Variables", *Psychological Reports*, III, p. 15–28.

Nahinsky, Irwin D. (1958), "The Relationship Between the Self-Concept and the Ideal-Self Concept as a Measure of Adjustment", *Journal of Clinical Psychology*, XIV, p. 360–364.

Nahinsky, Irwin D. (1966), "The Self-Ideal Correlation as a Measure of Generalized Self-Satisfaction", *The Psychological Record*, XVI, p. 55–64.

Nunnally, J. (1968), *Psychometric Theory*, McGraw Hill, New York.

Rinn, J.L. (1961), "Q-Methodology An Application to Group Phenomena", *Educational and Psychological Measurement*, XXI, No. 2, Summer, p. 315–329.

Rogers, Carl (1951), *Client Centered Therapy: Its Current Practice, Implications, and Theory*, Houghton Mifflin, Boston, Massachusetts.

Rogers, Carl (1954), "Changes in the Maturity of Behaviour as Related to Therapy" *Psychotherapy and Personality Change*, Carl Rogers and Rosalind Dymond Editors, University of Chicago, Chicago, Illinois.

Rummell, R.J., "Understanding Factor Analysis", *Journal of Conflict Resolution*, XI, No. 4.

Siegel, Sidney (1956), *Non-Parametric Statistics*, McGraw Hill Book Company, New York.

Appendix : The Job Aspect Q-Sort — Initial Form

A. Intrinsic Job Aspects

    1. Recognition and appreciation

    2. Self-respect

3. Creativity and self-expression
4. Freedom and independence of action and planning
5. Participation in decisions
6. Pride in accomplishment

Supervisory Job Aspects

7. Availability of superiors for support and consultation
8. Encouragement and cooperation by superiors
9. Delegation of authority by superiors
10. Consideration and fairness in dealing with superiors
11. Technical competence and ability of superiors

Working Conditions

12. A large and adequate faculty club and related recreational facilities
13. The geographical location and the community in which the university is located.
14. Attractive and clean university surroundings
15. Temperature and ventilation of work area
16. Adequacy and condition of university facilities
17. Convenient and adequate parking facilities

Wages

18. Relationship of university position to personal factors, motives and values.
19. Competitive or market oriented wage
20. Frequency and predictability of wage increases
21. Fairness or equitableness of compensation
22. The amount of pay, income, salary or earning derived from a university position

Opportunities for Advancement

23. Opportunity for professional development
24. Overall promotion policies
25. Opportunity for advancement in rank upon merit
26. Promotion from within the university
27. Opportunity for advancement in social position

Security

28. The stability of the university as a work environment
29. A feeling of being valued by the university
30. An ability to influence the administrative processes of the university
31. Tenure of job position
32. Steadiness of employment

Company and Management

33. The structure and size of the university
34. Cooperation and assistance of the administration
35. The interest of the administration in an individual faculty member
36. An interpretation of the fairness, intentions and good sense of the administration

37. Administrative procedures and policy
38. The university's foresight and planning

H. Social Aspects of Work

39. Work which is undertaken in an atmosphere of cooperation and good effort
40. Inter- and intra-department relations
41. A work effect which is characterized by a team balance
42. Congenial co-workers on and off the job
43. Competent co-workers
44. Pride in belonging to a balanced work group

I. Communication

45. Availability of information dealing with new university developments
46. Manner and fashion in which instructions and orders are conveyed
47. Availability of informational on university personnel policies and procedures.
48. Availability of information on university lines of authority and policy

J. Security-Based Fringe Benefits

49. Provisions made by the university for vacations and holidays
50. Provisions made by the university for meeting personal emergencies
51. University structured retirement programs
52. University programs which provide for illness and accident protection
53. Provisions made by the university for income protection

K. Supportive Work Aspects

54. A (Faculty) Secretarial help for research, writing and preparation for public contacts
54. B (Administrators) Secretarial help for administrative duties
55. A (Administrators) The use of management trainees and subordinates to lighten the routine portion of work
55. B (Faculty) The use of graduate assistants to lighten the routine portion of work
56. Sabbatical leaves for further professional development
57. Private office facilities
58. Financial support and assistance in research activities and research time
59. University support for professional meetings and academic development
60. Educational privileges, fellowship programs, and consultation opportunities aided by the university

PART II

6

The Internal Labor Market as a Stochastic Process*

Thomas A. Mahoney

George T. Milkovich

**Industrial Relations Center
University of Minnesota**

Introduction

The concept of the internal labor market has received increasing attention in recent years. The existence of the infernal labor market has been acknowledged by labor economists for some time, but it only recently has received any analytical development characteristic of economic analysis.

The growing importance of the internal labor market has provided an impetus for development of a number of operational techniques for analysis of this market. The increasing reliance upon the internal labor market and limited interaction with labor markets external to the firm creates need for improved manpower casting and planning.[1] Manpower administrators and labor market analysts both recognize the increasing need for models of the internal labor market to supplement the existing models of traditionally external labor markets.[2]

Internal Labor Market Concepts

Concepts of the internal labor market tend to reflect economic models of markets in general. Markets generally are perceived as performing the functions of pricing and allocating resources among competing demands; the internal labor market is conceptualized as performing these same functions. The internal labor market is conceptualized as an administrative unit, however, and not as the "place where exchange takes place, where the "laws" of supply and demand apply." The forces which operate and determine the pricing and allocation of labor in the internal labor market are perceived to be different from the forces identified in the more general market model. Administrative determination of the pricing and allocation of labor in the internal market implies a degree of isolation and independence from the forces of supply and demand operating in the competitive market model. Rather, the internal labor market is conceptualized as a complex or

* The work reported here has received support from the University of Minnesota's Industrial Relations Center and Graduate School. Preparation of this paper was aided in part by ONR Contract No. N00014-68-A-0141-0003. The following individuals also participated in the research: Paul Nystrom, Kenneth Wheeler, David Dimick, Thomas Robertson, Dennis Nolan, and Barbara Classen.

"web of rules" determining manpower pricing, allocation and development.[3] These rules are viewed more as a function of custom, tradition, negotiation or administrative policy than as a function of competitive market forces.

The internal labor market is characterized with boundaries, a boundary separating it from external market forces, and boundaries isolating sub-markets within the internal labor market. All of the boundaries are penetrable, since manpower must be recruited into the internal labor market as well as into the component sub-markets, but recruitment tends to be restricted to specific jobs which serve as "entry ports". Interaction with forces of the external labor market is restricted to these entry port points of exchange. The number and location of these entry ports are determined through administrative action and probably are influenced by the job structure/technology of the firm and by the condition of the external market.

The allocation process of the internal labor market is evidenced in the patterns of movement of manpower among jobs, occupations, and administrative units. Sub-markets of the internal labor market can be identified (conceptually or empirically) in terms of both horizontal and vertical dimensions of movement. Priorities for movement of manpower presumably are specified in the complex of rules. Criteria for these priorities may include skill, ability, job tenure, company tenure, or related measures. The general concept of the internal labor market is depicted diagrammatically in Figure 1.

OCCUPATIONAL CAREER LADDERS

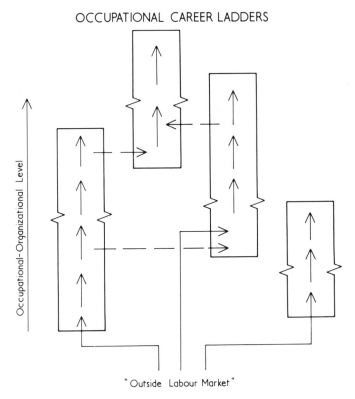

FIG. 1. Conceptualization of Internal labor market

Stochastic Process Models

Various stochastic process models have been explored in recent years for potential relevance in the analysis of the internal labor market.[4] The existence of sub- markets and job groups hierarchically ordered in terms of manpower flow sequences suggests conceptualization of the internal labor market as a series of queues moving through different job states or as a Markov process with probabilistic flows among job states. Conceptual applications of mathematical models have been developed and manipulated to determine the implications of different set of priorities for movement and of different rates and patterns of movement. Markovian models have been suggested for purposes of manpower forecasting, predicting future distributions of manpower within the market. Stochastic process models also have been suggested for simulation of the internal labor market and the exploration of impact of alternative manpower policies and strategies.

Applicability of stochastic process models to analysis of the internal labor market is unsettled. There have been relatively few empirical investigations of the applicability of the models within the corporate labor market. At the conceptual level, queueing approaches appear to provide the most realistic depiction of the internal labor market.[5] Manpower is recruited into the firm in one or another entry states. Each entry state can be viewed as a waiting line for servicing through movement to one or more other job states which, in turn, serve as waiting lines for further movement. The complex of rules for movement provide queue discipline; each individual is ordered in a queue on the basis of skill, seniority, or some other criterion. Individuals in a job state may be ordered in one or more queues for movement to different job states and may be ordered differently in the various queues. Complete application of queuing models is conceptually possible in a simulation model; analytical treatment of the model would be impossible without gross abstraction. Although there have been some noteworthy applications of queuing models to the analysis of manpower mobility within an internal labor market, most students have preferred to cast the internal labor market into a Markovian process model.

Markovian models have been applied in various investigations of mobility — industrial mobility, labor turnover, inter-generational mobility.[6] The essential characteristics of Markovian models — a finite set of states, successive time intervals or experiments, and movement among the states expressed in terms of probabilities — have rather direct analogies in the internal labor market. States can be defined as job groupings such that manpower are relatively easily transferred among jobs within the state; state boundaries reflect barriers to movement such as skill differentials, salary differentials or requisite personal characteristics. Transition probabilities of mobility can be defined as rates of flow between job states during fixed time intervals. Because of these rather direct analogies, there have been a number of conceptual applications of Markovian models to manpower mobility within the internal labor market.

Several issues of applicability arise in attempts to apply Markovian models in the analysis of internal labor markets. The Markovian model assumes that the probability of movement in any period is dependent solely upon the state of location at the start of the period. If we define states as job groupings, we know that this assumption is not valid. The probability of movement of any individual in the internal labor market is dependent upon the process through which he reached the current assignment as well as various personal characteristics. Thus, for example, the complex of rules governing allocation in the internal labor market would assign varying probabilities of movement to different individuals located within the same state; individuals within the state are queued in order of priority for movement. While states might be defined such that the probability of movement is equal for every individual in the state, this would require such a proliferation of states that applications of the model would be unappealing. Some variation of the Mover-Stayer models might be developed as an alternative, but these also would increase the complexity of application. Certainly the estimation of transition probabilities through rates of flow between states as usually recommended can only be a gross indication of probabilities.

Another issue faced in empirical application of Markovian models concerns the stability of the transition matrix. Mathematical analysis of Markovian models depends heavily upon this assumption; forecasting applications of Markovian models also would appear to require this stability of transition matrices. Accounts of internal labor market processes suggest that transition probabilities among job states may vary by time period as the corporate demand for labor and the supply of labor in the external labor market vary. Some observers suggest that the firm adjusts to an increasing demand for labor by increasing rates of promotion within the firm; others suggest that the structure of the internal market also changes, that new entry ports will be opened up and employees recruited into the firm at various points in the structure.[8] Additionally, changes in policies concerning manpower allocation within the internal labor market would be expected to alter the probabilities of movement among job states. The amount of variation in transition probabilities which occurs in fact and the relevance of this change for Markovian analysis and forecasting are empirical issues which we examine in this study.

The Markovian model holds considerable appeal for application in the analysis of the internal labor market. Present descriptions of the internal labor market are largely verbal and non-manipulable.. We report here an attempt to apply Markovian models in the analysis of the internal labor market of a large corporation. Our objectives in this application were two: (1) to explore the analytical relevance of the model in the depiction and simulation of the internal labor market, and (2) to examine the accuracy and usefulness of the Markovian model for manpower forecasting.

Application

Description of the Site and Data

The firm cooperating in this study is a large multiple-line insurance company, the world's largest insurer in one of these lines. Founded in 1922, the firm now employs about 23 000 persons in 21 geographically decentralized locations and about 6000 agents. During the period covered by the study, 1958 –1968, the firm grew from an employee count of 8729 to an employee count of 17 853. Much of the geographic decentralization also occurred during this period. The work force of the firm is divided into three relatively distinct groups:

1. the clerical work force consisting of file clerks, typists, secretaries, and

machine operators;

2. the sales force, agents, who provide services to the firm on contract;

3. the managerial-technical-professional work force consisting of supervisors, managers, underwriters, claims agents, and staff and service specialists..

Movement of personnel among these three work forces is almost non-existent; consequently, we can treat them as participants in three distinct and separate labor markets within the firm. The managerial-technical-professional labor market was selected for analysis. This work force more than doubled from 1958 to 1968, the period of study. It grew proportionately from 37 per cent (3246/8729) of the office and administrative work force to almost 45 per cent (7992/17853).

Records of employee distribution reports are maintained and were available. These records provided annual "snapshots" of the work force as of January 1st each year. These records indicate employee name, identification, job assignment salary, sex, and date of hire. These records were used in the measurement of manpower flows between time intervals, the measures later used in the estimation of transition probabilities.

State Definitions

States for the Markovian analysis were defined in accordance with the general concept of the internal labor market. States were sought such that jobs grouped into a single state were relatively comparable in terms of requirements and such that movement among the jobs was common. State boundaries were set to reflect barriers to movement generally believed to exist in the firm. The resulting job groupings and state boundaries reflect three criteria, all barriers to movement:

1. skill-function similarity — jobs grouped within a state tended to be similar in skill level and function performed

2. responsibility level — state boundaries within a skill-function grouping reflect significant breaks in the responsibility demanded; generally, these responsibility levels parallel job evaluation levels

3. organizational variation — the firm was organized in three subsidiary companies which were believed to comprise sub-markets with relatively little flow of manpower among them despite similarities in jobs and skill demands.

Twenty-three job states (groupings) were established using the above criteria. These states are depicted in Figure 2.

One issue confronted in the definition of states concerned the treatment of locations "outside the labor market". Conceptually, such a state is required to complete the possible states of location; manpower moves into and out of the internal labor market as well as among the states within the market. Three states are recognized "outside the labor market", two as time 1 locations (rows) and one as time 2 location (column). Individuals enter the internal market by transfer from one of the other internal markets or by recruitment from outside the corpor-- ation. Entries in each of these rows depict the distribution of entrants among job states.. Individuals leave the internal market by leaving the firm, Exit. This Exit state is treated operationally as a trapping state, anyone who leaves the labor

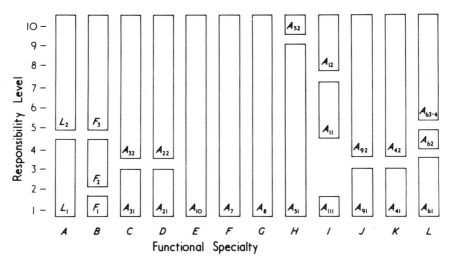

FIG. 2. Job Assignment States

FIG. 3. Transition Probability Matrix, 1958/59

	EXIT	L_2	L_1	F_3	F_2	F_1	A_{12}	A_{11}	A_{52}	A_{51}	A_{10}	A_7	A_8	$A_{63\text{-}4}$	A_{61}	A_{62}	A_{32}	A_{31}	A_{111}	A_{92}	A_{91}	A_{22}	A_{21}	A_{42}	A_{41}
EXIT	1.00																								
L_2	.04	.96																							
L_1	.06	.16	.78																						
F_3	.02			.98																					
F_2	.04			.08	.86	.02																			
F_1	.27				.11	.62																			
A_{12}	.05						.90	.05																	
A_{11}							.02	.95									.02					.02			
A_{52}							.15			.85															
A_{51}																									
A_{10}											1.00														
A_7								.04			.96														
A_8	.05												.95												
$A_{63\text{-}4}$	.06	.01					.02							.91	.01										
A_{61}	.16													.03	.78	.03									
A_{62}	.12														.13	.75									
A_{32}	.07															.02	.91								
A_{31}	.12											.01	.01		.01	.01	.01	.83			.01	.01			
A_{111}	.33												.01	.13	.02				.46		.05				
A_{92}	.02						.01													.97					
A_{91}	.15															.02				.07	.76				
A_{22}	.03																					.97			
A_{21}	.09																					.02	.89		
A_{42}	.03						.03																	.97	
A_{41}	.08																		.02						.90
Transfers			.13	.04	.10		.06						.01			.19					.36		.10		
Recruits			.02			.01							.01	.58	.24				.13						

market remains separated. While conceptually incorrect, this treatment results in reasonably accurate estimates of transition probabilities.

Data Generation

Data sought for the Markov model are probabilities of movement from one job state to another during a specified time interval. Time intervals of one year were established in this application. We reasoned that annual rates of movement likely would be more stable than rates observed over shorter periods of time, and that the annual period was short enough that it was unlikely that any individual would make more than one move during the period. The annual time interval also was judged to be most relevant for manpower planning purposes.

Probabilities of mobility were estimated from rates of movement among the job states during the annual time interval. We have used two alternative models for data generation in related applications. In the situation described here, annual employee distribution reports were available which indicated for each job in the firm the name, sex, salary, seniority, and organization code of all incumbents. Distribution reports for successive dates were compared to identify every shift of employees, and rates of flow among states were calculated from these. An alternative model works with individual job histories, identifies every movement across state boundaries, then sums these data across individuals and calculates rates of flow as before. Eleven distribution reports were available for the years 1958 –1968, permitting generation of ten matrices of transition probabilities. These data provide the basis for the analyses and findings reported below.

Findings – Descriptive

The Markovian matrix format provides a descriptive summary of the internal labor market structure. Examination of the 1958 – 1959 origins and destinations matrices reveals rather clearly the structure of the corporate labor market. Essential characteristics of the conceptual model of the internal labor market appear in these empirical descriptions. Entry ports, occupational and organization-- al sub-markets, and restricted channels of movement are shown in these matrices.

As expected, organizational and occupational sub-markets are indicated by the relatively restricted channels of movement within the firm. Sub-matrices F can be identified within the destinations matrix such that vertically and horizontally adjacent sub-matrices are zero (or near zero) matrices as in the diagram below. Manpower flows among job states are restricted largely to states within the

$$
\begin{array}{c|c|c}
 & 0 & \\
\hline
0 & F & 0 \\
\hline
 & 0 & \\
\end{array}
$$

sub-matrix F; these states comprise a sub-market. These sub-markets are indicated on the 1958 – 1959 destination matrix; thirteen such sub-markets are indicated. One state, A_{111}, is not classified within any of the sub-markets. This state appears to be a general entry state feeding to various sub-markets. Two of the sub-markets are organizational in nature, the remainder are occupational. Occupationally, job states within the two organizational sub-markets, L_i and F_i, are quite similar to job states in other sub-markets, but the organizational barriers to mobility apparently restrict the flow of manpower between these similar states. The sub-markets identified in this analysis are analogous to empirically derived occupational families, they result from the complex of rules governing manpower allocation within the internal labor market and need not reflect similarity of skill requirements.

Entry states through which manpower is recruited into the labor market are identified in the Transfer and Recruit rows of the matrix. Entrants to the labor market are obtained through "transfers" from other labor markets within the corporation and "recruiting" from the external labor market. Some of the sub-markets, A_{4j}, A_{3j}, A_{10}, A_{6j}, are more dependent upon the external market than other sub-markets; other sub-markets, A_{2j}, A_{9j}, and A_{5j}, recruit only from other sub-markets or other labor forces within the firm. Over the years under study, the state A_{111} was a primary entry port into the labor market despite the fact that it wasn't used during 1958. Both the number of entry states and the number of persons recruited through them varied from year to year; the average number of entry states which appeared over the years under study was eleven.

Every job state is a potential exit state, a state from which manpower leaves the market. Examination of the conditional probabilities of exiting in the matrix indicates that the exit rate varies considerably, ranging from zero to almost sixty per cent. Again, this evidence bears out experiential knowledge about the internal labor market. Exit rates from entry port states are higher than exit rates from terminal or destination states as we would predict from knowledge of relationships of turnover and tenure.

Employee career paths also are indicated in the Markovian matrix. Most employee career paths are restricted by the sub-market boundaries already noted. An individual enters an occupational sub-market and progresses upward in that occupation until he leaves the firm. Two states can be noted, A_{111} and A_{31}, which feed into several sub-markets, however, and which constitute states similar to a "labor pool" for the managerial-technical-professional labor market in this firm.

The Markovian matrix provides a useful format for the description and analysis of corporate internal labor markets. It describes in a simple format the sub-market boundaries, the entry ports and the career paths resulting from the complex of rules governing manpower allocation in the internal labor market. This description and the measures derivable from it provide an opportunity to assess the behavior of internal labor markets in response to changing conditions in the external labor market and the economic efficiency of the administrative rules established for the allocation and utilization of manpower resources.[9]

Findings — Predictive

One of the attractions of Markovian analysis lies in the possibility of generation of future distributions of manpower using the matrix of transition probabilities.[10] Various conceptual analyses assume a regular Markov process and work out implications of some future steady state of transition probabilities. These applications depend upon constancy of the transition probability matrix over time and upon existence of a regular chain. Whether or not these assumptions are valid involves both conceptual and empirical issues. Some internal labor market analysts maintain that the internal labor market structure is quite stable over time and that all adjustments are made by varying the rates of input at the entry ports. Other analysts maintain that the structure itself varies with changes in the external market and that the openness of the market as well as rates of flow among job states vary considerably over time. We are not aware of any empirical tests of these hypotheses.

We hypothesized in this application that the internal labor market structure would vary over time and that the assumption of constancy of the Markovian matrix would not be met. Changes in growth rate, technology and job design, organization and reporting structure and qualifications for recruitment into the corporation over the ten year period of analysis were believed to have been sufficient to cause change in the transition probabilities. A test of the hypothesis of constancy of transition probabilities developed by Anderson was conducted for the entire time period under study. Assuming the data observed in the firm were produced by a Markov process, each of the matrices generated provides estimates of the P_{ij} underlying the process. These estimates of P_{ij} are given by:

$$\hat{P}_{ij;t} = \frac{n_{ij}(t)^*}{n_{i(t-1)}}.$$

Given the various sets of observations, the maximum likelihood estimate $\hat{P}_{ij}$ of the transition probabilities P_{ij} are:

$$\hat{P}_{ij} = \frac{\sum_{t=1}^{T} n_{ij}(t)}{\sum_{t=1}^{T} n_{i(t-1)}} = \frac{\sum_{t=1}^{T} n_{ij}(t)}{\sum_{t=0}^{T}\sum_{j=1}^{T} n_{ij}(t)}$$

The maximum likelihood estimate [MLE] of the P_{ij} probabilities is presented in Figure 4.

The likelihood ratio criterion λ is used to test the hypothesis of constancy of the estimates $\hat{P}_{ij}$. The value $-2 \log \lambda$ is distributed as χ^2 with $(T-1) m(m-1)$ degrees of freedom for large n. The value λ approaches zero rapidly in our analysis and is infinitesimal when $t = 4$. Calculation of the significance of λ when $t = 3$ indicates a significance level of < 0.001. Thus we reject the hypothesis of constancy of transition probabilities over time in this analysis. This aspect of the internal labor market structure, the rate of manpower flows among alternative assignments, is not stable over time. As indicated later, the magnitude of this instability is less than might be expected.

direction and degree of error in forecasts made using the transitional probability matrices. Forecasting accuracy was assessed in several ways. The transitional probability matrix for the period 1958 − 1968 was generated empirically from the ten years of experience, $\tilde{P}_{ij} = \frac{n_{ij}(1968)}{n_i(1958)}$. This 1958/1968 matrix representing

"reality" was compared with forecasts based upon two methods. One, a single period matrix was raised to the tenth power

$$[\tilde{P}_{ij}] = [P_{ij}(1958/1959)]^{10}$$

---

* This notation differs slightly from that used in the following paper by Forbes. Here $n_{ij}(t)$ is the number moving from i to j between $t-1$ and t; in Forbes' paper $n_{ij}(t)$ relates to the period $t, t+1$ (Eds.)

EXIT	EXIT	L_2	L_1	F_3	F_2	F_1	A_{12}	A_{11}	A_{52}	A_{51}	A_{10}	A_7	A_8	$A_{63\text{-}4}$	A_{61}	A_{62}	A_{32}	A_{31}	A_{111}	A_{92}	A_{91}	A_{22}	A_{21}	A_{42}	A_4
L_2	.04	.95	.01																						
L_1	.11	.10	.78																						
F_3	.03			.95	.01																				
F_2	.09			.06	.83											.01									
F_1	.45			.01	.23	.31																			
A_{12}	.02						.96	.01			.01														
A_{11}	.03						.03	.92			.01														
A_{52}	.03						.03		.94																
A_{51}	.07								.06	.85			.01												
A_{10}	.04										.92	.01										.01			
A_7	.04							.01				.93											.01		
A_8	.06							.01					.89			.01						.01	.01		
$A_{63\text{-}4}$	.04							.01						.93	.01										
A_{61}	.15													.03	.80	.02									
A_{62}	.10							.01						.01	.09	.80									
A_{32}	.03							.02				.01	.01	.01			.90			.01		.02			
A_{31}	.08							.01					.01	.01	.03	.01	.05	.74			.09	.01	.01		
A_{111}	.24							.03				.01	.01		.07	.01			.45	.01	.01	.12		.03	
A_{92}	.02							.01												.95	.01				
A_{91}	.10							.01					.01		.01					.05	.80				
A_{22}	.02							.01					.06				.01					.81	.07		
A_{21}	.09												.09									.08	.72		
A_{42}	.02																							.94	.02
A_{41}	.08							.01																.08	.82

FIG. 4. Maximum Likelihood Estimate of Transition Probabilities

as an estimate of the actual 1958/1968 matrix of shifts. Second, the maximum likelihood estimate of the transition matrix, [MLE], was raised to the tenth power as another estimate of the 1958/1968 matrix

$$[\tilde{P}_{ij}] = [\text{MLE}]^{10}$$

Visual comparison of these matrices was sufficient to point up major differences and statistical testing of the differences was not warranted. Compared with the actual 1958/1968 matrix, the [1958/1959]^{10} matrix predicts fewer types of moves, 109 as compared with the 148 types observed. Additionally, the single period matrix raised to the tenth power over-predicts exits from the labor market. The exit of manpower from the labor market is over-predicted because rates of flow from the organization are used to estimate probability of exiting. In reality, the probability of exiting from the labor market is closely related to tenure and the assumption of constant probability of exiting grossly over-estimates the proportion of manpower who will leave the labor market. Compared with the [1958/1968] matrix, the [MLE]^{10} over-estimates the range of types of moves that will be made, 230 as compared with 148 types of moves. This results from the [MLE] matrix reflecting all of the single period movements which occurred during the ten years, both movements by persons in the process in 1958 and those entering the process in later years. Predicted exit rates in this comparison again are higher than actual exit rates for the same reason as before.

A second check of forecasting accuracy was made using the maximum

	EXIT	L_2	L_1	F_3	F_2	F_1	A_{12}	A_{11}	A_{52}	A_{51}	A_{10}	A_7	A_8	A_{63-4}	A_{61}	A_{62}	A_{32}	A_{31}	A_{111}	A_{92}	A_{91}	A_{22}	A_{21}	A_{42}	A_{41}
EXIT																									
L_2	.17	.79	.02						.02																
L_1	.37	.42	.17	.01									.01										.01		
F_3	.08			.82	.05		.03		.03																
F_2	.27			.56	.14															.02				.02	
F_1	.79			.11	.08									.02											
A_{12}	.05						.86				.05			.05											
A_{11}	.15						.30	.43	.02	.04	.02					.02						.02	.02		
A_{52}	.36						.04	.04	.16	.36			.04												
A_{51}																									
A_{10}	.17						.04				.74	.04													
A_7	.12							.12				.72	.04												
A_8	.10								.05	.05			.79												
A_{63-4}	.29						.02	.09			.01			.55	.04										
A_{61}	.59													.18	.20	.03									
A_{62}	.60			.01										.09	.10	.19									
A_{32}	.14			.02			.26						.05			.02	.44			.07					
A_{31}	.35			.01	.01		.01		.04				.02	.05	.01	.04	.02	.21	.10	.01	.09	.04		.01	.01
A_{111}	.61										.01	.01				.04	.08	.01	.08	.01	.05	.06	.04		
A_{92}	.15								.11	.01	.01		.09							.58	.03	.02			
A_{91}	.03	.01		.03					.02		.02	.01	.03				.05		.02	.46	.31	.03			
A_{22}	.21			.03					.15				.09									.53			
A_{21}	.15			.01					.02				.50			.01						.01	.22	.08	
A_{42}	.26												.06				.03							.57	.09
A_{41}	.33										.02						.02							.33	.29

FIG. 5. Observed Ten-Year Transition Probabilities, 1958/1968

likelihood estimate of the transition matrix [MLE] to generate single year projections of manpower distributions (1959, 1964, and 1968) for comparison with actual distributions for those years,

$$[n_j(t)] = [n_{i(t-1)}] \text{[MLE]}$$

$$t = 1959, 1964, 1968.$$

In a sense, this was rather a check on the constancy of transition probabilities than a check on forecasting accuracy since the [MLE] was derived using data for the entire period 1958–1968. Differences between the projected and actual distribution vectors are presented in Table 1. Errors of prediction were made for 6.4 per cent of the manpower in the 1959 distribution, 208 of 3241 persons. The largest single error was made in over-estimating exits, 27 persons or 6.8 per cent of actual exits. While the magnitude of error was smaller in all other states, the proportion of error occasionally was larger due to a smaller base. Errors of prediction were made for 4.5 per cent of the manpower in the 1964 distribution, 242 of 5405 persons. The largest single error occurred in state A_{21} where the number of assignments was under-estimated by 51 persons, 18.9 per cent of actual assignments. Errors of prediction were made for 10.7 per cent of manpower in the 1968 distribution, 793 of 7358 persons. This relatively large error arose from almost equal and balancing errors in two states, A_8 and A_{21}; manpower in state A_8 was under-estimated by 194 persons and manpower in state A_{21} was over-estimated by 185 persons. A check with the firm revealed that

FIG. 6. Ten-Year Transition Probabilities Estimated from 1958/1959

EXIT	EXIT	L_2	L_1	F_3	F_2	F_1	A_{12}	A_{11}	A_{52}	A_{51}	A_{10}	A_7	A_8	$A_{63\text{-}4}$	A_{61}	A_{62}	A_{32}	A_{31}	A_{111}	A_{92}	A_{91}	A_{22}	A_{21}	A_{42}	A_{41}
L_2	.32	.68																							
L_1	.41	.51	.08																						
F_3	.22			.78																					
F_2	.37			.38	.24	.01																			
F_1	.80			.09	.10	.01																			
A_{12}	.33						.39	.24									.02			.02					
A_{11}	.82						.09	.61					.01				.09			.12					
A_{52}	.17						.48	.14	.19								.01			.01					
A_{51}																									
A_{10}											1.00														
A_7	.02						.13	.02	.17			.67													
A_8	.42												.58												
$A_{63\text{-}4}$	.43	.02					.01	.08						.40	.03		.01			.01					
A_{61}	.78							.01						.07	.11										
A_{62}	.75													.03	.13	.08									
A_{32}	.55													.01	.06	.01	.38								
A_{31}	.65										.01	.04	.02		.03	.02	.03	.15		.01	.01	.01			
A_{111}	.77											.01	.02	.01	.02	.04	.02	.01	.08	.01	.01	.01			
A_{92}	.19						.01	.07									.01			.73					
A_{91}	.68							.01							.01	.02				.22	.06				
A_{22}	.26																					.74			
A_{21}	.59																					.10	.32		
A_{42}	.66						.01	.20									.01			.02				.75	
A_{41}	.57																				.05				.36

approximately 190 assignments had been transferred from the A_{21} occupational state to the A_8 occupational state during the year, which accounted for this seeming error; a more reliable occupational classification would have prevented the error. Omitting these errors of classification, the remaining errors of predictions would have amounted to about 5.6 per cent of the persons. In general, errors of prediction were relatively small, suggesting that, although the transition matrix was not constant over the period, the MLE of the transition matrix provides a fair description of the internal labor market during the ten years of study.

Ten-year projections of the 1958 manpower distribution vector were generated using the 1958/1959 matrix of P_{ij} estimates and using the maximum likelihood estimate of the P_{ij}

$$[n_{j(t)}] = [n_{i(t-10)}][P_{ij}]^{10}, t = 1968$$

and

$$[n_{j(t)}] = [n_{i(t-10)}]^{10}, \text{MLE}]^{10}, t = 1968.$$

These projections were compared with the observed 1968 distribution vector of manpower in the internal labor market in 1958. These comparisons are presented in Table 2. As suggested from the single year projections, considerable error appears in the ten-year projections, errors are made for 36.4 per cent of the persons using the MLE matrix and for 47 per cent of the persons using the 1958–1959 matrix. The [MLE], since it was based upon the entire ten-year history, is somewhat more accurate than the single [1958/1959] observation. It is interest-

Mahoney, Milkovich

	EXIT	L2	L1	F3	F2	F1	A12	A11	A52	A51	A10	A7	A8	A63-4	A61	A62	A32	A31	A111	A92	A91	A22	A21	A42	A41
EXIT																									
L_2	.36	.60	.03	.01																					
L_1	.59	.30	.09										.01									.01			
F_3	.29			.60	.05					.01	.02	.01				.01	.01								
F_2	.54			.23	.17						.01		.01	.01	.02										.01
F_1	.84			.08	.07									.01											
A_{12}	.22	.01		.64	.04			.05	.01		.02							.01							
A_{11}	.31			.16	.40	.01	.01	.06	.01		.01	.01						.02							
A_{52}	.20			.19	.01				.52	.01	.01														
A_{51}	.47			.04	.01				.21	.20	.01		.03			.01						.01	.01		
A_{10}	.23		.01	.01	.03	.03				.01	.45	.11	.05				.01	.03	.02	.01	.01				
A_7	.39			.01	.06	.01	.01					.46	.01			.01	.01	.01	.01						.01
A_8	.48				.02	.01	.03	.02					.34	.01	.01		.01			.02	.02	.02			
A_{63-4}	.35	.01		.01	.03	.04							.01	.50	.04	.01									
A_{61}	.71	.01		.01	.01	.01							.01	.09	.12	.03									
A_{62}	.68	.01		.01	.01								.01	.05	.12	.12									
A_{32}	.33			.01	.07					.02	.01	.03	.06	.01	.02		.34			.02	.06	.02			
A_{31}	.53		.01	.01	.02					.02	.01	.02	.04	.01	.05	.02	.10	.06		.02	.04	.02	.01	.01	
A_{111}	.68		.01	.01	.01					.01	.01	.02	.03	.01	.04	.01	.05	.03		.02	.03	.01	.01	.01	
A_{92}	.25		.01	.01	.01	.04				.01			.01	.01		.01			.01	.58	.02	.02	.01		
A_{91}	.56		.01	.01	.01					.01			.01	.02	.01	.02	.01		.01	.16	.12	.01	.01		
A_{22}	.38	.01		.01	.04					.01	.01	.01	.22	.01			.01		.01	.02	.01	.16	.08	.01	
A_{21}	.53	.01			.01					.01	.01		.20	.01		.01	.01		.01	.01	.01	.09	.07	.01	
A_{42}	.28		.01	.01	.02					.01			.01				.01					.01		.58	.07
A_{41}	.98		.01	.01	.01								.01				.01		.01					.30	.16

FIG. 7. Ten-Year Transition Probabilities Estimated from
Maximum Likelihood Estimate

ing to note that about half of the errors in both projections occur in the over-estimation of persons leaving the organization. The impact of over-estimation of exit rates in the transition matrix upon long-term projections is illustrated in regressions of the observed distribution of 1968 manpower upon the projected distribution generated with the [MLE]. This regression yields a line of best-fit.

$$Y = 35.75 + 0.725X$$

Omitting the exits from the regression, we obtain the following line of best-fit:

$$Y = -35.8 + 1.50X$$

Clearly the probability of exiting from the internal labor market varies with tenure. Probability rates of exiting estimated from the experience of employees distributed over various tenure categories are adequate for short-term projections of manpower, but they distort projections of long-term distributions of manpower. Attempts to correct these projections by sub-dividing entry states on the basis of tenure have proven unsuccessful to date in our work, although such a procedure would appear to have value.

Summary and Conclusions

An attempt was made in this paper to investigate the applicability of a Markovian model for the analysis of internal labor markets. The internal labor market model

State	1958 N	1959 Est. N	1959 N	Error N	Error %	1963 N	1964 Est. N	1964 N	Error N	Error %	1967 N	1968 Est. N	1969 N	Error N	Error %
L_2	52	57	63	−6	−9.5	97	102	100	2	2.0	105	115	115		
L_1	76	60	59	1	1.7	100	79	74	5	6.8	138	110	118	−8	−6.8
F_3	39	42	44	−2	−4.5	128	134	127	7	5.5	188	202	214	−12	−5.6
F_2	66	75	61	14	22.9	195	179	177	2	1.1	378	335	380	−45	−11.8
F_1	47	15	30	−15	−50.0										
A_{12}	21	23	24	−1	−4.2	59	62	62	0		66	70	66	4	6.1
A_{11}	54	55	60	−5	−8.3	75	79	75	4	5.3	83	90	87	3	3.4
A_{52}	25	23	23	0	0	103	103	102	1	.9	111	112	111	1	.9
A_{51}						97	89	89	0		117	108	113	−5	−4.4
A_{10}	23	23	25	−2	−8.0	64	61	61	0		83	78	74	4	5.4
A_7	25	27	26	1	3.9	49	50	47	3	6.4	56	55	64	−9	−14.1
A_8	19	32	19	13	68.4	44	74	44	30	68.2	81	114	308	−194	−62.9
A_{63-64}	251	280	267	13	4.9	396	433	443	−10	−2.3	601	652	632	20	3.2
A_{61}	1480	1229	1206	23	1.9	1930	1633	1618	15	.9	2726	2294	2336	−42	−1.8
A_{62}	220	210	218	−8	−3.7	662	572	551	21	3.8	1013	868	902	−34	−3.8
A_{32}	43	49	42	7	16.7	91	93	94	−1	−1.1	92	97	95	2	2.1
A_{31}	202	190	206	−16	−7.8	211	186	207	−21	−10.1	231	181	212	−31	−14.6
A_{111}	85	1	0	1		56	1	2	−1	−50.0	8	8		8	
A_{92}	93	98	104	−6	−5.8	172	184	169	15	8.9	185	201	191	10	5.2
A_{91}	190	172	149	23	15.4	395	334	341	−7	−2.1	494	409	416	−7	−1.7
A_{22}	34	40	35	5	14.3	68	84	71	13	18.3	171	167	137	30	21.9
A_{21}	110	87	99	−12	−12.1	290	219	270	−51	−18.9	277	216	31	185	596.8
A_{42}	35	37	34	3	8.8	58	60	61	−1	1.6	67	70	72	−2	−2.8
A_{41}	51	43	47	−4	−8.5	65	55	52	3	5.8	87	74	81	−7	−8.6
Exit		373	400	−27	−6.8		539	568	−29	−5.1		733	603	130	21.6
Total	3241	3241	3241	208	6.4	5405	5405	5405	|242|	4.5	7358			793	10.7

Table 1. Single Year Forecasts of Manpower Distribution Using Maximum Likelihood Estimate of Transition Probabilities
(Note: the notation $|X|$ means that X is the column total obtained by taking the modulus of each entry)

State	1968 N	MLE Est. N	Error N	Error %	58/59 Est. N	Error N	Error %
L_2	75	62	−13	−17.3	79	4	5.3
L_1	13	10	−3	−23.1	6	−7	−53.8
F_3	94	64	−30	−31.9	60	−34	−36.2
F_2	16	32	16	100	16	0	0
F_1							
A_{12}	42	36	−6	−14.3	33	−9	−21.4
A_{11}	84	61	−23	−27.4	94	10	11.9
A_{52}	7	16	9	128.6	11	4	57.1
A_{51}	26	13	−13	−50.0		−26	−100.0
A_{10}	29	23	−6	−20.7	25	−4	−13.8
A_7	23	26	3	13.0	27	4	17.4
A_8	104	61	−43	−41.3	16	−88	−84.6
A_{63-4}	425	281	−144	−34.0	215	−210	−49.4
A_{61}	347	236	−111	−32.0	215	−132	−38.0
A_{62}	84	74	−10	−11.9	68	−16	−19.0
A_{32}	71	42	−29	−40.9	16	−55	−77.5
A_{31}	23	20	−3	−13.0	40	17	73.9
A_{111}							
A_{92}	149	93	−56	−37.6	123	−26	−17.4
A_{91}	91	39	−52	−68.2	14	−77	−84.6
A_{22}	62	29	−33	−53.3	36	−26	−41.9
A_{21}	10	23	13	130	38	28	280.0
A_{42}	39	39	0	0	26	−13	−33.3
A_{41}	20	10	−10	−50.0	19	−1	−5.0
Exit	1404	1948	544	38.7	2135	731	42.1
Total	3238	3238	1180	36.4	3238	1522	47.0

Table 2. Ten-year Forecasts of Manpower Distribution Using Single-year and Maximum Likelihood Estimates of Transition Probailities
(Note: the notation $|X|$ means that X is the column total obtained by taking the modulus of each entry.)

is rich with intuitive and experiential concepts, but lacks operationality and rigor; the Markovian model is precise and capable of mathematical analysis but lacks institutional validity. Application of the Markovian model was attempted within the framework of a single corporate labor market.

Description of the internal labor market in terms of transition probability matrices was found useful. This format permits investigation of various characteristics attributed to the internal labor market — entry ports, sub-markets and the characteristics of their boundaries, and the "web of rules" governing allocation of labor within the firm. All of these were evidenced in examination of the transition probability matrices. Potential applications of a transition probability matrix to depict the internal labor market are numerous. Examination of the matrix points out operationally the boundaries of sub-markets internal to the firm, the degree of utilization of available manpower resources in staffing high level assignments, and probable career paths associated with entry states.

Once identified, sub-market boundaries can be changed to provide better manpower utilization, and selection and staffing criteria for entry positions can be specified on the basis of career implications.

As expected, we found that analysis of successive matrices indicated instability over time presumably reflecting changes in the rules governing manpower allocation. Short-term forecasts, single-year, made using the Markov an model and estimates of P_{ij} were reasonably accurate, while long-term forecasts, ten-year, were far less accurate. While this finding restricts the applicability of the model for long-term forecasts of manpower distributions, it does not restrict the use of the model for the analysis of implications of change in manpower allocation procedures. Our results confirm that even relatively minor alteration in the transition probability matrix compounds into sizable differences in the distributions of manpower forecast over a few time periods.

The relationship between turnover and tenure makes difficult the application of the Markovian model in the forecast of organizational and occupational distributions of manpower. Some means of taking this relationship into account without losing organizational-occupational specificity in the analysis and forecasts must be sought.

Finally, our results suggest that the Markovian model holds more potential for the analysis of internal labor market structures and the generation of implications of alternative market structures than it does for the more practical matter of generating manpower forecasts. Our results suggest that the student of labor markets has more to gain from application of the Markovian model than does the manpower recruiting function within the firm.

References

1. J. Walker, "Forecasting Manpower Needs", *Harvard Business Review*, March–April 1969; A Young, "Models for Planning Recruitment and Promotion of Staff", *British Journal of Industrial Relations*, 3:3, November 1965; E. Vetter, *Manpower Planning for High Talent Personnel*, Graduate School of Business Administration, University of Michigan, 1967.

2. V. Vroom and K. MacCrimmon, "Toward a Stochastic Model of Managerial Careers", *Administrative Science Quarterly*, XII, June 1968; T.W. Alfred, "Checkers or Choice in Manpower Management", *Harvard Business Review*, January–February 1967; M. Haire, "Approach to an Integrated Personnel Policy", *Industrial Relations*, February 1968.

3. J. Dunlop, *Industrial Relations Systems*, New York: Holt, 1958. Also see P. Doeringer, "Determinants of the Structure of Industrial Type Internal Labor Markets", *Industrial and Labor Relations Review*, 20:2, January 1967.

4. W. Dill, D. Gaver, and W. Weber, "Models and Modelling for Manpower Planning ", *Management Science*, XIII, December 1966; W. Gorham, "An Application of a Network Flow Model to Personnel Planning", *IEEE Transactions, Engineering Management*, September 1963; J. Hill, "A Consideration of Labour Turnover as the Resultant of a Quasi-Stationary Process", *Human Relations*, 4, 1951; C. Kossack and R. Beckwith, *The Mathematics of Personnel Utilization Models*, Personnel Laboratory, Wright Air Development Center, November 1959; J. Merck, *A Markovian Model for Projecting*

Movements of Personnel Through a System, Personnel Research Laboratory, Lackland AFB, March 1965.

5. W. Dill, D. Gaver, and W. Weber, *op. cit.*

6. See D.J. Bartholomew, *Stochastic Models for Social Processes*, New York: Wiley, 1967, for a general review of various models.

7. L. Goodman, "Statistical Methods for the Mover-Stayer Model", *American Statistical Association Journal*, December 1961.

8. See statements of J. Dunlop and G. Somers in *Work Force Adjustments in Private Industry — Their Implications for Manpower* Policy, *op. cit.*

9. See forthcoming doctoral dissertations of G. Milkovich and P. Nystrom, University of Minnesota, for these investigations.

10. See K. Rowland and M. Sovereign, "Markov Chain Analysis of Internal Labor Supply", *Industrial Relations*, November 1969.

11. T. Anderson, "Probability Models for Analyzing Time Changes in Attitudes", In P. Lazarsfeld, ed., *Mathematical Thinking in the Social Sciences*, Glencoe, Illinois: The Free Press, 1954.

7

Markov Chain Models
for Manpower Systems

An example and some comments on
testing for goodness of fit

A. F. Forbes

University of Kent at Canterbury (U.K.)

1. Introduction

The aims of this paper are twofold. First, to present typical data and values for
the flows and transition probabilities of a manpower system over a reasonable
span of time; in this case 8 years. Unfortunately very few data of the case study
type have been published. Second, to consider methods for testing the goodness
of fit of Markov Chain type models of manpower systems. Again little work appears
to have been done in this context. However, see the paper by Mahoney and
Milkovich model for the analysis of the internal labor market.

In section 2 the Markov chain model is briefly explained and the notation to be
used is defined. Two results relating to the model are given for use later in the
paper.

The data for the case study is introduced in section 3. The system considered
is the officer subsystem of the (British) Womens' Royal Naval Service (WRNS/0).
The data relates to a simple Markov transition model with states corresponding to
ranks. This model is later used as an example for the methods suggested for
testing goodness of fit.

In section 4, we consider the problem of testing the goodness of fit of Markov
chain models. In 4.1 the problem is defined and discussed. Three related aspects
are identified. First, the question of the validity of the model; that is whether the
model adequately describes the physical operation of the system. This is dealt
with in 4.2. The second aspect concerns the transition probabilities. An important question in this context is whether or not these remain constant over time.
Sections 4.3 and 4.4 consider problems of this sort; first by a simple graphical
method and then by means of goodness of fit statistics obtained by expressing
the data in the form of a contingency table. The third problem, dealt with in
section 4.4, relates to prediction, and in particular to evaluating predictions by
comparison with observed values and expected prediction errors.

2. The Model

The model is only briefly explained in this section. For a more detailed development see Bartholomew, Chapter 3.

2.1 Assumptions

A manpower system is considered to be composed of mutually exclusive and exhaustive classes or states, so that each member of the system may be in one and only one class at any given time. These classes may be defined in terms of any relevant variables. We shall be concerned with the number of members of the system in each of these classes at discrete points in time, and with the numbers (or flows) moving between these classes from one time point to the next. The system is open so that flows to and from the outside world are permitted. These correspond to wastage and recruitment respectively.

In the Markov chain model the flows are assumed to be governed by transition probabilities, and each class is homogeneous and independent with respect to these probabilities. That is each member of a class has the same probability of making a particular transition. And, furthermore, these probabilities operate independently. The basis of the Markov assumption is that the transition probabilities depend only on the class or state occupied at present. This should be borne in mind when defining the classes.

2.2 Notation

The notation to be used is defined as follows:

T calendar time, $T = 0, 1, 2 \ldots$ In the example $T = 1959, 1960$, etc.;

k the number of classes within the system. These will be numbered $i = 1, 2, \ldots, k$, and $i \equiv w$ will be used for a wastage flow, $i \equiv r$ for a recruitment flow;

$n_i(T)$ the number in class i at time T;

$p_{ij}(T)$ the probability that a member of class i makes a transition to class j in the time interval $(T\text{-}1, T)$

$r_i(T)$ the probability that a recruit arriving during the interval $(T\text{-}1, T)$ is in class i at time T;

$R(T)$ the number of recruits who arrive during the interval $(T\text{-}1, T)$ and who remain at time T;

$n_{ij}(T)$ the flow from $i \to j$ in $(T\text{-}1, T)$ i.e. the number of members of class i at time $(T\text{-}1)$ who are in state j at time T.

We shall find it convenient to define

$$\mathbf{n}(T) = [n_i(T)], \ \mathbf{P}(T) = [p_{ij}(T)]', \ \mathbf{r}(T) = [r_i(T)],$$

where the vectors are column vectors.

The flows during the period $(T\text{-}1, T)$ for a two state system may be represented diagrammatically as follows:

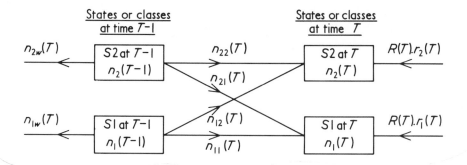

2.3 The equation and some comments

The equation of the model relating the expected number at time T, $\bar{n}(T)$, to the number at time $(T-1)$, $n(T-1)$, in terms of the parameters of the model is

$$\bar{n}(T) = \mathbf{P}(T).n(T-1) + R(T).r(T). \tag{1}$$

Substitution of the expected state vector $\bar{n}(T-1)$ for $n(T-1)$ allows the equation to be used recursively. Thus $\bar{n}(T)$ may be expressed in terms of some initial distribution, $n(0)$, and the intermediate parameter values $\mathbf{P}(t)$, $R(t)$, $r(t)$ where $t = 1, 2, ..., T$.

Note that the equation is deterministic since it gives only the expected numbers. If the model is viewed stochastically a similar equation may be derived (see Pollard [9]) giving the variances and covariances as well.

Two interesting results concerning the model are as follows:

RESULT 1 The flows from class i during the time period $(T-1, T)$ may be considered as a random variable with a multi-nomial distribution. That is, for each $i = 1, 2, ... k$, and using the usual notation.

$$n_{ij} \sim \text{Multinomial } \{n=n_i(T-1), p_j=p_{ij}(T)\},$$

where $p_{ij}(T)$ takes all non zero values, including $p_{iw}(T)$, the probability of leaving. Denote the number of these possible flows by $m(i)$.

The proof follows immediately from the form of the model and the conditions on the transition probabilities.

RESULT 2 The $n_{ij}(T)$ $i=1, 2, ... k$, w, and the number of recruits into each class form a set of sufficient statistics for the model during the period $(T-1, T)$.

PROOF Since $n_{ij}(T)$ $j=1, 2, ... k$, w are sufficient statistics for the multinomial variables of Result 1, Result 2 follows directly.

Result 1 is useful when considering the flows stochastically, and is the basis of Pollard's extension of equation (1). Result 2 relates to the data requirements of the model and implies that the transition tables detailed in 3.2 are sufficient.

3. The Example

The object of this section is to describe the system and the model and to present the data.

3.1 The WRNS/O system and the model

Fig. 1 shows the grade or rank structure of the WRNS/O system. This is a simple progressive system, with recruits entering only into the bottom grade and promotion only to the grade immediately above. There are various strict constraints in terms of seniority, length of service and age, for service, recruitment, promotion and retirement. These are detailed in Table 1.

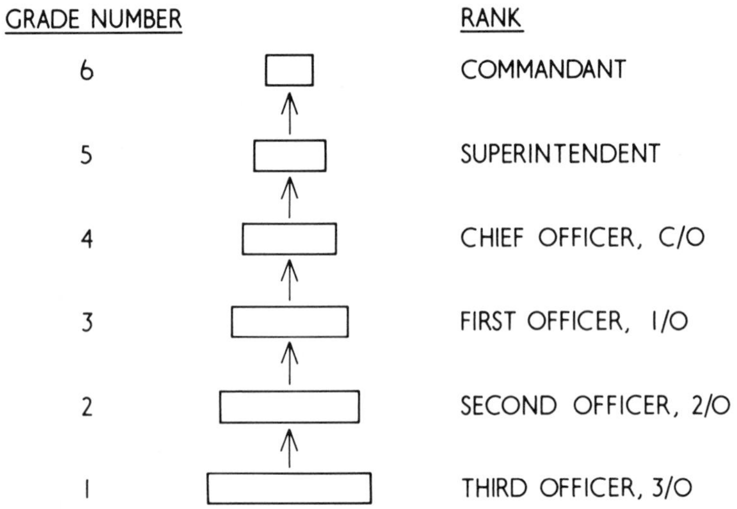

GRADE NUMBER   RANK

6   □   COMMANDANT

5   □□   SUPERINTENDENT

4   □□□   CHIEF OFFICER, C/O

3   □□□□   FIRST OFFICER, I/O

2   □□□□□   SECOND OFFICER, 2/O

I   □□□□□□   THIRD OFFICER, 3/O

FIG. 1. WRNS/O System: Grade (or Rank) Structure

We shall consider the simple model with classes corresponding to grades, except that the top 3 grades (i.e. numbers 4, 5 and 6 in Fig. 1) are grouped together into one class, giving four classes in all. The commandant (grade 6) remains in office for exactly three years. This induces a non random flow contrary to the basic Markov assumptions. The grouping of the top three grades is an attempt to avoid this and the small numbers in these grades.

Although Markov chain models of manpower systems often have classes defined exclusively in terms of grades this is by no means necessary. As stated above any relevant variables may be used (see for example Young and Almond [10]). This particular model was chosen because of its simplicity and convenience for illustrating the techniques discussed in section 4. However the constraints of Table 1 imply that the Markov assumptions might not be realistic. The question of the validity of the model is discussed in detail in 4.2. For the present we simply note that the relative stability of the system helps the Markov assumptions, and that the small numbers involved make it difficult to define many classes.

3.2 The data

Table 2 gives the service distributions, $n_i(T)$, the leavers, $n_{iw}(T)$, the promotees, $n_{i\,i+1}(T)$, and the recruits for the period 1959-67.

RECRUITMENT	Recruits must be at least 20½ years with 6 months service as a Rating, or at least 21 years.		
	The Maximum Age Limit for recruitment is the 29th birthday		
PROMOTION	To SECOND OFFICER	2½–7 years Seniority with Min. age of 24 and Max. age of 37.	
	To FIRST OFFICER	4–12 years Seniority with Min. age of 28 and Max. age of 42.	
	To CHIEF OFFICER	3–15 years Seniority with Min. age of 31 and Max. age of 48.	
	To SUPERINTENDENT	5–12 years Seniority with Min. age of 36 and Max. age of 52.	
RETIREMENT		Max. Age Limit	Length of Service
	THIRD OFFICER	37th Birthday	7 years including Probationary Time
	SECOND OFFICER	45th Birthday or	20 years as an Officer, whichever is later
	FIRST OFFICER	48th Birthday or	15 years in the Rank, whichever is earlier
	CHIEF OFFICER	52nd Birthday	12 years in Rank
	SUPERINTENDENT	55th Birthday	7 years in Rank

TABLE 1: WRNS/O SYSTEM: FLOW CONSTRAINTS

The flows for each year could equally well have been expressed in the form of transition tables. For example the transition table for 1961 is

$$
\begin{array}{c}
\text{Grade at end of 1960} \\[4pt]
\begin{array}{cccccc}
 & 1 & 2 & 3 & 4 & r \\
\begin{array}{c} \text{Grade} \\ \text{at} \\ \text{end} \\ \text{of} \\ 1961 \end{array}
\begin{array}{c} 1 \\ 2 \\ 3 \\ 4 \\ w \end{array}
\left[\begin{array}{cccc|c}
85 & & & & 41 \\
14 & 63 & & & \\
 & 4 & 23 & & \\
 & & 0 & 11 & \\
\hline
15 & 13 & 3 & 1 & 1
\end{array}\right] ,
\end{array}
\end{array}
$$

where the flows in row "w" are leavers, and in column "r" are recruits. This format keeps the data for each year together, and the estimates for the transition probabilities are easily obtained by dividing each element by its column sum (see 4.2). The table also depicts, almost diagrammatically, the possible flows in the system, especially if non-possible flows are left blank and the possible but zero flows (if any) are entered as zeros. In this particular case the table has little advantage because of the limited number of possible flows within the system. The main advantage of Table 2 format is in being able to consider each flow over time (see 4.3). Note that by Result 2 the transition table is sufficient data for the model over the period $(T-1, T)$, and contains $\mathbf{n}(T)$ and $\mathbf{n}(T-1)$ as the column and row sums respectively.

With respect to the data for the model it is important to note that the flows are defined only by the classes occupied at the beginning and end of the year. For example, consider someone who is in grade 1 at the beginning of the year, is promoted to grade 2 during the year, and leaves before the end of the year. This person contributes only to the wastage flow from grade 1.

	TIME T GRADE i	1959	1960	1961	1962	1963	1964	1965	1966	1967
SERVICE $n_i(T)$	1	107	114	126	112	126	133	140	136	129
	2	81	80	77	83	82	78	77	76	74
	3	27	26	27	27	27	26	26	25	28
	4	10	9	8	8	8	8	8	9	8
	5	2	2	2	2	2	2	2	2	2
	6	1	1	1	1	1	1	1	1	1
	TOTAL	228	232	241	233	246	248	254	249	242
LEAVERS $n_{iw}(T)$	1		18	15	30	16	21	23	21	25
	2		8	13	6	10	13	9	11	9
	3		6	3		2		1	4	5
	4		1		1	1	1			1
	5		1							
	6			1			1			1
	TOTAL		34	32	37	29	36	33	36	41
PROMOTEES FROM $n_{i\ i+1}(T)$	1		13	14	13	12	10	9	14	16
	2		6	4	1	3	1	1	4	9
	3		1		1	1	2		1	1
	4		1	1			1			1
	5			1			1			1
RECRUITS TO $R(T)$	1		38	41(1)	29	42	38	39(1)	31(1)	34

TABLE 2: NUMBERS IN GRADES (SERVICE), AND FLOWS (LEAVERS, ecruits), PROMOTEES, RECRUITS), 1959–67.

The Service distributions are as at 31st December of the appropriate year.
The flows of Leavers, Promotees and Recruits happen during the year and are therefore shown aligned between the service/year columns. Thus the first two service columns give the state of the system at the end of 1959 and 1960 respectively. The first column of Leavers, Promotees, and Recruits represent the flows during 1960.

N.B. 1. Leavers and promotees are tabulated by grade at the beginning of the year

2. Blanks indicate zeros.

In terms of data analysis, a simple way of producing the transition tables is to define a variable containing the number in each class at each time point. The transition table for $(T-1, T)$ is then obtained by simply tabulating the variable at time $T-1$ against the variable at time T.

4. The Goodness of Fit

4.1 Introduction

Three stages may be identified in testing the goodness of fit of Markov chain models for manpower systems.

(i) First we consider the validity of the model in the sense of how well it represents the physical operations of the system. This involves evaluating the correctness of the Markov chain assumptions and is covered in 4.2

(ii) Having considered the validity of the model, the next step is to test assumptions and hypotheses concerning the values of the parameters $P(T)$, $R(T)$ and $r(T)$. Of these $r(T)$ is fixed in our example, and $R(T)$ is a single variable which may be dealt with by standard methods. We therefore concentrate on the transition probabilities $P(T)$ and the following two questions.

(a) Do the transition probabilities have specified values?

(b) Do the transition probabilities remain constant over time?

In section 4.3 a preliminary graphical analysis is suggested. This is relatively inexpensive in terms of effort and provides a useful check on the other analyses. Statistics to test both (a) and (b) above are derived in 4.4. These are related to those used in the usual chisquare goodness of fit tests. For question (b) a contingency table analysis is required.

(iii) Finally, after (i) and (ii), we consider the predictions of the model. Predicted and observed numbers in each class are compared in relation to their expected prediction errors by means of a chisquare statistic derived from multivariate normal theory.

4.2 Validity

The two main assumptions of Markov chain models are

(i) homogeneous classes,

(ii) independent transition probabilities.

For a class to be homogeneous each member must have the same probability of making any particular transition. Ideally therefore we should consider each type of flow, identify the relevant variables and then define the classes in terms of these. For example if both length of serice and grade were found to affect wastage, each grade should be subdivided to give classes defined by length of service within grade. Other factors influencing the choice of classes are

(i) the objectives of the model building exercise;

(ii) data availability and cost;

(iii) the assumptions to be made.

It is also worth remembering that the greater the number of classes, the smaller the number of people in each class and hence the poorer the estimates. In practice the number and form of the classes used will depend on a compromise between demands of the sort listed above.

If a class is non-homogeneous then the probability of a particular transition will vary from person to person within this class. The flow associated with this transition will therefore not be a Binomial variable, as assumed in the model, but will have the Binomial distribution of Poisson. Both these distributions have the same mean but the Poisson Binomial has a smaller variance. Therefore if the classes are non-homogeneous the Markov model will tend to overestimate the variances.

The classes of our example are defined in terms of grades. This is a rather broad classification and does not take into account any of the other variables usually associated with wastage and promotion, like age and length of service. Inevitably therefore the classes will tend to be non-homogeneous although other data on the system suggest this effect is not excessive.

The second main assumption is that the flows of the model are independent. In our example this is probably reasonable for the wastage, but if promotion is dependent on vacancies the promotion flows will depend on flows higher up the hierarchy (see 4.3). We are at present working on an extension of Markov chain models in which promotion flows are dependent on vacancies.

4.3 Transition Probabilities: Graphical Analysis

Using Result 1 the best (i.e. minimum variance) estimator for the transition probabilities is simply the transition proportion

$$\hat{p}_{ij}(T) = \frac{n_{ij}(T)}{n_i(T)}$$

Furthermore, using the multinomial distribution, the estimated standard error of estimation is

$$\text{se}\{\hat{p}_{ij}(T)\} = \left[\frac{\hat{p}_{ij}(T)\{1-\hat{p}_{ij}(T)\}}{n_i(T)}\right]^{\frac{1}{2}}.$$

In our example we shall be considering only grades 1 and 2. Grades 3 and 4 are rather small, and grades 1 and 2 are sufficient to illustrate the methods. Table 3 shows the flows from grades 1 and 2, the estimates for the transition probabilities and their estimated standard errors. The estimates are shown graphically in Figs. 3 and 4 together with an estimation interval corresponding to $\hat{p}_{ij}(T)\pm\hat{\text{se}}\{\hat{p}_{ij}(T)\}$. This interval is intended to give some indication of the likely error of each estimate. On the assumption that these estimates are normally distributed, these intervals contain the true values with a probability of approximately 0.7. For small values of $p_{ij}(T)$, the distribution of the estimates becomes very skew and the normal assumption unreasonable. In this case a transformation of the variables is recommended (see, for example, Cox [6] page 33). The horizontal dotted lines in the graphs represent the estimates.

$$\hat{p}_{ij} = \sum_{T} n_{ij}(T)/\sum_{T} n_i(T),$$

obtained from the pooled data. This is the estimate for the transition probability on the assumption that it is constant over time. Note that this estimate is also the weighted sum of the estimates for each year where the weights are proportional to $n_i(T)$, the number at risk each year. If $\hat{p}_{ij}$ were the true value, we would expect approximately 70% of the estimation intervals to intersect this dotted line.

It can be seen from Fig. 3 and 4, that the estimates for the wastage rates are reasonably distributed about $\hat{p}_{iw}$. Since there appears to be no systematic deviation or trend, these graphs suggest that $p_{iw}(T) = \hat{p}_{iw}$, a constant. Further data on the system (not given in this paper) show that within each of these grades the distributions of other variables related to wastage, such as length of service and age, remain fairly constant. This implies little variation in the wastage rate $p_{iw}(T)$, and checks with the conclusion above.

The interpretation of the graphs of the promotion rates is not so straightforward. In grade 1 the deviations of the promotion rate appear to be about right, but the actual values $\hat{p}_{12}(T)$ have a distinct V-shape with a minimum in 1965. The deviations for the promotion rates from grade 2 are difficult to interpret because the values are rather too small to use the symmetrical estimation interval. However, the values again show a distinct pattern, this time U-shaped.

The apparent non randomness and similarity of the promotion rates from these two grades suggest some sort of dependence. In section 4.2 it was suggested that in practice promotion would often depend, at least partially, on the vacancies in the grade above. In Tables 3, $V_i(T)$ is the number leaving the system from grade $(i+1)$ and above. If promotion was made only to fill vacancies, $V_i(T)$ would be the same as the number promoted from grade i. In order to compare the vacancies with the promotion rate, the vacancy rates $v_i(T) = V_i(T)/n_i(T)$ are also shown in Table 3 and Figs. 3 and 4. It can be seen that there is a fairly strong association between the two rates, which implies that the assumption of the independence of the flows is not satisfied in the case of promotion. This does not necessarily imply, however, that the model with constant promotion rates will not give reasonable predictions. The promotion rates will probably vary systematically and non-randomly, due to this dependence, but in the long run this may tend to average out.

4.4 Transition Probabilities: Hypothesis Testing

The theory given in this section is closely related to that of Anderson and Goodman [1], who were concerned with a closed Markov chain and $p_{ij} > 0$. Their results carry over quite straightforwardly to an open system where some p_{ij} are zero. Our model is a Markov chain with many observations in each of the initial states, and this is the type of process considered by Anderson and Goodman. Bartlett [3] and Billingsley [4] also deal with inference in Markov chains, but are concerned with those processes consisting of a single observation, i.e. a sequence of states.

4.4.1 Specified Probabilities

We consider first the case of testing whether the transition probabilities have particular, given, values. Define $J(i)$ to be the set of all values of j for which $p_{ij} > 0$. (We assume that $J(i)$ is independent of T). The number of states in $J(i)$ is then $m(i)$. Remember that $j \equiv w \in J(i)$.

The null hypothesis concerning specified transition probabilities from state i at time T may be written

$$H_0 : p_{ij}(T) = p_{ij}^0(T) \text{ for all } j \epsilon J(i) \text{ given } i, T.$$

Under this hypothesis the usual (Pearson) statistic

$$\chi^2(i, T) = \sum_{J(i)} n_i(T) . \frac{[\hat{p}_{ij}(T) - p_{ij}{}^0(T)]^2}{p_{ij}{}^0(T)} \qquad (2)$$

$$\sim \chi^2 \text{ on } [m(i) - 1] \text{ degrees of freedom.}$$

That is, for a large sample, statistic (2) has approximately a chi-square distribution on the stated degrees of freedom and may be used to test the hypothesis in the usual way. For detailed derivation of the statistic and its uses see, for example, Mood and Graybill § 12.10 [8].

TABLE 3: FLOWS FROM GRADES 1 & 2 FOR EACH YEAR 1960–67:
DATA FOR FIGS. 3 & 4

| | TIME, T (YEAR) | | | | | | | | |
	1960	1961	1962	1963	1964	1965	1966	1967	60–67
GRADE 1									
$n_1(T)$	107	114	126	112	126	133	140	136	997
$n_{11}(T)$	76	85	83	84	95	101	105	98	727
$n_{12}(T)$	13	14	13	12	10	9	14	16	101
$n_{1w}(T)$	18	15	30	16	21	23	21	25	169
$\hat{p}_{12}(T)$	.121	.123	.103	.107	.079	.068	.100	.115	.101
$\hat{p}_{1w}(T)$	.168	.132	.238	.143	.167	.173	.150	.180	.169
$\hat{se}\{\hat{p}_{12}(T)\}$	.032	.031	.027	.029	.024	.022	.025	.027	.010
$\hat{se}\{\hat{p}_{1w}(T)\}$	.036	.032	.038	.033	.033	.037	.030	.033	.012
$V_1(T)$	16	17	7	13	15	10	15	16	109
$v_1(T)$	.150	.149	.056	.116	.119	.075	.107	.118	.109
GRADE 2									
$n_2(T)$	81	80	77	83	82	78	77	76	634
$n_{22}(T)$	67	63	70	70	68	68	62	58	526
$n_{23}(T)$	6	4	1	3	1	1	4	9	29
$n_{2w}(T)$	8	13	6	10	13	9	11	9	79
$\hat{p}_{23}(T)$	.074	.050	.013	.036	.012	.013	.052	.118	.046
$\hat{p}_{2w}(T)$	.099	.163	.078	.120	.159	.115	.143	.118	.125
$\hat{se}\{\hat{p}_{23}(T)\}$	.029	024	.013	.020	.012	.013	.025	.037	.008
$\hat{se}\{\hat{p}_{2w}(T)\}$	.033	.041	.031	.036	.040	.036	.040	.037	.013
$V_2(T)$	8	4	1	3	2	1	4	7	30
$v_2(T)$	.099	.050	.013	.036	.024	.013	.052	.092	.047

$\hat{p}_{ij}(T) = n_{ij}(T)/n_i(T)$, $\hat{se}\{\hat{p}_{ij}(T)\} = \{\hat{p}_{ij}(T).[1-\hat{p}_{ij}(T)]/n_i(T)\}^{\frac{1}{2}}$;
$V_i(T)$ = the number of vacancies in grade $(i + 1)$ during $(T-1, T)$
       = total wastage from grades $i + 1$, $i + 2$, ..., k during $(T-1, T)$
$v_i(T)$ = the vacancy rate = $V_i(T)/n_i(T)$.

Forbes

When considering state i over all time periods, the null hypothesis becomes

$$H_0 : p_{ij}(T) = p_{ij}{}^0(T) \text{ for all } j \in J(i), \ T \text{ given } i,$$

and the statistic

$$\chi^2(i) = \sum_T \chi^2(i, T) \tag{3}$$

$$\sim \chi^2 \text{ on } T.[m(i)-1] \text{ degrees of freedom.}$$

If we were interested in whether the transition probabilities from state i had specified constant values over time, then we would test $p_{ij}{}^0(T) = p_{ij}{}^0$.

For the whole process (i.e. all states) at time T

$$H_0 : p_{ij}(T) = p_{ij}^0(T) \text{ for all } j \in J(i), \ i \text{ given } T,$$

with statistic

$$\chi^2(T) = \sum_i \chi^2(i, T) \tag{4}$$

$$\sim \chi^2 \text{ on } \sum_i [m(i)-1] \text{ degrees of freedom.}$$

Finally for the whole process over all time periods

$$H_0 : p_{ij}(T) = p_{ij}^0(T) \text{ for all } j \in J(i), \ i, \ T,$$

and the statistic

$$\chi^2 = \sum_T \sum_i \chi^2(i, T) \tag{5}$$

$$\sim \chi^2 \text{ on } T. \sum_i [m(i)-1] \text{ degrees of freedom,}$$

under this null hypothesis.

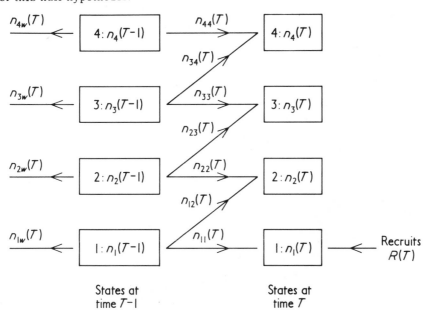

FIG. 2. Flow Diagram of the Model showing the flows during the period $(T-1, T)$

Markov chain models

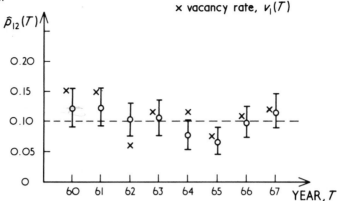

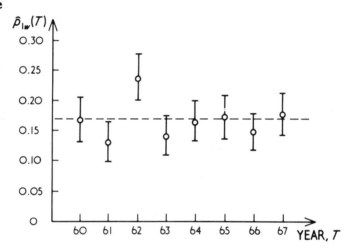

FIG. 3. Grade 1 Transition Probabilities (see also Table 3)

Statistics based on the likelihood ratio statistic may also be derived to test each of the foregoing hypotheses, since the flows are multinomially distributed and the $\hat{p}_{ij}(T)$ are the maximum likelihood estimates. The likelihood ratio for the hypothesis associated with statistic (2) is

$$\lambda(i,T) = \prod_{J(i)} \left[\frac{p_{ij}(T)}{\hat{p}_{ij}(T)} \right]^{n_{ij}(T)} \tag{6}$$

On this hypothesis

$$\chi^2(i,T) = -2 \log_e \lambda(i,T)$$

$$\sim \chi^2 \text{ on } [m(i)-1] \text{ degrees of freedom.}$$

Statistics analogous to (3), (4) and (5) may be similarly derived. The Pearson and likelihood-ratio statistics are asymptotically equivalent. Note that the Pearson statistic is of the form $\Sigma(O-E)^2/E$, and the likelihood ratio statistic of the form $-2\Sigma O \log\{E/O\}$ where E,O are expected and observed values respectively.

Forbes

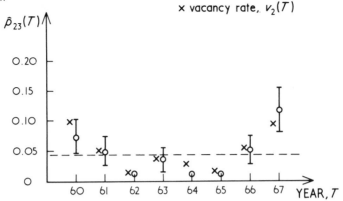

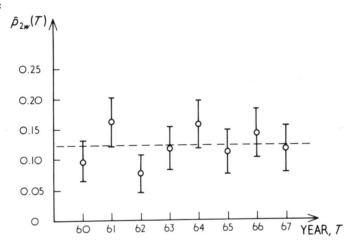

FIG. 4. Grade 2 Transition Probabilities (see also Table 3)

4.4.2 Time-homogeneous probabilities

The hypothesis that the transition probabilities for state i remain constant over time may be written

$$H_0 : p_{ij}(T) = p_{ij} \text{ for all } j \in J(i), \ T \text{ given } i.$$

As we shall see in the next section the data may be presented in such a way that this hypothesis of time-homogeneous transition probabilities is equivalent to the hypothesis of no association in a contingency table. The statistic for testing this hypothesis may therefore be written

$$\chi^2(i) = \sum_{T} \sum_{J(i)} n_i(T) \frac{[\hat{p}_{ij}(T) - \hat{p}_{ij}]^2}{\hat{p}_{ij}} \tag{7}$$

$$\sim \chi^2 \text{ on } (T-1)[m(i)-1] \text{ degrees of freedom.}$$

The intuitive connection between this result and (3) is that we have replaced $p_{ij}^0(T) = p_{ij}^0$ by our "best" estimate $\hat{p}_{ij}$. This involves estimating $[m(i)-1]$ independent parameters and this number of degrees of freedom is therefore lost.

For the whole process over all time periods

$$\chi^2 = \sum_i \chi^2(i) \qquad (8)$$

$\dot{\sim} \chi^2$ on $(T-1) \sum_i [m(i)-1]$ degrees of freedom.

Again the likelihood ratio approach may also be used. In this case

$$\lambda(i) = \prod_T \prod_{J(i)} \left[\frac{\hat{p}_{ij}}{\hat{p}_{ij}(T)} \right]^{n_{ij}(T)} \qquad (9)$$

4.4.3 Some Examples

We confine our attention to testing for time homogeneous transition probabilities for grades 1 and 2. Tables 4 and 5 show the flows from grades 1 and 2 for each of the years 1960–67, and both tables present the data in the form of contingency tables. If the transition probabilities have changed over time then the distribution in the columns will vary. That is there will be evidence of non-homogeneity amongst the columns. Thus we may use statistic (7) to test this hypothesis.

From Table 4, $\chi^2(1) = 10.18$, and on the null hypothesis this comes from a chi-square distribution with 14 degrees of freedom. This value is not significant, so overall there is no evidence to suggest that the transition probabilities from grade 1 are not constant.

The statistics $\chi^2(1,T)$ shown in the last row of Table 4 were calculated from the 3×2 contingency tables formed by comparing column T with all the other columns combined. Thus for 1965 we have

T j	1965	All other years	
1	101	626	727
2	9	92	101
w	23	146	169
	133	864	997

giving $\chi^2(1, 1965) = 1.92$. On the hypothesis that the transition probabilities for year T are no different from "all other years", $\chi^2(1, T)$ has a chi-square distribution on $[m(i)-1] = 2$ degrees of freedom. The statistic may therefore be used to test whether the transition probabilities remain constant during each particular year. This is important because if only one or two years varied, the effect could be masked by the other years and not show up in the overall chi-square value, $\chi^2(i)$. In Table 4 none of the $\chi^2(1, T)$ values are particularly significant. The largest is in 1962 and is significant at the 10% level. This is about what one would expect if the transition probabilities were constant.

The statistics $\chi^2(1,j)$ in the last column of Table 4 are the row equivalents of $\chi^2(1,T)$. That is, they are the chi-square values obtained from the 2×8 contingency tables formed from row j and all other rows combined. As statistics they may be used to test whether the transition probabilities for a particular flow remain constant over time. On this hypothesis they have a chi-square distribution on 7 degrees of freedom. None of the values in Table 4 are significant. The idea of obtaining chi-square values associated with each column and each row is similar to the partitioning of the overall chi-square value, (see Maxwell [7]).

In Table 5, the overall statistic $\chi^2(2) = 21.29$ is rather large, being significant at the 10% level. The values for each year are quite reasonable except for $\chi^2(2, 1967)$ which is very significant (at the 1% level). This is mainly due to the promotion flow in that year. Looking at $\chi^2(2,j)$ we find that promotion shows a significant variation over the years. Some of the values in Table 5 may be rather small for a contingency table analysis, although the size of the table should compensate for this, (see Maxwell, p 46 [7] and Cochran [5]).

Summarising the results, there appears to be no strong evidence that grade 1 does not have constant transition probabilities, except possibly during 1962. In Grade 2, the wastage probabilities appear constant over time, but the promotion rates seem to change significantly. These results are in general agreement with the conclusions drawn in 4.3.

TABLE 4 : FLOWS FROM GRADE 1 FOR EACH YEAR 1960–67 IN CONTINGENCY TABLE FORMAT

The flows are into states j at time T

j \ T	60	61	62	63	64	65	66	67	TOTAL	$\chi^2(1,j)$
1	76 (78)	85 (83)	83 (92)	84 (82)	95 (92)	101 (97)	105 (102)	98 (101)	727	5.49
2	13 (11)	14 (12)	13 (13)	12 (12)	10 (13)	9 (14)	14 (14)	16 (14)	101	3.72
W	18 (18)	15 (19)	30 (21)	16 (19)	21 (21)	23 (23)	21 (24)	25 (24)	169	6.44
TOTAL	107	114	126	112	126	133	140	139	997	
$\chi^2(1,T)$	0.54	1.73	4.99[†]	0.65	0.81	1.92	0.47	0.54	$\chi^2(1)=10.18$	

TABLE 5 : FLOWS FROM GRADE 2 FOR EACH YEAR 1960–67 IN CONTINGENCY TABLE FORMAT

The flows are into states j at time T

j \ T	60	61	62	63	64	65	66	67	TOTAL	$\chi^2(2,j)$
2	67 (67)	63 (66)	70 (64)	70 (69)	68 (68)	68 (65)	62 (64)	58 (63)	526	8.24
3	6 (4)	4 (4)	1 (4)	3 (4)	1 (4)	1 (4)	4 (4)	9 (4)	29	16.91*
W	8 (10)	13 (10)	6 (10)	10 (10)	13 (10)	9 (10)	11 (10)	9 (10)	79	4.29
TOTAL	81	80	77	83	82	78	77	76	634	
$\chi^2(2,T)$	2.13	1.29	4.26	0.23	3.19	2.36	0.37	10.46**	$\chi^2(2)=21.29$[†]	

N.B. Brackets contain expected numbers. Chi-square values computed from Pearson's formula, i.e. $\chi^2 = \Sigma (O-E)^2/E$.

[†] denotes significance at 10% level, * at 5%, ** at 1%, for the appropriate chi-square distribution.

4.5 Predictions

4.5.1 Theory

The model may be used to predict the numbers in each state as an expected vector $\bar{\mathbf{n}}(T)$ [from equation (1)], and a variance-covariance matrix $\Sigma(T)$ [from Pollard's theory], where $\bar{\mathbf{n}}(T)$ and $\Sigma(T)$ are functions of the initial distribution vector $\mathbf{n}(O)$ and the intermediate parameter values $\mathbf{P}(t)$, $R(t)$, $\mathbf{r}(t)$ for $t = 1, 2, \ldots,$ T, (see section 2.3).

The grade sizes are the sums of multinomial flows, so using the normal approximation it follows that

$$\sim \mathbf{n}(T) \stackrel{\sim}{\sim} N\{\bar{\mathbf{n}}(T), \Sigma(T)\},$$

where $\sim \mathbf{n}(T)$ denotes the random variable, and the approximation depends on the size of the sample. Using a standard result of multivariate normal theory,

$$\chi^2_k(T) = [\mathbf{n}(T) - \bar{\mathbf{n}}(T)]'. \Sigma(T)^{-1}. [\mathbf{n}(T) - \bar{\mathbf{n}}(T)], \tag{10}$$

$$\stackrel{\sim}{\sim} \chi^2 \text{ on } k \text{ degrees of freedom,}$$

where $\mathbf{n}(T)$ is the observed state vector at time T.

Statistic (10) may now be used in the usual way to evaluate predictions in relation to their expected errors. Notice however that we cannot separate this evaluation from the testing of the model since the predictions are made on the assumptions that

(i) the model is valid in the sense used in 4.2,

(ii) the parameters are as used in the predictions.

If the predictions are poor this implies that either one or both these assumptions are false. Consider the effect on statistic (10) of a relaxation of these assumptions.

(a) Non-homogeneous classes. This would imply less variance for the class sizes that predicted by the model (see 4.2), and hence smaller values than expected for statistic (10).

(b) Non-independence of flows. The effect in this case will depend on the form of the dependence. In our example, promotion depends on the number of vacancies, which will therefore tend to decrease the variation of the class sizes. Again this implies smaller values than expected for statistic (10).

(c) Incorrect parameter values. Predictions using these are likely to be further from the observed values than we would otherwise expect. This implies larger values than expected for statistic (10).

The sensitivity of the statistic to these assumptions is not known; some simulations would enable these effects to be quantified.

Note that the usual statistic of goodness of fit,

$$(O - E)^2 / E = \sum_i \frac{[n_i(T) - \bar{n}_i(T)]^2}{\bar{n}_i(T)}$$

is not applicable because the $n_i(T)$ are not independent. See for example the relatively large covariance terms in the variance-covariance matrices of Table 6.

Predictions

Observed	Expected	Variance-Covariance matrix

$$\mathbf{n}(64) = \begin{bmatrix} 133 \\ 78 \\ 26 \\ 11 \end{bmatrix} \quad \bar{\mathbf{n}}(63 \to 64) = \begin{bmatrix} 127.6 \\ 83.2 \\ 27.1 \\ 10.6 \end{bmatrix} \quad \sum(63 \to 64) = \begin{bmatrix} 47.07 & & & \\ -10.18 & 23.59 & & \\ 0 & -3.03 & 6.52 & \\ 0 & 0 & -0.66 & 1.78 \end{bmatrix}$$

$$\mathbf{n}(65) = \begin{bmatrix} 140 \\ 77 \\ 26 \\ 11 \end{bmatrix} \quad \bar{\mathbf{n}}(63 \to 65) = \begin{bmatrix} 128.7 \\ 84.4 \\ 27.2 \\ 10.2 \end{bmatrix} \quad \sum(63 \to 65) = \begin{bmatrix} 71.47 & & & \\ -12.63 & 39.27 & & \\ -0.32 & -4.47 & 11.32 & \\ & -0.07 & -1.01 & 3.13 \end{bmatrix}$$

$$\mathbf{n}(66) = \begin{bmatrix} 136 \\ 76 \\ 25 \\ 12 \end{bmatrix} \quad \bar{\mathbf{n}}(63 \to 66) = \begin{bmatrix} 129.5 \\ 85.5 \\ 27.3 \\ 9.9 \end{bmatrix} \quad \sum(63 \to 66) = \begin{bmatrix} 84.17 & & & \\ -12.22 & 50.47 & & \\ -0.60 & -5.03 & 14.93 & \\ -0.01 & -0.16 & -1.18 & 4.17 \end{bmatrix}$$

$$\mathbf{n}(67) = \begin{bmatrix} 129 \\ 74 \\ 28 \\ 11 \end{bmatrix} \quad \bar{\mathbf{n}}(63 \to 67) = \begin{bmatrix} 130.1 \\ 86.6 \\ 27.5 \\ 9.6 \end{bmatrix} \quad \sum(63 \to 67) = \begin{bmatrix} 90.82 & & & \\ -11.01 & 58.87 & & \\ -0.75 & -5.09 & 17.69 & \\ -0.02 & -0.24 & -1.23 & 4.97 \end{bmatrix}$$

For the predictions the parameters of the model had the following (constant) values estimated from 1960–63 data:

(i) The transition matrix, $P = \hat{P}(60-63) = \begin{bmatrix} .715 & & & \\ .113 & .841 & & \\ & .044 & .869 & \\ & & .028 & .894 \end{bmatrix}$

(ii) The number of recruits $\tilde{R}$ has mean $= 37.5$, and variance $= 21.4$

(iii) The initial distribution, $\mathbf{n}(0) \equiv \mathbf{n}(63) = [126, 82, 27, 11]'$

The values for statistic (10) are:

YEAR	1964	1965	1966	1967
From 1963 as origin (A)	1.86	2.98	3.52	3.18
Single year steps (B)	1.86	1.43	2.57	3.47

4.5.2 Some examples

Consider the data divided into two parts corresponding to the two periods 1960–63 and 1964–67. We shall use the data for 1960–63 to estimate the parameters of our model and to make predictions for 1964–67. The observed and predicted grade sizes will then be compared by means of statistic (10). Two methods of prediction will be used.

(A) In the first we predict $\bar{n}(T)$ for each of the years 1964–67, starting each time with the observed 1963 distribution as the initial one, and using the expected intermediate values. Diagrammatically this may be represented as follows.

A. Predictions from 1963 as origin

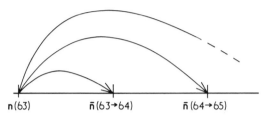

(B) The second involves predicting each year separately starting with the observed distribution of the previous year as the initial distribution. This gives a series of one year jumps and may be represented as follows,

B. Single year steps

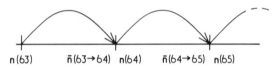

Table 6 contains the observed and expected grade sizes and the variance-covariance matrices for the predictions [using method (A)] for 1964–67. These were calculated using the parameter values shown in Table 6, which were estimated from the 1960–63 data. Also shown in this table and in Fig. 5 are the values for statistic (10) calculated from predictions based on both methods (A) and (B). The values derived from method A are represented by $\times$ in the figure, and are shown connected. This is because they are serially associated since the predictions at any time use the intermediate values of the predictions. Statistic (10) for Method A therefore gives a continuing measure of how well the model fits the process. In our example this statistic has a chi-square distribution with 4 degrees of freedom (providing the assumptions hold) and significance levels for this distribution are shown in Fig. 5 as dotted lines. Note that Fig. 5 can be used in the manner of a control chart if we consider the statistic ($\times$) as describing a random walk. If the path crosses the boundaries, as defined by the desired significance levels, then the process may be considered out of control in the sense that the assumptions may no longer hold. For example if the statistic wandered over the 5% line, say, we could be fairly confident that the parameters were incorrect (see 4.5.1). If we were using a constant transition matrix the implication would be that this had changed.

The statistic obtained by using the predictions based on Method B may be interpreted in a similar way. This time however the predictions for each year are independent so the statistic gives a separate measure for the process for each year.

110

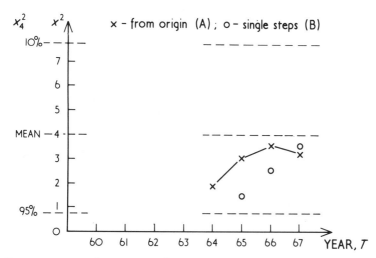

FIG. 5. x^2 values [Statistic (10)] from Predictions for 1964–67 using $\hat{P}(60-63)$
See Table 6

Taken as a whole the values shown in Fig. 5 are rather less than expected, although it should be remembered that the chi-square distribution on 4 degrees of freedom is fairly skew, so the modal (i.e. most likely) value is less than the mean. The number of observations is also rather small. The "less than expected" size of the statistic could be due to the non-homogeneity and non-independence which have already been shown to exist. One great disadvantage of this statistic is that although it can be used to imply that the assumptions do not hold, it cannot be used to imply that they do. For example if the validity assumptions and the parameter values were both incorrect, there would be a simultaneous increasing and decreasing effect which might tend to cancel out and give similar values to those obtained when the assumptions and parameter values are correct.

If the parameters of the model are estimated from the whole period 1960–67 and the initial distribution is taken as 1959, then the statistic may also be used to give some idea of the fit of the model to the whole data. This time however the estimated parameter values used to obtain the predictions, depend on the observed values, so that the predicted and observed values are not independent as before. The effect of this will be to remove some degrees of freedom from the chi-square distribution of the statistic. No theoretical solution is offered for the number of degrees of freedom lost, but at an intuitive level we may employ the following argument. The total number of independent parameters estimated in our example is 9. That is 7 in the transition matrix and 2 for the number of recruits (mean and variance). Since the data relates to a period of 8 years, the number of parameters estimated each year is 9/8 and this is the number of degrees of freedom lost. Hence, we would expect statistic (10) to have a chi-square distribution with $4-(9/8) \doteq 3$ degrees of freedom. Some simulations would provide a useful check on this result.

Table 7 gives details of the parameter values estimated over the period 1960–67, together with the values of statistic (10) obtained from predictions based on these parameter values. Statistic (10) is shown graphically in Fig. 6. The eight independent values giving a measure for each year [using predictions (B)] are

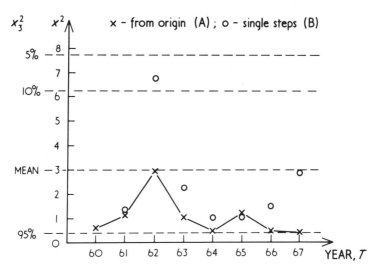

FIG. 6. x^2 values [Statistic (10)] from Predictions for 1960–67 using $\hat{P}$ (60–67)
See Table 7

again generally less than one might expect. As before this is probably due to a certain amount of non-homogeneity and non-independence. 1962 stands out as an odd year and this checks with the analyses of 4.3 and 4.4. The values of the statistic based on prediction Method A, which give a continuing measure of the process, are also small overall. There is a tendency for these values to decrease over the period 1960–67. This is as expected since the predicted values for 1967

TABLE 7: VALUES OF STATISTIC (10) FOR WHOLE PERIOD 1960–67

For the predictions the parameters of the model had the following (constant) values estimated from the whole period 1960–1967.

(i) The transition matrix, $P = \hat{P}$ (60-67)

$$= \begin{bmatrix} .729 & & & \\ .101 & .830 & & \\ & .046 & .867 & \\ & & .033 & .902 \end{bmatrix}$$

(ii) The number of recruits R has mean $= 36.5$
variance $= 17.25$

(iii) The initial distribution, $\mathbf{n}(O) \equiv \mathbf{n}(59)$
$= [107, 81, 27, 13]'$

The values for statistic (10) are:

YEAR	1960	1961	1962	1963	1964	1965	1966	1967
From 1959 as origin (A)	0.57	1.15	2.92	1.00	0.42	1.14	0.44	0.32
Single year steps (B)	0.57	1.34	6.79	2.20	1.00	1.02	1.46	2.83

using $\hat{P}$ (60–67) are likely to be closer in terms of the variance-covariance matrix, than the predictions for earlier years using the same $\hat{P}$ (60–67).

5. Conclusion

In the example there appears to be some non-homogeneity of classes and some non-independence of flows, but on the whole the model fits fairly well. The transition matrix is also reasonably constant especially considering how crudely the classes are defined. However, the WRNS/O system is particularly stable, well managed and close to equilibrium; other systems have not shown such a good fit.

One of the main reasons for a goodness of fit analysis is not just to accept or reject the model, but to appreciate where and why the model does not fit. Wherever possible one should be aware of the shortcomings of a model when interpreting the results.

A useful piece of further work would be to test these methods against some simulations. In particular this would given some insight into the sensitivity of statistic (10) to relaxations of the assumptions. Simulations could also be used to check the number of degrees of freedom lost by statistic (10) when it is used on data from which the parameters have been estimated (4.5.2).

Finally I should like to thank the Womens' Royal Naval Service for permission to use their system as an example, and for their help and cooperation in obtaining the data.

References

1. Anderson, T.W. and Goodman, L.A. (1957), "Statistical Inference about Markov Chains", *Ann. Math. Statistics*, 28, 89–109.

2. Bartholomew, D.J. (1967), *Stochastic Models for Social Processes*, Wiley, Chichester & New York.

3. Bartlett, M.S. (1955), *An Introduction to Stochastic Processes with special reference to methods and applications*, Cambridge University Press.

4. Billingsley, P. (1961), "Statistical methods in Markov Chains", *Ann. Math. Statistics*, 32, 12–40.

5. Cochran, W.G. (1954), "Some methods of strengthening the common χ^2 test", *Biometrics*, 10, 417–51.

6. Cox, D.R. (1970), *Analysis of Binary Data*, Methuen, London.

7. Maxwell, A.E. (1961), *Analysing Qualitative Data*, Methuen, London.

8. Mood, A.M. and Graybill, F.A. (1950), *Introduction to the Theory of Statistics*, McGraw-Hill, New York.

9. Pollard, J.H. (1966), "On the use of the direct matrix product in analysing certain stochastic population models", *Biometrika*, 53, 397–415.

10. Young, A. and and Almond, G. (1961), "Predicting distributions of staff", *Computer J.*, 3, 246–250.

8

A Generalised Network Model for Training and Recruiting Decisions in Manpower Planning*

A. Charnes	**University of Texas**
W. W. Cooper	**Carnegie-Mellon University, Pittsburgh**
R. J. Niehaus	**Office of Civilian Manpower Management, U.S. Navy Dept.**

---

1. Introduction

Models for manpower planning previously devised for the U.S. Navy's Office of Civilian Manpower Management have all utilized goal programming constructs with embedded Markoff processes. These models — referred to as "OCMM Models" — are here extended to include training elements along with related constraints.

A "goal programming model"[1] with iterated Markov elements to allow explicit consideration of transitions, exits, retirements, etc. in manpower planning over a sequence of periods was first introduced in [1]. As noted in the introduction to [1], the initial model formed one part of a total research effort on the part of the U.S. Navy's Office of Civilian Manpower Management (OCMM). This model — which we shall hereafter call the "OCMM Model" — has since been elaborated in a variety of directions including explicit allowance for predicted retirements within certain age or service categories and allowance for dynamically varying Markovian elements from period to period.[2] Other parts of the research program enunciated in [1] for the OCMM Models involve relating the multiple goals (e.g., the enunciated manpower ceilings) to tasks that need to be performed as well as introducing training possibilities to recruitment and job transfers in order to meet (as closely as possible) the specified goals.[3]

* This report was prepared as part of the activities of the Management Sciences Research Group at Carnegie—Mellon University under Contract NONR 760 (24) NR 047—048 with the U.S. Office of Naval Research. The research was also partly supported by ONR Contract No. NR 047—021, Task N00014—67—A—0126—0008, and the Center for Cybernetic Studies at the University of Texas. Reproduction in whole or in part is permitted for any purpose of the U.S. Government.

The authors are indebted to Wlodzinierz Szwarc (Carnegie—Mellon) for a careful review which yielded many helpful suggestions.

1 See [1] Appendix B and Chapter X for an explanation and development of the ideas of goal programming.

2 See, e.g., [5]

3 Actually some of this has already been done in an earlier phase of this research program — [8] — and in a way that takes account of on-the-job learning and dynamic organization design (and redesign) to allow for accumulating experience as well as formal training, etc.

In this report we propose to develop a first analytical model which explicitly provides for training as well as outside recruitment and job transition possibilities. We further propose to do this in a way which provides access to a variety of techniques such as "parametric variation" and "duality evaluations" [4] in order to facilitate experimentation with manpower program possibilities. In this way we shall be able to bring the power of linear programming to bear in evaluating optimal tradeoff possibilities and their resulting manpower mix and planning consequences. We shall then also be able to coordinate "career management" and "manpower planning" (and other parts of personnel planning) [5] by allowing for possible variations in manpower mixes and tradeoff possibilities in recruitment, transfer and training. Naturally, we shall want to accomplish this in a context that also considers other constraints such as financial budgets, supply and recruitment limitations imposed by policy or the environment at various times and also considers, of course, various kinds of limitations on training facilities. All except the last of these constraints have, however, already been included for explicit treatment in one or more versions of the OCMM Models. Hence we shall here relate these constraints to their predecessor developments in order to be able to utilize some of the results already secured.

2. Modeling Strategies

In a manpower planning context it is natural to want to consider modeling for training in a way that allows for the effects of training and the selection of trainees on the manpower mixes which will be available in the years that follow such training. [6] This will be done here in a manner that provides direct contact with the goal programming developments in prior OCMM Models. A convenient way to accomplish this is to posit that the effect of training may be represented by a *different* matrix of transition rates which will then apply to personnel who have been selected for training. Then we can split the population into two groups — *viz.*, those selected for training in a specified period and those who are not selected for training. The latter group may then transit in accordance with a "training" matrix while the former transit in accordance with "manpower" matrices of the kind we have previously utilized. [7]

With the wanted contacts with previous OCMM models thus established it is not necessary to treat again all of the previously developed types of constraints and stipulations and their related possibilities of variation and evaluation. Facilities as well as funds limitations on training capacities must be considered, of course, for training possibilities in each period. To continue to relate this to the previous developments, however, we shall here formulate only the funds limitation for explicit consideration. Situations where *no*

4 See [1], Chapters I and VI, for further explanations of these terms.

5 *Vide* [9].

6 Such effects should, of course, be interpreted as probabilistic projections when Markoff processes are being utilized in planning for a sequence of periods.

7 See [3] and [5] where similar devices were used to obtain refinements for retirement and related considerations. The latter developments, including extensions to dynamically varying Markoff elements are, of course, also available for use in these OCMM models (as noted in our introduction).

Charnes, Cooper, Niehaus

facilities are available can then be modeled from a budgetary standpoint as having zero dollars available for that type of training.[8] In an analogous manner, period-by-period cost constraints may also be imposed for outside recruitment and, of course, we may then also continue to impose an overall budgetary constraint on salaries, and extend this part of the previous OCMM models to include costs for recruiting and training as well as salary costs, etc., to be considered in each period, as desired.

In this same spirit we shall also preserve contact with the previous goal programming developments in our formulation of this model's objective. Thus we shall specify one part of this objective in terms of meeting a stipulated collection of manpower planning goals "as closely as possible", while staying within the constraints specified for each period in the planning horizon. We shall also extend the previously utilized objectives by including additional elements directed toward minimizing the total costs of outside recruitment and internal training. This extension is of interest in its own right, of course, but it also has the additional advantage of providing further insight for evaluating the relative weights assigned to deviations from other goals along with simultaneous evaluations of training-recruitment costs and tradeoffs.[9]

Finally, we shall also want to utilize the types of transformations and reductions available from our prior research in order to develop special structures which would otherwise remain latent and, perhaps, unutilized for the computational advantages that such special structures can supply.[10] Indeed, the formulations we shall employ will give rise to a model structure which further generalizes the "network type" model relations that have been elaborated in [1].[11] In fact, we may regard the developments which we shall employ here as representing still *further* generalizations of the generalized network models presented in [1] but, to avoid a proliferation of terminology, we shall refer to this model, too, as a "generalized network type model".

3. Definitions and Development of Generalized Network Type

The above modeling strategy may be given analytical form as follows. Let [12]

$$x_{ij}(t) = \text{number of personnel assigned to "job type } i\text{"}$$
from "source j", *without* assignment to additional training in period t.

$$y_{ij}(t) = \text{number of personnel assigned to "job type } i\text{"}$$
from "source j" *with* assignment to training

(1.1)

8 Alternatively, a lack of facilities can also be reflected in the training transition matrix by introducing zero rates of transition into certain parts of matrix and various combinations of budget and transition rate possibility may also be employed, of course.

9 Of course, total salary and related cost considerations will also be available for evaluation, too, via the budgetary constraints.

10 See, e.g., the discussion of "model types" in [1] Chapter 1 and ff.

11 *Vide*, e.g., Chapter XVII in [1].

12 As explained in [2], the terms "job type" and "source" are intended to comprehend distinctions between claimants or activities (for the same job or position) and recruitment or assignemnt in different geographical regions — and possibly other characteristics, too, if desired.

so that

$$x_{ij}(t) + y_{ij}(t) = \text{total number of personnel to be} \quad (1.2)$$
$$\text{assigned to job type } i \text{ from source}$$
$$j \text{ in period } t.$$

Thus, as indicated in the preceding section, the number of personnel obtained from source j may be summed and further distinguished between those assigned directly to job type i and those assigned to training for job type i. This will be done for each of the periods $t = 0, 1, 2, \ldots, N$ comprehended in the horizon for which manpower is being undertaken.

At time $t = 0$, the number of persons already in job type i may be represented by a known constant

$$a_i = \text{number of personnel in job type } i \quad (2)$$
$$\text{within the organization at } t = 0.$$

Furthermore, to simplify notation, we may consider a_i as one of the components of a vector "a" comprehending all pertinent job types and, correspondingly, let

$$x^j(t) = \begin{bmatrix} x_1(t) \\ \cdot \\ \cdot \\ \cdot \\ x_{nj}(t) \end{bmatrix}, \quad y^j(t) = \begin{bmatrix} y_1(t) \\ \cdot \\ \cdot \\ \cdot \\ y_{nj}(t) \end{bmatrix} \quad (3)$$

represent vectors with n components for each of the job types $i = 1, \ldots, n$.

In proceeding toward our model objectives we shall want to allow for transfers between job types and also for the possibility that persons recruited for training in one category may subsequently transit to some other category. Thus, in keeping with previous developments, we introduce the Markoff matrix,[13] M, with elements

$$M_{il} = \text{proportion of those in job } l, \text{ without training} \quad (4)$$
$$\text{in job } l, \text{ who will transit to job } i.$$

Then we introduce another matrix, T, with elements

$$T_{il} = \text{proportion of those in job } l \text{ with training in} \quad (5)$$
$$\text{job } l \text{ who will transit to job } i.$$

---

13 Actually we will modify the usual Markoff representation and, just as we have done before, we omit one row and column to allow for the fact that in these OCMM Models entrance into the system is to be determined by reference to decisions on recruitment. Note, unlike other manpower planning and analyses which use Markoff processes, the decision variables and objectives are set forth explicitly along with other constraints, including policy limitations, etc.

In order to bring the desired type of generalized network relations into prominence, we proceed as follows. For any period t, we can let

$$x(t) = \text{vector of personnel within the organization who are } not \text{ being trained.}^{14}$$

$$y(t) = \text{vector of personnel within the organization who are being trained.}$$

$$z(t) = \text{vector of personnel from } outside \text{ the organization who are being brought in.} \tag{6.1}$$

Then we introduce the following types of relations,

$$z(1) + Mx(0) + Ty(0) = x(1) + y(1) \tag{6.2}$$

wherein $z(1)$ represents the vector of personnel recruited from outside while $Mx(0) + Ty(0)$ represents the transfer via jobs and training from inside and the whole splits into the two new vectors $x(1)$ for personnel not being trained and $y(1)$ for personnel who are being trained in period 1. The sum $x(1) + y(1)$ then represents the total number employed in each job type in period 1.

An evident extension of these developments now produces

$$a = x(0) + y(0)$$
$$0 = -Mx(0) - Ty(0) + x(1) + y(1) - z(1)$$
$$0 = -Mx(1) - Ty(1) + x(2) + y(2) - z(2) \tag{7.1}$$

and so on via

$$0 = -Mx(t-1) - Ty(t-1) + x(t) + y(t) - z(t)$$
$$0 = -Mx(t) - Ty(t) + x(t+1) + y(t+1) - z(t+1)$$

where $z(0) \equiv 0$.[15] Reference to this structure suggests incidence relations of the generalized network variety. Of course, the indicated incidences are on vectors $x(t)$, $y(t)$ and matrices M and T but the representations (7.1) and (7.2) nevertheless display a structure which lends itself to this symbolism and related interpretations as a further generalization of these generalized network concepts and developments which we have previously used to advantage for serving computational efficiencies. See [1] Chapter XVII ff.

4. Additional constraints and objectives:

Other constraints will also be needed, however, to allow for limitations on training and recruitment. As indicated in preceding sections, we want to relate these to previously utilized formulations of budgetary limitations in OCMM models. Thus, we continue from (6.1) and introduce the following "training constraints"

$$K^1(t)\ y(t) \leqslant d^1(t) \tag{8}$$

where $K^1(t)$ is a matrix of the costs for training for each job type and source

14 See [8] for developments in which job type assignments are also effected for their training potential on *other* types of jobs at subsequent times.

15 Evidently we can also replace M and T by time-dependent Markoff matrices as in [5] and [8].

at time t and $d^1(t)$ is a stipulated vector of limitations imposed on such expenditures.

In this same vein we may also represent the constraints on outside recruitment via

$$K^2(t)\, z(t) \leqslant d^2(t) \qquad (9)$$

where $K^2(t)$ is a matrix of recruitment costs at time t and $d^2(t)$ is a corresponding vector of stipulations.

Finally we insert budget constraint on total salaries, as in previous OCMM models,

$$c^T(t)\,[x(t) + y(t)] \leqslant B(t)$$

where

$$
\begin{aligned}
c^T(t) \;=\; & \text{transpose of the vector of salaries to be paid} \\
& \text{for each job type in period } t. \\
B(t) \;=\; & \text{budget limitation (a scalar) on total salaries} \\
& \text{which may be paid in period } t. \qquad (10)
\end{aligned}
$$

The above constraints may be adjoined to those exhibited in the preceding section. Then letting

$$f_k(t) \;=\; \text{prescribed ceiling for } k^{\text{th}} \text{ type of manpower}$$

$$\mu_{kT} \;=\; \text{weight assigned to deviation from } k^{\text{th}} \text{ manpower} \quad (11)$$
$$\text{ceiling in period } t.$$

we can formulate the objective for this model as

$$
\min \sum_{t=1}^{N} \; \sum_{k} \mu_{kt} \; | \, e_{I_k}^T \, [x(t) + y(t)] - f\,(t) \, | \; +
$$
$$
+ \sum_{t=1}^{N} \; \mu_{ot}\,[\alpha^T y(t) + \beta^T\, z(t)] \qquad (12)
$$

where α^T and β^T represent vectors (transposed) containing the recruiting and training costs elements to be considered in the objective while

$$
e_{I_k}^T \equiv \left(\,\underset{i \, x \, I_k}{0} \quad , \quad \underset{i \, x \, I_k}{1}\,\right) \qquad (13)
$$

is a vector which has zeros in all components except those which are the unity elements. The latter, i.e., the values of unity, are in the positions that correspond to the kth type of manpower.

5. Matrix and structure:

Drawing the elements of the preceding two sections together we may obtain the matrix represented in Table 1. This may be used for developing direct or dual relations if desired but here we have only utilized the direct variable $x(t)$, $y(t)$ and $z(t)$ as defined and developed in the preceding section.[16] Such extensions will require replacing the (nonlinear) absolute value terms in (12) by

16 These developments implicitly utilize transformations and reductions first introduced in [5] for simplifying matters and making the underlying structure apparent as a guide to computational and interpretative development.

their linear programming equivalent via the usual "goal programming" reductions.[17] This has been done in the preceding papers in this series, however, and hence need not be repeated here.

With this structure now being available the stage is set for further interpretation and extensions. This will be done in a supplemental report, however, and made more concrete by means of a simple numerical example and just as was done for the reports finally incorporated in [5] this will be accompanied by related computations and solution results. The portrayal in Figure 1, then, completes this stage.

6. Addendum : Some extensions and interpretations :

This paper concludes with a numerical example and some further points suggested at the TIMS Conference. First we observe that this model involves embedded Markoff processes and hence is probabilistic in character. The interpretations need to be arranged accordingly and so do some of the further extensions that are possible. To detail all of these is beyond the scope of the present paper and the immediate applications possibilities. We shall proceed only via a very simple example and develop it only to a degree that will help to suggest some of these further possibilities, For this development we revert to the simpler cases of the earlier OCMM models — see, e.g., [2] and [4] — in which no training transitions are included for explicit consideration. We also restrict the example to one involving only one source and two job types with matrix

$$M = \begin{bmatrix} 0.7 & 0.1 \\ 0.2 & 0.6 \end{bmatrix} \tag{14}$$

This matrix details the probabilities of the transitions which may be effected *from* the column, $l = 1, 2$, *to* the row, $i = 1, 2$, for the job types associated with these indices. It may be thought of as a matrix of "Markoff type" adjusted for the fact that we want to use it as part of a goal programming model in which new entrants into the system are effected via the decision variables $x_{ij}(t)$ — wherein the values assigned to each such x denote the number of recruits from source j for job type i in each period t. See (1) ff. To accomodate the wanted variation from ordinary uses and developments in Markoff analyses, we have introduced the convention of omitting the column of the matrix that is usually allotted for the new entrant probabilities. We have also omitted the row for the existing probabilities [18] and thereby obtained a characterization in which the matrix, M, is square.

In the simple case being considered here, there are only two job types and one source being considered for the decision variables $x_{ij}(t)$. Hence, we can eliminate the index j (which is needed only when there is more than one source that must be identified) and write

17 See Chapter X in [1] for a general development including geometric interpretations and analytical developments of the theory underlying these reductions.

18 These may always be retrieved, if wanted, as the difference between unity and the corresponding column sum in m.

STRUCTURAL ELEMENTS

STIPULATIONS	x(0)	y(0)	x(1)	y(1)	x(2)	y(2)	⋯	x(N-1)	y(N-1)	x(N)	y(N)	z(1)	z(2)	⋯	z(N)
$=$ q	1	-1													
O	$-M$	$-T$	1	-1								-1			
O			$-M$	$-T$	1	-1							-1		
$\vdots$ O								$-M$	$-T$	1	1				-1
$\geq$ $d^1(1)$				$K^1(1)$											
$d^1(2)$						$K^1(2)$									
$\vdots$ $d^1(N)$											$K^1(N)$				
$\geq$ $d^2(1)$												$K^2(1)$			
$d^2(2)$													$K^2(2)$		
$\vdots$ $d^2(N)$															$K^2(N)$
$\geq$ $B(1)$			$c^T(1)$	$c^T(1)$											
$B(2)$					$c^T(2)$	$c^T(2)$									
$\vdots$ $B(N)$										$c^T(N)$	$c^T(N)$				

Fig. 1. Manpower Planning Relations. Note: $x(t)$, $y(t)$, $z(t) > 0$, all t.

$$X(1) = \begin{bmatrix} x_1 \ (1) \\ x_2 \ (1) \end{bmatrix} = \begin{bmatrix} 1 \\ 0 \end{bmatrix} \tag{15}$$

when a plan calls for hiring one person for job type 1 and none for job type 2 in period 1. We distinguish these planning decisions from the corresponding variates by writing the latter as

$$\hat{X}(1) = \begin{bmatrix} \hat{x}_1 \ (1) \\ \hat{x}_2 \ (1) \end{bmatrix} \tag{16}$$

with values to be determined via random processes generated from (14).

To clarify this last statement we commence with the initial state vector

$$a^T = (a_1, a_2) = (1, 1) \tag{17}$$

and then restrict our immediate attention to discrete state possibilities which can be generated from (17) via (14). These states and their corresponding probabilities are obtained from (14) and (15). For instance, for job type 1, we obtain $P[x, (1) = 0 | a_i = 1, a_2 = 1] = q_{11} q_{12} = (1 - p_{11})(1 - p_{12}) = 0.27$. as the probability of this event. This and the other probabilities are thus evaluated via . . .

$$P[\hat{x}_1(1) = 0 \mid a_1 = 1, a_2 = 1] = (1 - .7) \times (1 - .1) = \qquad = .27$$
$$P[\hat{x}_1(1) = 1 \mid a_1 = 1, a_2 = 1] = .7 \times (1 - .1) + (1 - .7) \times .1 = .66$$
$$P[\hat{x}_1(1) = 2 \mid a_1 = 1, a_2 = 1] = .7 \times .1 = \qquad = .07$$
$$\text{Total} \ \ \overline{1.00}$$
$$\tag{18}$$

Applying these probabilities to the corresponding states produces

$$E \ \hat{x}_1 \ (1) = .27 \times 0 + .66 \times 1 + .07 \times 2 = .80 \tag{19}$$

for the expected value. Alternatively, the straightforward matrix computation,

$$Ma = \begin{bmatrix} .7 & .1 \\ .2 & .6 \end{bmatrix} \begin{bmatrix} 1 \\ 1 \end{bmatrix} = \begin{bmatrix} .8 \\ .8 \end{bmatrix} \tag{19.2}$$

gives this same expected value for job type 1 (and job type 2) for period 1.

This is, of course, the expected value that results only from the initial state vector for the job types given in (17). The planned values for the decision variables, however, can also be aligned with this kind of probabilistic development via

$$M^\circ X \ (1) + M^1 a = \begin{bmatrix} 1 \\ 0 \end{bmatrix} + \begin{bmatrix} .8 \\ .8 \end{bmatrix} = \begin{bmatrix} 1.8 \\ 0.8 \end{bmatrix} \tag{20}$$

where we have used the $X \ (1)$ values given in (15). Here $m^\circ = I$, the identity matrix. The latter can be accorded the interpretation of a Markoff matrix, too, in which the transition probabilities are unity on the diagonal and zero elsewhere.[19] This means that there is unit probability of remaining in the job type

19 These are so-called "trapped state" probabilities.

for which the corresponding personnel components of X (1) were recruited during period 1. Under this interpretation an expected value is also obtained which may be added to those secured via the transitions effected from the components of a in period 0. The resulting sums provide the expected number of occupants for each job type that the plan will provide for period 1. Expression (20) can then be interpreted accordingly.

Of course, other probabilistic aspects may also need to be considered and a development that will suggest some of these possibilities may also be synthesized from this same very simple example.

From the computations in (17) we may, for instance, observe that

$$P[\hat{x}_1(1) \geqslant 1 \mid a_1 = 1, a_2 = 1] = .73. \tag{21}$$

If this is not satisfactory then either the initial components in the vector, a, must be altered or else the matrix of transition probabilities must be adjusted[20] — or, possibly, both of these might be done in various combinations.[21] For example, if we altered (17) to:

$$a^T = (a_1, a_2) = (2,1) \tag{22}$$

we would obtain

$$
\begin{aligned}
P[\hat{x}_1(1) = 0 \mid a_1 = 2, a_2 = 1] &= .3 \times .3 \times .9 &= .081 \\
P[\hat{x}_1(1) = 1 \mid a_1 = 2, a_2 = 1] &= 2(.7 \times .3 \times .9) + .3 \times .3 \times .1 &= .387 \\
P[\hat{x}_1(1) = 2 \mid a_1 = 2, a_2 = 1] &= .7 \times .7 \times .9 + 2(.7 \times .3 \times .1) &= .483 \\
P[\hat{x}_1(1) = 3 \mid a_1 = 2, a_2 = 1] &= .7 \times .7 \times .1 &= \underline{.049} \\
& \text{Total} &= \underline{1.000}
\end{aligned}
\tag{23}
$$

This gives

$$P[\hat{x}_1(1) \geqslant 1 \mid a_1 = 2, a_2 = 1] = .919 \tag{24}$$

and also

$$E\,\hat{x}_1(1) = .081 \times 0 + .387 \times 1 + .483 \times 2 + .049 \times 3 = 1.5. \tag{25}$$

Compared with (19.1) and (21) the alteration in initial conditions when proceeding from (17) to (22) increases the expected value and the probability for this job type, as exhibited in (25) and (24).

Of course, the expected cost of the latter result will also be increased, in general, and this, too, needs to be considered by the model — over the entire horizon. For instance, this increase may make it possible to reduce the value

20 Perhaps by behavioral science research designed to ascertain how the relative attractiveness of these job types may be altered to produce higher and lower transition probability values in selected categories. (Note that in this view a guide for such behavioral science research is thereby automatically supplied for the simultaneous consideration of career management and manpower planning.)

21 Depending on their relative costs and the further benefits that might attend each such alteration. Notice, for instance, that the use of these models for manpower planning can also affect the psycological attitudes and job-preparation propensities that personnel may subsequently display and these possibilities, too, need to be considered in a comprehensive program of personnel research.

of $x_1(1) = 1$ in (15) with resulting benefits later on. The point to bear in mind here, in any event, is that the OCMM models have been developed for use in a context such as the U.S. Department of Defense's Program-Planning and Budgeting Systems (PPBS), which envisions a 5 year plan — or forecast of such plans — tied into corresponding fiscal-monetary, and other, requirements. This, in turn, confines these models to a use of only "zero order decision rules" — to use the terminology of "chance constrained programming,"[22] but, of course, other applications may admit of access to o her classes of decision rules[23] as well.

To state all of this in a different manner, the distinctions we have elsewhere introduced for dealing with "planning" as contrasted with "control" and "operating" aspects of management are here omitted.[24] That is, it is assumed that the controls are perfect and that what is wanted is a detailing of manpower plans and related decisions over some specified future time horizon. This does not mean that possibilities for subsequent modification of these plans are eliminated. It also does not mean that the fact that such plans are formed in a probabilistic context is ignored. It only means that the relevant planning decisions are all to be specified numerically — including even those parts which are used to control the underlying probabilities and their related risks — so that, e.g., they may be coordinated[25] with the other plans and considerations that are being obtained, perhaps from other parts of the Department of Defence. organization.:.

The significance of these characterizations may be clarified, perhaps, by extending the immediately preceding developments. We shall do this by showing how such probabilistic considerations may be dealt with via values assigned to the decision variables (in earlier periods), but without entering into the complex chains of conditional probability computations that can attend these extensions in their many varieties.

Notice, for instance, that the alteration from (17) to (22) has produced a change in the probability distribution for the period 1 states. Similarly, the $X(1)$ choices can also produce different probability distributions for the possible states in period 2 — as well as in the combinations for compounding still other probability distributions in subsequent periods. This suggests that, in a manner analogous to the DEMON models,[20] constructs of chance-constrained programming can also be brought to bear in order to "constrain out" any of these distributions that are considered to be undesirable — e.g., with reference to the risk properties associated with their tails. For instance, via expressions of the form

$$P[\hat{x}_1(2) \geqslant k \mid a_1, a_2, x_1(1), x_2(1)] \geqslant \alpha \tag{26}$$

22 See, e.g., [20]

23 See, e.g., [24]

24 See, e.g., Preface and Chapter 1 in [1].

25 It must be remembered that budgets perform *coordination* as well as *control* and *planning* function.

26 The reference is to models developed in cooperation with J.K. DeVoe and D.B. Learner (then at Batten, Barton, Durstine & Osborn, Inc.) for use in marketing new products. See, e.g., [21] and [22].

A Model for Training and Recruiting Decisions

one may assure that k, a prescribed minimum number of "experienced personnel",[27] will be available for assignment in job type 1 at the start of period 2. This minimum value is to be assumed with a specified probability, $0 \leqslant \alpha \leqslant 1$. With a_1 and a_2 given this means that the choices of $x_1(1)$ and $x_2(1)$ must be made in a way that eliminates all of the probability distributions which do not satisfy these conditions. This can be done via expressions of the form

$$(M)_1^2 \ a + (M)_1 \ X \ (1) \geqslant h \ (\alpha \ k) \tag{27}$$

in which $(A)_i$ refers to the ith row of any matrix, A, while h depends on the α and k prescribed in (26). In principle, expressions such as (27) may be ascertained in advance[28] from the original probability data but, as a practical matter, recourse to approximation procedures and specially devised computer routines will need to be designed for these purposes. Similar controls may also be imposed on the distributions for $\hat{x}_2(2)$ and these may continue into subsequent periods, too, in a variety of ways.

References

[1]   Charnes, A. and W.W. Cooper, *Management Models and Industrial Applications of Linear Programming* New York : John Wiley and Sons, Inc., 1961.

[2]   Charnes A., W.W. Cooper and R.J. Niehaus, "A Goal Programming Model for Manpower Planning", in John Blood, ed. *Management Science in Planning and Control* New York : Technical Association of the Pulp and Paper Industry, 1968.

[3]   Charnes A., W.W. Cooper, R.J. Niehaus and W.N. Price "Application of Computer Assisted Techniques to Manpower Planning, "*Civilian Manpower Management* III, No. 3, Sept. 1969.

[4]   Charnes A., W.W. Cooper R.J. Niehaus and D. Sholtz "A Model and a Program for Manpower Management and Planning, *Computer Impact on Engineering Management* Pittsburgh : Instrument Society of America, 1968.

[5]   Charnes A., W.W. Cooper, R.J. Niehaus and D. Sholtz "A Model for Civilian Manpower Management and Planning", in "Models of Manpower System; A.R. Smith (Ed) London : English University Press, 1970

[6]   Charnes A., W.W. Cooper, R.J. Niehaus and D. Sholtz "Measurement of Personnel Movement", *Civilian Manpower Management* III, No.1, March 1969.

[7]   Charnes A., W.W. Cooper, R.J. Niehaus and D. Sholtz "A Systems Approach to Manpower Management and Planning" *Civilian Manpower Management* forthcoming Winter, 1970 Washington : U.S. Navy Office of Civilian Manpower Management.

27 i.e., experienced in the organization, although not necessarily in this particular job type. (Some of these persons may have transited from the $x_2(1)$ choices in period 1 as well as the initial members of this second job type given by a_2.)

28 We are not addressing considerations such as the existence of solutions, etc., which may arise when inequalities such as (26) or (27) are inserted into these goal programming models.

[8] Charnes A., W.W. Cooper, R.J. Niehaus and A. Stedry "Static and Dynamic Assignment Models with Multiple Objectives and Some Remarks on Organization Design", *Management Science*, Applications Vol. 16, June, 1969.

[9] Dunnette, M. *Personnel Selection and Placement* Belmont, Calif: Wadsworth Publishing Co., Inc., 1966.

[10] Gaylord, R.H., A.J. Farina and P. Spector "Operational Analyses of the Naval Personnel System: Part I, Development of a Personnel System Model" Pittsburgh: American Institute for Research, 1965.

[11] Gaylord, R.H., A.J. Knetz, "Operational Analysis of the Naval Personnel System: Part II, Development and Testing of a Machine Simulation of Personnel Operations", Pittsburgh: American Institute for Research, 1965.

[12] Haire, M. "An Approach to an Integrated Personnel Policy", *Industrial Relations* Vol. 8, No. 2 Feb., 1968.

[13] Ijiri, Y., *Management Goals and Accounting for Control* Amsterdam: North Holland Publishing Co., 1965.

[14] Johnson, E. *Studies in Multiobjective Decision Models*, Monograph No. 1, Economic Research Center in Lund, Sweden.

[15] Robinson, J. and N. Tarbox, "Manpower Planning" Pittsburgh: Carnegie–Mellon University, Graduate School of Industrial Administration, April, 1970.

[16] Rowland, K.M. and M.G. Sovereign, "Markov-Chain Analysis of Internal Manpower Supply", *Industrial Relations*, Vol. 9, No. 1, Oct., 1969.

[17] Scoville, T.G. "A Theory of Jobs and Training", *Industrial Relations*, Vol. 9, No. 1, Oct., 1969.

[18] Vroom, V. and K. MacCrimmon, "Toward a Stochastic Model of Managerial Career Development: Research Proposal", *Administrative Science Quarterly*, March, 1968.

[19] Weber, W. *Toward an Integrated Model for Manpower Planning*, Ph.D. Thesis Carniegie–Mellon University Graduate School of Industrial Administration, 1969.

[20] Charnes, A. and W.W. Cooper, "Deterministic Equivalents for Optimizing and Satisficing Under Chance Constraints", *Operations Research* 11, 1963 pp. 18–39.

[21] Charnes A., W.W. Cooper, J.I. DeVoe and D.B. Learner "DEMON, Mark II: An Extremal Equations to New Products Marketing" *Management Science*, Theory Series, 14 No. 9, May, 1968 pp. 513–524.

[22] Charnes A., W.W. Cooper, J.L. DeVoe and D.B. Learner "DEMON: A Management Model for Marketing New Products", *California Management Review*, Fall, 1968, XI, No. 1, pp. 31–46.

[23] Charnes A., W.W. Cooper and G.H. Symonds "Cost Horizons and Certainty Equivalents: An Approach to Stochastic Programming of Heating Oil Production", *Management Science*, Vol. 4, No. 3, 1968.

[24] Charnes A. and M.J.L. Kirby, "Optimal Decision Rules for the E-Model of Chance Constrained Programming", *Cahiers du Centre d'Etudes dee Recherche Operationnelle* 8, No. 1, 1966.

[25] Eisner, M.J. "On Duality in Infinite-Player Games and Sequential Chance-Constrained Programming", Ph.D. Thesis, Cornell University, Department of Operations Research, Ithaca, N.Y. Jan., 1970.

[26] R.S. Kaplan and J.V. Soden, "Admissible Decision Rules for the E-Model of Chance-Constrained Programming", Technical Report No. 47, Department of Operations Research, Cornell University, Ithaca, N.Y., June, 1968.

[27] Kortanek, K.O. and J.V. Soden, "On the Charnes–Kirby Optimality Theorem for the Conditional Chance-Constrained E-Model", *Cahiers du Centre d'Etudes de Recherche Operationnelle*, Vol. 8, 1967, pp. 87–98.

[28] Smith, D.V. "Programming Under Risk: A Bibliography" Harvard University Center for Population Studies, Cambridge, Mass., June, 1969.

[29] Walkup, D. and R. Wets, "A Note on Decision Rules for Stochastic Programs," *Journal of Computer and Systems Sciences*, Vol. 2, 1968, pp. 305–311.

Appendix

Let $p_{ij} \geq 0$, $i = 1, \ldots, n$, represent elements in a "Markoff type" matrix and define $q_{ij} = 1 - p_{ij} \geq 0$ for every i,j. Let x_j be the value (discrete) of the jth component, $j = 1, \ldots n$, of any state vector and let $P(\hat{x}_i = k)$ represent the probability that $\hat{x}_i$, the ith random variable generated from these x_j andıd p_{ij}, will assume the integer value $k = 0, 1, 2, \ldots, y; \ y \equiv \Sigma^n_{j-1} x_j$. Then

$$\sum_{j=1}^{n} p_{ij} x_j = \sum_{k=0}^{y} k \, P(x_i = k) = E \, \hat{x}_i, \tag{1}$$

where E represents the expected value operator.

This theorem, which is utilized in the immediately preceding text, does not seem to be readily available in the literature that deals with Markoff processes.[1] We will therefore prove it here, after some preliminary definitions and developments.

In our case,[2]

$$P(\hat{x}_i = k) = \sum_{C_k^y} \prod_{j=1}^{n} C_{r_j}^{x_j} p_{ij}^{r_j} q_{ij}^{x_j - r_j} \tag{2}$$

where the indicated summation is over all of the C_k^y terms for which $r_1 + r_2 + \ldots + r_n = k$ and r_j is the number of x_j appearing in the latter sum and

---

1 Possibly because a good deal of the classical literature in this area is based on natural science examples and models from physics and biology which are observation rather than decision oriented. (They also do not deal with constrained relations and their Markoff matrices have $\underset{j}{\Sigma} \, p_{ij} = 1$.)

2 Extensions to continuous cases and higher moments are possible but will not be developed here.

Charnes, Cooper, Niehaus

$$C_{r_j}^{x_j} = \begin{cases} \dfrac{x_j!}{r_j!\,(x_j - r_j)!}, & x_j \geq r_j \\ 0, & \text{otherwise} \end{cases} \tag{3}$$

where $x_j! = x_j\,(x_j - 1)\,(x_j - 2)\,\ldots\,1$. Also, "$\Pi$" represents "product" as in

$$\prod_{j=1}^{n} C_{r_j}^{x_j}\, p_{ij}^{r_j}\, q_{ij}^{x_j - r_j} =$$

$$= C_{r_1}^{x_1}\, p_{i1}^{r_1}\, q_{i1}^{x_1 - r_1} C_{r_2}^{x_2}\, p_{i2}^{r_2}\, q_{i2}^{x_2 - r_2} \ldots C_{r_n}^{x_n}\, p_{in}^{r_n}\, q_{in}^{x_n - r_n} \tag{4}$$

Using the above definitions and developments our proof will now be developed in a way that relates it directly to the preceding text. We also want to develop it in a manner that naturally relates it to familiar uses of the moment generating functions for binomial distributions. We therefore commence with the case for which the Markoff-type matrix is 1×1 with a single element, p, and write[1]

$$(pt + q)^x = \sum_{k=0}^{x} t^k\, C_k^x\, p^k\, q^{x-k} \tag{5}$$

Differentiating with respect to t gives

$$xp\,(pt + q)^{x-1} = \sum_{k=0}^{x} k t^{k-1}\, C_k^x\, p^k\, q^{x-k} \tag{6}$$

and setting $t = 1$ then produces

$$xp = \sum_{k=0}^{x} k\, C_k^x\, p^k\, q^{x-k} = \sum_{k=0}^{x} k\, P\,(\hat{x} = k) \tag{7}$$

so that (1) evidently holds for the 1×1 Markoff type matrix.

To relate (1) specifically to the example in the preceding text we establish

$$\sum_{j=1}^{2} p_{ij}\, x_j = \sum_{k=0}^{y} k\, P\,(\hat{x}_i = k) \,;\, y \equiv x_1 + x_2, \tag{8}$$

where $i = 1, 2$ in the 2×2 matrix with elements p_{ij} and $p_{ij} + p_{ij} = 1 - i$, $j = 1, 2$. For a proof in this case we extend the above development via the binomial moment generation functions,

$$\prod_{j=1}^{2} (p_{ij}\, t_j + q_{ij})^{x_j} = \prod_{j=1}^{2} \sum_{r_j=0}^{x_j} t_j^{r_j}\, C_{r_j}^{x_j}\, p_{ij}^{r_j}\, q_{ij}^{x_j - r_j}. \tag{9}$$

The total differential for this expression gives

---

[1] We define $0^0 = 1$ so that, e.g., fully stochastic (ordinary) Markoff matrices are also included.

$$x_1 p_{i1}(p_{i1}t_1 + q_{i1})^{x_1-1}(p_{i2}t_2+q_{i2})^{x_2}dt_1 +$$

$$+ x_2 p_{i2}(p_{i1}t_1 + q_{i1})^{x_1}(p_{i2}t_2+q_{i2})^{x_2-1}dt_2 = \tag{10}$$

$$= \left[\sum_{r_1=0}^{x_1} r_1 t_1^{r_1-1} C_{r_1}^{x_1} p_{i1}^{r_1} q_{i1}^{x_1-r_1}\right]\left[\sum_{r_2=0}^{x_2} t_2^{r_2} C_{r_2}^{x_2} p_{i2}^{r_2} q_{i2}^{x_2-r_2}\right]dt_1 +$$

$$+ \left[\sum_{r_1=0}^{x_1} t_1^{r_1} C_{r_1}^{x_1} p_{i1}^{r_1} q_{i1}^{x_1-r_1}\right]\left[\sum_{r_2=0}^{x_2} r_2 t_2^{r_2-1} C_{r_2}^{x_2} p_{i2}^{r_2} q_{i2}^{x_2-r_2}\right]dt_2 .$$

This is an identity in the dt's. Hence we may equate coefficients, so that, at $t_1 = t_2 = 1$,

$$\sum_{j=1}^{2} p_{ij} x_j = \sum_{r_1=0}^{x_1}\sum_{r_2=0}^{x_2}(r_1+r_2) C_{r_1}^{x_1} C_{r_2}^{x_2} p_{i1}^{r_1} q_{i1}^{x_1-r_1} q_{i2}^{x_2-r_2} p_{i2}^{r_2} =$$

$$= 0 C_0^{x_1} C_0^{x_2} p_{i1}^{0} q_{i1}^{x_1} q_{i2}^{x_2} p_{i2}^{0} + \ldots + k\sum_{s=0}^{k} C_{k-s}^{x_1} C_s^{x_2} p_{i1}^{k-s} q_{i1}^{x_1-(k-s)} q_{i2}^{x_2-p} p_{i2}^{p} +$$

$$+ \ldots + (x_1+x_2) C_{x_1}^{x_1} C_{x_2}^{x_2} p_{i1}^{x_1} q_{i1}^{0} q_{i2}^{0} p_{i2}^{x_2} =$$

$$= \sum_{k=0}^{x_1+x_2} k\left[\sum_{s=0}^{k} C_{k-s}^{x_1} C_s^{x_2} p_{i1}^{k-s} q_{i1}^{x_1-(k-s)} q_{i2}^{x_2-s} p_{i2}^{s}\right] \tag{11}$$

or, in the notation of (1) and (2), above,

$$\sum_{j=1}^{2} p_{ij} x_j = \sum_{k=0}^{y} k\, P(\hat{x}_i = k) = \sum_{k=0}^{y} k\sum_{C_k^y}\prod_{j=1}^{2} C_{r_j}^{x_j} p_{ij}^{r_j} q_{ij}^{x_j-r_j} \tag{12}$$

where, as indicated for (2), the second of the latter sums is to be considered over all of the C_k^y terms for which $r_1 + r_2 = k$. The derivation leading to (12) then shows that the theorem is also true in this case for *either* $i = 1, 2$.

The general case can evidently be obtained by a direct extension of the above arguments ... viz,

$$\prod_{j=1}^{n}(p_{ij}t_j + q_{ij})^{x_j} = \prod_{j=1}^{n}\left(\sum_{r_j=0}^{x_j} t_j^{r_j} C_{r_j}^{x_j} p_{ij}^{r_j} q_{ij}^{x_j-r_j}\right).$$

Then differentiating and setting all $t = 1$ produces

$$\sum_{j=1}^{n} p_{ij} x_j = \sum_{r_1=0}^{x_1}\sum_{r_2=0}^{x_2}\ldots\sum_{r_n=0}^{x_n}(r_1+r_2+\ldots r_n)\prod_{j=1}^{n} C_{r_j}^{x_j} p_{ij}^{r_j} q_{ij}^{x_j-r_j} =$$

$$= 0\prod_{j=1}^{n} C_0^{x_j} p_{ij}^{0} q_{ij}^{x_j} + \ldots + (x_1+x_2+\ldots+x_n)\prod_{j=1}^{n} C_{x_j}^{x_j} p_{ij}^{x_j} q_{ij}^{0}$$

$$= \sum_{k=0}^{y} k\sum_{C_k^y}\prod_{j=1}^{n} C_{r_j}^{x_j} p_{ij}^{r_j} q_{ij}^{x_j-r_j} = \sum_{k=0}^{y} k\, P(\hat{x}_i = k).$$

Q.E.D.

9
A Stochastic Programming Model for Manpower Planning

M. El Agizy

IBM Corporation
Armonk, New York

Summary

In this paper we describe a system for manpower planning in the face of uncertain requirements. The problem is to select manpower levels over a time horizon, by optimizing some effectiveness criterion, subject to certain operational and policy constraints. The inputs to the model are future workloads characterized by their statistical distributions. The outputs are full-time employee levels and the associated retraining and hiring programs, temporary employee levels, planned overtime, and subcontract work.

Our analysis has two parts: first a multi-stage stochastic programming model to determine the optimal manpower plan, by minimizing the expected costs over the planning horizon; and, second, a statistical procedure for estimating workload distributions by skill and by time period. The statistical procedure and programming models are developed as parts of a unified system which has been in operation for several months.

1. Introduction

Scope

This paper deals with the problem of direct manpower planning by skill for a manufacturing unit. In the broad sense, a manpower plan is a specification of the number of personnel by skill and type that are needed to satisfy work requirements over a finite planning horizon. The importance of this planning area stems from the direct impact of manpower allocation decisions on product cost. The problem is aggravated, particularly in advanced technology industry, by the uncertainties in future workloads. In the absence of reliable methods of prediction, manpower planning is a problem of decision making in the face of uncertain requirements.

In direct manpower planning, future requirements lend themselves to a degree of definition and measurement. For the type of manufacturing facility considered here, a common unit of workload and production capacity is man-hours at standard productivity. However, without loss of generality, the unit of workload we use is the number of man-hours equivalent to a full-time company employee working regular hours.

The manufacturing plant under investigation is responsible for production of several products. Commitments frequently limit management's ability to adjust work requirements to suit available manpower resources. Consequently, we will assume that workload requirements for any period are to be satisfied during that period. The work force is usually classified in major skill categories common to more than one product. Several alternatives are available to the decision maker to change the productive capacity and satisfy the typically fluctuating and uncertain requirements. These include retraining employees to perform a new skill, hiring new full-time employees, hiring temporary employees, working overtime, subcontracting work, and idling employees. These options can be exercised subject to some operational and policy constraints.

Workload Forecasts

Based on market forecasts, shipping schedules, unshipped orders, inventory on hand, in process work, etc., net production schedules are established for each product. The workload by major skill category for each product is then estimated. The calculation of workload is based on net production schedule by product, ultimate hours per unit, manufacturing progress function, cycle time, effective scheduling days, vacation, absenteeism, etc. Computer procedures for generation of workload are generally available and are not described here as part of the system.

In manpower planning it is convenient to deal with the aggregate workload by major skill categories. This aggregation on all products is justified by the fact that employees with a specific skill can be transferred among products with minimal retraining costs. If specific products impose unique skill requirements, they should be identified and treated separately.

At the product forecast level we are dealing with several products with varying degrees of uncertainty in magnitude and timing that directly impact workload projections. Moreover, the workload is affected by a variety of controllable and uncontrollable factors such as product transfers, technology and engineering changes, learning, etc. These factors make accurate workload forecasting a very difficult task.

Fortunately, the manpower planner can compare actuals with historical workload forecasts to assess the forecasting errors. In section 3 we describe how to use such data to estimate the statisticall distributions of future workloads. These estimates can be modified by the manpower planner based on his judgment and experience.

Problem Description

The decision maker is faced with the problem of sequentially selecting the manpower levels to satisfy the workload in each period to optimize some effectiveness criterion. For any time period he has the following long and short-term decision alternatives to satisfy the workload:

- Retrain employees to perform a new skill
- Hire full-time employees
- Hire temporary employees
- Work overtime
- Subcontract work
- Allow employees to be idle.

Here, we assume (without loss of generality in formulating the model) that employee lay-off is not allowed. Reduction in manpower levels, however, can take place by (uncontrollable) attrition: voluntary separation, military leave, retirement, etc.

Several types of constraints that limit the number of new hires, retrained employees, temporary employees, and overtime employees equivalent by skill as well as the total number of full-time employees must be considered by the decision maker. These can be either operating or policy constraints. The maximum number of new hires and the maximum allowed overtime are examples of operating constraints. A policy constraint that impacts manpower decisions is the manpower ceiling imposed by management. This ceiling policy restricts the total number of full-time employees to a specific limit.

Problem Treatment

This problem area has received considerable attention in the literature and several approaches have been reported. First we refer to the work of Modigliani, Holn, Holt, Simon and Muth [1], [2], and [3] on producting planning, inventory and workforce. The network flow and linear programming models of Manne [4] and Hanssman and Hess [5] also treat the same problem area. In these references the work force is considered in aggregate rather than by skill in a deterministic formulation.

Other papers which deal mainly with the problem of manpower planning are by Charnes, Cooper and Niehaus [6] and Jewett [7]. In the former, the interactions between skills are recognized in a deterministic goal programming formulation. The latter author assumes an aggregate work force, explicitly treats the uncertain requirements as a finite set of mutually exclusive workloads with known probabilities, and uses dynamic programming as a solution technique. Our approach bears some similarity to these models, yet is distinctly different.

Specifically, our treatment is suitable for strategic and operational planning rather than for scheduling where inventory may be a significant consideration. The interactions among manpower skill categories as well as workload uncertainty by skill are recognized explicitly in our model. As described in section 2, the problem is formulated as a multi-stage stochastic program that minimizes the expected cost over the planning horizon. A statistical procedure for estimating workload distribution by skill and time period is given in section 3. Our treatment also emphasizes the development of an operational system as a management tool for manpower planning that combines the statistical and optimization models into a unified program. This system and our experience with it are described in the last section.

2. Model Formulation

The model formulated in this section is described as follows: A decision maker can choose the level of full-time company employees, by skill, in any of a finite number of time periods. This is accomplished by retraining on-board experienced employees or by hiring new employees, subject to operational and policy constraints. For our purposes, full-time employees are either experienced with at least one time period with the company or they are considered to be newly hired. We assume that recruiting and training can be accomplished immediately, and that survival or attrition rates, by skill, are known for each period. The workloads for different skills, to be satisfied during a period, are assumed to be random variables with known probability distributions. In each period, the number of full-time employees is decided upon before the workload is observed. If the realized workload exceeds the number of full-time employees, the shortage is balanced by overtime, temporary employees, and subcontract work. On the other hand, some employees are idle if the number of employees exceeds the workload. An economic problem arises because the costs associated with an increase in full-time employees may be offset by reductions in the expected costs of balancing the workload.

Let w_{jt} denote the number of experienced employees with skill j ($j=1, ..., n$) at the end of period t ($t=1, ..., T$), and y_{jt} denote the number of newly hired employees at the beginning of period t, with a maximum value d_{jt}. Also, let x_{ijt} be the number of full-time employees with skill i ($i=1, ..., n$) at the beginning of period t who will be trained and assigned to skill j during the period, and c_{ijt} denote the maximum value x_{ijt} can assume. At the beginning of a period the number of experienced employees plus new hires must equal the total number of employees to be retrained from that skill to all other skills; that is,

$$\sum_{i=1}^{n} x_{jit} = w_{jt-1} + Y_{jt}, \; c_{ijt} \geqslant x_{ijt} \geqslant 0, \; d_{jt} \geqslant Y_{jt} \quad 0, \tag{1}$$

where w_{j0}, the number of initial employees with skill j, is prescribed.

Let p_{it} be the conditional probability that an employee with skill i will be in service in period t, given that he is in service in period $t-1$. We assume that this probability (survival rate) is known and does not depend on the skill to which the employee may be trained. Clearly the w_{jt} satisfy

$$w_{jt} = \sum_{i=1}^{n} p_{it} x_{ijt}. \tag{2}$$

The manpower ceiling policy restricts the total number of full-time employees, at the end of a period, to a certain level denoted by b_t (may be the same for all t); that is,

$$\sum_{j=1}^{n} \sum_{i=1}^{n} p_{it} x_{ijt} \leqslant b_t. \tag{3}$$

For period t, let the workloads for all skills be denoted by the random vector $Z_t = (Z_{1t}, ..., Z_{jt}, ..., Z_{nt})$. Also, let $f_t (\zeta_{1t}, ..., \zeta_{jt}, ..., \zeta_{nt})$ and $f_{jt} (\zeta_{jt})$ denote the joint and marginal distribution functions of the workloads, respectively. We assume that Z_t is statistically independent of $Z_{t-1}, ..., Z_1$, and that $f_{jt} (\zeta_{jt})$ is normally distributed with known mean and variance for all j and t.

In addition to the symbols defined before, we need the following:

α_{ijt} = cost of a full-time employee with skill i to be trained and assigned to skill j:

β_{jt} = cost of a new hire with skill j:

e_{1jt} = cost of processing one unit of skill j workload by temporary employees:

e_{2jt} = cost of processing one unit of skill j workload by overtime for on board employees:

e_{3jt} = cost of processing one unit of skill j workload by subcontract work;

δ_{1jt} = maximum allowable ratio of workload processed by temporary employees to that processed by on-board employees with skill j;

δ_{2jt} = maximum allowable ratio of workload processed by overtime to that processed by on-board employees with skill j;

ψ_t = total cost incurred in period t.

The total cost incurred in period t includes the costs of (i) full-time employees (productive or nonproductive) and their retraining, (ii) new hires, and (iii) balancing the discrepancy between the workload and on-board employees. The latter cost, which is composed of the costs of temporary employees, overtime and subcontract work, is a function of the on-board employees w_{jt} and the workload realization ζ_{jt}. We denote the cost of balancing skill j workload by the function $\phi_{jt}(\zeta_{jt}, w_{jt})$. Hence ψ_t is given by

$$\psi_t = \sum_{j=1}^{n} \{ \sum_{i=1}^{n} \alpha_{ijt} x_{ijt} + \beta_{jt} Y_{jt} + \phi_{jt}(\zeta_{jt}, w_{jt}) \}. \qquad (4)$$

The workload to be processed by temporary employees and by overtime is restricted to be less than or equal to $\delta_{1jt} w_{jt}$ and $\delta_{2jt} w_{jt}$, respectively. However, no limit on the amount of subcontract work is assumed. If the realized workload is greater than the on-board employees, the decision maker applies the balancing options as needed in the most economical order. For our particular problem, we will assume that $e_{3jt} \geqslant e_{2jt} \geqslant e_{1jt} \geqslant 0$ for all j and t. If however, the realized workload is less than the on-board employees, no additional cost is incurred for idle time because all regular time (productive or nonproductive) costs are already taken into account. Hence, $\phi_{jt}(\zeta_{jt}, w_{jt})$ can be defined as follows:

$$\phi_{jt}(\zeta_{jt}, w_{jt}) = \begin{cases} 0 & \text{if } \zeta_{jt} \leqslant w_{jt}; \\ e_{1jt}(\zeta_{jt} - w_{jt}) & \text{if } w_{jt} < \zeta_{jt} \leqslant (1 + \delta_{1jt}) w_{jt}; \\ e_{1jt} \delta_{1jt} w_{jt} + e_{2jt} [\zeta_{jt} - (1 + \delta_{1jt}) w_{jt}] \\ \qquad \text{if } (1 + \delta_{1jt}) w_{jt} < \zeta_{jt} \leqslant (1 + \delta_{1jt} + \delta_{2jt}) w_{jt}; \\ (e_{1jt} \delta_{1jt} + e_{2jt} \delta_{2jt})) w_{jt} + e_{3jt} [\zeta_{jt} - (1 + \delta_{1jt} + \delta_{2jt}) w_{jt}] \\ \qquad \text{if } \quad (1 + \delta_{1jt} + \delta_{2jt}) w_{jt} < \zeta_{jt}. \end{cases} \qquad (5)$$

This function is plotted in Figures 1(a) and 1(b) with w_{jt} and ζ_{jt} as parameters, respectively. It can be checked that necessary and sufficient conditions for convexity of $\phi_{jt}(\zeta_{jt}, w_{jt})$ in w_{jt}, for every value of ζ_{jt}, are $e_{3jt} \geq e_{2jt} \geq e_{1jt} \geq 0$.

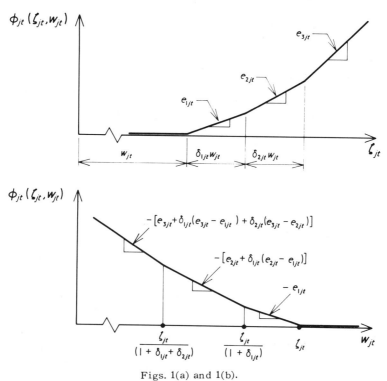

Figs. 1(a) and 1(b).

Now the decision maker's problem is to determine x_{ijt}, Y_{jt}, and w_{jt} that satisfy (1), (2) and (3) and minimize the expected cost for all periods. To summarize, we want to determine

$$\min E \sum_{t=1}^{T} \sum_{j=1}^{n} \{ \sum_{i=1}^{n} \alpha_{ijt} x_{ijt} + \beta_{jt} Y_{jt} + \phi_{jt}(\zeta_{jt}, w_{jt}) \}$$

subject to the following constraints:

$$\sum_{i=1}^{n} x_{ijt} - Y_{jt} - \sum_{i=1}^{n} p_{it-1} x_{ijt-1} = 0;$$
$$\sum_{i=1}^{n} p_{it} x_{ijt} - w_{jt} = 0; \qquad (6)$$
$$\sum_{j=1}^{n} \sum_{i=1}^{n} p_{it} x_{ijt} \leq b_t;$$

$c_{ijt} \geq x_{ijt} \geq 0$, $d_{jt} \geq Y_{jt} \geq 0$, $i = j = 1, \ldots, n$ and $t = 1, \ldots, T$; where E denotes expectation with respect to $Z_1, \ldots, Z_T$; $\sum_{i=1}^{n} p_{io} x_{ijo} = w_{jo}$ (the number of employees with skill j initially on board, is prespecified); and $\phi_{jt}(\zeta_{jt}, w_{jt})$ is defined by (5).

Since we are assuming that the random vector Z_t is stochastically independent of $Z_{t-1}, \ldots, Z_1$, it follows that the decision variables w_{jt}, y_{jt} and x_{ijt} do not depend on the realized workloads. Hence, our objective function can be written as

$$\min \sum_{t=1}^{T} \left\{ \sum_{j=1}^{n} \left(\sum_{i=1}^{n} \alpha_{ijt} x_{ijt} + \beta_{jt} Y_{jt} \right) + E_{Z_t} \sum_{j=1}^{n} \phi_{jt}(\zeta_{jt}, w_{jt}) \right\}. \tag{7}$$

Moreover, since ϕ_{jt} is only a function of ζ_{jt}, it follows that

$$E_{Z_t} \sum_{j=1}^{n} \phi_{jt}(\zeta_{jt}, w_{jt}) = \sum_{j=1}^{n} E_{Z_{jt}} \phi_{jt}(\zeta_{jt}, w_{jt}). \tag{8}$$

That is, the order of expectation with respect to Z_t and the summation with respect to j can be interchanged if we know, as assumed earlier, the marginal distribution of Z_{jt}. Using (7) and (8) our objective function is reduced to

$$\min \sum_{t=1}^{T} \sum_{j=1}^{n} \left\{ \sum_{i=1}^{n} \alpha_{ijt} x_{ijt} + \beta_{jt} Y_{jt} + E_{Z_{jt}} \phi_{jt}(\zeta_{jt}, w_{jt}) \right\}. \tag{9}$$

All terms in (9) are linear with the exception of $E_{Z_{jt}} \phi_{jt}(\zeta_{jt}, w_{jt})$, which is a convex, separable function of w_{jt}. This is an immediate consequence of the fact that the expectation of a convex function is also convex [8]. The expectation function, with notation simplified by suppressing the subscripts j and t, is written as

$$E_Z \phi(\zeta, w) = \int_{w}^{(1+\delta_1)w} e_1(\zeta-w)f(\zeta)d\zeta + \int_{(1+\delta_1)w}^{(1+\delta_1+\delta_2)w} e_2(\zeta-w)f(\zeta)\,d\zeta \tag{10}$$
$$+ \int_{(1+\delta_1+\delta_2)w}^{\infty} e_3(\zeta-w)f(\zeta)d\zeta.$$

In addition to being convex, this function is monotone decreasing in w. This can be demonstrated by showing that its first partial derivative with respect to w is nonpositive for all w.

As assumed earlier, $f(\zeta)$ is a normal distribution with known mean and standard deviation respectively, μ and σ. Define η as

$$\eta = \frac{(\zeta-\mu)}{\sigma}. \tag{11}$$

with a standard normal distribution denoted by $h(\eta)$. Also, let $H(a)$ denote the cumulative distribution of η, and $\bar{H}(a) = 1-H(a)$. From (11) we get

$$\left[\zeta = \sigma\eta + \mu, \qquad d\zeta = \sigma d\eta \qquad \text{and } h(\eta)\,d\eta = f(\zeta)d\zeta. \right] \tag{12}$$

Substituting in (10), using (12) and simplifying, we finally get

$$E_Z\phi(\zeta, w) = e_1\sigma h\left[\frac{w-\mu}{\sigma}\right] + (e_2-e_1)\sigma h\left[\frac{(1+\delta_1)w-\mu}{\sigma}\right] \quad (13)$$

$$+ (e_3-e_2)\sigma h\left[\frac{(1+\delta_1+\delta_2)w-\mu}{\sigma}\right] + e_1(\mu-w)\,\bar{H}\left[\frac{w-\mu}{\sigma}\right]$$

$$+ (e_2-e_1)(\mu-w)\,\bar{H}\left[\frac{(1+\delta_1)w-\mu}{\sigma}\right] + (e_3-e_2)(\mu-w)\,\bar{H}\left[\frac{(1+\delta_1+\delta_2)w-\mu}{\sigma}\right].$$

Knowing that $E_Z\phi(\zeta, w)$ is convex monotone decreasing in w, we can approximate it by a piece-wise linear convex function [9] as follows. For different values of w, say $a_0, a_0+a_1, \ldots, a_0+a_1+\ldots+a_L$, we compute $E_Z\phi(\zeta, w)$, and let the corresponding values be $b_0, b_1, \ldots, b_L$ [see Figure 2]. We assume that a is a desired or logical lower bound on w, and that the value of the function at $a_0+a_1+\ldots+a_L$, namely b_L, is approximately zero. This latter condition can be guaranteed by taking $a_0+a_1+\ldots+a_L$ large enough, e.g., $\mu+2\sigma'$. As shown in Figure 2, let the polygonal approximation of the expectation function be defined by the points $P_0, P_1, \ldots, P_L$ and let the slopes of the line segments be $-\gamma_l$ $(l = 1, \ldots, L)$. Hence the function can be represented as follows:

$$E_Z\phi(\zeta, w) \sim b_0 - \sum_{l=1}^{L} \gamma_l u_l; \quad (14)$$

$$w = a_0 + \sum_{l=1}^{L+1} u_l;$$

$$a_l \geq u_l \geq 0 \text{ for } l = 1, \ldots, L, \text{ and } u_{L+1} \geq 0.$$

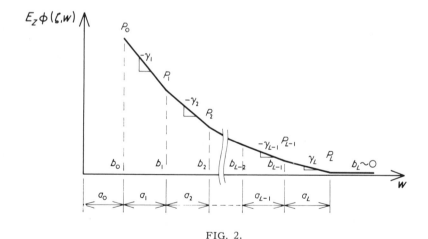

FIG. 2.

Substituting (14) in (9) after reinstating the subscripts j and t, program (6) can be approximated by the following equivalent linear program

$$\min \sum_{t=1}^{T} \sum_{j=1}^{n} \{ \sum_{i=1}^{n} a_{ijt} x_{ijt} + \beta_{jt} Y_{jt} - \sum_{l=1}^{L} \gamma_{ljt} u_{ljt} \} + Q_0$$

subject to

$$\sum_{i=1}^{n} x_{jit} - y_{jt} - \sum_{i=1}^{n} p_{it-1} x_{ijt-1} = 0; \qquad (15)$$

$$\sum_{i=1}^{n} p_{it} x_{ijt} - \sum_{l=1}^{L+1} u_{ljt} = a_{0jt}$$

$$\sum_{j=1}^{n} \sum_{i=1}^{n} p_{it} x_{ijt} \leqslant b_t;$$

$$c_{ijt} \geqslant x_{ijt} \geqslant 0, \; d_{jt} \geqslant Y_{jt} \geqslant 0, \; a_{ljt} \geqslant u_{ljt} \geqslant 0, \; u_{L+1jt} \geqslant 0,$$

where $i = j = 1, ..., n$, $t = 1, ..., T$, $l = 1, ..., L$, $\sum_{i=1}^{n} p_{i0} x_{ij0}$ is respecified,

and $Q_0 = \sum_{t=1}^{T} \sum_{j=1}^{n} b_{0jt}$.

Several aspects of our model formulation are of particular interest. First, we do not necessarily have to assume that training and assignment are allowed from any skill to all other skills, as indicated by equations (1) and (2). More realistic alternatives within our general formulation are to allow only upgrading of skills or upgrading to the next higher level skill in any time period. Also, the variables y_{jt} can be used for both hiring and layoff by simply assuming that it is non-restricted and that the associated cost has a V-shape. Second, while the assumption that the random vector Z_t is stochastically independent of $Z_{t-1}, ..., Z_1$, is essential for solving the problem yet the shape of the marginal distribution $f_{jt}(\zeta_{jt})$ need not be normal. Third, it can be shown, using a non-singular linear transformation, that program (15) has the matrix structure of a weighted distribution problem with generalized upper bounds. In the absence of a special algorithm to solve this class of problems we can, of course, use the simplex algorithm.

3. Estimation of Workload Distribution Functions

In the previous section we assumed that the marginal distribution functions of workloads during future time periods are known (see Figure 3). Here, we show how the characteristics of each distribution function, namely the parametric form, the mean, and the variance, can be estimated.

The forecasting process is described as follows: At any time period k the actual workload is observed, then the forecaster estimates the workloads in periods $k + 1, ..., k + t, ..., k + T$, where t $(t = 1, ..., T)$ denotes the forecast lead time. This process is repeated each period at forecast time.

The periodic observation of the workload as a time series can be described by components such as "trend," "cycle," "seasonal" and "irregular." The irregular component is the unpredictable variation that can be described by a probability distribution. There are too many factors, with complex interactions, to allow the derivation of an equation that describes the process underlying the workload data. The approach we take here is simply to assume that the forecaster does understand the process and can estimate the workload except for the irregular component.

A stochastic programming model

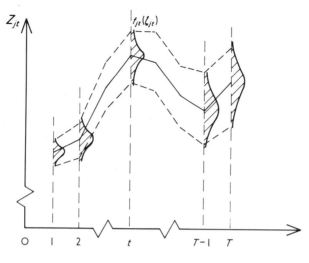

FIG. 3.

We use the term relative error in its mathematical sense to mean the actual workload minus the forecast divided by the forecast. We assume that the forecaster's relative error is a function of the forecast lead time and that it is independent of the time at which the forecast is made [10]. This assumption is intuitively appealing since one would expect that the relative error increases with forecast lead time, independent of forecast time. Moreover, we assume that the relative error in one period is independent of the relative errors in the preceding periods.

As in the previous section, let Z_t and $f_t(\zeta_t)$ denote the random workload periods from the forecast time for a particular skill and its corresponding marginal distribution. Here we have dropped the subscript j denoting the skill to avoid cumbersome notation. Also, let v_t be the true value of the underlying process, which we shall never know, and ϵ_t be the random relative error. Then Z_t is the sum of two components, the true process v_t and the irregular component $v_t \epsilon_t$, i.e.,

$$Z_t = v_t (1 + \epsilon_t). \tag{16}$$

To characterize $f_t(\zeta_t)$ we need to estimate the distribution of ϵ_t. The data from which one can do this are past observations of forecast errors. Let the actual workloads observed at time period k ($k = 1, \ldots, K$) be denoted by ζ_k and let the forecasts made at that time be denoted by $\hat{v}_{k, k+t}$ where $t = 1, \ldots, T$. (The accented symbol $\hat{v}$ indicates an estimated value.) By examining historical data

El Agizy

we can compare the workload observed at time k, ζ_k, with the forecast made t periods earlier, i.e., $\hat{v}_{k-t,k}$ for $t = 1, ..., T$. We define the relative error at time k, which depends on the lead time of the forecast, as

$$e_{kt} = \frac{\zeta_k - \hat{v}_{k-t,k}}{\hat{v}_{k-t,k}} \qquad \text{for } k = 1, ..., K \text{ and } t = 1, ..., T. \qquad (17)$$

Since we assume that the relative error is a function of the lead time t and is independent of k, e_{kt} is a random sample from the distribution of ϵ_t. From historical data we have $(K-t)$ sample points of this distribution. The mean and variance of ϵ_t, denoted by μ_{ϵ_t} and $\sigma^2_{\epsilon_t}$, are estimated by the sample mean and variance which are given by

$$\bar{e}_t = \frac{1}{K-t} \sum_{r=t+1}^{K} e_{rt} \qquad (18)$$

and

$$s_t^2 = \frac{K-t}{(K-t-1)} \frac{1}{K-t} \left(\sum_{r=t+1}^{K} e_{rt}^2 - \bar{e}_t^2 \right) \qquad (19)$$

On examining the random sample of the relative error, we hypothesized that the parametric form of the distribution of ϵ_t was normal. A χ^2 test was then used to substantiate this hypothesis.

Having estimated the characteristics of the distribution of the relative error, we can, given the workload forecast in period t, characterize the distribution of workload. Let the forecast for the workload t periods ahead be $\hat{v}_t$; then from (16) we have

$$Z_t = \hat{v}_t (1 + \epsilon_t). \qquad (20)$$

It follows from (20) that the mean and variance of Z_t are given by

$$\mu_{Z_t} = \hat{v}_t (1 + \mu_{\epsilon_t}), \text{ and } \sigma^2_{Z_t} = \hat{v}_t^2 \sigma^2_{\epsilon_t}. \qquad (21)$$

Since ϵ_t is normally distributed, then from (20) Z_t is also normally distributed with mean and variance estimated as

$$\mu_{Z_t} \sim \hat{v}_t (1 + \bar{e}_t), \text{ and } \sigma^2_{Z_t} \sim \hat{v}_t^2 s_t^2. \qquad (22)$$

In our statistical approach, to eliminate the bias from workload forecasts and estimate the error distribution, we used historical relative errors rather than the forecast error. This is particularly convenient since historical data may not be available except for total workload. In this case, we can use the total workload data with the assumption that the random relative errors for the workload by skill and total are the same. Here again, given that future forecasts are made by skill, our approach is still applicable.

4. Application, System Description and Experience to Date

Here we give a numerical example to illustrate the manpower planning model. In addition we describe how the techniques were developed as parts of an operational planning system and our implementation experience to data.

To illustrate the technique and to make the model inputs and solution outputs more specific we consider a simple numerical example: The planning problem consists of four time periods and the workforce is classified into two categories – nontechnical and technical employees. The workload means and standard deviations as well as the survival rates by skill and by time period are stipulated in Table 1.

TABLE 1

Time Period	Skill j					
	1 (Nontechnical)			2 (Technical)		
t	μ_{1t}	σ_{1t}	p_{1t}	μ_{2t}	σ_{2t}	p_{2t}
1	730	51	0.972	470	32	0.980
2	600	48	0.972	380	30	0.980
3	740	67	0.995	500	45	0.982
4	650	65	0.995	430	43	0.982

For this numerical example we ignore limits on hiring and training activities, i.e., d_{jt} and c_{ijt} are assumed to be vary large. We also assume that the manpower ceiling b_t is 1000 for all time periods. The number of initially available employees, the minimum number of onboard employees and the maximum allowed ratios δ_{1jt} and δ_{2jt} for all time periods are given in Table 2.

TABLE 2

Skill j	Initial employees	Minimum on-board employees	Temporary employees	Overtime
	w_{jo}	a_{ojt}	δ_{1jt}	δ_{2jt}
1	580	450	0.05	0.10
2	350	300	0.05	0.10

Finally, the costs for each period (in units of $1000) of full-time employees and their retraining, hiring, temporary employees, overtime and subcontract work shown in Table 3.

TABLE 3

Skill j	c_{1jt}	c_{2jt}	β_{jt}	e_{1jt}	e_{2jt}	e_{3jt}
1	3.5		0.3	3.0	4.0	4.5
2	4.0	4.5	0.6	4.0	5.0	5.5

In our example we do not allow training from skill 2 to skill 1.

The computer solution of this manpower planning problem using our approximation model, with manpower values rounded to the nearest integer, is summarized in Tables 4 and 5.

We notice that the manpower ceiling was reached only in period 3 and that no retraining took place in any of the periods. We avoid giving any interpretation or making any conclusions from this solution since the model data is purely hypothetical.

TABLE 4: Nontechnical Manpower (skill $j = 1$)

Description		1	2	3	4
			t		
Available employees		580	604	587	603
New hires	Beginning	41	0	26	2
Employees trained to Technicals	of period	0	0	0	0
Total assignment to Nontechnicals		621	604	613	605
Losses		17	17	10	8
Available employees		604	587	603	597
Expected temporary employees	End of	30	13	30	30
Expected overtime	period	60	0	60	23
Expected subcontract work		36	0	47	0
Expected workload		730	600	740	650

TABLE 5: Technical Manpower (skill $j = 2$)

Description		1	2	3	4
			t		
Available employees		350	370	362	397
New hires	Beginning	27	0	42	0
Employees trained to Nontechnicals	of period	0	0	0	0
Total assignment to Technicals		377	370	404	397
Losses		7	8	7	7
Available employees		370	362	397	390
Expected temporary employees	End of	18	18	20	19
Expected overtime	period	37	0	40	21
Expected subcontract work		45	0	43	0
Expected workload		470	380	500	430

System Description and Experience to Date

The system, shown schematically in Figure 4, has four major programs.

1. *Forecasting Error Analysis Program* Inputs are historical forecasts and actual workloads, and outputs are forecast percent errors, means, and standard deviations for different forecast lead times. Moreover, for a given workload forecast by skill, this program estimates the unbiased workload and the standard deviation of the associated error distribution.

2. *Matrix Generator and Input Report Program* Inputs are workload means and standard deviations, attrition rates, number of initially available employees, and cost data by skill and period. The Matrix Generator Program assembles all variable and row names, matrix coefficients, right-hand side values, and bounds, in a format acceptable to IBM/360 "Mathematical Programming System" (commercially available). This program has been designed to handle up to ten skills and twenty five time periods. It has arithmetic capabilities to make certain calculations required in generating the matrix coefficients. The Input Report Program assembles the input data in a management-readable input report.

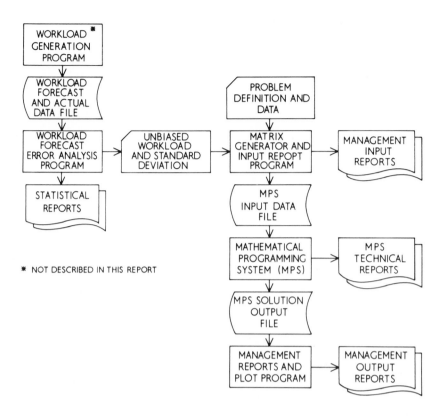

FIG. 4.

3. *Mathematical Programming System* (*MPS*) Input is generated by the previous program, and output is the solution of the approximate linear programming model. The solution is displayed in a series of technical reports to be used by those responsible for the operation of the model.

4. *Management Reports and Plots Program* Input is the MPS optimal solution, and outputs are management reports that show the optimal manpower levels, number of employees retrained, number of newly hired employees and number of attributed employees (rounded to the nearest integer) by period and skill. Moreover, the reports show the difference between the expected workload (should it materialize) and on-board employees would be satisfied by temporary employees, overtime and subcontract work.

This system was designed with emphasis on a correct balance between the sophistication of the analytical tools and ease of implementation and interpretation. The input data requirements are kept to a minimum. Several options are available for users to draw from, based on their problem solving needs. Although not described in this paper, a deterministic version of this model is made available to the user as part of the system.

Several features of this computer system are of particular interest. A total system approach, responsive to the user needs was emphasized in the development. Special programs were written for input and output reports, the statistical calculations and the matrix generation to capitalize on the properties of subject mathematical formulation. Also, the system was developed in a modular construction for ease of debugging as well as improving each module. The complete system is written in FORTRAN to facilitate understanding and for compatibility with the IBM Mathematical Programming System.

The need for a quantitative technique for manpower planning was suggested by a manufacturing planning staff. The development of this system was accomplished in cooperation with one manufacturing plant. Model assumptions, concepts, and input/output requirements were reviewed at different stages of development. The system was first demonstrated and adopted in January 1970 by the manufacturing plant to displace the existing judgemental methods of manpower planning. Since that time several case studies have been made and the system has been used for two modes of operation – updating and evaluation. The updating mode is used for operating and strategic planning during each planning cycle. The development of a plan is usually the end result of several case studies. The evaluation mode encompasses all the problem solving activities – the "what if" type problems.

Since the system was first demonstrated other manufacturing plants have adopted it as a tool for manpower planning. This was accomplished through an extensive effort of presentations made to management levels responsible for developing or approving manpower plans. As part of these management briefings, a typical manpower planning problem with real data was discussed and the advantages of this quantitative method were emphasized. The computer input and output reports, designed for easy interpretation, received favorable response. In addition to user's manuals, training of technicians was necessary for system implementation and solution interpretation. Several constructive comments were made to facilitate the use of the system from a user's point of view.

Operationally, the most time consuming part of applying this technique is the collection of cost data. However, this effort is usually rewarded with meaningful manpower plans that offer significant payoffs. Sensitivity analyses for several manpower plans indicated that the optimal solution was not sensitive to certain cost parameters. This suggests that it is not necessary to do extensive research to determine these costs with a high degree of precision.

Our experience with implementation so far has been adequate for sizeable benefits. Qualitatively, we can say that the system has been responsive to the planning needs as demonstrated by the expanding usuage. More acceptance is anticipated as management and present users gain confidence and experience with the tool.

References

1. Modigliani, F. and Hohn, F., "Production Planning Over Time and the Nature of the Expectation and Planning Horizon," *Econometrica*, Vol. 23, 1955, pp. 46–66.
2. Holt, C.C., Modigliani, F., and Simon, H.A., "A Linear Decision Rule for Production and Employment Scheduling," *Management Science*, Vol. 2, No. 1, 1955. pp. 1–30.

3. Holt, C.C., Modigliani, F., Muth, J.R., and Simon, H.A., *"Planning Production, Inventories and Work Force,"* Prentice-Hall, Englewood Cliffs, New Jersey, 1960.

4. Manne, A.S., "A Note on the Modigliani-Hohn Production Smoothing Model," *Management Science*, Vol. 3, No. 4, 1957, pp. 371–379.

5. Hanssmann, F., and Hess, S.W., "A Linear Programming Approach to Production and Employment Scheduling," *Management Technology*, January, 1960, pp. 46–51.

6. Charnes, A., Cooper, W.W., Niehaus, R.J., "A Goal Programming Model for Manpower Planning," *Management Science in Planning and Control*, John Blood, Jr. editor, New York, Technical Association of the Pulp and Paper Industry, STAP No. 5, 1969, pp. 79–93.

7. Jewett, R.F., "A Minimum Risk Manpower Scheduling Technique," *Management Science*, Vol. 13, No. 10, 1967, pp. 578–592.

8. Dantzig, G.B., "Linear Programming under Uncertainty," *Management Science*, Vol. 1, 1955, pp. 456–567.

9. Dantzig, G.B., *"Linear Programming and Extensions,"* Princeton University Press, 1963, pp. 484–486.

10. Brown, R.G., *"Smoothing, Forecasting and Prediction of Discrete Time Series,"* Prentice-Hall, Englewood Cliffs, New Jersey, 1963, pp. 271–273.

10

Manpower Modelling:
A Study in Research and Development*

A. E. Gear, J. S. Gillespie, A. G. Lockett, A. W. Pearson

Manchester Business School

Summary

In situations which involve decisions regarding recruitment policy as well as allocation of manpower resources to current opportunities there may be a need to consider not only the returns from particular resource allocations in the shorter term, but also the longer term implications of present day recruitment decisions. An example of this type of situation is met in R & D laboratories. If the blend of scientific manpower types in a laboratory is not keeping pace with the changing nature of the R & D opportunities the organisation may find itself unable to undertake certain desirable R & D work when the time comes.

The paper describes a model of this type of problem based on a mathematical programming approach which allows the inclusion of multiple types of manpower and other resources. The model is aimed at assisting the decision-taker to allocate resources to the present list of project opportunities, as well as recruitment policy in the various manpower grades over time. The model can incorporate features associated with: short term resource allocation decisions; natural wastage of manpower over time; training of manpower; the occurrence of future opportunities not known in detail at "time now"; and the ability of certain types of manpower to undertake activities normally assigned to other manpower types.

An application of the model, using data from an actual industrial R & D situation, is described. Difficulties associated with data collection and solution interpretation are discussed, and some preliminary conclusions outlined.

1. Introduction

Models based on linear programming have been described as aids to optimal programme planning in research and development laboratories where a scarcity of some resource types, typically scientific and technical manpower, may be the limiting factor. The foundations of these models were laid by Beattie[3] and Bell[4] and later developed by Allen[1] and Lockett[6].

* This study was sponsored by the Programme Analysis Unit, a joint unit of the Ministry of Technology and the United Kingdom Atomic Energy Authority.

The data requirements of these models may be summarised as:

(1) definition of a series of laboratory resources likely to be in short supply; usually different types of skilled manpower, time on certain facilities such as testing apparatus or pilot plant, money under one or more accounting heads.

(2) prediction of the overall availabilities of each type of resource in each of a number of time periods from the present, which together make up the overall planning period under consideration.

(3) estimation of the resource requirements of each distinct opportunity, whether potential or on-going, in each time period.

(4) estimation of the expected net benefit of each opportunity, if undertaken, in terms of the objective(s) of the organisation.

If one accepts the general suitability of models with this structure in certain R & D types of situation, considerable problems still arise in connection with the data requirements. The problem examined in this paper is how to define overall availabilities of manpower resources as a function of time. This problem is complicated by the fact that various manpower movements and transfers can take place in each future time period included in the model, so that only the availabilities at time now are accurately known.

For example, movements within the R & D system may result from the learning process, leading to promotions. Some types of manpower (or individuals) may, in an emergency, be flexible enough to carry out the activities "normally" allotted to other sorts of personnel. Transfers between R & D system and its environment may arise through recruitment and wastage, as well as from occasional transfers to and from other functional areas within the organisation.

An additional complication, which in general applies to any resource allocation model extending over future time, is how to take account of "future opportunities" for which detailed information is presently lacking. If the procedure of setting aside an increasing proportion of the overall availabilities of resources in future time periods is adopted, then this also modifies the manpower availability calculations.

Due to the complexity of the above processes, considered together, it appears useful to construct a manpower model of an R & D laboratory as an adjunct to a resource allocation model. This approach has the advantage of providing the decision-maker with information on which to base his resource allocation and recruitment decisions.

Nemhauser[9] has developed a dynamic programming model based on this philosophy, while both linear and dynamic programming formulations have been suggested by Purkiss.[11] Other mathematical programming models aimed at optimising manpower planning decisions have been described for a variety of applications by Maki,[7] Morgan,[8] Thelwell[12] and Patz.[10] An advantage to an organisation of using models of this kind is the integrative effect that results from the need for close co-operation between the personnel function and the functional area concerned.

In order to initially test these ideas, data from an industrial research and development situation has been obtained, and incorporated into a linear programming formulation extending over several time periods into the future. The model is deterministic in the sense that certain manpower flows connected with wastage and promotion are given average values based on past experience, rather than being treated as stochastic variables.

In the following section a simple manpower model is developed. The manpower model is incorporated into a resource allocation model of the practical situation in section 3, where also the results of a number of manipulations of this model are presented. Numerical details of the case study is not given in order to concentrate attention on the formulation of the problem.

Some implications of including the effects of future opportunities are briefly analysed in section 4, and some preliminary conclusions from what is an on-going study are given in the final section.

2. Manpower Model

In this section a deterministic model of a manpower system consisting of only two types of personnel is developed. Models of more complex systems with more than two manpower types and with additional flow interactions, may be constructed along idential lines. A model of this type has been developed, for example, by Duffett.[5] The development is in terms of finite difference equations which connect overall availabilities in time period p with those in time period $p + 1$.

Consider two manpower types, A and B with effective availabilities A_p and and B_p in time period $p(p = 1, 2, \ldots k, \ldots, p)$, where p is the number of time periods making up the overall planning period from the present ($p = 1$). Let variables r_p and s_p represent the amounts of recruitment in period p to the manpower categories A and B respectively, which effectively becomes available for use in period $p + 1$. Let variable L_p and M_p represent the amount of wastage in period p from A and B respectively, which takes effect in period $p + 1$.

In this situation, it is supposed that category B represents a senior level to that of A, and that staff from A may be up-graded to B as they gain experience. Accordingly a variable, U_p is introduced to represent the amount of up-grading from A to B in period p, taking practical effect in period $p + 1$. The situation is depicted in figure 1 for time periods $p = 1, 2$.

Recurrence equations which relate the availabilities in successive periods for the types of manpower may be written:

$$\left. \begin{array}{l} A_{p+1} = A_p + r_p - L_p - U_p \\ B_{p+1} = B_p + s_p - M_p + U_p \end{array} \right\} \tag{1}$$

It it is assumed that the loss and up-grading rates can be represented by the deterministic linear expressions:

$$\left. \begin{array}{l} L_p = \alpha A_p \\ M_p = \beta B_p \\ U_p = \gamma A_p \end{array} \right\} \tag{2}$$

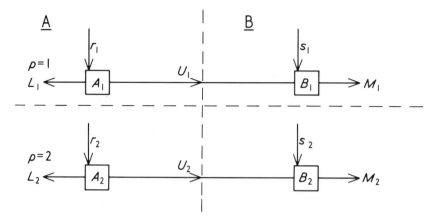

Fig. 1. Manpower movements in periods $p = 1, 2$.

where the loss rates α and β and the up-grading rates γ are constants independent of time, then combining the groups of equations (1) and (2) results in the equations (3), from which the availabilities of manpower of each type in each period can be calculated in terms of the initial availabilities, A_1 and B_1, and the recruitment variables, r_p and s_p.

$$A_p = A_1(1 - \alpha - \gamma)^{p-1} + \sum_{k=1}^{p-1} (1 - \alpha - \gamma)^{p-k-1} r_m, \quad 2 \leqslant p \leqslant P$$

$$\tag{3}$$

$$B_p = B_1(1 - \beta)^{p-1} + \sum_{k=1}^{p-1} (1 - \beta)^{p-k-1} (s_k + \gamma A_k), \quad 2 \leqslant p \leqslant P.$$

As the equations (3) are linear, A_p and B_p can be used as availabilities in linear or mixed integer programme. It would be preferable to treat the recruitment variables as integers, but useful outputs can be obtained by treating them as continuous. An application of this approach is described in the following section.

3. R & D Case Study

The case study described in the following sections forms a part of a larger study aimed at developing and assessing quantitative models as an aid to decision-making in a variety of R & D situations.

3.1. Laboratory Environment

The case study covers all the non-mandatory R & D projects, both on-going and proposed, of a division of an electrical and electronics engineering organisation. The division is primarily concerned with the development and manufacture of specialised electronic components and devices, usually based on established scientific principles and knowledge.

Proposals for projects to be considered by the R & D section of the division usually come from senior R & D management, and sometimes from sales and marketing personnel. The proposals are usually stimulated by the identification

Gear, Gillespie, Lockett, Pearson

of a potential market need or gap which lies within a field of expertise of the division. Thus fairly detailed proposals in terms of technical and commercial objectives are defined at the outset. The technical objectives of each project are in terms of one or more electrical/mechanical/thermal/size characteristics, while the commercial objectives are often established in terms of works cost per item.

The division has relatively little freedom to set the selling price per item, as this is largely determined by a complex set of market factors external to the division. However, there is uncertainty regarding the way these factors will operate, and hence considerable uncertainty regarding the profitability of a particular project, if undertaken.

3.2 Project Evaluation

As it is not the objective of this paper to emphasise the method by which each project in the list under consideration for inclusion in the programme was evaluated, it is only briefly described here.

For each project, the R & D resource requirements in eight periods, each of three months duration from the present, were estimated by the project managers likely to be concerned. Apart from general overheads which would be incurred anyway, the direct resource requirements resulting from the decision to undertake an R & D project were summarised in terms of man-weeks for various categories of skilled manpower as well as some capital costs. Manpower costs were not subtracted from the eventual project benefits on the grounds that the decision to employ laboratory staff had already been taken, making manpower a committed cost.

After the R & D stage, a number of technical outcomes were predicted by the project managers concerned, each with a subjective probability attached. The technical outcome achieved largely determined the production cost per item, while the selling price, as mentioned earlier, is largely market determined and was considered as a stochastic variable at the time of project evaluation. Because the uncertainties regarding cost and selling prices meant that it could be unprofitable to proceed with the project into production, after completion of the R & D stage, a "decision to manufacture" decision point was built into the evaluations on a go/no go basis. The approach to the project evaluations was based on the use of a decision-tree structure for each project. This allowed the expected monetary net present value of each project to be calculated, and used in the linear programming formulation.

3.3. R & D Manpower Model

A preliminary analysis of the R & D situation showed that for the project opportunities under consideration the only types of scarce resource were likely to be certain categories of R & D personnel. Thus the problem appeared to be how best to utilise R & D manpower over time on some or all of the projects in order to maximise the overall net present value of the benefits to the division.

The problem became one of defining appropriate manpower categories, and defining the major manpower movements and transfers. Discussion with the

R & D Director and his deputy, who were not included in the manpower model, led to the isolation of two different manpower categorisations, with uncertainty as to which was the more appropriate.

The alternatives, referred to as categorisations I and II, are explained with the aid of figures 2 and 3 respectively. These figures show both the basic manpower categories and the major inputs and outputs connected with them. In both models, the manpower categories are in terms of:

Supervisors: experienced scientists and technologists able to lead teams on one or more projects.

Scientists: a mixture of graduate physicists and chemists.

Electricians: technicians with skill in the design, construction, development and testing of electronic circuitry and equipment.

Technicians: laboratory assistants with general practical skills.

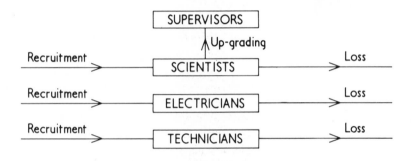

Fig. 2. Manpower Categorisation I

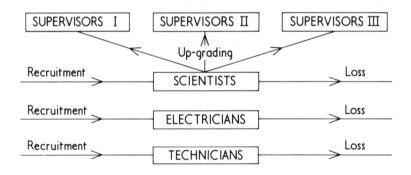

Fig. 3. Manpower Categorisation II

In categorisation II the supervisor category has been sub-divided into three blocks, instead of the one block for categorisation I. This was because it was realised that three types of supervisors, who would normally be expected to control projects only in their own field of technical expertise, were recognised by the R & D Director and his deputy. Given some learning time, say 1–3 months, then a supervisor of one type could acquire sufficient knowledge in another technical field to start managing projects in that field. In order to explore the value of adopting a policy of increasing the flexibility of supervisors, both manpower models were developed.

Recruitment possibilities, and an average loss rate for scientists, electricians and technicians were included in both manpower models. Promotion to the supervisory level from among the scientists was included. In categorisation II it was assumed that one third of the up-graded scientists would enter each of the supervisory blocks. Direct recruitment to, or loss from, the supervisory grades was extremely rare and not included.

3.4. Mathematical Model

A formulation of the above situation as a linear programming problem is presented in this section. The model, which contains variables associated with alternative versions of each project, and with recruitment of manpower into various categories, is composed of the following relationships:

(a) Inequalities to ensure that each project cannot be selected in more than one version, at most, which takes the form:

$$\sum_{j=1}^{m_i} x_{ij} \leqslant 1, \quad i = 1, 2, \ldots, n. \tag{4}$$

where x_{ij} = a variable representing version j of project i ($i = 1, 2, \ldots, n$) and $j = 1, 2, \ldots, m_i$)

n = total number of projects

m_i = number of versions of project i.

(b) Inequalities to ensure that the availability of scientists is not exceeded in any of the eight planning periods which take the form:

$$\sum_{i=1}^{n} \sum_{j=1}^{m_i} a_{ijp} \, x_{ij} \leqslant A_p \tag{5}$$

where p = period number ($p = 1, 2, \ldots, 8$),

A_p = effective overall availability of scientist manpower in time period p,

a_{ijp} = requirement of scientific manpower for version j of project i in period p.

In accordance with the manpower model developed in section 2, A_p is given by,

$$A_p = A_1 (1 - \alpha - \gamma)^{p-1} + \sum_{k=1}^{k=p-1} (1 - \alpha - \gamma)^{p-k-1} \, r_k \tag{6}$$

for all periods after the first ($2 \leqslant p \leqslant 8$). In equation (5),

A_1 = availability of scientific manpower in period $p = 1$

α = average rate of loss of scientific manpower per period as a fraction of total availability in the immediately preceding period.

γ = average rate of up-grading to the supervisory category of scientific manpower per period as a fraction of total availability in the immediately preceding period

r_k = amount of recruitment of scientists in time period
$p = k\,(k = 1, 2, \ldots , 8)$

(c) Inequalities to ensure that the availability of supervisors is not exceeded in any time period, of the form,

$$\sum_{i=1}^{n} \sum_{j=1}^{m_i} b_{ijp}\, x_{ij} \leqslant B_p \tag{7}$$

where B_p = overall availability of supervisors in period p,

b_{ijp} = requirement of scientific manpower for version j of project i in period p.

In equation (7), B_p is given by,

$$B_p = B_1 + \gamma \sum_{k=1}^{k=p-1} A_k, \quad 2 \leqslant p \leqslant 8 \tag{8}$$

where B_1 = availability of supervisory manpower in period $p = 1$

A_k = availability of scientific manpower in period $p = k$ as given by equation (6).

(d) Inequalities to ensure that the availability of electricians is not exceeded in any period of the form:

$$\sum_{i=1}^{n} \sum_{j=1}^{m_i} c_{ijp}\, x_{ij} \leqslant C_p \tag{9}$$

where C_p = availability of electricians in period p

c_{ijp} = requirement of electricians for version j of project i in period p

In the above, C_p is given by,

$$C_p = C_1(1 - \beta)^{p-1} + \sum_{k=1}^{k=p-1} (1 - \beta)^{p-k-1} s_k, \quad 2 \leqslant p \leqslant 8 \tag{10}$$

where C_1 = availability of electricians in period $p = 1$

β = average rate of loss of electricians per period as a fraction of the overall availability in the immediately preceding period

s_k = amount of recruitment of electricians in time period $p = k$

(e) Inequalities to ensure that the availability of technicians is not exceeded in any period. These are identical in form to those of (10) above, requiring the introduction of the following variables:

D_1 = availability of technicians in period $p = 1$

δ = average rate of loss of technicians per period as a fraction of the overall availability in the immediately preceding period.

t_k = amount of recruitment of technicians in time period $p = k$.

(f) Inequalities to ensure that the overall recruitment of all categories in year 1 (time periods $p = 1, 2, 3$); in year 2 (time periods $p = 4, 5, 5, 7$); and in the final period covered by the model ($p = 8$), do not exceed specified total amounts. That is;

$$\sum_{p=1}^{p=3} (r_p + s_p + t_p) \leqslant R_{1,3} \tag{11}$$

$$\sum_{p=4}^{p=7} (r_p + s_p + t_p) \leqslant R_{4,7} \tag{12}$$

$$(r_8 + s_8 + t_8) \leqslant R_8 \tag{13}$$

where $R_{1,3}$, $R_{4,7}$ and R_8 represent the maximum total recruitment to the laboratory in year 1, year 2, and in the final period. Recruitment in the final period $p = 8$, is assumed to become available in period $p = 9$, which is the first period beyond that covered by the model.

(g) Two relationships to ensure that the longer term (time period $p = 9$) proportions of different types of manpower do not fall outside certain boundaries which the laboratory director feels will be approximately optimal. These feelings are based on predictions of the longer range market opportunities in the technological area covered by the division. The predictions are no more than judgements based on experience of the area regarding the general types of future R & D project opportunities which will arise more than two years from the present time. The first period 9 constraint is an inequality to ensure that the ratio of scientists to supervisors does not exceed 3:1 in the long term:

$$3(A_8 + r_8) \leqslant B_8 \tag{14}$$

The second of these constraints is an equality to ensure that the ratio of scientists to electricians plus technicians is 1:1. That is;

$$(A_8 + r_8) = (C_8 + s_8) + (D_8 + t_8) \tag{15}$$

(h) An objective function of the form:

$$\text{MAX}\left[\sum_{i=1}^{n} \sum_{j=1}^{m_i} x_{ij} \, b_{ij} - \sum_{p=1}^{p=8} (r_p V_{rp} + s_p V_{sp} + t_p V_{tp}) \right]$$

where b_{ij} = the net present value of the benefits of version j of project i, if undertaken, and using a discount ratio, α_0.

V_{rp} = the net present value of the cost of employing one unit of scientific manpower from time period p. Similarly for V_{sp} and

V_{tp} . Values for the coefficients, V_{rp}, V_{sp}, V_{tp} were calculated using the normal discounting formula,

$$V_{rp} = \int_{p}^{p+S_r} v_r \, e^{-\alpha_0 T} dT.$$

where S_r = the average stay time in the organisation,

v_r = the cost of employment per unit time, assumed to be independent of time in the above.

3.5. Data Summary

It is not the intention to present all the data which relates to the practical study in this section, but only a summary. This allows the objective of the paper of presenting a particular formulation in application to be maintained.

Seven projects were involved in the case study. As several of the projects were included in more than one mutually exclusive R & D version, this meant a total of 15 project versions. Differences between the versions, together with the expected benefit of each version are presented in table 1. Some project versions arose from re-defining inter-dependent projects in a more aggregated form.

In table 2 the data which was used to calculate the coefficients in the model concerned with wastage and up-grading rates, limitations on recruitment, and the cost of employment are summarised.

3.6. Results

The model described in the preceding section was analysed as a linear programming problem. This meant that both the project variables, x_{ij}, and the recruitment variables, r_p, s_p, t_p, could take fractional values.

The model was analysed in a number of ways in order to test for significant changes in the solution with respect to:

(1) the adoption of either manpower model as described in section 3.3.

(2) the addition of recruitment variables, together with wastage and up-grading, to a basic resource allocation model including only project version variables.

(3) the inclusion of the two constraints which define limits to the longer term (period 9) manpower profield of the laboratory.

In table 3, solutions to the model numbered 1 to 6 are presented. Solutions 1 to 3 apply to manpower categorisation I in which supervisors are grouped together; solutions 4 to 6 apply to categorisation II in which supervisors are separated into three categories.

Solutions 1 and 4 apply to a basic resource allocation model in which no manpower availabilities are assumed to remain constant through each time period and set equal to their first period values.

Gear, Gillespie, Lockett, Pearson

Table 1. Project Versions

Project Version		Description of Project Version in Terms of Timing and rate of Resource Usage	Expected Benefit (Money Units)
i	j		
1	1	starting first period.	69
2	1	starting first period.	35
3	1	starting first period.	234
3	2	starting third period.	216
3	3	starting fifth period.	201
4	1	starting first period, slow rate of working	30
4	2	starting first period, fast rate of working	82
4	3	starting first period, medium rate of working	76
5	1	starting third period.	43
5	2	starting fifth period.	40
6	1	starting first period, fast rate of working	205
6	2	starting first period, slow rate of working	189
6	3	starting third period.	171
7	1	starting second period.	353
7	2	starting fourth period.	337

Table 2. Coefficient values in model

Coefficients	Value
α	1 in 20 per annum
β	1 in 20 per annum
γ	1 in 10 per annum
δ	1 in 5 per annum
$R_{1,3}$	3 men
$R_{4,7}$	4 men
R_8	1 man
v_r, v_s, v_t	£5,000 per annum
α_0	14%

Solutions 2 and 5 apply to the basic model with manpower recruitment wastage and up-grading included, but excluding period 9 profile constraints.

Solutions 3 and 6 apply to the basic model with manpower recruitment, wastage and up-grading included, and with period 9 profile constraints added.

3.7. Discussion of Results

Examination of the solutions shown in table 3 reveals some significant features which are summarised below:

(1) Significant difference exists between equivalent solutions of the two manpower categorisations, that is between solutions: 1 and 4, 2 and 5; 3 and 6. The value of the objective function drops by 26%, 10% and 9% respectively as a result of subdividing the supervisory category into

Project Variables		MANPOWER CATEGORISATION I			MANPOWER CATEGORISATION II		
Project Number (i)	Project Version (j)	Solution 1 (Basic)	Solution 2 (Basic + Manpower)	Solution 3 (Basic + Manpower + Long-Term Constraints)	Solution 4 (Basic)	Solution 5 (Basic + Manpower)	Solution 6 (Basic + Manpower + Long-Term Constraints)
1	1	1.0	0.9	0.8	0.4	1.0	0.7
2	1	1.0	1.0	1.0	1.0	0.8	1.0
3	1	0.4	0.4	0.3	0.5	0.3	0.2
3	2	0.5	0.6	0.7	0.5	0.5	0.5
3	3	0.1	0.0	0.0	0.0	0.2	0.3
4	1	0.0	0.0	0.0	0.0	0.0	0.0
4	2	0.0	0.0	0.2	0.1	0.2	0.3
4	3	0.5	0.3	0.8	0.9	0.2	0.7
5	1	0.7	0.3	0.0	0.4	0.0	0.0
5	2	0.3	0.2	0.0	0.6	0.8	0.4
6	1	1.0	1.0	1.0	0.0	0.2	0.2
6	2	0.0	0.0	0.0	0.7	0.7	0.7
6	3	0.0	0.0	0.0	0.0	0.0	0.0
7	1	0.1	0.2	0.0	0.0	0.0	0.0
7	2	0.9	0.8	1.0	0.7	0.9	0.9
Recruitment variables in numbers of men							
r_1 (scientists, period 1)		0.0	0.0	1.1	0.0	0.6	1.5
r_2 (scientists, period 2)		0.0	0.1	0.2	0.0	0.0	0.0
r_6 (scientists, period 6)		0.0	0.0	1.3	0.0	0.0	1.4
r_8 (scientists, period 8)		0.0	0.0	1.0	0.0	0.0	1.0
Value of objective function		947	902	821	749	823	758

Table 3. Solutions of model of case study. Recruitment variables absent from table do not appear in the basis of any of the solution.

three categories. The magnitude of the difference is reduced when wastage, recruitment and up-grading are included. In terms of the project versions, the preferred version of project 6 changes from version 1 to version 2 when the supervisors are sub-divided. Both these versions consume resources in the first time period, but at differing rates, so that a different "time now" allocation for this project results from adoption of the alternative manpower models.

(2) When recruitment variables are included, recruitment of scientific manpower is indicated in one or more of the periods 1, 2, 6, 8. The amount of recruitment in period 8 is up against its limit, in the cases where the longer term (period 9) laboratory constraints are applied. Note that recruitment of technicians and electricians does not appear in any of the solutions.

(3) In the main, the same project versions appear in all solutions, although the values of the fraction selected change. Project versions $ij = 41$ and 63 are never selected, while project 3 is always fully selected in the sum of its versions.

(4) All of the projects appear in at least one fractional version in all of the solutions. The solutions are indicating different "optimal" schedules for each project. The solutions, with fractions of projects and of men appearing, may not always be capable of interpretation by the decision-taker concerned. For comparison, the model has been solved for manpower categorisation I requiring the project version variables to take values of zero or unity only. These solutions, labelled to 9, are shown in table 4. It may be seen that projects 3 and 4 are missing from solution 7, project 5 is missing from solution 8, and project 1 from solution 9.

(5) In solution 2, little recruitment has been "selected". The value of this solution is lower than that of solution 1 because wastage and up-grading are included.

(6) None of the solutions 1 to 6 are bounded by limitations on the amounts of recruitment set for periods 1–3 and 4–7.

4. Future Opportunities

No allowance has been made for the effects of future project opportunities, not appearing in the present list of projects, but likely to arise during the two year period covered by the model. Some allowance has been made for opportunities expected to arise beyond the two year period by means of the longer term laboratory profile constraints.

A way of allowing for future opportunities which arise during the period covered by a planning model has been suggested by Lockett.[6] This method involves apportioning the overall availabilities of resources in future time periods between those available for opportunities on the present list and those available for future opportunities.

It seems reasonable to hypothesise that, as time goes by, an increasing proportion should be set aside for future opportunities. One simple assumption would be that the additional amount to set aside in period $p + 1$ for future

PROJECT VARIABLES		MANPOWER CATEGORISATION I		
Project Number (i)	Project Version (j)	Solution 7 (Basic)	Solution 8 (Basic + Manpower)	Solution 9 (Basic + Manpower + Long-term Constraints)
1	1	1 (1.0)	1 (0.9)	0 (0.8)
2	1	0 (1.0)	1 (1.0)	1 (1.0)
3	1	1 (0.4)	0 (0.4)	1 (0.3)
3	2	0 (0.5)	1 (0.6)	0 (0.7)
3	3	0 (0.1)	0 (0.0)	0 (0.0)
4	1	0 (0.0)	0 (0.0)	1 (0.0)
4	2	0 (0.0)	0 (0.0)	0 (0.2)
4	3	0 (0.5)	1 (0.3)	0 (0.8)
5	1	1 (0.7)	0 (0.3)	0 (0.0)
5	2	0 (0.3)	0 (0.2)	1 (0.0)
6	1	1 (1.0)	1 (1.0)	1 (1.0)
6	2	0 (0.0)	0 (0.0)	0 (0.0)
6	3	0 (0.0)	0 (0.0)	0 (0.0)
7	1	0 (0.1)	0 (0.2)	0 (0.0)
7	2	1 (0.9)	1 (0.8)	1 (1.0)
Recruitment Variables in Numbers of Men				
r_1		0.0 (0.0)	1.5 (0.0)	0.7 (1.1)
r_2		0.0 (0.0)	0.0 (0.1)	0.0 (0.2)
r_6		0.0 (0.0)	0.0 (0.0)	3.8 (1.3)
r_8		0.0 (0.0)	0.0 (0.0)	0.0 (1.0)
s_4		0.0 (0.0)	0.1 (0.0)	0.0 (0.0)
s_6		0.0 (0.0)	0.0 (0.0)	0.2 (0.0)
t_5		0.0 (0.0)	0.0 (0.0)	0.7 (0.0)
t_6		0.0 (0.0)	0.1 (0.0)	0.0 (0.0)
t_7		0.0 (0.0)	1.4 (0.0)	0.0 (0.0)
Value of Objective function		888 (947)	862 (902)	737 (821)

Table 4. Integer solutions for manpower categorisation I. For comparison, the fractional solutions from table 3 are shown in brackets.

opportunities is proportional to the effective availability for present opportunities in period p. A relationship of this type could be added to the manpower transfer relationships (equation (2)) and built into the linear programming formulation.

The probable effects of increasingly reducing the availabilities of resources for the present list of opportunities with time into the future would be to not only alter the resource allocation part of the solution, but also to increase the amounts of recruitment, especially in later time periods.

Gear, Gillespie, Lockett, Pearson

5. Conclusions

The extension of resource allocation models in R & D to incorporate manpower flows due to processes such as manpower wastage, up-grading, recruitment, and to allow for future opportunities appears to be useful. However, a great number of assumptions have been implicitly and explicitly included in the foregoing model.

It is particularly important to investigate whether a deterministic development, using average flow values, is appropriate. The uncertainties connected with manpower movements in R & D may well be at least as great as those associated with the technical and commercial uncertainties surrounding R & D projects themselves. In this case, stochastic models along the lines of those described by Bartholomew,[2] for example, could prove of value.

As the numbers of men involved in this example are small stochastic aspects are probably important, though it is arguable that for planning purposes only the expectations matter. However, the objective function is likely to be subject to a good deal of fluctuation. In these circumstances it would be interesting to discover a strategy which was relatively immune to chance events with small probabilities, such as the loss of key staff.

A major problem encountered during the case study was to decide how, and in what degree of detail, to model the manpower system. Two aspects of this arise in the categorisation of personnel and in the definition of the important manpower flows. Until a number of case studies have been attempted, answers to these problems are unlikely to be forthcoming. A conceptual problem arose during the study regarding the definition of a benefit horizon for project returns and for employment costs following recruitment. It seemed reasonable to calculate project returns to a common point in the future, but to calculate employment costs over an expected length of stay.

The model seeks to aid decisions relating to recruitment and resource allocation at a fairly detailed level. When it is the overall level of effort which is being decided other methods such as those developed by Jones[4] may sometimes be more appropriate. Such methods seek to arrive at stable investment levels with appropriate balance between areas, but do not assist with detailed manpower considerations within these limits.

References

1. Allen, D.H., & Johnson, T.F.N., "Evaluation of a Project Selection Model". Paper presented at a conference titled 'Practical Aids to Research Management' organised by the R & D Study Group of the Operational Research Society, February, 1970.

2. Bartholomew, D.J. *Stochastic Models for Social Processes*, J. Wiley & Sons, 1967.

3. Beattie, C.J., "Allocating Resources to Research in Practice" in *"Applications of Mathematical Programming Techniques"*, Ed. E.M.L. Beale, English Universities Press, 1970.

4. Jones, P.M.S., and Hunt, H. "An Outline of Evaluation as Practised by the Programmes Analysis Unit". *Programmes Analysis Unit Report M12*, H.M.S.O. London, 1969.

5. Duffett, R.H.E. "A Quantitative Approach to Company Manpower Planning". *Manpower and Applied Psychology*. Vol. 3., p. 11–22, 1969.

6. Lockett, A.G., and Gear, A.E. "Programme Selection in Research and Development". Submitted for publication to the *Journal of Management Science*, Application Series.

7. Maki, D. "A Programming Approach to Manpower Planning". *Industrial and Labour Relations Review*, p. 397–405, April, 1970.

8. Morgan, R.W. "Manpower Planning in the Royal Air Force: an exercise in Linear Programming" in *Models of Manpower Systems*, Englishlish Universities Press, 1971.

9. Nemhauser, G.L., and Nuttle, H.L.W. "A Quantitative Approach to Employment Planning". *Journal of Management Science*, Vol. II. No. 8, (Series 8) p. 155–162, 1965.

10. Patz, A.L. "Linear Programming Applied to Manpower Management". *Industrial Management Review*. Vol. II, No. 2, 1970.

11. Purkiss, C.J., and Richardson, J.Z. "Planning Recruitment and Training in the Steel Industry". *B.I.S.R.A. Operational Research Department* Open Report No. OR/41/68. 1968.

12. Thelwell, R. "An Evaluation of Linear Programming and Multiple Regression for Estimating Manpower Requirements". *Journal of Industrial Engineering*, Vol. XVIII, No. 3. p. 227–236, 1967.

11
A Simulation Model for Manpower Management

C. W. Walmsley

Imperial Chemical Industries Limited

Introduction

There are many decisions affecting the development and deployment of individuals within an organisation, which should be related to the overall corporate objectives. Lack of overall compatibility between the various activities arises because the relationships are very complex and even when people with experience attempt to thrash out strategies, there is room for differences of opinion over what will be the effect of various policies.

This difficulty is particularly evident when organisations are static in the total numbers they employ, but are dynamic in that technological and other changes are continually taking place. As a result, the relevant importance of the various skills and functions are always changing. When the organisation is also concerned to provide acceptable careers and not to engage in "hire and fire" policies, the problems can appear insurmountable.

This paper describes a model which is used as a background against which Managers and Personnel Department can operate knowing that the individual decisions being made are compatible with one another and with long range corporate activities.

Corporate Planning

For this paper, it is assumed that a Corporate Plan exists and can produce a projected task for each part of the organisation which in turn can be broken down into the number of people required identified by major skill groups and by level.

In practice the development of a corporate plan is an iterative process, which requires information on the human factors involved for two main reasons:

(i) The corporate plan should be influenced by the likely strengths and weaknesses of the organisation, including those directly resulting from a study of the people who are and could be employed.

(ii) The corporate plan should take into account the cost implications of proposals, and the cost of employing people can be a very large part of the costs of the organisation.

The Simulation Model

The "stock" of manpower in an organisation at any particular point of time, and the "flows" during various time periods, constitute a system, the study of which can help to resolve some of the problems mentioned above. This is the system which we have modelled.

The model developed is a simulation one. The transaction used is the individual who passes through the processes of Recruitment, Promotion and Leaving.

A simulation model was built because it was felt that to build a sufficiently realistic model, a degree of complexity was required which made an analytical solution unlikely. For alternative approaches see Bartholomew. [1]

The rest of this paper describes the various processes used in the model.

Wastage

In the model, the individual can leave the system in one of three ways:

Voluntary Leaving, Natural Causes and Transfers Out. These are largely self explanatory but have been defined precisely for our analysis.

The most important of these is Voluntary Leaving and a great deal of work has been done by others in analysing this characteristic. The usual conclusion is that for each category of entrant ("cohort"), the completed length of service distribution is log-normal. This we found to be broadly true, but in practice, we decided initially to use a simpler model.

We divided the staff into categories according to grade and department. All female clerk/typists were treated as one category regardless of grade or department. Then the number of categories were reduced by combining grades to form 4 groups of grades, and departments to form 5 groups of departments. Finally, all those in Management grades were treated as one category regardless of department. The final structure used was as shown in Figure 1.

Within each category we analysed the past behaviour of staff in terms of whether they stayed or left during a year according to the number of completed years of service at the beginning of that year. Again to reduce the number of groups being considered, and thus obtain a reasonable number of observations, we aggregated staff with different length of service into one of 6 groups: 0, 1, 2–3, 4–7, 8–15 and 16 years and over. This resulted in us obtaining for each category, and each length of service, a probability of leaving during any year. This has proved to give a very accurate forecast of voluntary leaving.

Individuals also leave the system because of natural causes, the most usual of which is Normal Retirement, but death in service, early retirement, etc are also covered. Incidentally, in our analysis a woman leaving to have a child is classified as voluntary and not a natural cause! Retirement age is obviously a control parameter and so one has to be able to examine the effects of changing it.

As a result of past analysis, leaving due to natural causes is sufficiently infrequent to be ignored as a possibility for those under 50, and for those over 50 is made a function of age only.

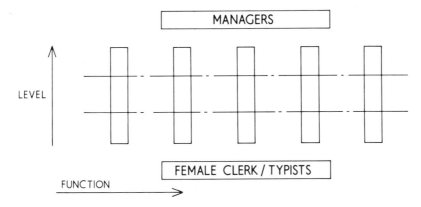

Transfers Out (and Transfers In), are Management control parameters, and link the model of one area with that of another. Eventually, we hope to set up a programming model to optimise these, but currently we supply to the model details of these transfers in terms of number of people, their age range and their apparent potential i.e. of those who are to transfer. After a few runs, these may be changed in the light of the results suggested by the model. It is therefore essential that the model should include within it all areas with frequent transfers.

Promotions

Originally we attempted to model promotion in a way very similar to that for voluntary leaving. This attempt failed because we could not find parameters which enable one to predict promotion. This is not surprising because one would think that the probability of promotion is some sort of function of the number of vacancies in the grade above and of the capabilities of those eligible for promotion.

Price[4] has tackled this problem by using promotion rules which seem reasonable to Management which are based on an "ability factor". We have taken this concept slightly further by basing our rules for deciding who is to be promoted on the apparent potential of each candidate. The concept of the apparent potential arises from the idea of Salary Progression Curves, which are described in the next section.

Salary Progression Curves

The model relies upon the hypothesis that one can find a family of curves relating age to remuneration which are virtually constant over time. This idea arose from the work of Jaques.[2] However, to be able to do this, one has first to postulate a shape. After studying plots of individual salary histories made on Earnings Progression Paper as drawn up by Glacier Institute of Management, we decided to fit a curve of the following form to each individual's history:

$$y_t = a + bx_t + cx_t^2 \qquad (1)$$

where
$$y_t = \mathrm{Log}\,(S_t/I_t) \qquad (2)$$

and S_t = Total Remuneration of the individual in tth year.

I_t = Salary Index applicable to the tth year (see below).

x_t = Age of individual in tth year.

a, b & c are parameters applicable to the individual.

The problem of what is the right Salary Index to use to correct for salary inflation is a difficult one, and I will return to this later. Initially we used the Index which is implied by the Glacier Institute's method of plotting the curves.

Using Multiple Regression, we fitted these curves to the salary history of a randomly selected stratified sample of about 60 individuals who have been with us for more than 10 years. This could have introduced bias because no one who had left was considered, nor was anyone with short length of service. On the other hand, it was felt that curves obtained in this way would be more suitable for use in our model as those who had become dissatisfied with the organisation were excluded and we avoided giving an excessive weight to the early years in a career.

In this way we obtain an a_i b_i and c_i for each individual i. The error can be defined as the difference between the actual remuneration received by the individual in a particular year and the corresponding remuneration calculated from the best fitting curve

$$y_{it} = a_i + b_i x_{it} + c_i x_{it}^2 + e_{it} \tag{3}$$

The method of fitting used assumed that e_{it} are distributed normally with mean error equal to zero, and that there is no correlation between successive errors. These assumptions will be discussed later.

When a cumulative frequency distribution of errors in a particular year for all individuals was drawn, it became apparent that a bias has been introduced by the Index Numbers used to allow for the general levels of earnings. This could be dramatically observed in some years when the vast majority (or even all) the errors had the same sign. A correction procedure had to be devised. The method selected was to adjust the Index for the year where the absolute value of the mean error was greatest. A new set of a_i b_i and c_i were then generated and the procedures as far as this point repeated until the mean errors for each year were all close to zero.

We obtained a relationship between each set of a_i, b_i and c_i by Linear Regression:

$$b_i = m_1 a_i + k_1 \tag{4}$$

$$c_i = m_2 a_i + k_2 \tag{5}$$

Finally, we settled for some combination of two basic log parabola curves:

S to denote a curve $\quad y_{it} - (\eta + \theta x_{it} + \kappa x_{it}^2) = 0 \tag{6}$

and S' to denote a curve $y_{it} - (\alpha + \gamma x_{it} + \epsilon x_{it}^2) = 0 \tag{7}$

combined such that $\quad \lambda_i S + (1 - \lambda_i)S' = 0 \tag{8}$

which expanded is

$$y_{it} = \lambda_i \eta + (1 - \lambda_i)a + [\lambda_i \theta + (1 - \lambda_i)\gamma]x_{it} + [\lambda_i \kappa + (1 - \lambda_i)\epsilon]x_{it}^2 = 0 \quad (9)$$

re-arranging and replacing some variables results in

$$y_{it} = a + \lambda_i \beta + (\gamma + \lambda_i \delta)x_{it} + (\epsilon + \lambda_i \zeta)x_{it}^2 \quad (10)$$

where $\qquad \beta = \eta - a, \quad \delta = \theta - \gamma \quad$ and $\quad \zeta = \kappa - \delta$

an alternative version of (10) is

$$y_{it} = (a + \gamma x_{it} + \epsilon x_{it}^2) + \lambda_i(\beta + \delta x_{it} + \zeta x_{it}^2) \quad (11)$$

After some tedious algebra, which I do not intend to reproduce here, one can specify the sets of values for $a\ \beta\ \gamma\ \delta\ \epsilon$ and ζ which are consistent with m_1, m_2, k_1, k_2.

Of particular interest to us is the locus of the apex of these Log Parabola curves i.e. the particular age/salary combination at which the individuals reach their peak earnings (in comparison with the Index representing the general levels of earnings). This provides us with a measure of the potential of an individual and this potential is represented by the parameter λ_i. Inspection of equation (10) shows that the range of λ_1 can be adjusted by altering the relative values of $a\ \beta\ \gamma\ \delta\ \epsilon$ and ζ. (This is equivalent to replacing 1 in (8) by a constant).

A program in conversational mode has been written to enable us to adjust these parameters to obtain a λ_i in any given range; the "bench marks" were chosen such that 0 indicates a person who has reached a certain low potential at an early age and 100 indicates a person who reaches a potential of a managerial position towards the end of his working life.

In the final stage of the calculation of a suitable set of parameters, an iterative procedure was used:

Step 1 Using current values of the parameters, calculate for each individual using a Linear Regression. See (11).

Step 2 Using these values of λ_i obtain another estimate of the parameters using a Multiple Regression. See (10).

Step 3 Adjust these parameters by means of the conversational mode program to give λ_i in the designed range. Then repeat Step 1.

This random search is obviously inefficient and could give rise to oscillations. This did at first occur but was very much reduced by inserting a term in $\lambda_i y_{it}$ in (10). The coefficient of this was always very small but it did help stabilise the iterative procedure.

When we reached a point where we ceased to obtain any improvement in the fit measured by the variance of the difference between calculated and observed points, we stopped.

To test these curves as predictors, a further sample of individuals was selected and their salary history in 1956–8 used to obtain 3 estimates of λ_i for each person. These were averaged and the result used to calculate the expected salary for 1967. Those compared so well with the actual values, for those over 30 in 1957, that we felt that the curves could safely be used to predict salaries in the future. Up-dating the curves by the same method 3-years later has confirmed that they are only slowly changing their shape.

Two theoretical problems remained. The first is that the curves are symmetrical about the apex and hence predict that a person's remuneration (corrected for salary inflation) t years after he has reached his peak will be falling at the same rate as it was climbing t years before the apex. This problem is however more theoretical than practical. In practice, it is sufficiently realistic to say that once a person has reached his peak he stays in the same grade. This can be adopted in the simulation.

The second theoretical problem concerns the fact that the errors are not distributed normally and that the errors in successive years are correlated. The correlation coefficient was calculated and the technique used by Naylor [3] used to simulate it. The distribution of error used in the simulation was a Log Normal one, and the variance of this was obtained from a subsidiary simulation in which we tried various values until we observed the same pattern of distribution and correlation of errors as had been observed in the sample.

Promotion for those Under Thirty

As mentioned above, Salary Progression Curves are not such good predictors of progression for those under 30. There is not of course anything magic about that age. The inaccuracy diminishes with age from about 25 onwards. However, further investigation was felt to be necessary. The method used was to allocate to each individual over 30, an apparent potential based on the person's current age and salary. This could then be used as the dependent variable in correlations with various features of his position several years earlier as the independent variables.

It became apparent that in this age range, the company grade structure and the associated payments policy were influencing the pattern of salary progression and masking the effect of 'potential'. The population of persons under 30 in a particular grade at a particular age and at a particular time were studied knowing the mean and variance of their eventual apparent potential. Following discussions about the correlations and trends using random numbers, we observed the model was programmed to allocate an apparent potential to each person under 30 in the Organisation. Also from discussions, we obtained some suitable promotion rules whereby these people were to reach the salary progression curve implied by this apparent potential.

Recruitment

In building a model for Manpower Management, it must be remembered that Recruitment cannot be obtained by straight extrapolation of the past history. For one thing, it is the most important single variable which can be controlled by Management to obtain the required mix of people in the organisation. Secondly, it is affected by changes in the external environment, and such changes are at present very radical. One example is the proposed raising of the school leaving age and another is the recent explosion in the number of school leavers.

As a guide to what has happened in the past, we obtained the probability distribution of the apparent potential of those over 30 grouped by characteristics which we knew about at the time of engagement. The most important of these is the correlation between Apparent Potential and Educational Achievement. We found that the higher the educational achievement prior to joining, the higher is the Apparent Potential. There may even be mechanisms at work to assure this is the case. However, much more interesting was the shape of the distributions and their range. This indicated that there was considerable overlap and that even the lowest band of educational achievements was giving us a proportion of people with high apparent potential.

It is easy to say that conditions nowadays are different, but this analysis enables us to make subjective assessments of the value in terms of potential of various recruitment sources, and later on, check back on it. The fact that there is such a long time delay may not be critical unless the environment changes a lot faster than we believe it is doing.

Currently the model after completing the simulation of a particular year, selects from the available sources that recruitment which will bring the number employed up to the establishment given.

The Overall Model

The foregoing sections have described how Wastage, Promotion and Recruitment are modelled. These various processes are brought together in a simulation of the system where the basic transaction is movement of the individual and the basic time period is one year.

The first process through which the transaction passes is that of Wastage, and, by using the probabilities obtained by the method described above, the individual either leaves the system for one of the three categories of reason, or stays within it.

Given that the individual stays within the system, the next process considered is that of Promotion. According to what vacancies there are, and what are the apparent potentials of the individuals competing for these vacancies, the promotion is given to particular individuals. Following this, a new salary is associated with each individual transaction, and the apparent potential is updated.

When the progress of all the individuals already within the system has been simulated for one year, the Recruitment is simulated. According to the number of vacancies and the possible sources available, new individuals are created. This involves allocating an age and apparent potential to each one according to specified frequency distributions.

Use of Model

I believe that from the brief description which I have given, it is apparent that this model is very rich in that it is capable of considerable development to meet different demands and also that it fits very well into the sort of planning activity which goes on in a Personnel Department.

A Simulation Model for Manpower Planning

The major use of the model is that it ensures that the current strategy and tactics for recruitment and Career Development (and, by implication, some Training) are compatible with the longer term objectives or the organisation. It shows up areas where we are likely to be weak, and also areas where we are likely to be embarrassed by having more people than there are jobs.

Future Work

From a Management Scientist's point of view there are two areas which have not yet been tackled, but which ought to be considered.

First, we do not yet know enough about the dynamic characteristics of the total system if this model was used in the decision making process.

Secondly, the model is very clumsy to use when there are Transfers or alternative possibilities of Recruitment to consider. There appears to be a good case for developing a programming model using expected values for use alongside this Simulation Model.

Acknowledgements

I would like to express my appreciation for the advice which I received from the Institute of Operational Research during the development of this work. In particular for introducing me to Salary Progression Curves.

This work would not have been possible without support from the Management and Personnel Department of Imperial Chemical Industries Limited (Paints Division) for which I am very grateful.

References

1. Bartholomew, D.J., *Stochastic Models for Social Processes*, Wiley, 1967.

2. Jaques, E., *Equitable Payment*, Pelican, 1967.

3. Naylor, T.H., et alia, *Computer Simulation Techniques*.

4. Price, P.C., "Mathematical Models of Staff Structure Evolution" in:— *Aspects of Manpower Planning* Edited by D.J. Bartholomew and B.R. Morris, English Universities Press. 1971.

PART III

12

A Theory of Macroscopic Labour Absorbing and Labour Releasing Innovation Effects

F. E. Burke, Donald J. Clough

**University of Waterloo,
Ontario**

Summary

This paper outlines a tentative theory to describe some important labour
absorbing and labour releasing phenomena associated with employment
implications of certain kinds of innovation effects in industrial countries.
The theory is based on the following main premises: (1) equilibrium conditions
of supply and demand do not exist, (2) demands cannot be estimated independently
of supplies, (3) there exist sets of short-run "capacity" constraints on industry
outputs, (4) there exist sets of "demographic" constraints on labour inputs,
(5) there exist sets of government "policy" constraints on some industry inputs
and outputs.

Effects of technological innovations are defined as either changes in production
functions* or changes in technological constraints, or both. Effects of social-
political innovations are defined as shifts in either demographic constraints
or government policy constraints, or both. A proper set of fixed industry
production functions* and other constraints then specifies a "short-run feasible
production region". A sequence of discrete-time innovation effects similarly
specifies a "long-run feasible production region". Because of inter-industry
dependencies (e.g., as displayed in Leontieff input-output models), an innovation
effect in one industry may have effects on outputs, or technological coefficients,
and hence on labour inputs, in one or more industries. These are here called
the labour-releasing and labour-absorbing effects of innovations.

One important feature of the theory is that it describes only feasible production
regions (production possibilities) and does not explain how an economy generates
a unique production solution within the feasible region. Another feature is that
final demands are not defined at all. Instead, feasible consumptions (domestic
consumption plus investment plus net exports) are displayed as feasible values
of slack variables that depend on the feasible industry outputs and inter-industry
input-output relations.

It is noted that in some cases the sets of constraints define a relatively

---

* "production function" is used in the broad sense of empirically found aggregate
relations between factors and products, instead of the more narrow notion of the
optimal output related to input factors in a given state of technology.

small feasible production region, and also a relatively small feasible consumption region. In such cases the theory may account for the appearances of linearities in production functions between narrow limits defined by the constraints. The theory may also account for the appearance of stability of outputs and consumptions over time, since they may be severely constrained within narrow limits. The theory may also help to account for the rather long time delays observed between an innovation and its chain of effects.

Introduction

This paper proposes a tentative theory to deal with some employment effects of a variety of technical changes. We start from the observation that constraints imposed on economies by government policies and regulations, and by the decisions of major corporations, play an increasing role compared with the free interplay of economic forces tending to equilibrium. We then note that recent macro-economic work of empirical character (e.g. Solow [1] and his numerous intellectual progeny) assigns to technical changes a place second in importance as a factor only to labour, while capital seems, in this view, to take a poor third place in developed economies. Last, we are not happy with explicit or implied notions of equilibrium (and the attendant apparatus of separate demand and supply sides) as part of empirical work. This is partly due to the impossibility of observing when or if equilibrium occurs, and partly due to observations (e.g. Salter's [1]) that over 20 years may elapse between best practice and average practice attainments of productivity of well defined outputs (e.g. pig iron). We feel, in consequence, that the attainment of equilibrium is apt to be out-paced by technological possibilities — which create new, unattained "equilibria". We also feel that this feature renders the notion of a production function (stating the maximum output related to input factors for a given state of technology) suspect as a tool of empirical investigation.

It is well known that technological change, employment and their relations to macro-economic questions have a long and complex history. To oversimplify, up to the 1920's discussion attempted to elucidate the role of capital, the 1930's the pressing questions of cyclical relations between employment, investment and demand, and the early post-war years the questions of structural employment effects. More recently, relations of growthmanship and science policy have been emphasized. In all of these contributions, assumptions of continuity, optimality, or equilibrium have been central, and often employment effects of technical changes have been assumed away on grounds of exogeny or dogma. This has been done in spite of the fruitful view (from any empirical perspective) of Simon [1] that decision makers "satisfice" rather than optimize, and in the face of conspicuous failures of planned economic policies for growth based on such powerful assumptions. As a single constraint may render an optimal consideration invalid, we are motivated to attempt a model based on a substantially revised set of assumptions.

This paper defines "technological innovation" in terms of changes in the parameters of a dynamic Leontieff input-output model with fully specified constraints. Models of the Leontieff type describe economic systems in which the outputs of industries are themselves used as inputs to other industries. A variety of static and dynamic models of the Leontieff type have been dealt with in the literature, from both theoretical and empirical points of view. The reader is referred especially to works of W.W. Leontieff [1], [2], [3], and also to the extensive theoretical analysis of selected references given by Michio Morishima [1].

An early discussion with a similar aim was Herbert A. Simon's [2] "effects of technological change in a linear model" in 1951. Professor Simon noted that in economic history the term "technological change" had generally been applied to any change in the methods of production used in an economy, and that the concept of technological change had been somewhat narrowly represented as a shift in a production function. In his definition, Simon suggested that a technological change may result from (i) an improvement in an existing process for making a commodity, (ii) the partial or total replacement of an old input resource by a new one, or (iii) the production of a new consumers' good not previously in existence. Simon's model (ibid.), while formally containing constraints, largely assumes their importance away, and the objective function implied in his formulation retains the aim for optimality that we find empirically questionable. Our aim, then, is to build on these past contributions with an emphasis on constraints and their shifts due to technological innovations.

An Input-Output Model

Definition of Parameters

$k_{ij}(t) \geqslant 0$,   stock of capital good i held by industry j at time t, (units), Note $i, j = 1, 2, \ldots, n$.

$y_{ij}(t) \geqslant 0$,   amount of capital good i absorbed by industry j to service current production in period starting at time t, out of stock available at time t, (units).

$x_{ij}(t) \geqslant 0$,   amount of output of industry i absorbed by industry j in current production in period starting at time t, (units).

$x_{j}(t) \geqslant 0$,   total output of commodity j in period starting at time t, (units).

$a_{ij} \geqslant 0$,   input-output coefficient, the amount of output of industry i absorbed by industry j in current production of one unit of output j, (units/unit).

$b_{ij} \geqslant 0$,   capital-input coefficient, the amount of capital good i absorbed by industry j to produce one unit of output j, (units/unit).

$\tau_{ij} \geqslant 1$,   time constant, the average length of life of capital good i held by industry j, (expressed in time periods). The reciprocal $1/\tau_{ij}$ is taken as the depreciation rate of capital goods, where $0 < 1/\tau_{ij} \leqslant 1$.

$d_{ij}(t) = k_{ij}(t)/\tau_{ij}$,   depreciation of capital good, the maximum amount of capital good i held by industry j at time t that can be absorbed in production, (units). Note $\tau_{ij} \geqslant 1$.

$z_j(t) > 0$,   amount of manpower (labour) employed by industry j in current production in period starting at time t, (man-hours).

$m_j > 0$,   manpower input coefficient, the amount of manpower employed by industry j in current production of one unit of output j, (man-hours/unit).

$L(t) > 0$,   total amount of manpower available for the period starting at time t, (man-hours).

$c_j(t) \geqslant 0$,   consumption of good j in period starting at time t, (units).

Corresponding to the above elements we write matrices $\mathbf{k}(t)$, $\mathbf{y}(t)$, $\mathbf{x}(t)$, $\mathbf{a}$, $\mathbf{b}$, τ, $\mathbf{d}(t)$, and column vectors $\mathbf{x}(t)$, $\mathbf{z}(t)$, $\mathbf{m}, \mathbf{c}(t)$. We denote a transposed matrix with a prime (e.g., $\mathbf{a}'$, $\mathbf{z}'(t)$, $\mathbf{m}'$).

Input-Output Accounting Relations

The technological coefficients are related to inputs and outputs as follows:

$$a_{ij} = x_{ij}(t)/x_j(t), \quad \text{for } i, j = 1, 2, \dots, n. \tag{1}$$

$$b_{ij} = y_{ij}(t)/x_j(t), \quad \text{for } i, j = 1, 2, \dots, n. \tag{2}$$

$$m_j = z_j(t)/x_j(t), \quad \text{for } j = 1, 2, \dots, n. \tag{3}$$

Suppose outputs are restricted by the availability of stocks of capital goods (e.g., plant capacities). These constraints may be shown in terms of upper limits on capital good depreciation, as follows:

$$b_{ij} x_j(t) = y_{ij}(t) \leqslant d_{ij}(t) = k_{ij}(t)/\tau_{ij} \leqslant k_{ij}(t)/\tau_{ijP'} \tag{4}$$

for $i, j = 1, 2, \dots, n$. Here a parameter $(1/\tau_{ijP})$ is an upper limit on the rate at which a capital good may be used up. Two cases arise: (1) A capital good may be depleted naturally, whether or not is is used as an input to production, in which case $\tau_{ij} = \tau_{ijP}$ is a specified physical time constant and the constraint is expressed as an inequality,

$$x_j(t) \leqslant k_{ij}(t)/b_{ij}\tau_{ij}, \quad \tau_{ij} = \tau_{ijP}. \tag{5}$$

(2) A capital good may be depleted only if it is used as an input to production, in which case we write the equality

$$x_j(t) = k_{ij}(t)/b_{ij}\tau_{ij}, \quad \tau_{ij} \geqslant \tau_{ijP}. \tag{6}$$

In this latter case we can treat τ_{ij} as a function of $x_j(t)$ in the following expressions. Since $n - 1$ of the constraints indexed by $i = 1, 2, \dots, n$ are redundant, one of them may be considered as critical and we can write (4) as follows:

$$x_j(t) \leqslant \underset{i = 1, 2, \dots, n}{\text{minimum}} \{ k_{ij}(t)/b_{ij}\tau_{ij} \} = x_{jK}(t), \tag{7}$$

for $j = 1, 2, \dots, n$. Here x_{jK} denotes the upper limit on output imposed by the capital goods constraints.

The outputs are also restricted by the availability of manpower, as follows:

$$\sum_{j=1}^{n} m_j x_j(t) = \sum_{j=1}^{n} z_j(t) \leqslant L(t). \tag{8}$$

If we assume some immobilities of manpower in the short run (one time period, fixed constraints) there may be an effective ceiling on manpower available to each industry. Thus we write as follows:

$$x_j(t) = z_j(t)/m_j \leqslant z_{jL}(t)/m_j = x_{jL}(t), \tag{9}$$

for $j = 1, 2, \ldots, n$. Here $z_{jL}(t)$ denotes the upper limit on manpower available as input to industry j, and $x_{jL}(t)$ denotes the corresponding upper limit on output j imposed by the manpower constraint (the subscript L denoting labour).

Either the capital or labour constraint is redundant and one of them is critical, so that we reduce them as follows:

$$x_j(t) \leqslant \min\{x_{jK}(t), x_{jL}(t)\} = x_{jKL}(t), \tag{10}$$

for $j = 1, 2, \ldots, n$. Here $x_{jKL}(t)$ denotes the upper limit on output j imposed by the critical capital or labour constraint.

The equation of balance says that the total stock of capital good i at time t, *minus* the depreciation of that capital good, *plus* the total output, *minus* the amount of output required by other industries, *minus* the amount of output required for consumption, equals the total stock of capital good i at time $t + 1$. Thus we write

$$\sum_{j=1}^{n} k_{ij}(t) - \sum_{j=1}^{n} d_{ij}(t) + x_i(t) - \sum_{j=1}^{n} a_{ij} x_j(t) - c_i(t) = \sum_{j=1}^{n} k_{ij}(t+1) \tag{11}$$

for $i = 1, 2, \ldots, n$, This can be rewritten as follows:

$$x_i(t) - \sum_{j=1}^{n} a_{ij} x_j(t) - c_i(t) - \sum_{j=1}^{n} [k_{ij}(t+1) - k_{ij}(t)] = \sum_{j=1}^{n} d_{ij}(t), \tag{12}$$

for $i = 1, 2, \ldots, n$. This is called *the basic accounting equation*.

Additional Policy Constraints

The input-output accounting relations shown above describe the technology of production, but do not include relations to describe (1) constraints on final consumptions, capital accumulations and total outputs imposed as a result of government policies, and (2) constraints linking capital accumulation with outputs, imposed as a result of management decisions in the industries concerned.

Suppose that total outputs are exogenous parameters which cannot be set at levels greater than the constraints imposed by manpower availability and capital capacities (available stocks of capital goods). In this case the sum of final consumption and change in stocks of capital goods (investment) is the residual left over after satisfying inter-industry production requirements. If outputs are set as high as possible, the residual will be as large as possible. But there still remains the problem of dividing the residual between consumption and investment.

Suppose that total outputs are fixed, say at the upper limits imposed by manpower and capital capacity constraints. Suppose also that final consumptions of goods are exogenous parameters. If these are set too high, they may violate the accounting relations and therefore may not be feasible. If they are set at some high levels, all the industries could produce at full capacity and still not have enough left over to increase stocks of some capital goods (after satisfying final consumption and inter-industry requirements for current goods). In this case there would be a negative accumulation of stocks of some capital goods, which would cause a tightening of constraints on production in the following period.[*]

Suppose that total outputs are fixed, say at capacity limits, but this time the changes in capital stocks are exogenous parameters. If changes in capital stock are large (positive), all the industries could produce at full capacity and still not have enough left over to satisfy "normal" final consumptions. In this case there would be a short-run sacrifice of consumption in favour of a positive accumulation of stocks of capital goods. These positive increments amount to a relaxation of the capital constraints on production in the following period, so that outputs may be increased in the future (provided that the manpower constraints are not binding).

If the manpower constraints are binding some outputs, excess capital accumulation is wasteful because depreciation will continue whether or not the capital goods are utilized to capacity. On the other hand, if capital constraints are binding some outputs, manpower may not be utilized to capacity and unemployment may result.

The problem is to identify that set of additional constraints, resulting from government policies and industrial management policies, which will allow feasible short-run solutions of the input-output accounting relations and will simultaneously satisfy specified social and economic criteria (e.g., full employment, stable growth of outputs).

Let us assume that there exist some identified rigidities (in many cases irreversibilities) of government policies that are manifested as effective floor levels or ceilings on the final consumptions, capital accumulations and total outputs of some commodities (or services). For example, by its taxation policies the government may affect capital accumulation. By its monetary policies (e.g., credit restriction policies) it may affect final consumption. The government is both a final consumer of some goods and an industry that uses up inputs of some goods in the production of other goods (or services). For example, by its foreign aid policies the government may effectively place lower limits on the consumption (export) of some commodities (e.g., engineering of dams in Asia). By its provision of certain welfare, defence, postal, forestry and other services it may effectively operate as an industry, and as a matter of policy (or legislative constraint) may set a lower limit on the total outputs of some of its services. As an industry, the government may also accumulate

---

[*] In control theory terms, this is a positive feedback effect which would drive stocks of some capital goods toward low levels at which some exogenous consumptions become infeasible.

capital goods (e.g., park facilities, transport aircraft) and stockpiles of goods for long-run storage that may be considered as capital goods required to produce the same kind of output goods in later periods, (e.g., strategic metals and some agricultural commodities). By its agricultural subsidy policies, for example, the government may effectively place some limits on the outputs of some agricultural commodities.

Taking all of such government policies and operations into consideration, along with certain known "subsistence level" consumptions of some goods, and employment goals, we write the following constraints:

$$x_{jP} \leqslant x_j(t) \leqslant x_{j\bar{P}}, \qquad j = 1, 2, \ldots, n. \tag{13}$$

$$c_{jP} \leqslant c_j(t) \leqslant c_{j\bar{P}}, \qquad j = 1, 2, \ldots, n. \tag{14}$$

$$e\, L(t) \leqslant \sum_{j=1}^{n} m_j x_j(t), \qquad 0 < e < 1. \tag{15}$$

Here e is the minimum fraction of manpower force to be employed. The subscript P denotes lower Policy limit and the subscript $\bar{P}$ denotes upper Policy limit. For some goods $x_{jP} = 0$, and $x_{j\bar{P}}$ is unlimited (∞). It should be noted that some of these constraints may be redundant or may render some of the earlier ones redundant. (It should also be noted that some government policies concerning stockpiling are effected through a selection of the b_{ij} and τ_{ij} values under its control.)

Either the capital-manpower constraint (10) or the upper policy constraint on output (13) is redundant, and one of them is critical, so that we can reduce them as follows:

$$x_j(t) \leqslant \min\{x_{jKL}, x_{j\bar{P}}\} = x_{jKL\bar{P}}, \tag{16}$$

for $j = 1, 2, \ldots, n$.

Now let us consider management decision rules, which may be motivated partly by market conditions (short-run or long-run profit expectations) and partly by government policies (e.g., affecting employment, taxes, subsidies, wages, prices, tariff protection, contracts for goods). Suppose that rules exist that provide a definite link between investment in capital goods and total outputs. For purposes of illustration, consider the following relationship for example:

$$k_{ij}(t+1) - k_{ij}(t) = \tau_{ij} b_{ij} [x_j(t) - x_j(t-1)], \tag{17}$$

for $i, j = 1, 2, \ldots, n$. This rule says that the specified change in capital good i held by industry j is proportional to the most recent change in output of industry j. The constant of proportionality is the coefficient τ_{ij} times the capital-input coefficient b_{ij}.

Recapitulation of Input-Output Relations

Combining the input-output accounting relations and the additional constraints, we obtain the following set of relations to be satisfied (where τ_{ij} is given by either (5) or (6)):

$$x_i(t) - \sum_{j=1}^{n} [a_{ij} + \tau_{ij} b_{ij}] x_j(t) - c_i(t) =$$

$$= \sum_{j=1}^{n} k_{ij}(t)/\tau_{ij} - \sum_{j=1}^{n} \tau_{ij} b_{ij} x_j(t-1), \quad i = 1,2,\ldots,n. \tag{18}$$

$$x_j(t) \leqslant x_{jKL\overline{P}}, \qquad\qquad j = 1,2,\ldots,n. \tag{19}$$

$$c_j(t) \leqslant c_{j\overline{P}}, \qquad\qquad j = 1,2,\ldots,n. \tag{20}$$

$$x_j(t) \geqslant x_{jP}, \qquad\qquad j = 1,2,\ldots,n. \tag{21}$$

$$c_j(t) \geqslant c_{jP}, \qquad\qquad j = 1,2,\ldots,n. \tag{22}$$

$$\sum_{j=1}^{n} m_j x_j(t) \leqslant L(t). \tag{23}$$

$$\sum_{j=1}^{n} m_j x_j(t) \geqslant e L(t), \qquad 0 < e < 1. \tag{24}$$

In the above relations let us assume that $x_j(t)$ and $c_j(t)$ are *variable* parameters and that all other symbols denote *constant* parameters whose values are fixed and known for time t, all non-negative.

Once the constant parameters are specified, three cases arise: (1) There is no feasible solution for the $x_j(t)$ and $c_j(t)$ because some constraints are contradictory (i.e., the constraints define disjoint sets rather than a linear convex set). In this case one or more of the policy constraints may have to be relaxed, since the accounting relations that describe production technology must be satisfied.* (2) There is a unique solution. This seems to be a trivial case because it is implausible that a fortuitous selection of the constant parameters would yield a unique solution. (3) There is an infinite set of feasible solutions because the constraints define a linear convex set of points. In this case the question arises "which of the infinity of solutions *occurs* or *should occur*?"

Suppose that the constraints do define a convex polyhedron, such that an infinity of solutions exist. The polyhedron may be quite "narrow" in each dimension, so that all possible solutions are "almost the same". In this case the economy is *so tightly constrained* that only small variations in the $c_j(t)$ and $x_j(t)$ are feasible. If the final consumptions are very tightly constrained, the outputs will adjust to satisfy the input-output accounting relations. On the other hand, if outputs are tightly constrained, the final consumptions will adjust to satisfy the input-output relations. It seems plausible that for some goods the outputs are tightly constrained, while for others the final consumptions are tightly constrained.

Now suppose the government has a policy of maintaining high employment, and will take actions necessary to achieve the goal. The parameter e represents

---

* This is a feature of the model that relates to feasibility and infeasibility in *planning*. Infeasible plans are changed to feasible ones because real economic activities do go on.

a lower limit on employment. For example, $e = 0.95$ indicates a government goal to maintain at least 95 percent employment. Note that the employment constraint delineates a "narrow" region and may severely constrain outputs and consumptions.

Price Relations

Let us assume that the production period for each output is one period, and let us define the following additional parameters:

$p_i(t) \geq 0$, price of current good i, in terms of labour; current wages $= 1$, (man-hours).

$q_i(t) \geq 0$, price of capital good i, in terms of labour (current wages $= 1$). Note that this is the current replacement price, (man-hours).

$0 < r < 1$, interest rate on both fixed capital stocks and working capital tied up one period in current production, (decimal fraction).

The unit cost of good j produced by industry j, in terms of labour (current wages $= 1$), is then given as follows:

$$p_j^*(t + 1) = \sum_{i=1}^{n} a_{ij} p_i(t) + \sum_{i=1}^{n} [d_{ij}(t)/x_j(t)] q_i(t) + m_j \tag{25}$$

$$+ r \left\{ \sum_{i=1}^{n} a_{ij} p_i(t) + \sum_{i=1}^{n} [k_{ij}(t)/x_j(t)] q_i(t) + m_j \right\}$$

for $j = 1, 2, \ldots, n$. Note that the cost at time $(t + 1)$ depends on the value of inputs of goods at time t, the value of depreciation of capital at time t, the value of labour inputs at time t, and the interest (on investment) values of inputs of goods, capital stocks and manpower. Given the values $p_j^*(t + 1)$, the prices for time $(t + 1)$ may be specified as follows:

$$p_j(t + 1) = f_j p_j^*(t + 1), \quad \text{for } j = 1, 2, \ldots, n. \tag{26}$$

$$g_j(t + 1) = g_j p_j^*(t + 1), \quad \text{for } j = 1, 2, \ldots, n. \tag{27}$$

where $f_j > 0$, $g_j > 0$ are parameters to be decided by managers. In the simplest case $f_j = 1$ and $g_j = 1$, indicating no profit-taking.

Catalogue of Alternative Production Processes

Suppose a particular production process for good j (industry j) is completely described by a set of vectors $\boldsymbol{\tau}_j^a$, $\mathbf{b}_j^a$, $\mathbf{a}_j^a$ and a scalar m_j^a, where

$$\boldsymbol{\tau}_j^a = \begin{pmatrix} \tau_{1j}^a \\ \tau_{2j}^a \\ \cdots \\ \tau_{nj}^a \end{pmatrix} \qquad \mathbf{b}_j^a = \begin{pmatrix} b_{1j}^a \\ b_{2j}^a \\ \cdots \\ b_{nj}^a \end{pmatrix} \qquad \mathbf{a}_j^a = \begin{pmatrix} a_{1j}^a \\ a_{2j}^a \\ \cdots \\ a_{nj}^a \end{pmatrix} \tag{28}$$

(Bold-face type denotes a vector or matrix). Suppose that there exist α_j distinctly different production processes that are technologically feasible, indexed by $\alpha = 1, 2, \ldots, \alpha_j$. Then we can write the following matrices $(j = 1, 2, \ldots, n)$:

$$\boldsymbol{\tau}_j' = (\boldsymbol{\tau}_j^1, \boldsymbol{\tau}_j^2, \ldots, \boldsymbol{\tau}_j^{\alpha_j}) \quad \text{and} \quad \boldsymbol{\tau} = (\boldsymbol{\tau}_1', \boldsymbol{\tau}_2', \ldots, \boldsymbol{\tau}_n') \tag{29}$$

$$\mathbf{b}_j' = (\mathbf{b}_j^1, \mathbf{b}_j^2, \ldots, \mathbf{b}_j^{\alpha_j}) \quad \text{and} \quad \mathbf{B} = (\mathbf{b}_1', \mathbf{b}_2', \ldots, \mathbf{b}_n') \tag{30}$$

$$\mathbf{a}_j' = (\mathbf{a}_j^1, \mathbf{a}_j^2, \ldots, \mathbf{a}_j^{\alpha_j}) \quad \text{and} \quad \mathbf{A} = (\mathbf{a}_1', \mathbf{a}_2', \ldots, \mathbf{a}_n') \tag{31}$$

$$\mathbf{m}_j' = (\mathbf{m}_j^1, \mathbf{m}_j^2, \ldots, \mathbf{m}_j^{\alpha_j}) \quad \text{and} \quad \mathbf{M} = (\mathbf{m}_1', \mathbf{m}_2', \ldots, \mathbf{m}_n') \tag{32}$$

We shall call the set of four matrices $\mathbf{X}_j = (\boldsymbol{\tau}_j, \mathbf{b}_j, \mathbf{a}_j, \mathbf{m}_j)$ the *catalogue of feasible alternative production processes* for good j, and the set $\mathbf{X} = (\boldsymbol{\tau}, \mathbf{B}, \mathbf{A}, \mathbf{M})$, the catalogue of feasible alternative production processes for all goods.[*]

A particular production process β may be selected from the catalogue for good j by the operator $\boldsymbol{\delta}_j^\beta$, where

$$\boldsymbol{\delta}_j^\beta = \begin{pmatrix} \delta_{1\beta} \\ \delta_{2\beta} \\ \ldots \\ \delta_{\alpha_j \beta} \end{pmatrix} \quad \text{and} \quad \boldsymbol{\Delta} = \begin{pmatrix} \delta_1^\alpha & 0 & \ldots & 0 \\ 0 & \delta_2^\beta & \ldots & 0 \\ \ldots & \ldots & \ldots & \ldots \\ 0 & 0 & \ldots & \delta_n^\eta \end{pmatrix}. \tag{33}$$

Here $\delta_{\alpha\beta} = 0$ if $\alpha \neq \beta$, and $\delta_{\beta\beta} = 1$, is the Kronecker delta function. For example, the operator applies as follows to the catalogue of current input-output vectors for good j:

$$\mathbf{a}_j^\alpha = \mathbf{a}_j' \, \delta_j^\alpha. \tag{34}$$

The operator also applies as follows to the catalogue of current input-output vectors for all goods $(j = 1, 2, \ldots, n)$:

$$\begin{aligned} \mathbf{A}\boldsymbol{\Delta} &= (\mathbf{a}_1' \delta_1^\alpha, \mathbf{a}_2' \delta_2^\beta, \ldots, \mathbf{a}_n' \delta_n^\eta) \\ &= (\mathbf{a}_1^\alpha, \mathbf{a}_2^\beta, \ldots, \mathbf{a}_n^\eta) \\ &= \mathbf{a}_\Delta \end{aligned} \tag{35}$$

Thus $\mathbf{A}\boldsymbol{\Delta} = \mathbf{a}_\Delta$ is a particular $n \times n$ matrix of current input-output coefficients selected from the catalogue of input-output coefficients for all goods. Similarly, we write a capital-input matrix $(n \times n)$,

$$\begin{aligned} \mathbf{B}\boldsymbol{\Delta} &= (\mathbf{b}_1' \delta_1^\alpha, \mathbf{b}_2' \delta_2^\beta, \ldots, \mathbf{b}_n' \delta_n^\eta) \\ &= (\mathbf{b}_1^\alpha, \mathbf{b}_2^\beta, \ldots, \mathbf{b}_n^\eta) = \mathbf{b}_\Delta, \end{aligned} \tag{36}$$

and a matrix of capital depreciation time constants $(n \times n)$,

---

[*] This notion of a catalogue of processes is adopted from Morishima (1964).

$$\mathbf{T\Delta} = (\tau_1' \, \delta_1^\alpha, \, \tau_2' \, \delta_2^\beta, \dots, \tau_n' \, \delta_n^\eta)$$

$$= (\tau_1^\alpha, \, \tau_2^\beta, \dots, \tau_n^\eta) = \mathbf{\tau_\Delta}, \qquad (37)$$

and a vector of manpower inputs

$$\mathbf{M\Delta} = (\mathbf{m}_1' \, \delta_1^\alpha, \, \mathbf{m}_2' \, \delta_2^\beta, \dots, \mathbf{m}_n' \, \delta_n^\eta)$$

$$= (m_1^\alpha, \, m_2^\beta, \dots, m_n^\eta) = \mathbf{m_\Delta}. \qquad (38)$$

Matrix Formulation with Alternative Production Processes

For convenience let us define the elements $v_{ij}^\alpha = b_{ij}^\alpha \, \tau_{ij}^\alpha$, and the corresponding matrices.

$$\mathbf{v}_j^\alpha = \begin{pmatrix} v_{1j}^\alpha \\ v_{2j}^\alpha \\ \dots \\ v_{nj}^\alpha \end{pmatrix} = \begin{pmatrix} b_{1j}^\alpha \, \tau_{1j}^\alpha \\ b_{2j}^\alpha \, \tau_{2j}^\alpha \\ \dots\dots \\ b_{nj}^\alpha \, \tau_{nj}^\alpha \end{pmatrix} \qquad (39)$$

$$\mathbf{v}_j' = (\mathbf{v}_j^1, \mathbf{v}_j^2, \dots, \mathbf{v}_j^{\alpha_j}) \qquad (40)$$

$$\mathbf{V} = (\mathbf{v}_1', \mathbf{v}_2', \dots, \mathbf{v}_n') \qquad (41)$$

$$\mathbf{V\Delta} = (\mathbf{v}_1' \, \delta_1^\alpha, \mathbf{v}_2' \, \delta_2^\beta, \dots, \mathbf{v}_n' \, \delta_n^\eta)$$

$$= (v_1^\alpha, v_2^\beta, \dots, v_n^\eta) = \mathbf{v_\Delta}. \qquad (42)$$

Similarly let us define the elements $d_{ij}^\alpha(t) = k_{ij}(t)/\tau_{ij}^\alpha$, and the corresponding matrices

$$\mathbf{d}_j^\alpha(t) = \begin{pmatrix} d_{1j}^\alpha(t) \\ d_{2j}^\alpha(t) \\ \dots\dots \\ d_{nj}^\alpha(t) \end{pmatrix} \qquad (43)$$

$$d_j'(t) = (\mathbf{d}_j^1(t), \mathbf{d}_j^2(t), \dots, \mathbf{d}_j^{\alpha_j}(t)) \qquad (44)$$

$$\mathbf{D}(t) = (\mathbf{d}_1'(t), \mathbf{d}_2'(t), \dots, \mathbf{d}_n'(t)) \qquad (45)$$

$$\mathbf{D}(t)\mathbf{\Delta} = \mathbf{d_\Delta}(t). \qquad (46)$$

Corresponding to a particular selection (operator $\mathbf{\Delta}$) from the catalogue of technologically feasible production processes, we rewrite the relations (18) through (24) in matrix form as follows:

$$(\mathbf{I} - \mathbf{a}_\triangle - \mathbf{v}_\triangle)\, \mathbf{x}(t) - \mathbf{c}(t) \;=\; \mathbf{d}_\triangle(t)\, \mathbf{i} - \mathbf{v}_\triangle \mathbf{x}(t-1) \tag{47}$$

$$\mathbf{x}(t) \;\leqslant\; \mathbf{x}_{CL\overline{P}} \tag{48}$$

$$\mathbf{c}(t) \;\leqslant\; \mathbf{c}_{\overline{P}} \tag{49}$$

$$\mathbf{x}(t) \;\geqslant\; \mathbf{x}_P \tag{50}$$

$$\mathbf{c}(t) \;\geqslant\; \mathbf{c}_P \tag{51}$$

$$\mathbf{m}_\triangle \mathbf{x}(t) \;\leqslant\; L(t) \tag{52}$$

$$\mathbf{m}_\triangle \mathbf{x}(t) \;\geqslant\; e.L(t) \tag{53}$$

where all the elements of the vectors and matrices are non-negative, and where $\mathbf{I}$ is an $n \times n$ identity matrix and $\mathbf{i}$ is an n-dimensional column vector of 1's.

Technological Innovation

Let us consider eight main categories of technical or policy changes, as follows:

(1) *New ways of making good* j. We characterize a change in production process for good j by a change in the operator $\boldsymbol{\delta}_j^\alpha$ to $\boldsymbol{\delta}_j^\beta$. The result may be a simultaneous change in depreciation time constants, capital-input coefficients, current input-output coefficients, and the manpower-input coefficient, from $\boldsymbol{\tau}_j^\alpha, \mathbf{b}_j^\alpha, \mathbf{a}_j^\alpha, m_j^\alpha$ to $\boldsymbol{\tau}_j^\beta, \mathbf{b}_j^\beta, \mathbf{a}_j^\beta, m_j^\beta$. If $\tau_{ij}^\beta < \tau_{ij}^\alpha$, then $d_{ij}^\beta > d_{ij}^\alpha$ and the depreciation constraint on output (4) is relaxed. Similarly, if $b_{ij}^\beta < b_{ij}^\alpha$, the same depreciation constraint (4) is relaxed. If $a_{ij}^\beta < a_{ij}^\alpha$, less input of current good i is required. In all of the cases above, the basic accounting equation also changes. If $m_j^\beta < m_j^\alpha$, the upper limit for the corresponding labour constraint changes, $x_{jL}^\beta(t) > x_{jL}^\alpha(t)$.

(2) *New ways of storing, maintaining and utilizing stocks of capital goods.* We characterize such an innovation by a change of a depreciation time constant from τ_{ij}^α to τ_{ij}^β. If $\tau_{ij}^\beta < \tau_{ij}^\alpha$, the corresponding depreciation is changed from d_{ij}^α to $d_{ij}^\beta > d_{ij}^\alpha$, and the corresponding constraint on output is relaxed. The basic accounting equation also changes. For example, suppose that an improved method of management reduces equipment waiting times in queues (e.g., trucks waiting in queues at shovels and crushers in open-pit mining). This would result in greater effective utilization of the equipment, thus shifting the constraint imposed by the availability of equipment. At the same time, equipment in use more hours per day would be subject to more wear and tear, hence increased real depreciation. Note that the capital-input coefficient may or may not change when τ_{ij} changes. This case of a change in τ_{ij} is a special case of a new way to make good j, discussed above.

(3) *Transfer of capital goods from one industry to another.* We characterize a transfer from industry j to industry h by the following changes:

$$k_{ij} \rightarrow k_{ij}^* \,, \quad \text{where} \quad k_{ij}^* \;=\; k_{ij} - \Delta k_i \tag{54}$$

$$k_{ih} \rightarrow k_{ih}^* \,, \quad \text{where} \quad k_{ih}^* \;=\; k_{ih} + \Delta k_i \,.$$

The effect is that the capital constraint for industry j is tightened, while the constraint for industry h is relaxed.

(4) *Merger of two or more industries.* In the case of a complete merger of industries j and h, their jointly held capital goods may be shared in joint production, and constraints of the following type may apply.

$$b_{ij} \, x_j(t) + b_{ih} \, x_h(t) \leq d_{ij}(t) + d_{ih}(t), \tag{55}$$

for $i = 1, 2, \ldots, n$. In such cases the simple constraints (7) have to be replaced by a more complicated set.

(5) *Invention of a new good,* $j = n + 1$. We characterize the invention of a new good by an expansion of the list of goods (industries) to include $j = n + 1$, and an expansion of the corresponding catalogue of production processes to produce the new good $j = n + 1$. After adding to the catalogue, in some cases an accumulation of capital goods to some critical level is required before production can begin, so that $k_{i, \, n+1}(t)$ may increase over one or more periods for some i, while $x_{n+1}(t) = 0$. In other cases, a stock of capital goods may be transferred from production of one good (industry), $j \neq n + 1$ to the new good (industry), $j = n + 1$, so that production can begin immediately. The effect of introducing a new good is to absorb some resources (capital, labour, current goods) that would otherwise be available for production of other goods, thus tightening constraints on some outputs as well as changing the basic accounting equation. Note that this effect may be observed *even if there is no immediate final consumption of the new good.* There may be necessary a time of capital-goods accumulation before production can begin, and a time of subsequent absorption of the entire output by other industries which may use it either as capital or current input to new processes of their own. (This "trigger effect" is described below.)

(6) *Invention of new technology which may be feasible but not necessarily economical for production of an existing good.* We characterize such an addition to *knowledge* by the addition of a new production process, denoted by $(a_j + 1)$ to the catalogue of feasible production process vectors for good j (industry j). Whether or not a particular feasible production process is selected for use depends on both the constraints on production and the decisions of entrepreneurs. Knowledge of the *existence* of feasible alternative ways to produce a good j may affect policies of government and industries designed either to discourage or encourage the selection of a particular production process by industry j. The invention of new technology (accumulation of knowledge) requires an input of resources to a "research and development industry" and an output of services from that industry to all other industries. These services may be considered as capital goods to be accumulated for possible future use in production (e.g., in the form of patents, designs, secret recipes, and so on).

(7) *Invention of a new consumption use for an existing good or a new good.* We characterize changes in potential consumption uses (*tastes*) by changes in the limits on consumption, c_{jP} and $c_{j\bar{P}}$.

(8) *Invention of new government policies, or new applications of old policies to regulate outputs and consumptions.* We characterize changes in such policies by changes in the limits of consumption, c_{jP} and $c_{j\bar{P}}$, and outputs x_{jP} and $x_{j\bar{P}}$. Such policies may constrain manpower (immigration, retraining), consumption (taxes, subsidies, credit regulation), capital accumulation and output, and selection of production processes. The policies may consist of a combination of many fiscal and monetary strategies.

In addition to the effects of each of these categories of technical or policy changes on shifts of constraints, we note their implications for labour inputs. These implications can be inferred only if a particular change is adopted because it is perceived to provide relevant advantages* to adopters.

Categories (1), (2) and (3) will be adopted only if the new set of parameters will require less labour input for the same output compared with the old set of parameters. Where the move is to more capital intensive technology, this is obvious. In (3), where capital input saving may appear to dominate, adoption either implies an accompanying labour saving as more appropriate equipment is made available for some processes, or at least implies (with a lag not greater than τ) a decrease in labour input to the respective capital industry. We call all such effects of technical change "labour releasing".

On the other hand, categories (5), (6) and (7) similarly absorb resources not otherwise used in the macro system, and again allowing for lags at most, the input primarily absorbed is labour. We shall refer to these categories as "labour absorbing" effects of technological change.

In categories (4) and (8) the effects may be either labour absorbing *or* releasing. Thus where mergers lead to economies of scale without constraints on consumption, the effect is labour releasing. Where the economies of scale are accompanied by certain changes in monopoly (or monopsony, oligopoly) conditions leading to constraints on consumption, labour absorbtion may be the net effect. Changes of policies and regulation often are (and with improvements in understanding should increasingly be) devised to be either labour releasing or labour absorbing so as to remove distortions of the macro-economy resulting from undesirable constraints.

Now let us consider an *internal trigger effect* of a technical or policy change. Suppose, for example, that the critical output constraint for industry j currently is the constraint on available manpower, such that

$$x^{\alpha}_{jKL\bar{P}} \;=\; x^{\alpha}_{jL} \;<\; x^{\alpha}_{jK} \;<\; x^{\alpha}_{jP}. \tag{56}$$

Suppose that industry j makes a change in its production process, denoted by a change from δ^{α}_{j} to δ^{β}_{j}. Suppose that the manpower input coefficient is thereby reduced from m^{α}_{j} to $m^{\beta}_{j} < m^{\alpha}_{j}$. We call this a *short-run labour releasing*

---

* The nature of such advantages is taken for granted here, partly so that a discussion of objectives to be optimized need not be given while we are only concerned to determine feasible sets of solutions, and partly because the nature of advantages of a technical change belongs to micro-economic theories which are entirely beyond the scope of this paper.

A related issue, concerning the labour elasticity of consumption, is a multi-period consideration to be dealt with in a subsequent paper.

innovation. Suppose that this labour-releasing innovation shifts the manpower constraint (9) so that the capital-input constraint now becomes critical, as follows:

$$x_{jKL\bar{P}}^{\beta} \; = \; x_{jK}^{\beta} \; < \; x_{jL}^{\beta} \; < \; x_{j\bar{P}}^{\beta} . \tag{57}$$

If the capital-input constraint is binding, output cannot be increased in the short run unless another production innovation occurs simultaneously either to reduce the critical capital-input coefficient b_{ij}, or to increase the critical rate of utilization of the capital good, $1/\tau_{ij}$. However, the output may be increased in the long run if additional capital accumulations tend to relax the binding capital-input constraint. Suppose that the critical capital-input constraint is shifted either in the short-run by a production innovation or in the long-run by capital accumulation, so that the manpower constraint again becomes critical and binding. Then the industry may be motivated to make another short-run labour-releasing innovation and a new cycle of internal changes is triggered in industry j. A sequence of short-run labour-releasing innovations over more than one time-interval may be referred to as innovations in a *long-run labour releasing industry*.

In a situation of "ideal" allocation, the manpower, capital and policy constraints on output should be equal and *not quite binding*, as follows:

$$x_{jKL\bar{P}} \; = \; x_{jK} \; = \; x_{jL} \; = \; x_{j\bar{P}} \tag{58}$$

and

$$x_j(t) \; = \; x_{jKL\bar{P}} \; - \; \epsilon \tag{59}$$

where ϵ is an arbitrarily small positive number. In this case the resource constraints are *balanced*. In practice, such constraints may never be in balance and there may be a continuing sequence of constraint shifts resulting from a continuing chain-reaction of innovations, each one triggering the next. This is the *internal trigger effect* for an industry j.

Now let us consider the effect of a technical or policy change of one industry on another. We call this an *external trigger effect* of one industry on another. For simplicity let us consider only two industries (goods) i and j. Suppose that industry j makes a production innovation, such that either its capital-input coefficient or its current input-output coefficient for good i is increased. In this case the total output of industry i may have to be increased to meet the inter-industry consumption. However, suppose that industry i's output is restricted by a critical and binding capital constraint. In this case industry i may respond in the short run by making a production innovation that is designed to relax the critical capital constraint. Alternatively, it may respond in the long run by accumulating capital to relax the constraint. If industry i's critical capital good is good j, it may make a production innovation to reduce its input requirements for capital good j, thus reducing the inter-industry demand for good j. In response, industry j may reduce its capital accumulation of good i.[*] Thus an innovation by one industry may be *counter-balanced* by a triggered innovation in another industry, in the sense that the net long-run effect on outputs may be *smaller* than expected. On the other hand, depending on which constraints are

---

[*] In control theory terminology, this is a *negative feedback effect*.

critical and binding, an innovation by one industry may trigger an innovation by another such that inputs and outputs for both *increase* in the long run.[*] In any event, increases or decreases in outputs may be limited by capital, labour and policy constraints, at least in the short run, no matter what innovations are introduced.

As an example of another kind of external trigger effect, suppose that two industries i and j share the same manpower pool of size $M_{(i,j)}$. Manpower inputs for the two industries are subject to a joint constraint of the form

$$m_i^a x_i(t) + m_j^a x_j(t) \leqslant M_{(i,j)}. \tag{60}$$

Suppose that industry j makes a labour releasing innovation, reducing its manpower input coefficient from m_j^a to $m_j^\beta < m_j^a$, and simultaneously changing its capital-input coefficients so that its capital constraint is tightened, $x_{jK}^\beta < x_{jK}^a$. Suppose that the capital constraint is binding on industry j's output after the innovation, so that it must embark on a capital accumulation programme. In turn, the capital accumulation triggers an increase in inter-industry consumptions of the output of industry i. Then industry i may absorb the manpower released by industry j, until the manpower constraint is again binding, as follows:

$$m_i^a x_i(t) + m_j^\beta x_j(t) = M_{(i,j)} \tag{61}$$

Industry i or j may then be motivated to make further labour-releasing innovations.

As an example of a short-term *labour absorbing* innovation, suppose a new industry (commodity) j is created, and this new industry requires an input of manpower from the same manpower pool as industry i. In this case a manpower constraint like (60) applies. Suppose that the manpower constraint is binding. Then industry i will be motivated to make a labour releasing innovation, changing m_i^a to $m_i^\beta < m_i^a$.

The internal and external trigger effects of sequences of innovations over time constitute an exceedingly complex process.

Numerical Example

Consider a simple two-industry hypothetical example. Suppose that all capital goods deteriorate whether used or not, so that $\tau_{ij} = \tau_{ijP}$, and all manpower is pooled.

Initial conditions for time $t = 0$, $t = 1$:

$$x_1(0) = 100, \qquad x_2(0) = 100$$
$$k_{11}(1) = 60, \qquad k_{12}(1) = 30$$
$$k_{21}(1) = 70, \qquad k_{22}(1) = 80$$

---

[*] This kind of reinforcement is called *positive feedback* in control theory.

Parameters for time $t = 1$:

$$m_1 = .10, \quad m_2 = .15 \quad M_{(1,2)}(1) = M(1) = 25$$

$$a_{11} = .25, \quad a_{12} = .50$$

$$a_{21} = .20, \quad a_{22} = .50$$

$$b_{11} = .10, \quad b_{12} = .04$$

$$b_{21} = .05, \quad b_{22} = .05$$

$$\tau_{11} = 5, \quad \tau_{12} = 5$$

$$\tau_{21} = 10, \quad \tau_{22} = 10$$

Policy constraints for time $t = 1$:

$$c_1(1) = 10, \quad 10 \leqslant c_2(1) \leqslant 30$$

Undetermined variables:

$$x_1(1) = x_1, \quad x_2(1) = x_2, \quad c_2(1) = c_2$$

Formulation of constraints:

Basic accounting equations, as in (18),

$$0.25x_1 - 0.70x_2 = -44$$

$$0.70x_1 + c_2 = 87.$$

Capital depreciation constraints, as in (7),

$$x_1 \leqslant \min\{120, 140\} = 120$$

$$x_2 \leqslant \min\{150, 160\} = 150.$$

Manpower constraint, as in (60),

$$0.10x_1 + 0.15x_2 \leqslant 25.$$

Policy constraints on consumption, as in (20), (22),

$$c_2 \geqslant 10, \quad c_2 \leqslant 30.$$

Feasible solutions for time $t = 1$: See Figure 1.

Figure 1 shows a plot of the constraints, on the coordinate axes x_1, x_2, and c_2. The line segment $A-C$ is a portion of the straight line defined by the basic accounting equations. The interior of the seven-faced polyhedron shown in Figure 1 is a linear convex region defined by the two capital constraints, two policy constraints on consumption, one manpower constraint and two non-negativity conditions (on x_1 and x_2), all of which are inequalities. The feasible solution region, which we shall call the *feasible production-consumption region*, is the line segment $A-B$, which lies entirely within the convex polyhedron. Point A corresponds to the solution $x_1 = 78.5$, $x_2 = 88$, $c_2 = 30$, at which the upper consumption constraint is binding and the other constraints are all slack. Point B corresponds to the solution $x_1 = 103.0$, $x_2 = 97.3$, $c_2 = 12.8$,

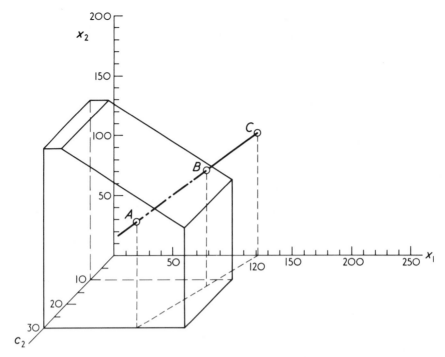

Fig. 1.

at which the manpower constraint is binding and all the other constraints are slack. Any convex combination of A and B is a feasible solution. In this example it is clear that the manpower constraint is critical and the capital goods are being wasted (depreciating without being fully used). There is an imbalance in the utilization of capital goods and manpower.

Let us suppose that the solution at Point A "occurs" or is somehow "adopted" by society. In this case additional consumption of good 2 is "preferred" to additional capital accumulation. The net effect on the stocks of capital goods at the beginning of time interval $t = 2$ can be computed from the capital investment relation (17). The values $k_{ij}(2)$ become initial conditions for time $t = 2$, as follows.

Initial conditions for time $t = 1$, $t = 2$ (given solution A at $t = 1$):

$$x_1(1) = 78.5, \quad x_2(1) = 88.0$$
$$k_{11}(2) = 49.2, \quad k_{12}(2) = 27.6$$
$$k_{21}(2) = 59.2, \quad k_{22}(2) = 74.0.$$

On the other hand, suppose that the solution at point B occurs. Then the initial conditions for the next period are as follows.

Initial conditions for $t = 1$, $t = 2$ (given solution B at $t = 1$):

$$x_1(1) = 103.1, \quad x_2(1) = 97.3$$
$$k_{11}(2) = 61.5, \quad k_{12}(2) = 29.5$$
$$k_{21}(2) = 71.5, \quad k_{22}(2) = 78.6.$$

Burke, Clough

Suppose that industry 2 introduces a labour-releasing innovation that becomes effective at time $t = 2$. Suppose the innovation reduces the manpower input coefficient but increases one of the capital input coefficients, as follows:

Parameters for time $t = 2$ (given solution B at $t = 1$)

$$m_1 = .10, \quad m_2 = .12 \text{ (new)}, \quad M(2) = 25, \quad c_1 = 10$$

$$a_{11} = .25, \quad a_{12} = .50$$

$$a_{21} = .20, \quad a_{22} = .50$$

$$b_{11} = .10, \quad b_{12} = .06 \text{ (new)}$$

$$b_{21} = .05, \quad b_{22} = .05$$

$$\tau_{11} = 5, \quad \tau_{12} = 5$$

$$\tau_{21} = 10, \quad \tau_{22} = 10.$$

Formulation of constraints for time $t = 2$ (given B at $t = 1$):

Basic accounting equations, as in (18),

$$0.25x_1 - 0.80x_2 = -51.8$$

$$0.70x_1 + c_2 = 85.0.$$

Capital depreciation constraints, as in (7):

$$x_1 \leqslant \min\{123, 143\} = 123$$

$$x_2 \leqslant \min\{98.5, 157\} = 98.5.$$

Manpower constraint, as in (60):

$$0.10x_1 + 0.12x_2 \leqslant 25.$$

Policy constraints, as in (20), (22):

$$c_2 \geqslant 10, \quad c_2 \leqslant 30.$$

Feasible solutions for time $t = 2$ (given solution B at $t = 1$):

Figure 2 is essentially the same as Figure 1, except that the constraints have been shifted. In this case the manpower constraint is redundant. Point D corresponds to the solution $x_1 = 78.5$, $x_2 = 89.5$, $c_2 = 30$. Point E corresponds to the point $x_1 = 107.1$, $x_2 = 98.3$, $c_2 = 10$. Any convex combination of D and E is a feasible solution. Suppose solution E occurs. In this case the lower policy constraint on consumption is binding, although the capital constraint on output x_2 is almost binding. The manpower use turns out to be

$$m_1 x_1 + m_2 x_2 = (.10)(107.1) + (.12)(98.3) = 22.5.$$

The "unemployment rate" in this case is 10%.

Conclusions

Modelling for feasible regions of outputs or consumptions, here undertaken explicitly for one time period, appears to show almost all that single period

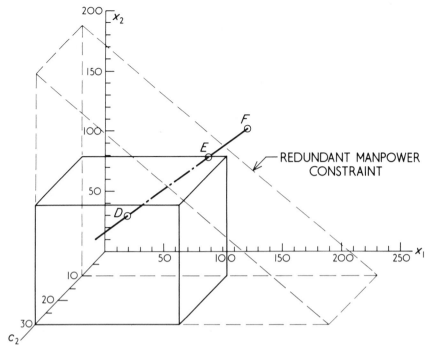

Fig. 2.

Leontieff models of the classical type discuss — particularly as regards effects of technical change. The explicit incorporation of a full set of constraints replaces, with advantage, assumptions of equilibrium models, shifts in production functions, and various assumptions about optimizing behaviour.

In an empirical situation, where growth-oriented Leontieff coefficients often cannot be estimated usefully (Morgenstern [1], Hatanaka [1]), and where continuity, optimality, or equilibrium assumptions destroy realism, the estimation of constraints may be more practical. A "feasible" region, while it theoretically contains an infinity of solutions, may be as close as the preceding considerations justify. Moreover, it is compatible with the powerful notions of "satisficing" proposed by Simon [1] *et al* to take the place of the infinite needs for information implied by true, empirical optima.

While we have defined price relationships, these do not appear meaningful beyond the first time period, when capital valuation problems seem to become intractable.

The explicit consideration of labour release and absorbtion (or their time displaced capital use analogues) resulting from shifts in constraints effected by technical changes, may not provide new conclusions (taken one by one). However it does provide an alternative model that has certain advantages in description and may be empirically testable. It seems a useful way to demonstrate connections between policies and decisions on the one hand, their consequences for resource utilization on the other.

The elaboration of trigger-effects, while these have been mentioned elsewhere, seems particularly natural in terms of constraint shifts, and highly appropriate to technological interactions of changes in products, processes or services.

Burke, Clough

It is clear that extension to quasi-dynamic models, while not demonstrated in this paper, is attractive and likely to lead to conclusions different from "optimal growth" models (e.g., as described by Morishima [1]). In an empirical sense, the existence of constraints is more likely to be discernable than "equilibria", which may take 5 to 30 years to establish, and therefore may become outdated by subsequent technical changes before they are reached.

There appear to be two characteristic time periods worth considering, to be more clearly discussed in future quasi-dynamic models, in which very "small" or "narrow" feasible regions may be expected. In the very short run, a very large number of otherwise variable items (e.g., number of employees, quantities of staple goods on order or *not* on order) are, in fact, fixed and therefore constraints upon output. Similarly, goods in shops (or *not* in shops) are, in fact, constraints on consumptions on this very short time scale. This feature may help to explain stabilities not otherwise readily derived from economic models. On the other hand, in the very long run, where τ's are small compared to the time horizon, the number of constraints may be smaller but capital may not be empirically distinguishable from lagged labour. For these long time horizons behavioural regularities may enter as binding constraints in a manner not readily accessible to other quantitative models.

Acknowledgements

The authors would like to thank the Canada Council for its continuing financial assistance in the form of a Killam Award for studies of innovation processes, and the National Research Council of Canada for its continuing financial support for industrial operations research.

References

Hatanaka, M.　　[1] *The workability of input-output analysis*, Ludwigshafen am Rhein, 1960.

Leontieff, W.W.　[1] *The structure of American economy, 1919–39*, New York, Oxford University Press, 1951.

　　　　　　　　[2] "Structural change", *Studies in the structure of the American economy*, by W.W. Leontieff and others, New York, Oxford University Press, 1953, p. 17–52.

　　　　　　　　[3] "Dynamic analysis", *Studies in the structure of the American economy*, by W.W. Leontieff and others, New York, Oxford University Press, 1953, p. 53–90.

Morgenstern, O. [1] *On the accuracy of economic observations.* 2d. ed. Princeton, N.J., Princeton University Press, 1950, 1963.

Morishima, M.　[1] *Equilibrium, stability, and growth: a multi-sectoral analysis.* Oxford, Clarendon Press, 1964.

Salter, W.E.G.　[1] *Productivity and social change.* Cambridge, Eng., Cambridge University Press, 1966. (University of Cambridge. Department of Applied Economics Monographs, no. 6)

Simon, H.A.   [1] *Administrative behavior: a study of decision-making process in administrative organization.* New York, The Free Press, (1945), 1965. 2d. ed.

                       [2] "Effects of technological change in a Leontieff model", in *Activity analysis of production and allocation*, ed. T.C. Koopmans, New York, Wiley, 1951, p. 260–281.

Solow, R.M.   [1] "Technical change and the aggregate production function", *Review of economics and statistics*, Vol. XXXIX (1957), p. 312–320.

13

Technological Manpower: Contribution made by an Analysis by Function to the Studies of Profitability in Manufacturing Industry

Gloria P. Ford

Ministry of Technology (U.K.)

Introduction

This exploratory paper derives from a pilot study carried out by the then Ministry of Technology in January 1968 and uses this limited data to suggest some of the progress which may be made with the results of a full survey. The data drawn from this pilot survey are not statistically representative. The purpose of the pilot was primarily methodological — to extend the work on classification of technological manpower undertaken by the Department in conjunction with some of the larger employers in Great Britain.

Definitions

Definition of function

Function is defined as a basic or structural sub-division of the activities of the company or other organisation.

2. The informal advisory panel set up by the Ministry of Technology defined two basic criteria: one, maximum flexibility offered by a multi-axis system of classification; two, distinction between the man and the job. Although the second criteria follows naturally from the first it was found to be an essential discipline to state it separately.

3. **Function** meets both of these criteria. In particular it is addressed to the job rather than the man. It gives us the sub-division of jobs into the major structural sub-divisions of the company. If, at a later stage of analysis, we look at the men occupying those jobs, we get a picture of the way in which they are being used.

4. Five major sub-divisions are defined for a business enterprise:

> **Commerce,**
> **Research and development**
> **Production**
> **General management**
> **Services**

The five major sub-divisions are defined by a list of typical sub-activities. It is visualised that although within a company the sub-activities might vary slightly in name and in content, they would still be identifiable as belonging to a particular major sub-division.

The data available

5.   The data now available on the results of analysis by function, although of great interest in potential, is strictly limited in coverage.

QSEs

6.   The data covered persons holding degrees or equivalent qualifications in engineering, technology and science (QSEs). This universe was chosen to match the other data already available to the Ministry of Technology. [1]

Coverage

7.   Analyses by function are available for twenty-eight companies or representative parts of companies. These data are drawn from a pilot study carried out in January 1968, which was designed as a methological rather than statistical exercise. The aggregrates are not representative of all industry. Nevertheless the individual results are of interest, to show the interaction of function and other economic indicators for these small groups of companies.

Company codes

8.   Great care has been taken to ensure the confidentiality of the data supplied by the companies who kindly co-operated in the study. Two letter codes have been assigned, of which the first letter represents percentage return on investment :

> companies earning 15 per cent and above are coded "A": companies earning over 10 per cent and under 15 per cent are coded "B":
> and those earning under 10 per cent are coded "C".

Density

9.   The concept of density of QSEs, in the sense of numbers of QSEs per 100 persons employed, has been used in analyses and reports of previous manpower surveys. It is convenient to look first at this crude measure of utilisation for the companies under consideration before going on to look at analysis by function.

10.   Of the twenty-eight companies making returns, twenty-four were used in this preliminary study. They shared a wide range of density, from 0.4 per 100 to 18.9 per 100. All companies chosen were "science-based" so the variation is a matter of some interest.

11.   In Table 1 below, the densities are shown for the twenty-four companies;

firstly all QSEs together; followed by qualifications in engineering, technology and science separately. Higher automated concerns are found to have a high density of QSEs while the more labour-intensive companies have a low density, sometimes under one per hundred. But apart from this observation, no very clear pattern emerges at this stage.

QSEs as a percentage of total employment in 24 companies

Per cent

	All QSEs	Engineering and technology	Science
BD	18.9	3.6	15.3
AB	18.5	8.8	9.8
AA	9.9	8.4	1.5
BJ	7.3	2.7	4.7
CB	6.9	5.1	1.7
AD	6.4	4.1	2.4
CC	6.2	1.7	4.5
CD	5.7	1.4	4.3
CF	5.7	2.4	3.3
OO	5.7	4.7	0.9
BG	3.6	2.0	1.6
EF	2.9	1.8	1.1
CA	2.6	1.2	1.4
BE	2.5	2.4	0.1
BB	2.4	2.1	0.3
BA	1.8	1.4	0.5
AC	1.5	1.4	0.1
AE	1.4	1.3	0.1
CG	1.4	1.2	0.2
BH	1.3	0.4	0.9
BC	1.1	0.5	0.6
CE	0.8	0.8	–
CH	0.7	0.5	0.2
BK	0.4	0.2	0.2
CJ	0.4	0.3	0.1

Table. 1. *Density.*

Relationship between density and profitability

12. The arguments for expanding the employment of QSEs in British industry, as for example, given in the report of the Swann Committee, [2] are in terms of the profitability of the business. It is therefore of interest to compare the density of the use of people with these qualifications with one measure of profitability — the return on investment.

13. The following table gives the density (QSEs employed per 100 employees) for the five companies in the survey with the highest rates of profitability in 1967/68.

Table 2. Density in five top companies.

Per Cent

	All QSEs	Engineering and technology	Science
AA	9.9	8.4	1.5
AB	18.5	8.8	9.8
AC	1.5	1.4	0.1
AD	6.4	4.1	2.4
AE	1.4	1.3	0.1

14. This comparison shows that there is no simple correlation between density and profitability. The most successful companies employed between 1.4 and 18.5 QSEs per 100. Looked at another way, Table 1 shows that the five highest densities were found in companies in the earning groups "B" and "C" as well as in "A".

Analysis by function

15. The results in Table 1 emphasise the purpose underlying the pilot study. Density, although indicative of the pattern across manufacturing industry is at best a blunt instrument; further studies need to be concentrated on *the use made* of QSEs within the company.

16. The concept of function is, of course, neither new nor untried in employer surveys. "Research and development" and "Other work" were included in the questionnaires used in surveys 1959, 1962, 1965 and again in 1968. However the satisfactory subdivision and definition of "Other work" did not become a practicable proposition before 1967, when the initiative came from industry and the collaboration of six major companies provided the nucleus.

17. Although only twenty-four companies are represented in this study, the quality of the data is more consistent than in previous surveys for the limits of each function have been set by very full definitions. Table 3 shows the analysis of 21,190 jobs occupied by QSEs in January 1968 by the five major functions. It is interesting to note that this group covers roughly 20 per cent of all QSEs employed in manufacturing industry.

18. Within this group of companies it is of interest that 43 per cent of QSEs were employed in jobs in R & D (compared with 35 per cent obtained in the 1968 survey). Of the remainder 3.2 per cent were in general management, 14.2 per cent in commerce, 33.0 per cent in production and 7 per cent in services.

QSEs in innovation

19. The credibility of the simple recipe for greater productivity, more expenditure of resources on research and development, has been eroded by recent comparative studies of expenditure patterns. As a result attention has been focussed on those activities responsible for guiding and transforming the results of R & D into new marketable products.

Table 3. Analysis of QSEs by function

	Number of QSEs	Per cent in each function
All QSEs in responding companies	21,190	100.0
General management	680	3.2
Commerce	3,010	14.2
Research and development	9,020	42.6
Production	7,000	33.0
Services	1,480	7.0

20. If more comprehensive data were available than that provided by the twenty-eight companies, then one would exploit the flexibility of the data in a full analytical model. One might for example, postulate a set of typical function patterns for each industry and run these against criteria of profitability.

21. With the limited data available, a simplified approach has been taken. The two functions "production" and "commerce" have been taken as an approximation to "innovation", that is the post-R&D activities. In practice, of course, some innovation in the wider sense, takes place during development so that this assumption is essentially an over-simplification for the purpose of analysis.

22. Within this particular group of companies, 47 per cent of all QSEs were working in these two functions (Table 3). The range (as reported) was from 12 per cent to 86 per cent. Table 7 gives the full range of results, distinguishing different levels of profitability in 1967/68 and giving a comparison with density of engineering qualifications within the company.

23. Figure 1 shows the percentage return on capital (y) plotted against the percentage of QSEs in innovation (x). A first examination of the scatter diagram and the line of regression of y on x which has been drawn, appear to support such intuitive postulates as "more profitable companies tend to be associated with a higher proportion of QSEs in innovation" or "to improve company profits, a substantial proportion of QSEs should be employed outside the R & D function".

24. Nevertheless, it cannot be emphasised too strongly that these results can do no more than illustrate the uses to which this new analysis might be put if the survey was on a much larger and more representative scale. Not only is the present sample of companies quite unrepresentative, but in some cases, the whole company is not covered. The pilot was designed to assess the *practicability* of the analysis and the companies who assisted Mintech were not pressed to cover all their establishments if this was inconvenient for them. The correlation coefficient was 0.58. At this value it is not possible to make any strong inference. It may however be regarded as indicative of a causal relationship which is worth further investigation on a multivariate basis with the results of a full survey.

25. The proportions of QSEs in innovation in the six most profitable companies

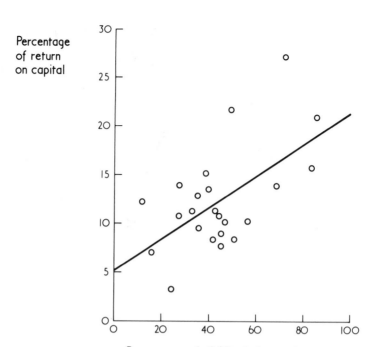

Percentage of QSEs in innovation

Fig. 1

in 1967/68 are shown in Table 4. It is of interest, that in this particular group, *all* the innovation ratios above 68 per cent are found among these six companies. (See also Table 7.)

Table 4. Proportion of QSEs in innovation

	All functions	Innovation	R & D	Other
	(Six top companies)			Per cent
AA	100	72	18	10
AB	100	49	39	12
AC	100	86	10	4
AD	100	83	2	15
AE	100	39	58	3
BA	100	68	18	14

Expansion in the number of QSEs required by 1971

26. The questionnaire also asked for the planned expansion in the employment of QSEs up to 1971. The expansion in innovation and R & D is shown below, so that

200

Ford

we can also examine the link between these two indicators of future trends.

The forecast annual rate of increase is shown for the six top companies and contrasted with the six showing the highest rates of increase reported (full results are shown in Table 8).

Table 5. Forecast annual rates of increase (1968 to 1971)

Per cent

	QSEs in innovation	QSEs in R & D
Six top companies		
AA	4.8	5.3
AB	3.7	3.9
AC	6.5	6.6
AD	2.2	–
AE	3.5	5.3
BA	2.6	6.3
Six highest increases		
BC	7.6	6.4
CE	8.7	12.4
BF	12.9	13.4
CJ	16.8	17.4
BH	19.1	21.1
BK	34.9	24.6

27. Points of interest in this table on forecasts are as follows: –

(i) None of the six top companies occur among the companies returning the six highest increases in QSE employment. The most profitable companies all have future requirements of under 7 per cent.

(ii) The four companies who forecast the highest increases in QSE employment are all in the lower part of the earnings scale (See also Table 7).

(iii) In 18 out of the 22 companies who were able to give future requirements, the percentage increase in R & D was greater than that for innovation.

28. A further interesting comparison can be made between the forecast increases and the current density. For this sample, Table 6 shows quite conclusively that the high forecast annual rates of increase all occur where the current density is low, in fact, below 1.5 per cent. The variation in the rates of increase forecast up to 1971 could be a matter of considerable importance. As seen from Table 6, companies with a "density" between 5.5 and 7 per cent show small increases (one a heavy decrease); the substantial increases are all observed in companies with a low density in 1968.

29. The concept of the "S curve increase" in density was first discussed in 1960 when long-term forecasts for QSEs in manufacturing industry were being

Table 6. Employment increases 1968 to 1971 compared with density in 1968.

	Per cent increase in innovation	Per cent Density of all QSEs
Smallest increases		
CB	−11.2	6.9
BJ	0.6	7.3
AD	2.2	6.4
CD	2.7	5.7
CC	3.6	6.2
Largest increases		
CE	8.7	0.8
BF	12.9	1.1
CJ	16.8	0.4
BH	19.1	1.3
BK	34.8	0.4

prepared. [3] Certain companies consulted in the process of this study, admitted "saturation" at around 7 per cent. The results from the pilot study suggest that this level may have a long-term significance. It is possible that companies tend to "level off" their recruitment as this density is reached. It can be seen too, from company detail in the limited pilot sample, that those companies who report a density above 7.5 per cent are in a rather special situation. Thus, it might be argued that 7.5 per cent currently represents the terminal flattening of the "S curve", a value which other companies, still on the rising portion of the curve, may be expected to reach in time, but seldom to pass unless QSEs are employed in non-traditional roles. (Computer companies and other companies concerned with very advanced technology could prove to be an exception to this rule).

Summary of the analyses

(i) There is no overall correlation between high density and high profitability (Table 1)

(ii) High density is observed in companies using automated processes, low density in the more labour-intensive or craft industries (paragraph 11).

(iii) In the 24 companies, the proportion of QSEs in R & D was 42.6 per cent, followed by 33 per cent in production and 14 per cent in commerce: that is, 47 per cent in the "innovation" functions.

(iv) Four out of the six most profitable companies had 68 per cent or more of their QSEs employed in innovation (Table 7)

(v) The twenty-four companies forecast changes in the numbers of QSEs in innovation ranging from −11 to +35 per cent between 1968 and 1971. (Table 8).

(vi) The six top companies are all forecasting annual increases in QSEs in innovation and R&D of less than 7 per cent.

(vii) The largest forecast increases in QSE employment observed in companies with a density below 1.5 per cent. This could suggest that these companies are on the steep part of the "S curve".

Table 7. QSE's employed on innovation
Analysis by return on capital 1967/68

Per cent

	Proportion of QSE's supporting innovation	Density of engineers in company
15 per cent or more		
AA	72	8.4
AB	49	8.8
AC	86	1.4
AD	83	4.1
AE	39	1.3
10 and under 15 per cent		
BA	68	1.4
BB	27	2.1
BC	40	0.5
BD	12	3.6
BE	33	2.4
BF	42	1.8
BG	27	2.0
BH	44	0.4
BJ	56	2.7
BK	47	0.2
Under 10 per cent		
CA	36	1.2
CB	45	5.1
CC	51	1.7
CD	42	1.4
CE	45	0.8
CF	16	2.4
CG	35	1.2
CH	24	0.5
CJ	34	0.3

Table 8. Expansion in the number of QSE's required by 1971.
Percentage annual rate of increase

Per cent

	Innovation	R and D
15 per cent or more		
AA	4.8	5.3
AB	3.7	3.9
AC	6.5	6.6
AD	2.2	–
AE	3.5	5.3
10 and under 15 per cent		
BA	2.6	6.3
BC	7.6	6.4
BD	4.2	5.7
BE	–	1.6
BF	12.9	13.4
BG	5.2	–0.6
BH	19.1	21.1
BJ	0.6	1.6
BK	34.9	24.6
Under 10 per cent		
CA	5.7	7.1
CB	–11.2	0.5
CC	3.6	4.2
CD	2.7	5.5
CE	8.7	12.4
CF	–	5.2
CH	4.2	7.0
CJ	16.8	17.4

Conclusions

Analysis by function is a valuable step forward in the study of utilisation and effectiveness (profitability) of deployment of QSEs. High on its list of attributes, appealing to both model builders and personnel managers, is the *capacity* for unambiguous definition. Function gives a new dimension to the consideration of manpower as a human resource. On the national scale it extends the information on how the stock of QSEs is being used: an essential prerequisite to planning. At the level of the firm the potential is even greater as part of an integrated system of management information.

References

1. *Report on the 1965 Triennial Manpower survey of engineers, technologists, scientists and technical supporting staff.* Cmnd. 3103. HMSO 1966.

2. *The Flow into Employment of Scientists, Engineers and Technologists.* Cmnd. 3760. HMSO 1968.

3. *The Long-term Demand for Scientific Manpower* Cmnd. 1490 HMSO 1961.

PART IV

14

Capacity Models in University Management[*]

Günter Menges   **Simon Fraser University, Canada**

Gert Elstermann   **University of the Saar, Germany**

I. Introduction and Summary

In the last decade, the universities in the Federal Republic of Germany have been confronted with an exploding demand for higher education which led to a rapid growth of the student population. In spite of expanding faculties and considerable investments in buildings and equipment, the admission of students had to be restricted in more and more fields of study (*numerus clausus*). In other fields of study, there is an unrevealed *numerus clausus* in the form of restricted admissions to laboratory courses, seminars etc. and of overcrowded libraries; this leads to queues of students and, at last, to a wasteful increase of the duration of studies.

It is to be expected that in a very few years the admissions to nearly all fields of study will be restricted at all institutions of tertiary education. Students will have to apply for admission at a central registration office[†] which, in a computer-based procedure, assigns students to institutions in co-operation with the faculties, taking into consideration the students' qualifications and preferences, the faculties' criteria for admission, and the educational capacity of the institutions in terms of student enrolment by field of study. The philosophy is now seriously discussed that every sufficiently qualified person should be granted the chance to get higher education; that, however, the free choice of both the field of study and the institution have to be abandoned; and that the distribution of students on fields of study should be controlled with respect to highly qualified manpower requirements of economy and society (cp. (2), p. 48).

In this situation, universities and federal and state agencies in the F. R. expressed the urgent need of capacity models for universities.

Capacity models are to serve three main purposes:

[*] The preparation of this paper was supported by *Wissenschaftliche Gesellschaft des Saarlandes e. V.* The authors are indebted to Mr. H. Rommelfanger for helpful comments and suggestions.

[†] This is already the case in the field of medicine (1).

First, the number of applicants who can be admitted to university education may be derived from the capacity of the institution as compared to actual enrolment, by department, field of study, or subject, respectively (*admissions management*).

Second, the validity of the departments' demands for additional resources, especially teaching personnel, may be examined and compared with respect to actual and potential teaching load of the departments (*funds allocation management*).

Third, future resource requirements may be estimated by means of a capacity model on the basis of enrolment forecasts (*planning*).

In order to serve these purposes, a capacity model should allow for the study of the mutual effects between the resources of a university (personnel and facilities), on the one hand, and the number of students, by level and field of study, who can be educated with these resources, on the other hand, at the same time taking into account the institutional and organizational factors influencing the educational processes within a university.

In the Federal Republic the following capacity models have been discussed:

(a) The Krings-Finkenstaedt formula (3), (4), (5), (6);

(b) the Rumpf formula (7);

(c) the method of calculation employed by the Science Council (8);

(d) the method of calculating the capacity of a psychology department by Heckhausen (9);

(e) the model by Mahrenholtz and Withum (10);

(f) the Dietze model (11) which employs transition matrices (cp. (12), (13));

(g) the Caspar model (14);

(h) the Braun-Hammer-Schmid model (15).

Based on those models, in this article a more comprehensive type of capacity model is developed which explicitly takes into consideration the *time structure* of the admissions optimization problem, making evident the close connection between admissions management and short-term planning. The admissions optimization problem is generalized to the problem of determining an optimal admission policy (for N admission periods) which is shaped in such a way that dynamic-programming techniques are applicable.

2. A Comprehensive Capacity Model

2.1. General

In the following we develop, on the basis of the models presented earlier, a more versatile and general capacity model. It is to simultaneously serve three main tasks:

> admissions management,
>
> funds allocation management,
>
> capacity planning,

and, at the same time, it considers the type and amount of statistical information a university should posses. We start the development of our model with a description of its components. Among its main components we may distinguish between "supply constituents", describing faculties and other resources as well as the curricula offered by the university, on the one hand, and "demand constituents" characterizing the student part of the problem, on the other hand.

2.2. "Supply Constituents" of the Model

A single course is denoted by $v_\mu (\mu = 1, \ldots, m)$; the set of all courses belonging to a certain curriculum C_k $(k = 1, \ldots, n)$ and to a certain study semester $f(f = 1, \ldots, n_k)$ of the k-th curriculum is denoted by V_{fk}. The set of all courses to be offered by the university with respect to the set C of all curricula is

$$V = \bigcup_{f=1}^{n_k} \bigcup_{k=1}^{n} V_{fk}.$$

By means of V_{fk} we can define C_k in the following form:

$$C_k = \{ V_{1k}, \ldots, V_{n_k k} \mid V_{fk} \subset V \}.$$

As a rule, V is more *and* less than the actual supply of courses in a certain semester, for there are courses which, although belonging to V, are not offered every semester, and there are courses not belonging to V which are actually offered. The latter type may be called supplementary courses; V^S. The courses actually offered are denoted by $v_\mu (\mu = 1, \ldots, m')$; their set is A.

Each element $v_\mu \in A \cup V$ is characterized by its number $w(v_\mu)$ of semester hours.

A faculty L is the set of the university's teachers $L_1, \ldots^{(a)}, L_s$. Every teacher L_a has a certain preference profile $\pi(L_a)$ which expresses his preference order on the set of courses V. Furthermore, every teacher L_a has a teaching obligation F_a (measured in semester hours) and an actual teaching load G_a with

$$G_a = \sum_{v_\mu \in V_a} w(v_\mu),$$

where V_a is the set of courses offered by teacher a:

$$\bigcup_{a=1}^{s} V_a = A.$$

A single $v_\mu \in A$ may belong to more than one V_a because one course might be given by two or more teachers. The teaching load should not exceed the teaching obligation:

$$G_a \leqslant F_a. \tag{2.1.}$$

Lastly, every teacher is qualified, or not, to teach the course $v_\mu \in V$. The "qualification variable" may be denoted by $\gamma_{a\mu}$ with

$$\gamma_{a\mu} = \begin{cases} 1 \text{ if } L_a \text{ is "officially"} \\ \quad \text{qualified to teach } v_\mu \\ 0 \text{ else} \end{cases}$$

The ordered set of $\gamma_{a\mu}$ forms the qualification matrix Γ with[*]

$$\Gamma = \begin{pmatrix} \gamma_{11}, \ldots, \gamma_{1m} \\ \cdot \\ \cdot \\ \cdot \\ \gamma_{s1}, \ldots, \gamma_{sm} \end{pmatrix}$$

The assignment problem "teacher — course" is solved by individual proposals and decisions of the faculty council, formally not accomplishable. Here, we do not inquire into the assignment process.

Another supply constituent is the set of rooms $R = \{r_1, \overset{(\delta)}{\ldots}, r_q\}$. To each room r_δ, there is attached a number of "stations" $z(r_\delta) = z_\delta (\delta = 1, \ldots, q)$. A "station" may be a seat in a classroom, or a place in a laboratory, etc. A room assignment mapping Φ assigns rooms to courses:

$$\Phi: R \to \mathscr{P}(A) \tag{2.2.}$$
$$r_\delta \mapsto \{v_{\rho_1}, \ldots, v_{\rho_n}\} \subset A$$

where $\mathscr{P}$ denotes the power set of A.

At the same time, this mapping brings about an attachment of stations to courses: To each course $v_\mu \in \{v_{\rho_1}, \ldots, v_{\rho_n}\} = \Phi(r_\delta)$ the number of stations $z_\delta = z(r_\delta)$ is assigned, which may be denoted by z_μ. The mapping Φ, practically seen, can be submitted to certain optimization techniques (time-table optimization programs; cp. (17)). This may lead to some (often unavoidable) diminution of individual privileges. In the present context the mapping (2.2.) is regarded as given. This assumption is, of course, a simplification, for in most cases the suboptimization problem of the time-table is closely linked with the overall problem of optimal capacity utilization.

The number of stations z_μ assigned to a course v_μ is not the only restriction imposed on the number of students who can be admitted to the course v_μ. Other restrictions stem from didactic considerations and from the teaching burden as far as it is not accounted for in the teaching load $w(v_\mu)$. We therefore introduce the variable e_μ which denotes the number of participants in course v_μ which is optimal from such considerations; the variable e_μ may be called the "didactic class size". The capacity number y_μ of the course v_μ is

$$y_\mu = \min(z_\mu, e_\mu). \tag{2.3.}$$

2.3. "Demand Constituents" of the Model

The demanding factor of the university is the student body. We denote the student body at time t by S_t. t is an element of a "relevance period" T.

---

[*] Γ may be generalized to a productivity matrix in which each element represents the productivity of assigning a teacher to a course; cp. (16).

T itself consists of three partly overlapping periods: T_1 = observation period, T_2 = short-term planning period, T_3 = long-term planning period. $T = T_1 \cup T_2 \cup T_3$; $T_2 \subset T_3$. T_2 is the period relevant for capacity determination and short-term planning in connection with capacity determination. T_3 is the period of long-term capacity considerations.

S_t is a column vector of the following form:

$$
S_t = \begin{pmatrix} \vdots \\ s_{fkt} \\ \vdots \end{pmatrix} \qquad
\begin{array}{l}
f = 1, \ldots, n_k \quad \text{(study semesters)} \\[4pt]
k = 1, \ldots, n \quad \text{(curricula)} \\[4pt]
t \in T
\end{array}
$$

For planning and admission purposes the model has to be a dynamic one, and thus we must incorporate the transition process of the students. This is accomplished by means of the transition matrix Q. For fixed $t \in T_1 \cup T_2$ the transition matrix of kth curriculum is

$$
Q^k = \begin{pmatrix}
0 & 0 & \ldots & 0 & 0 \\
q_{12}^k & 0 & \ldots & 0 & 0 \\
0 & q_{23}^k & \ldots & 0 & 0 \\
\vdots & \vdots & & \vdots & \vdots \\
0 & 0 & \ldots & q_{n_k-1,n_k}^k & 0
\end{pmatrix}
$$

Here, $q_{i,i+1}^k$ $(i = 1, \ldots, n_k - 1)$ denotes the rate of transition of the students in curriculum k from the i'th study semester to the $(i + 1)$'th study semester. The Q^k themselves are the diagonal elements of the overall transition matrix Q:

$$
Q = \begin{pmatrix}
Q^1 & 0 & \ldots & 0 \\
0 & Q^2 & \ldots & 0 \\
\vdots & \vdots & & \vdots \\
0 & 0 & \ldots & Q^n
\end{pmatrix}
$$

The non-diagonal elements of Q by definition are set equal to zero because, for the sake of simplicity, we assume that students do not change their field of study. This assumption may be called *assumption A*. The numerical values of the transition matrix which are taken from reality do contain cases of curriculum-changers and therefore a certain error has to be accepted when the transition numbers are used as *pure* transition rates within a curriculum.

Another and more important assumption is the time-stability of Q (*assumption B*), i.e. we assume that the student study behavior with respect to transition within the curriculum is stable; that the efficiency of the system "university" shows no change; and that there exist no relative changes in dropping-out from the university on hand.

The most important constituent on the demand side, the population of the new-enrolled students will, for the sake of simplicity, by definition be restricted to freshmen only, i.e. to that group of new-enrolled students who start their university study. This assumption may be called *assumption C*. We distinguish n subgroups corresponding to the different fields of study and compile the subgroups to the following admission vector for semester $t \in T_2$:

$$
Z^t = \begin{pmatrix} z_{11t} \\ 0 \\ \cdot \\ \cdot \\ \cdot \\ 0 \end{pmatrix} (n_1 - 1) \text{ times} \\ \begin{matrix} z_{12t} \\ 0 \\ \cdot \\ \cdot \\ \cdot \\ 0 \end{matrix} (n_2 - 1) \text{ times} \\ \cdots \\ \begin{matrix} z_{1nt} \\ 0 \\ \cdot \\ \cdot \\ \cdot \\ 0 \end{matrix} (n_n - 1) \text{ times}
$$

The neglect of those newly admitted students who are not freshmen produces an error similar in nature and gravity to that caused by assumption A.

Now we combine the admission vector Z_t and the overall transition matrix Q to a new matrix, which may be called flow matrix:

$$
M_t = (Z_t \mid Q), \ t \in T_2 .
$$

This combined flow matrix M_t, when post-multiplied by the student column vector for semester t

$$
\tilde{S}_t = \left(\frac{1}{S_t} \right), \ t \in T_2 ,
$$

yields the new student vector S_{t+1} for semester $t + 1$:

$$
M_t \cdot \tilde{S}_t = S_{t+1} . \tag{3.1.}
$$

Because of the zero elements in M_t caused by assumptions A and C we can simplify (3.1.) to the following system:

$$s_{1k,t+1} = z_{1kt}$$

$$s_{2k,t+1} = s_{1kt} \cdot q^k_{12}$$

$$\vdots$$

$$(k = 1, \ldots, n \, ; \quad t \in T_1 \text{ fixed}) \qquad (3.2.)$$

$$s_{n_k k, t+1} = s_{n_k-1, kt} \cdot q^k_{n_k-1, n_k}$$

The first step in the course of application of our model is the determination of estimates of the q's. The second step is forecasting the future freshmen numbers. As a rule, this is accomplished on the basis of high school graduation statistics and forecasts. As soon as one knows the q's and the future z's one can, by repeated application of formula (3.1), find a recursion system for the prediction of future student populations. The recursion system reads as follows:

$$M_t \cdot \tilde{S}_t = S_{t+1} \rightarrow \tilde{S}_{t+1}$$

$$M_{t+1} \cdot \tilde{S}_{t+1} = S_{t+2} \rightarrow \tilde{S}_{t+2}$$

$$\vdots \qquad (3.3.)$$

$$M_{t+i} \cdot \tilde{S}_{t+i} = S_{t+i+1} \rightarrow \tilde{S}_{t+i+1}$$

$$\vdots \qquad (t \in T_2).$$

If the admission numbers Z_t are held constant, i.e. if M_t is constant for all $t \in T_2$, then the student population becomes stationary after n_k semesters, $n_k \leqslant n(T_2)$.

After having, by means of system (3.3.), forecast the student populations, the problem arises of how to link those forecasts with the courses offered and thus to link the demand side with the supply side of the model. The answer is given by certain participation rates $p^f_{k\mu}(f = 1, \ldots, n_k; \ k = 1, \ldots, n \, ; \ \mu = 1, \ldots, m)$. $p^f_{k\mu}$ represents the proportion of students in study semester f and study field k who participate in course v_μ. The $p^f_{k\mu}$ form a matrix P

$$P = (p^f_{k\mu})$$

which may be called the participation matrix.

Its elements are gained by empirical studies. Post-multiplying the participation matrix by S_t we arrive at the student demand vector D_t:

$$D_t = P \cdot S_t \ (t \in T_2). \qquad (3.4.)$$

The elements of D_t show the distribution of students according to courses:

$$D_t = \begin{pmatrix} d_{1t} \\ \vdots \\ d_{mt} \end{pmatrix}(\mu) = \begin{pmatrix} p_{11}^1 & p_{11}^2 & \cdots & p_{21}^1 & \cdots & p_{n1}^{n_k} \\ p_{12}^1 & p_{12}^2 & \cdots & p_{22}^1 & \cdots & p_{n2}^{n_k} \\ \vdots & & & & & \\ p_{1m}^1 & p_{1m}^2 & \cdots & p_{2m}^1 & \cdots & p_{nm}^{n_k} \end{pmatrix} \cdot \begin{pmatrix} s_{11t} \\ s_{21t} \\ \cdot \\ \cdot \\ s_{12t} \\ \cdot \\ \cdot \\ s_{n_k n t} \end{pmatrix}$$

The participation matrix is a weak part in our system becuase it is by no means fixed but depends on many factors, mainly on the frequency or periodicity with which different courses are offered.

Another difficulty with respect to (3.4.) arises when this relation is to be used for capacity determination, i.e. for determination of S_t and with S_t the student admission numbers because the relationship between S_t and D_t is not unique: One and the same D_t may correspond to different vectors S_t.

If the participation matrix cannot be found or if its application seems not feasible one might try to come along with (2.3.1.) of the BHS model although that is a poor substitute.

2.4. Determination of Optimal Admission Numbers for One Period

After having fixed the supply and demand constituents of the model one faces the difficult problem of determining the number of students who can be admitted for study. In order to solve this problem the demand numbers $d_{\mu t}(\mu = 1, \ldots, m)$ are compared with the capacity numbers $y_\mu(\mu = 1, \ldots, m')$. The y_μ's correspond to the set A of actually offered courses. In a strict sense, A is time-dependent: A_t. We assume, however, that the system is stationary with respect to V (assumption D), and we define this stationarity in the following way:

$$V \subset A_t \text{ for all } t \in T_2,$$

i.e. within one semester all courses $v_\mu \in V$ which are required by the curricula are offered. So we consider the $y_\mu(\mu = 1, \ldots, m)$ corresponding to V:

$$d_{\mu t} \leq y_{\mu t} \text{ for all } \mu \text{ with } v_\mu \in V(t \in T_2) \tag{4.1.}$$

The system (4.1.) eventually restricts the number of students to be admitted. Starting from the $d_{\mu t}$'s one can, through the participation matrix P, determine the student vector S_t which allows one to identify the components of z_t. It will not be useful to solve equation (3.4.) for S_t by the matrix multiplication $S_t = p^{-1} \cdot D_t$. Instead we recommend determination of $z_{1kt}(k = 1, \ldots, n)$ with the help of systematic simulation.

Furthermore, an objective function is needed in order to determine the optimal number of admissions. We recommend the following objective function:

$$\sum_{k=1}^{n} f_k \cdot z^*_{1kt} = \max_{\{Z_t\}} \sum_{k=1}^{n} f_k \cdot z_{1kt} \qquad (4.2.)$$

where $z^*_{11t}, \ldots, z^*_{1nt}$ are the optimal admission numbers. We call

$$Z^*_t = \begin{pmatrix} z^*_{11t} \\ \cdot \\ \cdot \\ \cdot \\ z^*_{1nt} \end{pmatrix}$$

the optimal admission vector; f_k $(k = 1, \ldots, n)$ are weighing factors attached to each z_{1kt} $(k = 1, \ldots, n)$. The numerical determination of the factors f_k stems from considerations outside the model itself, e.g. concerning student demands, manpower requirements, or costs of a study place.

A special case of (4.2.) is $f_k = 1$ for all $k = 1, \ldots, n$:

$$\sum_{k=1}^{n} z^*_{1kt} = \max \sum_{k=1}^{n} z_{1kt}. \qquad (4.3.)$$

The problem of determing the optimal admission vector z^*_t is described by (4.2.) or (4.3.), respectively, together with (4.1.) as the system of constraints and with (3.4.) as the system which links (4.2.) and (4.1.); the full (3.4.) optimization problem reads as follows:

$$\sum_{k=1}^{n} f_k \cdot z^*_{1kt} = \max_{\{Z_t\}} \sum_{k=1}^{n} f_k \cdot z_{1kt}$$

subject to constraints

$$z_{1kt} \in \{0, 1, 2, \ldots\} \text{ for all } k = 1, \ldots, n \qquad (4.4.)$$

$$d_{\mu t} \leqslant y_{\mu t} \text{ for all } \mu \, | \, v_\mu \in V$$

$$S_t = P^{-1} \cdot D_t, \ Z_t \to S_t.$$

As soon as, by simulation, the optimization task (4.4) is fulfilled it is to be determined for which courses v_μ the equal sign holds in (4.1.); these courses are identified as bottle-necks which prevent the student population expanding The information concerning the bottle-necks is forwarded to the *funds allocation manager* who can now try to reallocate funds in such a way that the bottle-necks are eliminated as far as possible. We have to understand this task as an iteration process which repeatedly runs through (4.4.) with increased capacity numbers $y_{\mu t}$ for those courses which can be eliminated as bottle-necks. This reallocation process is not formalized here. So far the admission optimization process may be outlined by Fig. 1. Up to now the time-structure of the problem has not been duly regarded: the possibility of bottle-necks occuring in future semesters is explicitly to be taken into consideration. It is guaranteed that the students to be admitted for (calendar) semester t, Z^*_t, do not run into bottle-necks in t but there is no guarantee for the semesters to come: $t + 1, t + 2, \ldots$ Of course, this consideration is relevant only in the

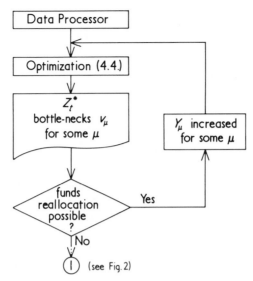

Fig. 1. Conceptual Diagram of Admissions Optimization

situation of an expanding student population, as we have it now.

In order to make sure that the students admitted now will not run into bottle-necks during their whole educational process, up to their graduation, a series of "*capacity overload checks*" with respect to T_2 has to be carried out.

After the optimization (4.4.) and, perhaps, the proper funds reallocation process have been performed Z_t^* is determined within a first round. Z_t^* of the first round may be denoted by $Z_t^{(1)}$ The corresponding student vector which includes $Z_t^{(1)}$ may be denoted by $S_t^{(1)}$ being the student vector which will be realized after the admissions $Z_t^{(1)}$ have taken place. Up to this stage $S_t^{(1)}$ is still hypothetical.

By means of the transition matrix Q the corresponding student vector for $t + 1$ is calculated:

$$\hat{S}_{t+1}^{(1)} = Q \cdot S_t^{(1)}. \tag{4.5.}$$

This vector $\hat{S}_{t+1}^{(1)}$ is incomplete insofar as it does *not* include freshmen (in $t + 1$). Now, by means of (3.4) and (4.1.) the "capacity overload check" is performed:

$$D_{t+1}^{(1)} = P \cdot \hat{S}_{t+1}^{(1)} \tag{4.6.}$$

$$d_{\mu, t+1}^{(1)} \leq y_{\mu, t+1} \quad \text{for all } \mu \mid v_\mu \in V. \tag{4.7.}$$

Here we have to distinguish two cases:

First, (4.7.) holds. Then the quasi-forecast of the student population and the capacity overload check are repeated with respect to $t + 2$(and $j = 1$); in a more general notation:

Menges, Flstermann

$$\hat{S}_{t+1}^{(j)} = Q^i . S_t^{(j)}$$

$$D_{t+i}^{(j)} = P . \hat{S}_{t+1}^{(j)}$$

(4.8.)

$$d_{\mu,\,t+i}^{(j)} \leqslant y_{\mu,\,t+i} \quad \text{for all } \mu \,|\, v_\mu \in V$$

$$\text{for } \{t,\dots,t+i\} \leqslant T_2, \quad i = 1, 2, \dots$$

$$j = 1, 2, \dots$$

Second, (4.7.) does not hold; the $v_\mu \in V$ for which $\nleqslant$ in (4.7) are identified as future bottle-necks. If the funds allocation manager succeeds in reallocating resources so that some relevant y_μ can be increased, (4.8.) is applied again for $i = 1$. If not, or if the reallocation process does not result in (4.7.) to hold, respectively, a new (hypothetical) admission vector

$$Z_t^{(2)} \leqslant Z_t^{(1)},$$

i.e. $\qquad\qquad z_{1kt}^{(2)} < z_{1kt}^{(1)} \quad$ for at least one k,

is to be fixed.

It cannot be formalized here how to determine those components of $Z_t^{(2)}$ which are smaller than the corresponding components of $Z_t^{(1)}$. It is rather a heuristic process which should use the information provided by the identification of those $v_\mu \in V$ for which $\nleqslant$ in (4.7.), in connection with (4.6.) and (4.5.). Given $Z_t^{(2)}$ the capacity overload check (4.8.) is repeated with $j = 2$.

The choice between different competing admission vectors $Z_t^{(j)}$ is made with respect to the objective function (4.2.) or (4.3.), respectively.

This process is continued until, within T_2, an overall optimal admission vector is determined.

The whole process (with the exception of the optimal determination of $Z_t^{(j)}$) is outlined in Fig. 2, which can be regarded as an extension of Fig. 1.

2.5. Determination of Optimal Admission Numbers for N Periods

If we expand the considerations of paragraph 2.4. to the case of more than one period it might be useful to shape the problem in such a way as to make dynamic-programming techniques applicable (cp. (18), § 26).

We interpret each semester $\tau(\tau = 0, 1, 2, \dots, N)$ as a stage of a student flow process. At each stage τ, this process is characterized by the student vector S_τ. The sequence

$$S = (S_0, S_1, \dots, S_N)$$

determines the flow of the process. In the present context we call S_0 the initial state of the process.

At each stage an optimal admission vector $Z_\tau^*(\tau = 1, 2, \dots, N)$ is to be chosen from the set of possible admission vectors $\mathcal{Z}_\tau$. $\mathcal{Z}_\tau$ is a set of vectors each of which consists of elements belonging to $\mathcal{N} = \{0, 1, 2, \dots\}$

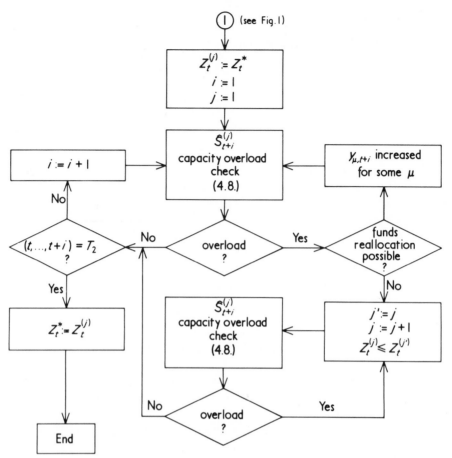

Fig. 2. Conceptual Diagram of Capacity Overload Check in Admissions Optimization

The sequence
$$Z = (Z_1, Z_2, \ldots, Z_N)$$

is called an *admission policy*. The problem is to find an optimal admission policy.

Our process is *Markovian* in that each student vector $S_\tau (\tau = 1, \ldots, N)$ depends only on the previous state $S_{\tau-1}, (\tau = 1, \ldots, N)$ and on the admission vector $Z_\tau (\tau = 1, \ldots, N)$. The transition from $S_{\tau-1}$ to $S_\tau (i = 1, \ldots, N)$ is expressed by the transformation (cp. (3.1.))

$$S_\tau = T(S_{\tau-1}, Z_\tau) (\tau = 1, \ldots, N). \tag{5.1.}$$

In choosing $Z_\tau (\tau = 1, \ldots, N)$ we have to observe that by the following restrictions

$$d_{\mu t} \leqslant y_{\mu t} \text{ for all } \mu \,|\, v_\mu \in V$$

$(t = \tau, \tau + 1, \ldots, \tau + N'; N' = \text{average duration of studies})$

$$D_\tau = P.(Q.S_{\tau-1} + Z_\tau) \tag{5.2.}$$

Menges, Elstermann

$$D_t = P \cdot \hat{S}_t \, (t = \tau + 1, \ldots, \tau + N')$$

$$(\text{cp. } (3.4.5.))$$

a set of admissible admission vectors

$$\mathfrak{z}_\tau(S_{\tau-1}) = \{Z_\tau\}$$

is defined. The set of all admissible policies, denoted by $\mathfrak{z}$, is the set of all sequences $Z = (Z_1, Z_2, \ldots, Z_N) \in \mathfrak{z}$ for which (5.2.) holds.

In dynamic programming the optimal policy is a function of the initial state S_0, and we denote these "policy functions" by $\tilde{Z} = (\tilde{Z}_1, \ldots, \tilde{Z}_N)$; for a state $\bar{S}_0$ we have:

$$\tilde{Z}(\bar{S}_0) = \bar{Z} \in \mathfrak{z}$$

$$Z: \{S_0\} \to \mathfrak{z}.$$

(5.3.)

The set of all policy functions is denoted by $\tilde{\mathfrak{z}} = \{\tilde{Z}\}$.

To each transformation from $S_{\tau-1}$ to $S_\tau (\tau = 1, \ldots, H)$ we attach a loss

$$\bar{\lambda}(S_{\tau-1}, S_\tau) \ (\tau = 1, \ldots, N)$$

or, because of (5.1.) and (5.3.),

$$\bar{\lambda}(S_{\tau-1}, S_\tau) = \lambda(S_{\tau-1}, Z_\tau) = \tilde{\lambda}(S_{\tau-1}, \tilde{Z}_\tau) \ (\tau = 1, \ldots, N).$$

The simplest way of expressing the losses $\lambda(S_{\tau-1}, Z_\tau)$ would be the use of the differences between the number of high school graduates H_τ willing to study, in the region relevant for the university on hand, and (cp. (4.2.))

$$\sum_{k=1}^{n} f_k z_{1kt} :$$

$$\lambda(Z_\tau) \propto (H_\tau - \sum_{k=1}^{n} f_k z_{1k\tau}) \ (\lambda = 1, \ldots, N).$$

(5.3.)

Another way is the use of a *Gaussian* loss function

$$\lambda(Z_\tau) \propto (H_\tau - \sum_{k=1}^{n} f_k z_{1k\tau})^2.$$

(5.4.)

Other forms are possible. (5.3.) and (5.4.) seem to be justified from the following point of view: Each high school graduate who though willing is not admitted to study means a "social loss". The greater the number of rejected applicants the greater is the "social loss".

In a more general way the loss function is not only dependent on the difference

$$H_\tau - \sum_{k=1}^{n} f_k z_{1k\tau}$$

but also on the number of students already enrolled. This philosophy, in addition, takes into consideration manpower requirement aspects. The general type of loss function may be expressed as follows:

$$\lambda(S_0, Z_\tau) \quad (\tau = 1, \dots, N). \tag{5.5.}$$

Now we have to aggregate the losses of the single stages. The simplest way of determining the total loss L would be:

$$L^N(S_0, \tilde{Z}) = \sum_{\tau=1}^{N} \tilde{\lambda}(S_{\tau-1}, \tilde{Z}_\tau) \tag{5.6.}$$

with (5.1.).

The admission policy function $\tilde{Z}^* \in \tilde{\mathfrak{z}}$ for which

$$L^N(S_0, \tilde{Z}^*) = \min_{Z \in \mathfrak{z}} L^N(S_0, \tilde{Z}) \tag{5.7.}$$

is the optimal one. And for a particular initial state $\bar{S}_0$ the optimal admission policy

$$\bar{Z}^* = \tilde{Z}^*(\bar{S}_0) \in \mathfrak{z}$$

is determined.

The Markovian property (5.1.) and the form of the overall loss function (5.6), together, allow for the application of dynamic programming.

We introduce the notations

$$\tilde{\mathfrak{z}}^n = \{\tilde{Z}^n\} = \{(Z_1, \dots, Z_n)\} \quad (1 \leqslant n \leqslant N)$$

and

$$L^n_{min}(S_0) = \min_{\tilde{Z}^n \in \tilde{\mathfrak{z}}^n} L^n(S_0, \tilde{Z}^n).$$

Then, the optimal policy functions $\tilde{Z}^*$ result from the following recursion system:

$$L^1_{min}(S_0) = \min_{\tilde{Z}_1 \in \tilde{\mathfrak{z}}^1} \tilde{\lambda}(S_0, \tilde{Z}_1)$$

$$L^{n+1}_{min}(S_0) = \min_{\tilde{Z}_{n+1} \in \tilde{\mathfrak{z}}^1} [\tilde{\lambda}(S_0, \tilde{Z}_{n+1}) + L^n_{min}(T(S_0, \tilde{Z}_{n+1}))] \tag{5.8.}$$

$$n = 1, \dots, N - 1.$$

3. References

1. Pressmar, D.B. (1969) "Die Verwendung eines elektronischen Daten-verarbeitungssystems bei der zentralen Zuteilung von Studienplätzen"; *Technische Mitteilungen AEG-Telefunken*, 5. Beiheft Datenverarbeitung, p. 6–14.

2. Habermas J. (1969) *Protestbewegung und Hochschulreform*; Suhrkamp, Frankfurt am Main.

3. Krings, H. (1969) "Zugang zu den Hochschulen"; *Wissenschaftsrecht – Wissenschaftsverwaltung – Wissenschaftsförderung*, Beiheft 3, p. 53–105.

4. Bessai, B., Elstermann, G., Lutz, H., and Redelberger, M. (1970) "Projektion des Lehrpersonalbedarfs einer Universität mit Hilfe der Krings-Finkenstaedt-Formel"; *Wissenschaftsrecht – Wissenschaftsverwaltung – Wissenschaftsförderung*, Vol. 3, p. 148–164.

5. Redelberger, M. (1969) "Kapazitätserhebungen in der Universität des Saarlandes"; *Planung und Organisation in der Hochschule*, Ed. H.J. Schuster, Universität des Saarlandes, Saarbrücken, p. 79–88.

6. Bessai, B., Elstermann, G., Lutz, H., and Redelberger, M. (1969) *Modellstudie zur Personalplanung an der Universität des Saarlandes bis zum Jahre 1975*; Ed. H.J. Schuster, Universität des Saarlandes, Saarbrücken.

7. Rumpf, H. (1969) "Über die gesellschaftliche Bedeutung und den Bedarf an wissenschaftlicher Ausbildung und die Berechnung von Ausbildungskapazitäten"; *Deutsche Universitätszeitung*, 1969, No. 17/18, p. 15–19.

8. Wissenschaftsrat (1967) *Empfehlungen des Wissenschaftsrates sum Ausbau der wissenschaftlichen Hochschulen bis 1970*; Mohr (Siebeck), Tübingen.

9. Heckhausen, H. (1968) "Die Ausbildungskapazität im Fach Psychologie: personeller Grundbestand und Berechnungsmodell"; *Psychologische Rundschau*, Vol. 19, p. 79–96.

10. Mahrenholtz, O., and Withum, D. (1969) *Zur Berechnung der Lehrbelastung wissenschaftlicher Hochschulen*; Technische Universität Hannover (mimeographed).

11. Dietze, H.–D. (1970) *Zur Kapazitätsermittlung an Universitäten*; Ed. H.J. Schuster, Universität des Saarlandes, Saarbrücken.

12. Gani, J. (1963) "Formulae for Projecting Enrolments and Degrees Awarded in Universities"; *Journal of the Royal Statistical Society*, Vol. 126, p. 400–409.

13. Stone, R. (1965) "A model of the Educational System"; *Minerva*, Vol. 3, p. 172–186.

14. Caspar, R., Bingert, A., Bayer, W., and Blahusch, F. (1968) *Ein Modell zur Ermittlung der Zulassungszahlen von Studienanfängern an einer wissenschaftlichen Hochschule*; Universität Stuttgart.

15. Braun, H., Hammer, G., and Schmid, K. (1969) "Ein Verfahren zur Ermittlung der Ausbildungskapazität wissenschaftlicher Hochschulen"; *Jahrbücher für Nationalökonomie und Statistik*, Vol. 182, p. 381–397.

16. Hatch, R.S. (1970) "Development of Optimal Allocation Algorithms for Personnel Assignment"; *Models of Manpower Systems*, Ed. A.R. Smith, English Universities Press, London, p. 383–397.

17. Bayer, W., Fischer, K., and Schneider, H.–J. (1969) *Anwendung des Stundenplanprogramms bei der Lehrraumbedarfsermittlung durch Simulation*; Ed. Zentralarchiv für Hochschulbau, Stuttgart.

18. Menges, G. (1969) *Grundmodelle wirtschaftlicher Entscheidungen*; Westdeutscher Verlag, Köln und Opladen.

15
Academic Competition

William P. McReynolds
**University of Waterloo,
Ontario**

Summary

Educational authorities sometimes restrict the number of students who are allowed
to make a certain transition, for example from secondary school to university.
Academic performance, as measured by some kind of test score, is often taken as
the criterion for deciding who will "pass". The educational planner must be concerned with the social implications of such a criterion where it operates differ-
entially on members of different socio-economic classes. In modelling an
academic competition, the author views the students as competing with each other
in some examination or battery of tests in such a way that each student receives
a unique ordinally ranked standing. In addition to this ordinal rank, students are
distinguished only by the socio-economic class to which they belong. The competition is viewed as a stochastic process, the outcome of which is an ordinally
ranked array of persons belonging to different classes. In the model, the expected
outcome of the competition depends only on the number of members of each class,
and a set of parameters called class-linked achievement factors. The model is a
biased urn model without replacement. In the degenerate case in which the
class-linked achievement factors are not different, the model reduces to a multivariate hypergeometric process. An example of such a process, using data for the
Province of Ontario, is given.

In attempting to apply Markov chain models to the flows of students in an
educational system, one is forced sooner or later to come to grips with the
difficult methodological problem of how to cope with dynamically changing
transition proportions in some particular sector of the system (see for example
Thonstad (1), Armitage and Smith (2)). Clough and McReynolds (3), and Clough
(4), suggested that the values that transition proportions may take are limited by
constraints imposed by authorities (who "supply" educational services) and by
constraints determined by the aggregate behavior of students (in exercising their
"demand" for educational services). McReynolds (5) later extended these notions
and applied them to transitions between the final year of secondary school and the
first year of universities, colleges, and other tertiary institutions. The post-

secondary transition may be described as occurring in three separable processes. The first of these is the academic competition, in which students compete by examinations or other means to achieve "standing" which is used as a criterion for selection by educational authorities. The second is the expression by the individual students for the courses of study which they would wish to pursue, and the third and final stage is the selection from among the candidates of those who will be admitted to each course and institution.

The subject of this present paper is the process of academic competition, as it is seen within the particular context of the post-secondary transition, subsidiary to a Markov chain flow model of an educational system.

The problem situation can be summarized briefly as follows. The main flow model will predict the number of persons belonging to each of several different socio-economic classes who can be expected to finish secondary school in a particular year. In order to predict the flows of students into post-secondary courses and institutions, it is necessary to be able to say how many persons from each class will become academically qualified for admission to each course. In general, to be able to consider the effects of different admissions policies, it is necessary to be able to determine the cumulative distribution of class-membership in descending order of academic standing.

The process that will be considered here is assumed to have certain specific properties. The occupants of the final year of secondary school (called the origin) are seen to compete with each other for standing by achieving grades on examinations, by taking tests, by term work or whatever. It is assumed that if one were to examine the documents of two students, one would always be able to say which one had the higher standing. (Later it will be seen that in practice the empirical results do not really depend on this tie-breaking rule). As a result of these assumptions, it is possible to view the students as competitors, who, within the limits of their own motivation, basic ability, work habits, environment and other factors, achieve some kind of rank or standing among their fellow competitors. Some student will stand first, some one second, and so forth, and each student will be given ordinal rank index number ϕ.

The origin has N occupants in a particular year*, of whom N_a belong to a general population class a, where $a = 1, 2, \ldots A$. After competing, they are ranked ordinally according to their achievement. Thus the person who stands first has rank number $\phi = 1$, the person who stands second $\phi = 2$, the person who stands 297th has $\phi = 297$ etc.

To illustrate the academic competition model, two distinctly different processes and models of them will be considered. In one process, an experimenter intervenes by allocating candidates randomly into classes $a = 1, 2, \ldots, A$, such that there are $N_1, N_2 \ldots, N_A$ candidates in the respective classes. In the other process, an experimenter identifies candidates as members of classes $a = 1, 2, \ldots, A$ on the basis of specified attributes (e.g. sex). The latter process is the one that occurs in reality, and its model is the one that is called the academic competition model.

---

* In the main flow model these variables would be indexed for time t, but such time dependence can be ignored in the present discussion.

Consider first a multiclass population in which the class membership is arbitrarily constructed, that is, one in which the population classes are defined by the toss of a coin, the roll of a die, or some other such way that bears absolutely no relationship to academic achievement, with N_a persons in class a, $a = 1, 2, ..., A$. In the flow model, nothing is known about an individual competitor except the class to which the person belongs. Now consider all the competitors in descending order of their standing in the competition, starting with the person who stands first, then the person who stands second and so forth. The set of all competitors constitutes a probability sample space, the examination of the class membership of a person having a particular rank is an experiment, and the class to which he belongs is the outcome of that experiment.

Since it has been assumed that class membership is not connected with standing, and since individuals are indistinguishable within a class, it is equally likely that the person who stands first in the competition is any one of the competitors. The probability of specification is uniform for all elements of the sample space, that is, for all competitors.

The student of probability theory will recognize that the process which has just been described is simply an urn model without replacement, and that this model is the foundation of the multi-variate hypergeometric process.

Let $k_a (\phi)$ denote the number of persons belonging to class a, $a = 1, 2, ..., A$, who obtain in the competition a rank index number less than or equal to ϕ, where $\phi = 1, 2, ..., N$. That is, $k_a (\phi)$ is the number of competitors from class a who stand among the top ranked ϕ competitors. The expected value of $k_a (\phi)$ is obtained by deriving the mean of the marginal distribution of $k_a (\phi)$ from the multivariate hypergeometric distribution. It is found to be (6, 7).

$$\mu(k_a (\phi)) = \frac{N_a}{N} \cdot \phi \qquad a = 1, 2, 3, ..., A. \tag{1}$$

This result can be interpreted in terms of a simple educational flow model. Suppose that entrance to higher education is restricted to the top ranked c competitors. For $\phi = c$, the expected number of persons from class a who will "pass" is $N_a c/N$, for $a = 1, 2, ..., A$. The transition proportion for any class a is just c/N. Thus the transition proportions are the same for all population classes when class membership is assumed to be unrelated to the academic competition.

The introduction of a probability model of the process of competition seems appealing. Although the ultimate interest is in the aggregate behavior of the competitors, if one is to speak of their ordinal ranking according to some criterion of academic achievement, such as the marks obtained on a set of examinations, then one is implicitly thinking of the competitors as individuals. At the same time, even if one knew a great deal about a specific competitor, one could not predict with certainty his performance in the competition, because there are many random factors which might influence the outcome of the competition, however slightly. Furthermore, one does not know all about every competitor; one only knows of those attributes which are used to define the class composition of the population. Members of the same class are, by definition, indistinguishable from each other before the competition determines their ordinal ranking. Another reason for resorting to a probability model in this instance is that the historical behavior of some students who have been observed will be used to predict the behavior of other students who have not yet been in the competition. Under these conditions, no matter how carefully the class definitions are drawn, a certain amount of random variation in the competitive abilities of their membership from year to year seems inevitable.

The probability model described above takes into account the very necessary feature that the outcome of the competition depends on the number of members in each population class, but it has built into it the unrealistic assumption that the standing obtained by an individual is entirely independent of his class membership. The next step in modeling refinement is to withdraw this restriction, and to allow the class membership to be linked with competitive achievement. Instead of random assignment of class membership, let the classes be defined on the basis of some specified attributes of the students which are known, and which are thought to be in some way related to academic performance. *Within* the classes so defined the competitive ability will be considered random, but it will no longer be assumed that there is no difference *between* classes. Class membership is treated as homogeneous; if more were known about the competitors additional partitions would be drawn.

The connection between class membership and standing must apply to each member of the class in the same way. That is, each member of a class derives the same relative stochastic advantage or disadvantage from his class membership as every other member of the same class. This relative advantage or disadvantage applies at the level of the individual, and consequently must not depend on the number of persons who are in the class at the time. The ordinally ranked standing of a randomly selected member of class a depends stochastically on two kinds of influences;

(1) a part which is independent of whatever advantage may be derived from belonging to a particular class, and which reflects only the number of members of each class, as in the previous model.

(2) a class linked factor which applies to each member of a class uniformly, and is independent of the number of competitors belonging to each class.

A stochastic model can be specified which embodies these additional requirements. Consider the competitors again in descending order of their standing in the competition. The person who stands first is selected from the set of all competitors, but here, unlike the earlier model, the probability of selection is not uniform for each person, but rather it depends on the population class to which a person belongs. The probability of selection for any person in any class a is the same as for any other person in that class, but it may not be the same for a person in some other class a".

The symmetry that exists in the earlier model is absent in this more general version. In the first case, where it was assumed that the probability of selection is uniform for all competitors, the probability of selecting a person from any class a as the person of rank $\phi + 1$ is conditional on the number of previous selections $k_a(\phi)$, $a = 1, 2, ..., A$, among the first ϕ persons. This conditional probability is denoted by $P_{\phi + 1}[a]$ and is given by

$$P_{\phi+1}[a] = \frac{N_a - k_a(\phi)}{\displaystyle\sum_{a=1}^{A}(N_a - k_a(\phi))} = \frac{N_a - k_a(\phi)}{N - \phi}, \quad a = 1, 2, ..., A. \tag{2}$$

In the more general (and more realistic) case the probability of selection is not assumed to be uniform for all competitors but only for competitors belonging to the same class. The constant of proportionality is written w_a where $a = 1, 2, ..., A$. The conditional probability $P_{\phi+1}[a]$ becomes

$$P_{\phi+1}[a] = \frac{(N_a - k_a(\phi))\, w_a}{\displaystyle\sum_{a=1}^{A}(N_a - k_a(\phi))\, w_a}, \quad a = 1, 2, ..., A. \tag{3}$$

The parameters w_a are independent of the number of competitors in each population class, and express the relative advantage or disadvantage that comes to a person by belonging to a particular class, in terms of his potential achievement in a particular competition. The term *class-linked achievement factors* has been coined to describe the parameters w_a. Note that the numerical factors are not yet determined uniquely, but that they may be scaled by any arbitrary multiplication factor without changing the probability expressions in which they appear. It is convenient to normalize them by stipulating their sum, e.g.

$$\sum_{a=1}^{A} W_a = 1.$$

Because of the dependence of selection probabilities on class membership through the bias introduced by the factors $w_1, w_2, ..., w_a$, the probabilities of the elementary sample points are in general different, and thus far it has not been possible to derive the probability distribution function and its moments as was possible for the more simple case which leads to the multi-variate hypergeometric distribution. In practice, fortunately, the inability to obtain explicit functional representation does not prevent the application of the probability model including class dependence to real competitions.

In the case of a competition involving a large number of competitors, an approximation can be utilized in order to estimate the class-linked achievement factors and hence compute the expected class distribution on the ordinally ranked array of competitors.

In equation (3) setting $\phi = \phi + \theta < N$, and manipulating gives

$$P_{\phi+\theta+1}[a] = \frac{(N_a - k_a(\phi))w_a\left(1 - \dfrac{k_a(\phi+\theta) - k_a(\phi)}{N_a - k_a(\phi)}\right)}{\displaystyle\sum_{a=1}^{A}(N_a - k_a(\phi))w_a\left(1 - \dfrac{k_a(\phi+\theta) - k_a(\phi)}{N_a - k_a(\phi)}\right)} \tag{4}$$

If the interval θ corresponding to an additional number of selections is kept sufficiently small, and if there remains a sufficiently large number of persons in each class whose standing has not been considered, then

$$\frac{k_a(\phi+\theta) - k_a(\phi)}{N_a - k_a(\phi)} \ll 1 \tag{5}$$

and, as an approximation,

$$P_\phi[a] = P_{\phi+\theta}[a]. \tag{6}$$

That is, for short intervals in which there are many unselected members of each class, the probability of selecting a member of class a can be treated as a constant. The expectation of the number of persons of class a selected in a short interval $(\phi, \phi+\theta)$ is approximately equal to $P_\phi[a]_\theta$. This is equivalent to the binomial approximation to the hypergeometric probability law, where for a small number of trials from a large population, sampling without replacement is approximated by sampling with replacement. This approximation is used later in the empirical analysis leading to the estimation of the class-linked achievement factors.

On the basis of theoretical considerations only, a probability model has been devised which describes the correspondence between class membership and the ordinal ranking of students on a set of competitive examinations. Before the model becomes anything but a theoretical exercise, it will be necessary to show that the parameters of the model are:

(a) *estimable*, in the sense that one can take the results of a real competition and compute the values of the class-linked achievement factors which must have been operative in that competition, to the extent that the probability model is a valid description of the real process;

(b) *sensitive*, in the sense that the class-linked achievement factors are in fact distinguishably different from each other when the classes are well defined;

(c) *reasonable*, in the sense that the class-linked achievement factors operate to endow relative advantage or disadvantage in the competitive process in the way that the class attributes are believed to operate;

(d) *usable*, in the sense that the estimated values of the w_a's can be used to simulate the results of other competitions (having different number of competitors) under the same general conditions.

In the absence of a data bank which was specifically designed for the purposes of this model, it was necessary to "make do" with the best data source available. In Ontario, a longitudinal study (8) was done using the scholastic records of all the approximately 90,000 students who entered high school in 1959. The individual records were made available for the purposes of this research. Several thousand of these students reached the final year of secondary school (Grade 13), and many of them wrote a set of examinations which were set and marked by central authorities. (Strictly speaking, not all of the students "competed" with each other since some of them were delayed by being required to repeat grades, but the form of the examinations was not greatly changed over the interval.)

Having chosen the Grade 13 examinations as the paradigm of competition, there remained three other fundamental choices to be made in the application of the probability model:

(1) the definitions of population classes.

(2) the criterion by which academic achievement is to be judged and individuals ranked.

(3) the interval θ and the residual number of unselected persons, that is $(N_a - k_a(\phi))$.

The choice of population classes must be consistent with those of the main flow model. In general, the classes are chosen to emphasize either differences in achievement or differences in personal preferences in education options. The attributes upon which the classes are based must be measurable, and if long range forecasting is to be attempted the class memberships also must be amenable to forecasting.

The criterion for academic achievement should be expressed, if possible, in the same form that is used in statements of admissions policies, promotion policies, scholarship policies, or other expressions of administrative policies in the educational system. For example, if the specific transitions being studied are from the final year of high school to the freshman year of college, and if the admission policies are stated in terms of achievement on a standardized college entrance examination, then the criterion which is relevant is the marks obtained on that examination. Similarly, if the admission policy is stated in terms of average of the best marks obtained in nine particular examination papers written over any number of years, then that is the appropriate criterion of academic achievement. A wide range of complex criteria are possible, as long as they can be used to rank the candidates ordinally, and as long as they are stated in a form that is relevant to educational policy statements and transition decisions.

The choice of the size of the interval θ involves a compromise between two different considerations. On the one hand, the interval should be as small as possible, so that the probability of selecting a person of any class a remains essentially constant over the interval. On the other hand, the interval should be as large as possible, in order to give the effect of having repeated samples at that constant probability, and in order to make the method insensitive to ties between competitors. The specific compromise which is made will depend to a large extent on the number of competitors and their respective class membership, the criterion of academic achievement and the class-linked achievement factors which are operative in the competition under study. The nature of this compromise will be clarified by the descriptions of the empirical analysis and the examples given. The number of persons who remain unselected in the process must be large compared with the size of the interval θ.

In the example, there are 18 population classes based on three factors; sex, mother's education, and community size. The sex variable has two levels, male and female. The highest educational attainment of the mother is divided into three categories; (1) did not complete high school, (2) completed high school but did not go to college, (3) took at least some college level studies. The size of the community is utilized as another attribute with three size ranges considered:

(1) communities of less than 6000 total population.

(2) communities between 6000 and 109 999 total population.

(3) communities of 110 000 or greater total population.

Table 1 summarizes the 18 class definition of the example and gives the population class code numbers.

TABLE 1: Class definitions and code numbers for 18-class
population used as example of competition.

Community Size	Mother did not complete high school	Mother completed high school	Mother had at least some college
less than 6000	Male – Class 1 Female – Class 10	Male – Class 4 Female – Class 13	Male – Class 7 Female – Class 16
6000 to 109 999	Male – Class 2 Female – Class 11	Male – Class 5 Female – Class 14	Male – Class 8 Female – Class 17
110 000 or more	Male – Class 3 Female – Class 12	Male – Class 6 Female – Class 15	Male – Class 9 Female – Class 18

The criterion used to rank the competitors in order of standing is the total marks obtained by an individual on his best nine examination papers written in Grade 13. In this example, the selection was restricted to those students who wrote at least nine papers (conforming approximately to the form of the University of Toronto admission criterion from that time). Rejection of the records of students who wrote less than nine examinations, or records which were incomplete or bore recognizable errors cut the sample down from over seventeen thousand to 9681. An interval of $\phi = 1000$ was chosen for the empirical analysis.

The first computational step was to ordinally rank the students according to the criterion of achievement by means of computer "sort" routine. Next, the competitors so ranked were divided into the appropriate intervals (indexed by j) of 1000 persons, and the number of members of each population class occurring in each interval were enumerated. Table 2 shows the results of this enumeration for the example. Here it can be seen that the method is insensitive to ties in the ordinal ranking of competitors, since what is really being observed in practice is the interval of 1000 persons into which an individual falls.

An entry in Table 2 is denoted by $x_a(j)$, $a = 1, 2, ..., A$, where j is the interval number, define as

$$j = 1, \quad 1 \leqslant \phi \leqslant 1000$$
$$j = 2, \quad 1001 \leqslant \phi \leqslant 2000$$

etc., down to
$$j = 10 \quad 9001 \leqslant \phi \leqslant 9681$$

and $x_a(j)$ is the number of competitors belonging to class a who are encountered in the j-th interval. Note that interval 10 is incomplete, containing fewer than one thousand persons, but for $j = 1, ..., 9$

$$\sum_{a=1}^{A} x_a(j) = 1000.$$

It will be noticed on Table 2 that for some classes (e.g. class 1) the entries $x_a(j)$ increase as j increases, while the entries decrease as j increases for some other classes (e.g. class 9). That is, class 1 is relatively under-represented at the high end of the achievement scale, and class 9 is relatively over-represented

McReynolds

Interval j

Class Number a	1	2	3	4	5	6	7	8	9	10
1	11	41	38	41	53	54	56	61	81	56
2	63	81	85	100	99	105	119	127	115	81
3	81	85	101	80	86	96	79	80	100	84
4	28	25	22	27	31	24	32	37	39	34
5	89	77	89	75	79	94	103	86	77	62
6	126	106	97	93	84	79	93	78	89	64
7	8	11	6	12	7	7	13	13	5	9
8	45	28	32	26	19	20	23	27	15	16
9	72	36	35	31	25	25	17	24	27	18
10	29	37	50	49	54	51	51	51	64	44
11	77	101	89	116	101	114	102	107	113	64
12	61	81	76	85	82	85	83	74	63	38
13	21	24	30	27	35	43	46	33	37	22
14	83	93	94	96	87	77	78	82	79	31
15	109	85	88	84	91	70	58	73	59	30
16	7	11	7	11	11	11	6	11	7	5
17	41	32	29	27	32	21	18	16	17	7
18	49	46	32	20	24	24	23	20	13	16

at the high end of the achievement scale. Table 3 gives the same data as Table 2 but in cumulative form, so that an entry in Table 3 is interpreted as $\sum_{j=1}^{i} x_a(j)$, where j is the interval number.

At the start of interval j, the number of members of any class a remaining to be selected is equal to the initial total number of that class, less those who have been selected, that is to say, $N_a - \sum_{j=1}^{j-1} x_a(j)$. At the end of interval j, the number remaining to be selected is, similarly $N_a - \sum_{j=1}^{j} x_a(j)$. Let $\bar{N}_a(j)$ denote the average number of persons of some class a from among whom selections are made in the j-th interval, that is,

$$\bar{N}_a(j) = \frac{1}{2}\left(N_a - \sum_{i=1}^{j-1} x_a(i) + N_a - \sum_{i=1}^{j} x_a(i) \right) \tag{7}$$
$$= N_a - \sum_{i=1}^{j-1} x_a(i) - \frac{1}{2} x_a(j).$$

If the size of the interval θ has been well chosen, then the probability of selection for members of class a is approximately constant over an interval (so long as there are many unselected members of each class) and equal to

Interval

Class Number	1	2	3	4	5	6	7	8	9	10
1	11	52	90	131	184	238	294	355	436	492
2	63	144	229	329	428	533	652	779	894	975
3	81	166	267	347	433	529	608	688	788	872
4	28	53	75	102	133	157	189	226	265	299
5	89	166	255	330	409	503	606	692	769	831
6	126	232	329	422	506	585	678	756	845	909
7	8	19	25	37	44	51	64	77	82	91
8	45	73	105	131	150	170	193	220	235	251
9	72	108	143	174	199	224	241	265	292	310
10	29	66	116	165	219	270	321	372	436	480
11	77	178	267	383	484	598	700	807	920	984
12	61	142	218	303	385	470	553	627	690	728
13	21	45	75	102	137	180	226	259	296	318
14	83	176	270	366	453	530	608	690	769	800
15	109	194	282	366	457	527	585	658	717	747
16	7	18	25	36	47	58	64	75	82	87
17	41	73	102	129	161	182	200	216	233	240
18	49	95	127	147	171	195	218	238	251	267

$$P_\phi[a] = \frac{w_a \bar{N}_a(j)}{\sum\limits_{a=1}^{A} w_a \bar{N}_a(j)} \qquad a = 1, 2, \ldots, A; \ 1000(j-1) < \phi \leqslant 1000j \quad (8)$$

$$= \frac{w_a \left(N_a - \sum\limits_{i=1}^{j-1} x_a(i) - \frac{1}{2} x_a(j) \right)}{\sum\limits_{a=1}^{A} w_a \left(N_a - \sum\limits_{i=1}^{j-1} x_a(i) - \frac{1}{2} x_a(j) \right)}.$$

The expected number of selections from class a' in a sequence of $\theta = 1000$ trials in the j-th interval is

$$P_\phi[a].\theta = P_\phi[a]\ 1000, \ 1000(j-1) < \phi \leqslant 1000j.$$

The sample estimate of this expectation is just $x_a(j)$. The probability of occurrence for a member of a on any trial in the j-th interval is given in equation (8). The estimate for the j-th interval of the class linked achievement factor w_a is written as $\hat{w}(j)$ and the factor $\sum\limits_{a=1}^{A} w_a \left(N_a - \sum\limits_{i=1}^{j-1} x_a(i) - \frac{1}{2} x_a(j) \right)$ is written $Q(j)$. This gives.

$$x_a(j) = \frac{\hat{w}_a(j) \left(N_a - \sum\limits_{i=1}^{j-1} x_a(i) - \frac{1}{2} x_a(j) \right)}{Q(j)} \times 1000 \qquad (9)$$

Cross-multipilication produces

$$\hat{w}_a(j) = \frac{x_a(j)}{1000} \cdot \frac{Q(j)}{\bar{N}_a(j)} \tag{10}$$

where, as usual, a refers to any population class 1, 2, ..., A.

Every variable on the right hand side of (10) is known exept $Q(j)$, and $Q(j)$ is a factor independent of the particular class a under discussion. By the normalization condition for the class-linked achievement factors,

$$\sum_{a=1}^{A} \hat{w}_a(j) = 1$$

$$Q(j) = \frac{1000}{\dfrac{x_1(j)}{\bar{N}_1(j)} + \dfrac{x_2(j)}{\bar{N}_2(j)} + \dots + \dfrac{x_a(j)}{\bar{N}_a(j)}} \tag{11}$$

Hence $Q(j)$ can also be expressed in terms of known quantities, and it is now possible to compute $\hat{w}_a(j)$ for $a = 1, 2, \dots, A$ and $j = 1, 2, \dots$. Table 4 shows the results of such a calculation using the data from the example. Each interval j in Table 4 gives an independent estimate of the class-linked achievement factors, but of course in the right-most columns ($j = 8, 9$, etc.) the approximation of repeated selection under equal probability is no longer valid. Variations in w_a within a row are statistical fluctuations which tend to be larger for smaller values of θ, the interval size.

In the example, the attributes of the students which were used to define the classes were chosen specifically because they were believed to be associated with educational achievement. It is interesting, however, to interpret the results without making this assumption a priori. The class-linked achievement factors can be thought of as observations on a random variable w, and the associated class attributes can be thought of as "treatments" which may or may not condition the random variable. If the treatments do not, in fact, condition the random variable, then the several observations of the random variable may be thought of as samples from the same population.

The technique of analysis of variance v as used to test the hypothesis that any apparent systematic differences in the class-linked achievement factors can be attributed to random variations introduced by the sampling and estimation. Each interval of size θ produces an independent estimate of the w's and is in this sense a replication of the experiment of sampling the random variable w, if the null hypothesis is true. The results of this test show that, if the hypothesis is correct, a highly unlikely event (well beyond the 1% confidence level for all the main effects of sex, mother's education and community size) has taken place. The null hypothesis is difficult to accept. This statistical inference must be weighed together with other evidence before any stronger conclusion can be drawn about the class-linked achievement factor.

Table 5 gives the mean values over the first seven intervals for the estimated class-linked achievement factors for the eighteen-class population used in the example. It remains to be decided how well these estimates satisfy the requirements for the empirical analysis that were set down earlier.

TABLE 4: Estimated class-linked achievement factors for 18-class population writing Ontario Grade 13 examinations [$w_a(i)$]. (Six decimal places are used for the benefit of readers who wish to repeat the calculations. It is not claimed that the factors are estimated with this degree of precision)

Class Number (a)	1	2	3	4	5	6	7	8	9
1	0.01058	0.03780	0.03531	0.03561	0.04399	0.04398	0.04345	0.04166	0.05644
2	0.03123	0.03946	0.04217	0.04761	0.04607	0.04859	0.05455	0.05599	0.05583
3	0.04557	0.04822	0.06028	0.04692	0.04953	0.05618	0.04564	0.04086	0.05018
4	0.04596	0.04106	0.03663	0.04256	0.04741	0.03566	0.04453	0.04626	0.04902
5	0.05293	0.04647	0.05612	0.04615	0.04752	0.05736	0.06532	0.05406	0.05152
6	0.06967	0.06166	0.06038	0.05777	0.05240	0.04973	0.04876	0.04647	0.05516
7	0.04301	0.06027	0.03402	0.06628	0.03848	0.03682	0.06804	0.07254	0.02924
8	0.09212	0.06192	0.07728	0.06428	0.04773	0.05029	0.05803	0.06941	0.04292
9	0.12292	0.06948	0.07422	0.06781	0.05620	0.05808	0.03846	0.04817	0.05764
10	0.02914	0.03632	0.05029	0.04783	0.05205	0.04956	0.04847	0.04370	0.05662
11	0.03809	0.05007	0.04572	0.05833	0.05093	0.05889	0.05339	0.05310	0.06306
12	0.04091	0.05490	0.05426	0.06025	0.05928	0.06473	0.06722	0.06134	0.06095
13	0.03195	0.03576	0.04549	0.03899	0.04895	0.06169	0.07014	0.05000	0.06143
14	0.05119	0.05889	0.06374	0.06600	0.06185	0.05712	0.05921	0.06212	0.07535
15	0.07363	0.06061	0.06764	0.06581	0.07530	0.06282	0.05325	0.06654	0.06668
16	0.03921	0.06269	0.04181	0.06452	0.06711	0.07296	0.04046	0.07191	0.05538
17	0.08737	0.07425	0.07440	0.07187	0.09351	0.07015	0.06441	0.05720	0.07375
18	0.09452	0.10016	0.08025	0.05098	0.06169	0.06538	0.06666	0.05867	0.03885

w_1	= 0.03582	w_{10}	= 0.04481
w_2	= 0.04424	w_{11}	= 0.05078
w_3	= 0.05034	w_{12}	= 0.05736
w_4	= 0.04197	w_{13}	= 0.04757
w_5	= 0.05313	w_{14}	= 0.05971
w_6	= 0.05862	w_{15}	= 0.06558
w_7	= 0.04956	w_{16}	= 0.05554
w_8	= 0.06459	w_{17}	= 0.07657
w_9	= 0.06959	w_{18}	= 0.07424

(a) The class-linked achievement factors w_a are *estimable*, in that the results of a real competition can be used to compute their values in the way that was described in the example.

(b) Table 5 shows that when the population classes are defined on the basis of attributes which influence scholastic achievement, the w_a's determined from the results of a real competition are distinguishably different from each other, spanning a range of value from 0.036 to 0.077 in the example. The difference among classes is clearly revealed by the class-linked achievement factors. Thus, the model appears to satisfy the requirement of *sensitivity*.

(c) Certain general observations can be made on the estimated CLAF's given in Table 5.

(i) The w_a's increase with community size. This would indicate that there is some advantage to competitors from larger communities in this particular competition. This may be derived from a greater incentive to gain admission to higher education, or from better teachers and social facilities or some other unidentified factors. Nevertheless, it is consistent with experience, and satisfies the requirement that the class-linked achievement factors be *reasonable*.

(ii) The w_a's increase with the highest education achievement of the competitor's mother. This would indicate that there is some relative advantage in the competition associated with having a well educated mother. This advantage might be produced by higher expectations placed on the student by the family, a higher value placed on education, a better study environment, inherited ability, cultural advantages, or other factors. Such an advantage would also appear to be reasonable.

(iii) There appears to be a slightly higher set of w_a's associated with girls than with boys. This is also reasonable when one considers the different educational behavior of the sexes which was revealed in their respective transition proportion matrices (5).

(d) Using the estimated class-linked achievement factors, it is possible to compute the expected number of persons from each class to be selected in ϕ trials.

At the start of some interval $j + 1$, the total number of occurrences of members of class a is $k_a(j\theta) = \sum_{j=1}^{j} x_a(j)$ and the probability that the next competitor

will belong to class a is, by equation (3).

$$P_{j\theta+1}[a] = \frac{(N_a - \sum_{i=1}^{j} x_a(i)) w_a}{\sum_{a=1}^{A} (N_a - \sum_{j=1}^{j} x_a(i)) w_a} \tag{12}$$

Making the approximation of equation (6) that

$$P_{j\theta+1}[a] = P_{j\theta+2}[a] = \ldots = P_{(j+1)\theta}[a] \tag{13}$$

over a small interval θ, the expected value of $x_a(j+1)$ is

$$E[x_a(j+1)] = P_{j\theta+1}[a] \cdot \theta \tag{14}$$

Thus for the first interval we have

$$F[x_a(1)] = \frac{N_a w_a}{\sum_{a=1}^{A} N_a w_a} \cdot \theta$$

and for the second interval,

$$E[x_a(2)] = \frac{N_a - E[x_a(1)] w_a}{\sum_{a=1}^{A} N_a - E[x_a(1)] \; w_a} \cdot \theta$$

and in general

$$E[x_a(j+1)] = \frac{\left(N_a - \sum_{i=1}^{j} E[x_a(i)]\right) w_a}{\sum_{a=1}^{A}\left(N_a - \sum_{i=1}^{j} E[x_a(i)]\right) w_a} \cdot \theta \tag{15}$$

In the following example, the interval size $\theta = 100$ was adopted, and equation (15) was used recursively to compute the expected number of persons in each population class for each interval of 100 persons. The estimated values of the w_a's was taken from Table 5 and the total number of competitors belonging to each class (N_a) was taken to be the same as in the actual competition described above. The results of this exercise are summarized in Table 6 in a form which is directly comparable with the original observations of Table 3.

To facilitate comparison between the observed cumulative distributions given in Table 3 and the simulated distribution given in Table 6, the same results have been plotted (directly from the computer on a Calcomp plotter) in Figures 1 through 6. It can be seen that the simulated values, represented by the continuous curves, adhere quite closely to the observed values which are represented by the × marks. It should be emphasized that this is not "curve fitting" in the sense that a polynomial of arbitrary order is parametrically adjusted to give the best fit of the observed data according to some such criterion as minimizing the sum of squares of deviations. The simulated cumulative distribution curves are produced directly from repeated applications of the stochastic relationship of Equation (15) which was obtained by elementary consideration of the process of competition. The simulated cumulative distributions are generated by this theoretical relationship

McReynolds

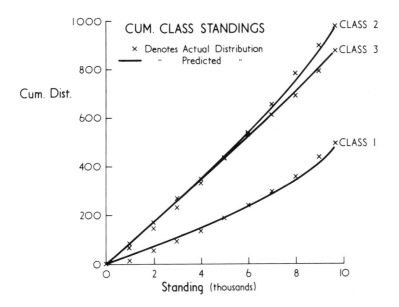

FIG. 1. Cumulative number of persons belonging to classes 1, 2 and 3 appearing among the top-ranked Ø competitors. Points were observed, curves were generated by competition theory.

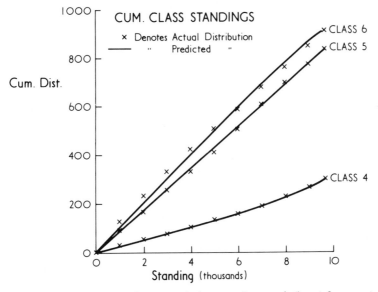

FIG. 2. Cumulative number of persons belong to classes 4, 5 and 6 appearing among the top-ranked Ø competitors. Points were observed, curves were generated by competition theory.

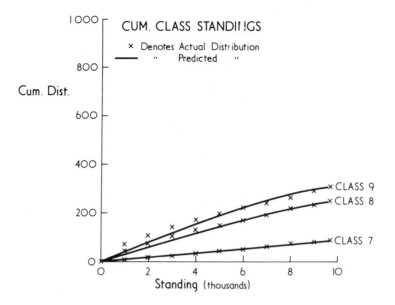

FIG. 3. Cumulative number of persons belonging to classes 7, 8 and 9 appearing among the top-ranked Ø competitors. Points were observed, curves were generated by competition theory.

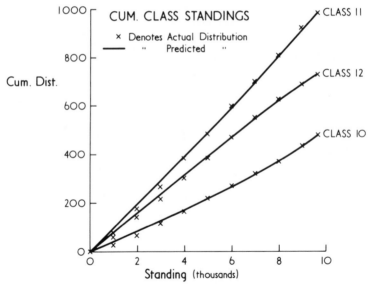

FIG. 4. Cumulative number of persons belonging to classes 10, 11 and 12 appearing among the top-ranked Ø competitors. Points were observed, curves were generated by competition theory.

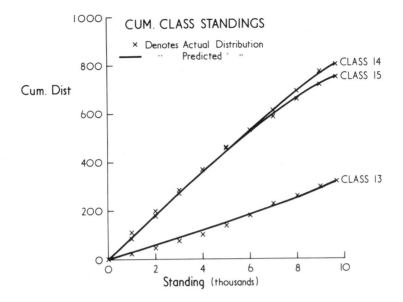

FIG. 5. Cumulative number of persons belonging to classes 13, 14 and 15 appearing among the top-ranked Ø competitors. Points were observed. curves were generated by competition theory.

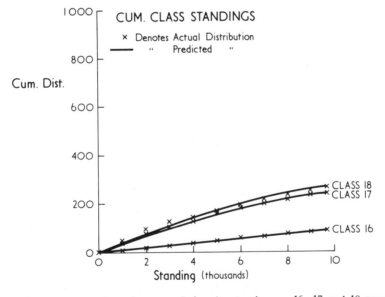

FIG. 6. Cumulative number of persons belonging to classes 16, 17 and 18 appearing among the top-ranked Ø competitors. Points were observed, curves were generated by competition theory.

Academic competition

239

TABLE 6: Simulated values of the cumulative number of persons of class a occurring up to and including interval j ($\theta = 100$).

Class Number	Interval 10	20	30	40	50	60	70	80	90
1	34.2	69.8	107.2	146.7	188.7	234.1	284.1	341.1	411·6
2	83.0	168.1	255.5	345.7	439.1	536.6	639.3	749.4	871.9
3	84.0	169.0	255.0	342.3	430.9	521.1	613.1	707.5	804.9
4	24.2	49.1	74.9	101.6	129.5	158.9	190.2	224.3	263.4
5	84.3	169.0	254.3	340.0	426.3	513.2	600.5	688.3	775.7
6	101.2	201.8	301.7	400.6	498.4	594.5	688.6	779.3	863.7
7	8.6	17.4	26.3	35.3	44.5	53.9	63.5	73.4	83.7
8	30.6	60.7	90.1	118.8	146.5	173.2	198.4	221.7	241.9
9	40.6	80.0	118.1	154.6	189.5	222.3	252.5	279.5	301.4
10	41.4	83.7	127.2	171.9	218.2	266.4	317.0	371.0	430.7
11	95.6	192.2	289.9	388.9	489.2	591.2	695.0	801.1	910.0
12	79.4	158.6	237.4	315.7	393.4	470.3	545.9	619.6	689.3
13	29.0	58.6	88.7	119.4	150.9	183.4	217.0	252.2	289.7
14	90.7	180.6	269.5	357.4	443.9	528.7	611.1	689.9	762.4
15	92.5	183.0	271.4	357.3	440.2	519.5	594.2	662.7	721.3
16	9.2	18.4	27.6	36.8	46.0	55.2	64.3	73.2	81.9
17	34.4	67.2	98.4	127.8	155.2	180.3	202.5	221.4	235.4
18	37.1	72.8	106.9	139.3	159.6	197.6	222.9	244.5	261.2

using only the known number of competitors belonging to each population class and the class-linked achievement factors which have been estimated. If the number of competitors belonging to the various population classes changed, but if the conditions of the competition were otherwise unchanged, the class-linked achievement factors would remain the same, but a different set of curves would be produced by the model.

Without having data from a series of such competitions it is not possible to determine how much the class-linked achievement factors might change from year to year. One might speculate, however, that if the nature of the competition appeared to be the same in terms of such external criteria as the curriculum, the method of testing, etc., then the class-linked achievement factors might very well be exceedingly stable over time. They are, after all, obtained by observations of the aggregate behavior of very large numbers of people. The w_a's represent the average stochastic relative advantage or disadvantage applying to all members of a population class.

The competition model was created in order to be able to predict the distribution of class membership with academic standing, because individual student preferences for various forms of higher education have been found to depend both on class and on standing. Preferences, in turn, are important for simulating transition flows in an educational system under various sets of educational policies. Having once been obtained, however, it appears that the competition model may have a number of other uses that were not originally envisaged. One such area of possible application is in the use of class-linked achievement factors as a statistic of competitive ability. For example, suppose that in addition to the usual attributes used to define population classes, an additional partition is drawn to divide each class into sub-classes on the basis of the type of school attended (e.g. Public, Separate, Private or graded and ungraded). Class-linked achievement factors estimated for the sub-classes would give a measure of how well each school type served to prepare various types of persons for the academic competition. Another application of potential importance is in the direct utilization of cumulative class distributions, both actual and simulated, to evaluate the social implications of certain policies. For example, if class definitions are based on economic attributes of the population, one could use the distribution curves to review whether academic scholarship awards were actually being made in accordance with stated social objectives of increasing socio-economic mobility through education.

Acknowledgements

This paper is based on work done by the author while a member of the faculty of the Department of Educational Planning, The Ontario Institute for Studies in Education. Substantial support from that institute is gratefully acknowledged. The work was also part of a Ph.D. dissertation for the Department of Industrial Engineering, University of Toronto. The author is grateful to Professor D.J. Clough, now Chairman, Department of Management Sciences, University of Waterloo, who served as his thesis advisor.

References

1. Thonstad, T. *Education and Manpower: Theoretical Models and Empirical Applications.* Report No. 4 of the Unit for Economic and Statistical Studies on Higher Education. University of Toronto Press, 1968.

2. Armitage, P., and Smith, C. "The Development of Computable Models of the British Educational System and Their Possible Uses," in *Mathematical Models in Educational Planning.* Paris: OECD, 1967.

3. Clough, D.J., and McReynolds, W.P. "State Transition Model of an Educational System Incorporating a Constraint Theory of Supply and Demand." *Ontario Journal of Educational Research*, 9, 1 (Autumn 1966).

4. Clough, D.J. "A Model for Education-Employment Systems Analysis." *Growth Project Paper GPP 252.* Department of Applied Economics, University of Cambridge, 1967.

5. McReynolds, W.P. *A Model for the Ontario Educational System.* Ph.D. Thesis, Department of Industrial Engineering, University of Toronto, 1969. Also available as *Educational Planning Occasional Paper No. 8*, Department of Educational Planning, The Ontario Institute for Studies in Education, 1969.

6. Wilks, S.S. *Mathematical Statistics.* John Wiley and Sons, 1961.

7. Parzen, E. *Modern Probability Theory and its Applications.* John Wiley and Sons, 1960.

8. *Carnegie Study of Identification and Utilization of Talent in High School and College.* Department of Educational Research, Ontario College of Education, University of Toronto.

16

A Constrained Multinomial Distribution Theory Relating Academic Achievement to Social Class

Donald J. Clough

**University of Waterloo,
Ontario**

Summary

Consider a population of students classified into mutually exclusive social classes $S_1, S_2, \ldots, S_J$ containing $n_1, n_2, \ldots, n_J$ students respectively. On the basis of aggregate examination marks the students are ordinally ranked and the ordinal scale is divided into ordered intervals $T_1, T_2, \ldots, T_I$ containing $m_1, m_2, \ldots, m_I$ students respectively. The number of students from social class S_j who obtain a rank in the interval T_i is x_{ij}, $i = 1, \ldots, I$ and $j = 1, \ldots, J$. This paper specifies a mathematical model based on the following set of hypotheses: (1) the numbers x_{ij} have a joint *constrained multinomial probability distribution*, (2) the numbers x_{ij} must satisfy accounting constraints imposed by the n_j and m_i, and linear constraints of the form $\theta_j = \Sigma_i a_i x_{ij}$, for $j = 1, 2, \ldots, J$, and (3) the observed set of number $\{x_{ij}^0\}$ will be close to the most probable (maximum entropy) set $\{x_{ij}^*\}$. The set of hypotheses is tested with data on Ontario Grade 13 academic rankings for 9681 students in eighteen defined social classes in the year 1964. An approximation formula is developed for predicting changes in the most probable arrangement of number $\{x_{ij}^*\}$ that result from changes in the parameters n_j, m_i and θ_j. The evidence supports the model and its set of hypotheses.

Preface

The mathematical model described in this paper was motivated by two considerations: (1) a particular need for a formula to predict academic standing of students from various social classes (aggregated and individually unidentified), as measured by ordinal rankings based on standard examination results, and (2) a general need for a theory or model to describe statistical regularities in observations of some social phenomena subject to constraints.

The need for a formula to predict relative academic standings on an ordinal scale arises because such ordinal ranking schemes are widely used as a basis for university admission practices. University admission officers commonly start at the top of a list of ordinally ranked applicants and allocate admissions by proceeding down the list until either all the available places in the university are filled (i.e., until a short-run *capacity constraint* is binding), or until a minimum acceptable passing mark is reached (i.e., until an *academic standards* policy constraint is binding). If a relatively large proportion of one population class is admitted and a relatively small proportion of another population class is admitted, such a result may be regarded by some people as *de facto* discrimination.

Academic administrators and public officials in many jurisdictions are evidently concerned about *de facto* discrimination, since it may be affected by changes in capacities (amounts, kinds and locations of educational facilities) and by changes in academic standards, as well as by changes in admissions practices and students' preferences.

For example, consider a simple example in which a population of senior high-school students is divided into two mutually exclusive categories, blacks and whites (or males and females, natives and immigrants, rich and poor). Suppose that all the students compete for places in a university system by writing the same set of entrance examinations, and they are all ranked on an ordinal scale on the basis of total marks achieved on the set of examinations. Suppose that the university admission practice is to start at the top of the list of ordinally ranked students and to allocate places by proceeding down the list until either all the available places are filled or a minimum acceptable passing mark is reached.

If a capacity constraint is binding, such that the number of university places available, u, is smaller than the number of academically qualified students on the ordinally ranked list, then the first u student will be admitted and the remaining students rejected. Suppose the result is that a relatively large percentage of the white population is admitted and a relatively small percentage of the blacks is admitted. In such an event the admission procedure based on academic standing may be regarded by some people as "discriminatory". (The implied measure of discrimination, relative proportions of whites and blacks admitted, is given only for purposes of illustration, without any attempt to justify it.) Some academic administrators and public officials may argue that such apparent "discrimination" is based on a widely accepted and objective academic criterion and is therefore justifiable. However, others may counter-argue that examinations are arbitrarily designed by professors who have been exposed to specific environmental and social conditioning. Their examinations, like I.Q. tests, may measure not only differences in specific categories of intelligence but also differences in environmental and social conditioning. In any event, it may be argued that an academic criterion alone is not relevant under prevailing political conditions and that some combination of criteria for "academic achievement" and " social equity" is relevant.

In reality, conditions are much more complicated than in the simple hypothetical case just considered. In a provincial system of higher education, for example, there may exist a large number of different kinds of academic programme (e.g., arts, engineering law) offered by a large number of universities. Admission criteria may differ from one programme to another or from one university to another and may be based on different sets of entrance examinations. In addition, individual students may state their own ordered preferences for programmes and universities. (For example, in the Province of Ontario, Canada, a student applying for admission to a university indicates his ordered preferences for four different combinations of programme and university, and each of the selected universities has an opportunity to accept or reject the applicant.) Whatever the condition might be, and whatever allocation models are considered, in almost all cases it is necessary to consider an ordinal ranking of candidates based on some standard entrance examination results, and in almost all cases the question of *de facto* discrimination arises.

This paper does not attempt to deal with the problem of causes and remedies for *de facto* discrimination, but only with the associated statistical problem of describing the most probable numbers of students from various social classes falling into ordered intervals on an ordinal ranking scale. The theory developed for fitting a set of estimating equations to data, subject to certain side constraints, may have much broader applicability to a variety of phenomena in the social sciences.

1. Introduction

Mathematical models based on constrained multinomial distributions and the "principle of maximum entropy" are not of recent origin. A review paper by Clough (1964) provides a brief account of historical developments by Clausius (1857) in thermodynamics and kinetic theory of gases, followed by Maxwell, Boltzmann, Planck, Gibbs, and others (1860–1900) in statistical mechanics, Szilard (1929), Shannon (1948), Brillouin (1956) and others in information theory, and Jaynes (1957), Good (1963), and others in engineering and decision-theory applications. A great deal has been made of the fact that particle systems naturally tend to a state of equilibrium at which "entropy is maximized", and workers such as Jaynes (1963) have suggested that other kinds of systems (e.g., inventory systems) exhibit similar behavior. Jaynes proposed that the principle of maximum entropy be assumed as a basis for making decisions in the absence of evidence. Good (1963) and Clough (1964) contended that the Jaynes' formalism was essentially an extension of Laplace's old "principle of insufficient reason" (assuming equiprobable events), and proposed that the principle of maximum entropy be invoked only as a heuristic for generating null hypotheses to be tested by experimental or observational evidence.

Consider a set of discrete random variables $v_1, v_2, \ldots, v_K$. Conventionally, the "principle of maximum entropy" is applied to the special case in which the r.v.'s have a joint probability density

$$f(v_1, \ldots, v_K) = K^{-n} n! / \prod_{k=1}^{K} v_k!$$

where

$$\sum_{k=1}^{K} v_k = n$$

and where additional side constraints may apply to the v_k. The entropy parameter in this special case is given by

$$H(v_1, \ldots, v_K) = - \sum_{k=1}^{K} v_k \ln v_k.$$

The "principle of maximizing entropy" generates that set of discrete values

v_1, v_2, ..., v_K which maximizes H subject to the specified constraints. In this paper the principle is used to generate a null hypothesis concerning the arrangements of students from various social classes on an ordinal scale of academic achievement.

2. Probability and Entropy Measures

Consider a population of students divided into social classes $S_1, \ldots, S_J$ containing $n_1, \ldots, n_J$ students respectively. Suppose the students are allocated into academic achievement classes $T_1, \ldots, T_I$ containing $m_1, \ldots, m_I$ students respectively. The classes S_j, $j = 1, \ldots, J$ are exhaustive and mutually exclusive, as are the classes T_i, $i = 1, \ldots, I$. It follows that

$$\sum_{j=1}^{J} n_j = \sum_{i=1}^{I} m_i = N. \tag{1}$$

The number of students allocated from social class S_j to achievement class T_i is denoted by x_{ij}.

Suppose that the process of allocating students from a social class to an academic achievement class is probabilistic and there are no restrictions on the numbers m_i that can occupy achievement classes. In this case there would be I^N possible ways to allocate N students into I achievement classes. Let us consider this set of I^N ways to allocate as a sample space S containing $w(S) = I^N$ sample points, each having the same probability measure, I^{-N}.

An *event* $E = \{x_{ij}; i = 1, \ldots, I; j = 1, \ldots, J\}$ is defined as a subset of sample points corresponding to the particular set of values x_{ij}. The number of sample points in E (numbers of ways the event can occur) is:

$$w(E) = N! / \prod_{\text{all } i, j} x_{ij}! , \quad \sum_i \sum_j x_{ij} = N. \tag{2}$$

Assuming equal probabilities for all sample points, the probability of the event E is

$$p(E) = w(E) . I^{-N}. \tag{3}$$

Suppose we want to determine the "most probable" event, that particular set of values x_{ij} having the largest probability of occurrence. Since maximimizing $\ln p(E)$ is the same as maximiming $p(E)$, where ln denotes the natural logarithm, we want to maximize the following:

$$\ln p(E) = -N \ln I + \ln N! - \sum_{i=1}^{I} \sum_{j=1}^{J} \ln x_{ij}! \tag{4}$$

If an integer z is large enough, say $z > 30$, Stirling's approximation can be used, as follows:

$$\ln z! = (z + \tfrac{1}{2}) \ln z - z + \ln \sqrt{2\pi}$$

Then:
$$\ln p(E) = \text{constant} - \sum_{i=1}^{I} \sum_{j=1}^{J} x_{ij} \ln x_{ij}. \tag{5}$$

The term on the right is called the entropy measure $\phi(E)$,*

---

* In particle physics, the entropy measure is defined on a set of states and is expressed as a function of the states. In information theory the entropy measure is defined on a probability density function and is a function of the probabilities (a parameter of the probability density function). See references (1) and (2) for the different treatments of entropy.

$$\phi(E) = -\sum_{i=1}^{I} \sum_{j=1}^{J} x_{ij} \ln x_{ij}. \tag{6}$$

Maximizing entropy $\phi(E)$ is the same as maximimizing probability $p(E)$. If there are no restrictions on the numbers m_i that can occupy the achievement classes, the maximum entropy (most probable) event E turns out to be as follows:

$$x_{ij}^* = n_j/I \, , \, i = 1, \, ..., \, I \text{ and } j = 1, \, ..., \, J \tag{7}$$

and

$$m_i = N/I \, , \, i = 1, \, ..., \, I.$$

Now suppose the numbers m_i are fixed, so that the numbers x_{ij} must satisfy the following fixed set of constraints C:

$$\sum_{i=1}^{I} x_{ij} = n_j \, , \, \text{for } j = 1, \, ..., \, J$$

$$\sum_{j=1}^{J} x_{ij} = m_i \, , \, \text{for } i = 1, \, ..., \, I. \tag{8}$$

$$\sum_{j=1}^{J} n_j = \sum_{i=1}^{I} m_i = N.$$

C is a subset of the sample space S. Denoting the number of sample points in C by $w(C)$, the *conditional probability* of a subset (event) E contained in C is given as follows:

$$p(E|C) = w(E)/w(C), \text{ for any } E \subset C, \, (E \cap C = E). \tag{9}$$

The most probable (maximum entropy) event in C is obtained by maximizing $\ln p(E|C)$ which is the same as maximimizing entropy $\phi(E)$, subject to the constraints (8).

The exact maximum entropy (most probable) event itself may have only a small probability of occurrence. However, a union of "near-maximum-entropy" events may have a large probability. Thus, there is a large probability that some set of x_{ij} values close to the maximum entropy set will occur. (Here probabilities are conditional, defined on C.)

Now suppose that in addition to constraints given by (8) there is also a set of constraints B as follows:

$$\sum_{i=1}^{I} a_i x_{ij} = \theta_j \, , \, \text{for } j = 1, \, ..., \, J. \tag{10}$$

Here the a_i are specified parameters representing unit values or "scores" for students allocated to academic achievement classes T_i . And θ_j is a total value or "total score" achieved by students of social class S_j. Each social class is thus characterized by a single parameter θ_j. The intersection of constraints (8) and (10) is described as the set $D = B \cap C$. Denoting the number of sample points in D by $w(D)$, the conditional probability of a subset (event) E contained in D is given by:

$$p(E|D) = w(E)/w(D), \text{ for any } E \subset D. \tag{11}$$

The most probable (maximum entropy) event in D is obtained by maximizing $\ln p(E|D)$, which is the same as maximimizing entropy $\phi(E)$, as given by equation (6), subject to constraints as given by (8) and (10).

3. Maximum Entropy Hypothesis

Let us entertain the null hypothesis that the event which is realized in the experimental application is the one having maximum probability of occurrence, or maximum entropy $\phi(E)$, given by (6), subject to constraints given by (8) and (10), and subject to the conditions that all x_{ij} are positive and large enough for the validity of Stirling's approximation. Under this hypothesis we have the following:

Theorem: The maximum entropy solution is

$$x_{ij}^* = \exp\left[-1 + \alpha_j + \beta_j + a_i \gamma_j\right], \tag{12}$$

where the α_i, β_j and γ_j are parameters to be determined by solving the constraint equations (8) and (10), for $i = 1, ..., I$, and $j = 1, ..., J$.

Proof: From (6), (8) and (10), we form the Lagrangian

$$L = -\sum_i \sum_j x_{ij} \ln x_{ij} + \sum_i \alpha_i \left[\sum_j x_{ij} - m_i\right]$$

$$+ \sum_j \beta_j \left[\sum_i x_{ij} - n_j\right] + \sum_j \gamma_j \left[\sum_i a_i x_{ij} - \theta_j\right], \tag{13}$$

where the $\alpha_i, \beta_j, \gamma_j$ are Lagrange multipliers, $i = 1, ..., I$ and $j = 1, ..., J$. Assuming that the x_{ij} are large enough that they can be approximated as continuous variables, we obtain the maximum point as follows:

$$\partial L / \partial x_{ij} = -\ln x_{ij} - 1 + \alpha_i + \beta_j + a_i \gamma_j = 0, \tag{14}$$

for $i = 1, ..., I$ and $j = 1, ..., J$. The Lagrange multipliers may be determined by substituting from (14) into the constraints (8) and (10).

Note: (a) In (10) a linear rescaling $a_i^* = r + s a_i$, $(r, s$ real), and $i = 1, ..., I$, will not change the form of the solution. (b) It can be shown that at most $I + 2J - 2$ of the constraint equations are linearly independent, and at least two of the $I + 2J$ parameters may be selected arbitrarily.

4. Prediction by Linear Approximation Method

Suppose that the numbers of candidates in social classes S_j, $j = 1, ..., J$, are either known or predicted to be n_j, $j = 1, ..., J$. The total population is $N = n_1 + ... + n_j$. Suppose also that an ordinal ranking scale is arbitrarily subdivided, as described earlier, into sets T_i, $i = 1, ..., I$, respectively containing m_i, $i = 1, ..., I$ candidates, where $N = m_1 + ... + m_I$.

Now suppose that the *relative scores* of the social classes are known from past experience to be θ_j^*, $j = 1, ..., J$. We want to apply a scaling $\theta_j = k\theta_j^*$ such that the constraint equations (10) are satisfied. We note that

$$\sum_i a_i x_{ij} = \theta_j = k\theta_j^* , \, j = 1, ..., J \tag{15}$$

$$M = \sum_i \sum_j a_i x_{ij} = \sum_i a_i m_i = \sum_j \theta_j = k \sum_j \theta_j^*. \tag{16}$$

From (16) we obtain

$$k = \sum_i a_i m_i / \sum_j \theta_j^*. \tag{17}$$

Given only the specified values of the m_i, n_j and θ_j, for $i = 1, ..., I$, and $j = 1, ..., J$, we want to predict the values x_{ij} using the maximum entropy hypothesis.

Approximation

For large numbers z, we note that the logarithmic function $\ln z$ can be approximated by a straight line:

$$\ln z \cong b + cz. \tag{18}$$

For example, in the range $30 \leqslant z \leqslant 150$ the following approximation is acceptable

$$\ln z \cong 3.29 + 0.0124 \, z \tag{19}$$

Some approximation errors for (19) are shown in the following table.

z	30	50	90	130	150
exact $\ln z$	3.40	3.91	4.50	4.86	5.01
approx. $\ln z$	3.66	3.91	4.41	4.90	5.15

The approximation is not very good for small values of z.

The approximate prediction formula is obtained by solving the constraint equation (8) and (10) and equation (14), employing the linear approximation

$$\ln x_{ij} \cong b + cx_{ij} , \; i = 1, ..., I \text{ and } j = 1, ..., J. \tag{20}$$

Substituting (20) into (14) we obtain an approximation formula

$$b + cx_{ij} = -1 + \alpha_i + \beta_j + a_i \gamma_j, \text{ all } i, j. \tag{21}$$

Summing (21) over j, and using (8) we obtain

$$Jb + cm_i = -J + J\alpha_i + \sum_j \beta_j + a_i \sum_j \gamma_j, \text{ all } i. \tag{22}$$

Because of linear dependencies in the constraint equations, we can arbitrarily select two parameters:

$$\sum_j \beta_j = 0 \text{ and } \sum_j \gamma_j = 0. \tag{23}$$

Setting $\quad \lambda = \sum_i a_i \text{ and } \mu = \sum_i a_i^2$, we obtain

$$\alpha_i = J^{-1} cm_i + (b+1) \tag{24}$$

$$\sum_i \alpha_i = J^{-1} cN + I(b+1) \tag{25}$$

$$\sum_i a_i \alpha_i = J^{-1} c \sum_i a_i m_i + \lambda(b+1) = J^{-1}c \sum_j \theta_j + \lambda(b+1) \tag{26}$$

Summing (21) over i, and using (8), we obtain

$$cn_j = -I(b+1) + \sum_i \alpha_i + I\beta_j + \lambda\gamma_j , \text{ all } j. \tag{27}$$

Multiplying (21) by a_i, summing over i, and using (10), we obtain

$$c\theta_j = -\lambda(b+1) + \sum_i a_i \alpha_i + \lambda\beta_j + \mu\gamma_j, \text{ all } j. \tag{28}$$

Substituting from (25) into (27) and from (26) into (28), and solving (27) and (28), we obtain

$$\beta_j = c(\lambda^2 - I\mu)^{-1}[\lambda(\theta_j - J^{-1}\sum_j \theta_j) - \mu(n_j - J^{-1}N)] \tag{29}$$

$$\gamma_j = -c(\lambda^2 - I\mu)^{-1}(\theta_j - J^{-1}\sum_j \theta_j) - \lambda(n_j - J^{-1}N)], \text{ all } j. \tag{30}$$

Substituting (24), (29) and (30) into (21), we obtain the solution

$$x_{ij}^* = J^{-1}m_i + (\lambda^2 - I\mu)^{-1}[(\lambda - Ia_i)(\theta_j - J^{-1}\sum_j \theta_j) - (\mu - \lambda a_i)(n_j - J^{-1}N)], \tag{31}$$

for $i = 1, ..., I$ and $j = 1, ..., J$. Note that the solution would be exactly the same under any linear transformation

$$a'_i = r + sa_i , \; (r, \; s \text{ real}),\tag{32}$$

$i = 1, ..., I$. This can be verified by substituing a'_i for a_i in equation (31). Note also that the solution would also be the same under any linear transformation

$$x'_{ij} = r + sx_{ij}, \; (r, \; s \text{ real}),\tag{33}$$

$i = 1, ..., I$ and $j = 1, ..., J$. Because of this latter property, the solution is independent of the values b and c specified in the linear approximation (20) and (21).

It is convenient to deal with *proportions* p_{ij} instead of numbers x_{ij}, where

$$p_{ij} = x_{ij}/n_j\tag{34}$$

for $i = 1, ..., I$ and $j = 1, ..., J$. These proportions are convenient for plotting and visual comparison purposes.

Application to Ontario Grade 13 data

In his Ph.D. thesis, *A Model for the Ontario Education System* (1969), W.P. McReynolds included a chapter on academic competition. In that chapter he described a probabilistic sub-model of academic competition as part of a larger flow model based on papers by Clough and McReynolds (1966) and Clough (1967). The model described in this paper is motivated by McReynolds' model but is quite different in structure. To test his model McReynolds used the average of nine examination marks for each of 9681 students at the Grade 13 level in Ontario high schools in 1964. These data were obtained from master computer tapes from the *Carnegie Study of Identification and Utilization of Talent in High School and College* (Jackson and Fleming, 1959–64). The same raw data used by McReynolds are used below to test the maximum entropy model developed in this paper.

McReynolds defined 18 social classes of students, corresponding to the 18 combinations of the following factors: sex, level of mother's education, and size of community. These eighteen classes are denoted S_j, $j = 1, ..., 18$, as shown in Table 1.

McReynolds ordinally ranked the 9861 students on the basis of their Grade 13 examination results (standings on the average of nine examinations). He then subdivided the ordinal scale into nine intervals of 1000 each and one interval of 681, corresponding to the ordinal ranks 1 to 1000, 1001 to 2000 ,..., 8001 to 9000, and 9001 to 9681. These ten ordered intervals, which we may call "scholastic achievement" classes, are denoted by T_i, $i = 1, 2, ..., 10$ for the purposes of this paper.

It is convenient to define "scores" or "mean ranks" a'_i for people in the ordered intervals: $a'_i = 500, 1500, ..., 8500, 9340$. The results will be the same if we rescale these scores to be $a_i = 1, 2, ..., 9, 9.84$ using a simple linear transformation $a_i = 0.5 + 0.001 \, a'_i$:

The observations x^0_{ij} from McReynolds' thesis are shown in Table 2. Observed proportions p^0_{ij} can be computed from McReynolds' data as follows:

TABLE 1: Social Class Index j

Community Size	Sex of Student	Mother did not complete high school	Mother completed high school	Mother had at least some college
less than 6000	male	1	4	7
	female	10	13	16
6000 to 110000	male	2	5	8
	female	11	14	17
more than 110000	male	3	6	9
	female	12	15	18

TABLE 2: McReynolds' Observations x_{ij}^0

Class S_j	Rank Order Interval T_i										n_j
	$i = 1$	2	3	4	5	6	7	8	9	10	
$j = 1$	11	41	38	41	53	54	56	61	81	56	492
2	63	81	85	100	99	105	119	127	115	81	975
3	81	85	101	80	86	96	79	80	100	84	872
4	28	25	22	27	31	24	32	37	39	34	299
5	89	77	89	75	79	94	103	86	77	62	831
6	126	106	97	93	84	79	93	78	89	64	909
7	8	11	6	12	7	7	13	13	5	9	91
8	45	28	32	26	19	20	23	27	15	16	251
9	72	36	35	31	25	25	17	24	27	18	310
10	29	37	50	49	54	51	51	51	64	44	480
11	77	101	89	116	101	114	102	107	113	64	984
12	61	81	76	85	82	85	83	74	63	38	728
13	21	24	30	27	35	43	46	33	37	22	318
14	83	93	94	96	87	77	78	82	79	31	800
15	109	85	88	84	91	70	58	73	59	30	747
16	7	11	7	11	11	11	6	11	7	5	87
17	41	32	29	27	32	21	18	16	17	7	240
18	49	46	32	20	24	24	23	20	13	16	267
m_i	1000	1000	1000	1000	1000	1000	1000	1000	1000	681	9681

$$p_{ij}^0 = x_{ij}^0/n_j^0 , \quad i = 1, ..., I \text{ and } j = 1, ..., J,$$

$$n_j^0 = \sum_{i=1}^{I} x_{ij}^0 , \quad j = 1.., J. \tag{35}$$

Corresponding values θ_j^0 are obtained from equation (10).

To test the model outlined in this paper, the *observed proportions* p_{ij}^0 were computed from McReynolds' data and *predicted proportions* p_{ij}^* were computed from the model equations (31) and (34). *Cumulative proportions* from the observations and the model predictions are shown in Table 3 and 5. Plots of cumulative numbers are shown in Figure 1, and plots of cumulative proportions are shown in Figure 2. It can be seen that the cumulative values tend to smooth out statistical variations

TABLE 3: Cumulative Proportions From McReynolds' Observations

Social Class	Rank Order Scale — Thousands										Class Total
	1	2	3	4	5	6	7	8	9	9.68	
1	.02	.11	.18	.27	.37	.48	.60	.72	.89	1.00	492
2	.06	.15	.23	.34	.44	.55	.67	.80	.92	1.00	975
3	.09	.19	.31	.40	.50	.61	.70	.79	.90	1.00	872
4	.09	.18	.25	.34	.44	.53	.63	.76	.89	1.00	299
5	.11	.20	.31	.40	.49	.61	.73	.83	.93	1.00	831
6	.14	.26	.36	.46	.56	.64	.75	.83	.93	1.00	909
7	.09	.21	.27	.41	.48	.56	.70	.85	.90	1.00	91
8	.18	.29	.42	.52	.60	.68	.77	.88	.94	1.00	251
9	.23	.35	.46	.56	.64	.72	.78	.85	.94	1.00	310
10	.06	.14	.24	.34	.46	.56	.67	.78	.91	1.00	480
11	.08	.18	.27	.39	.49	.61	.71	.82	.94	1.00	984
12	.08	.20	.30	.42	.53	.65	.76	.86	.95	1.00	728
13	.07	.14	.24	.32	.43	.57	.71	.81	.93	1.00	318
14	.10	.22	.34	.46	.57	.66	.76	.86	.96	1.00	800
15	.15	.26	.38	.49	.61	.71	.78	.88	.96	1.00	747
16	.08	.21	.29	.41	.54	.67	.74	.86	.94	1.00	87
17	.17	.30	.43	.54	.67	.76	.83	.90	.97	1.00	240
18	.18	.36	.48	.55	.64	.73	.82	.89	.94	1.00	267

TABLE 4: Parameter Values for Model Prediction Formula*

i	a_i	m_i	j	n_j	θ /n_j
1	1	1000	1	492	6.35
2	2	1000	2	975	5.82
3	3	1000	3	872	5.50
4	4	1000	4	299	5.87
5	5	1000	5	831	5.40
6	6	1000	6	909	5.06
7	7	1000	7	91	5.51
8	8	1000	8	251	4.72
9	9	1000	9	310	4.44
10	9.84	681	10	480	5.82
			11	984	5.50
			12	728	5.26
$I = 10$			13	318	5.77
$J = 18$			14	800	5.07
$N = 9681$			15	747	4.78
			16	87	5.26
			17	240	4.43
			18	267	4.41

* From McReynolds' data in Table 2. Note that $\theta_j = \theta_j^o = \sum_i a_i x_{ij}^o$

Clough

TABLE 5: Cumulative Proportions from Model Prediction Formula

Social Class	Rank Order Scale — Thousands										Class Total
	1	2	3	4	5	6	7	8	9	9.68	
1	.05	.11	.18	.26	.36	.47	.59	.73	.88	1.00	492
2	.08	.16	.25	.34	.44	.55	.66	.77	.89	1.00	975
3	.10	.19	.29	.39	.49	.60	.70	.81	.91	1.00	872
4	.07	.15	.23	.33	.43	.54	.66	.78	.92	1.00	299
5	.10	.20	.31	.41	.51	.61	.71	.82	.92	1.00	831
6	.12	.24	.35	.46	.56	.66	.76	.85	.94	1.00	909
7	.07	.15	.25	.36	.47	.60	.73	.88	1.00	1.00	91
8	.13	.26	.38	.50	.61	.71	.81	.90	.99	1.00	251
9	.15	.29	.42	.54	.65	.75	.84	.93	.99	1.00	310
10	.08	.16	.24	.34	.44	.55	.66	.78	.90	1.00	480
11	.10	.19	.29	.39	.49	.60	.70	.80	.91	1.00	984
12	.11	.22	.32	.43	.53	.63	.73	.83	.93	1.00	724
13	.08	.16	.25	.34	.45	.55	.67	.79	.92	1.00	318
14	.12	.24	.35	.46	.56	.66	.76	.85	.94	1.00	800
15	.14	.26	.39	.50	.61	.70	.80	.88	.96	1.00	747
16	.08	.18	.29	.39	.51	.63	.76	.90	1.00	1.00	87
17	.15	.29	.42	.54	.65	.76	.85	.93	1.00	1.00	240
18	.15	.29	.42	.55	.66	.76	.85	.93	1.00	1.00	267

between adjacent intervals T_i. This is a reasonable way to examine the results because a somewhat different subdivision of the ordinal ranking scale could lead to somewhat different variations of observations between adjacent intervals. The tables show a very close fit of the model to the observations for those social classes having moderate or large population sizes n_j. The fit is not very good for those social classes having small population sizes, but the error (due to the linear approximation) is very small in terms of numbers of students. We take the closeness of fit as evidence that seems to support the maximum entropy hypothesis. There is insufficient evidence to reject the hypothesis.

6. Some Conclusions

The maximum entropy hypothesis is plausible and the data from the Ontario Grade 13 case evidently support the hypothesis. We conclude that the academic achievements of the members of any of the specified social classes are random, and have maximum entropy arrangements on an ordinal ranking scale given approximately by equations (31). The relative academic achievements of the various social classes can be measured adequately by a set of parameters θ_j, one for each social class $j = 1, ..., J$. For obvious reasons we may call these the *Social Class Relative Achievement Parameters* (SCRAP).

Given the population sizes of specified social classes, and a set of SCRAP values projected from past experience, the ordinal rankings on an academic achievement scale can be predicted by equations (31). Such predictions may be useful in the formulation of admissions policies for academic institutions.

CUMULATIVE NUMBER X_j OF RANK ORDER $O(X_j)$
OR HIGHER FOR MALES OF NINE SOCIAL CLASSES

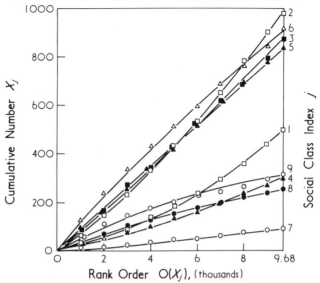

FIG. 1. Maximum Entropy Predictions compared with Actual Observations

CUMULATIVE PROPORTION P (X_j) OF RANK ORDER $O(X_j)$
OR HIGHER FOR MALES WHOSE MOTHERS DID NOT COMPLETE
HIGH SCHOOL.COMPARISON BY COMMUNITY SIZE

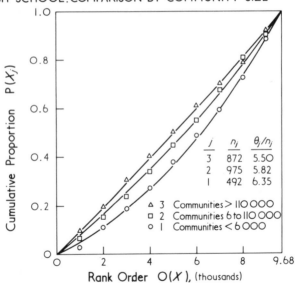

FIG. 2. Maximum Entropy Predictions Compared with Actual Observations

The main purpose of this exercise was to develop a *measure* of academic achievement, a *primitive theory*, and a *prediction formula*, and not specifically to analyze the Ontario data. However, the tabulated and plotted results are interesting and show very clearly that there are significant differences in academic achievements for the specified social classes.

The maximum entropy model may have much broader applicability to a variety of phenomena and problems in the social sciences which may be otherwise intractable. The main problem is to identify constraints which have a plausible interpretation and yield predictions that are consistent with observations.

Acknowledgements

The author is grateful to his colleague, Dr W.P. McReynolds, and the Ontario Institute for Studies in Education, for provision of sample data. The author is also grateful to the National Research Council of Canada for continuing financial support of research, and to the University of Waterloo President's N.R.C. Fund for a special grant for studies of academic administration.

References

1. Leon Brillouin, *Science and Information Theory*, New York: Academic Press, Inc., 1956.

2. Donald J. Clough, "Application of the Principle of Maximizing Entropy in the Formulation of Hypotheses", *CORS Journal*, Vol. 2, No. 2, December 1964.

3. Donald J. Clough and William P. McReynolds , "State Transition Model of an Educational System Incorporating a Constraint Theory of Supply and Demand' *Ont. Jour. Ed. Res.*, 9, 1 (Autumn, 1966).

4. Donald J. Clough, "A Model for Education — Employment Systems Analysis", *Growth Project Paper GPP 252, Dept. of Applied Economics, University of Cambridge.*

5. I.J. Good, "Maximum Entropy for Hypothesis Formulation, Especially for Multidimensional Contingency Tables", *Annals. of Math. Stat.* , Vol. 34, No. 3 (September, 1963).

6. Jackson and Fleming, *Carnegie Study of Identification and Utilization of Talent in High School and College* (1959–64) Ontario Institute for Studies in Education.

7. E.T. Jaynes, "New Engineering Applications of Information Theory", *Proc. First Symposium on Engineering Applications of Random Function Theory.* New York: Wiley, 1963.

8. E.T. Jaynes, "Information Theory and Statistical Mechanics", *Phys. Rev.*, Vol. 106 (1957), p. 620, and Vol. 108, p. 171; *Appl. Mech, Rev.*, Vol. 11 (1958), Rev. 2293.

9. W.P. McReynolds, *A Model for the Ontario Education System*, Ph.D. Thesis, University of Toronto, 1969.

10. C.E. Shannon, "A Mathematical Theory of Communication", *Bell System Tech. J.* , Vol. 27 (1948), pp. 379–423, 623–656.

11. C.E. Shannon and W. Weaver, *The Mathematical Theory of Communication.* Urbana: University of Illinois Press , 1949.

12. L. Szilard, *Z. Physik* , Vol. 53 (1929), p. 840.

13. M. Tribus, "Information Theory as a Basis for Thermo-Statics and Thermodynamics", *J. Appl. Mech.*, Vol. 28 (March 1961); p. 1–8; *Appl. Mech. Rev.*, Vol. 16, No. 10 (1963).

17

A Survey of Graduate Engineers of Cambridge University

R. W. Morgan
University of Cambridge

Very little is known about what happens to Engineering Graduates after they leave the University. Do they emigrate to the United States? Do they leave the Engineering profession altogether? Do they quickly go into management positions? Are they well paid? This survey obtains answers to these and other questions for Cambridge Engineering Graduates.

A survey of the graduate engineers of Cambridge University was carried out during the summer of 1968. Most surveys of this kind only look at current employment, but we decided to ask for details of employment from the year of graduation to the present, hoping to be able to detect trends in career patterns. Our sample consisted of 32 men who had graduated from Cambridge from each of the years 1948–1967, and was stratified so as to include 8 with firsts, 16 with seconds, and 8 with thirds from each year. Half the sample had done Part I in the year they graduated and half the year before..

Of the 640 questionnaires sent out, we received completed returns from 555 and partially completed returns from a further 23. This represents a 90% response which was spread very evenly over the 20 years, the best response being 32 out of 32 of those who took Part I in 1959, and the worst being 26 out of 32 who took Part I in 1963. The results fall naturally into three sections, Country of Residence, Occupation, and Salary.

Country of Residence

The Working Group on Migration, under Dr F.E. Jones, reached the following conclusions in its report, known as "The Brain Drain" report.

(i) The number of Engineers emigrating in 1966 was 42% of the supply three years earlier, and this figure is increasing.

(ii) The number returning to this country is also increasing but the net balance is a substantial increase in the numbers living abroad.

(iii) About half the emigrants are emigrating to North America.

Of course this report covers all engineering graduates while our survey covers only Cambridge graduates, and so they cannot be directly compared, Nevertheless our survey failed to confirm the Jones findings. There is no serious brain drain of Cambridge Engineering graduates and in so far as there is a brain drain it is not to North America.

Table 1 gives the present and expected future countries of residence of the entire sample. In 1968 84% of the sample were resident in the United Kingdom, and although a substantial number are unclear about where they expect to live in the future there is no evidence to suggest that this figure will change much. Fewer than 3% of the sample are resident in the United States of America and none of these are graduates of the last five years.

TABLE 1: Present and Expected Future Country of Residence

	Present	1970	1973	1978
U.K.	448	401	356	338
Armed forces	32	32	32	31
U.S.A.	17	17	14	13
Europe	18	13	7	6
Africa	13	13	4	0
Canada	9	5	2	3
Australia	8	9	8	7
South Africa	6	4	3	3
India, Pakistan, Ceylon and Thailand	5	5	5	4
West Indies	4	2	2	2
New Zealand	3	1	1	1
Hong Kong	3	2	2	0
Malaysia	2	1	1	0
Libya, Iraq and Iran	2	1	1	1
Japan	1	1	0	0
Brunei	1	1	0	0
Uncertain	0	64	134	163

Table 2 examines trends in the number of people living abroad. Of any one year's graduates there is an increase in the number living abroad over the years until after seven years about a quarter live abroad, but this is followed by a slow decline or at worst a levelling off. There has been an increase in both emigration and immigration but the total number living aboard has changed very little. If we may assume that the behavior of those who graduated prior to 1948 has been similar to those who graduated just after, we find that the percentage of graduates of the last twenty years living abroad has risen from about 12% to about 16%, that this change took place between 1958 and 1962, and that there has been no change since 1962.

Table 3 gives a breakdown by year of taking Part I into those who have always lived in the United Kingdom, those who have emigrated but returned, and those who have not yet returned. 68% of the sample have never left this country and 13% have not returned since leaving. The other 19% have returned to England to live although some have gone abroad again. On present trends it seems that half of our present graduates will live abroad at some time though most of them will re-

TABLE 2: Number (out of 30) of Graduates Living Abroad

Number of years after graduation

Year of Graduation	0	1	2	3	4	5	6	7	8	9	10	11	12	13	14	15	16	17	18	19
1948	0	0	0	2	2	2	3	4	5	4	3	3	3	3	3	7	5	5	5	4
1949	0	1	3	1	3	3	5	5	5	5	6	6	6	6	6	6	8	5	6	
1950	1	2	3	4	3	3	3	3	3	2	3	4	3	4	3	3	2	2		
1951	2	2	2	3	3	2	3	4	5	4	3	3	3	3	2	2	2			
1952	0	1	2	1	2	5	6	3	3	1	1	2	2	2	2	3				
1953	2	3	3	4	3	4	4	4	4	4	4	4	3	3	3					
1954	1	1	1	1	1	2	1	1	3	3	2	2	3	3						
1955	1	2	1	2	2	2	3	3	4	4	4	3	3							
1956	2	3	2	3	5	7	7	5	6	5	6	6								
1957	2	3	5	7	5	5	5	7	7	7	7									
1958	3	1	2	2	4	7	8	9	6	8										
1959	2	3	4	8	7	5	7	7	6											
1960	3	4	4	5	6	4	6	7												
1961	3	2	4	3	3	4	2													
1962	4	2	5	3	9	8														
1963	0	3	3	2	3															
1964	1	4	5	5																
1965	3	1	3																	
1966	4	3																		
1967	3																			

TABLE 3: Numbers Remaining in U.K. or Living Abroad

	Always in U.K.	Left but Returned	Not yet Returned
1947	5	4	2
1948	19	5	4
1949	16	6	3
1950	23	1	2
1951	15	5	3
1952	17	8	2
1953	21	4	2
1954	23	5	1
1955	19	4	4
1956	15	10	3
1957	16	8	5
1958	10	11	7
1959	22	4	6
1960	19	8	2
1961	21	6	4
1962	17	6	5
1963	14	6	6
1964	24	2	2
1965	23	5	1
1966	25	2	2
1967	12	0	3
	376	110	69

turn to this country. In the past the average period lived abroad before returning was 2 − 3 years.

We looked at the question of whether qualifications affect country of residence. The most striking finding was that those living in the United States are well qualified − 7 have Ph.D's and 6 have firsts out of a total of 17. Those with higher degrees are extremely likely to emigrate and most of them stay abroad, but those with firsts and no higher degree almost always come back. Emigrants to countries other than the United States are less well qualified than average.

We also looked at the incentives for leaving the U.K. and found that nearly all those who emigrated had an increase in salary which averaged £1000. Returning usually meant a drop in salary, the average drop being £250, but quite a lot of people got an increase for both moves. Those who went abroad and came back are slightly better paid now than their less adventurous contemporaries. Nearly everyone had an increase in job responsibility on going out and on coming back. Marital status seems to be relatively unimportant except that men who already have a family when they emigrate usually emigrate permanently.

Occupation

The Report of the Working Group on Manpower for Scientific Growth under Professor Swann expresses concern about the flow of our most able graduates into higher education and research instead of into industry and schools. We found that of the graduates from the 1964 − 7 period none went into school teaching confirming the Swann report but it seems that Cambridge sends far more graduates into industry than most other universities. The Swann report says that about 60% of graduates in technology go into industry and 20% into higher education and research, and that of firsts only 40% go into industry while 45% go into higher education and research. We found that at Cambridge 73% go into industry and 14% into higher education and research, and that of firsts 63% go into industry and only 33% into higher education and research.

We also compared our findings with the Ministry of Technology Survey of Professional Engineers in 1966, and some of the questions used were taken directly from the report of that survey. We found that our graduates who classified themselves as engineers are working in the same fields in roughly the same proportions as the Engineering Profession as a whole, but that our graduates are in more responsible posts than average. In Table 4 the job status varies from A, Junior Engineering functions, to F, Top Management.

TABLE 4

Age	Cambridge Graduate Percentages in							Mintech Survey Percentages in						
	A	B	C	D	E	F	above F	A	B	C	D	E	F	above F
Under 25	28	32	35	5	0	0	0	16	41	40	2	1	0	0
25−29	1	14	37	27	18	3	0	4	19	59	15	4	0	0
30−34	0	0	15	44	32	5	4	2	7	45	31	12	2	1
35−39	0	0	8	23	42	20	7	1	4	29	34	26	5	1
40−44	0	0	2	18	39	36	5	1	2	20	30	34	11	3

Of course not all our graduates are working as engineers. The breakdown is given in Table 5.

TABLE 5

As engineers or within the engineering industry	383
University teaching or research	51
Management services	42
Armed forces	31
Students	17
School teaching	11
Other	20
	555

The expansion of universities in recent years has attracted a large number of graduates into university teaching out of industry. As the expansion slows we can expect that fewer of our graduates will become university teachers. The expansion of the computer industry and the numbers of jobs for systems analysts and operational researchers can be expected to gain momentum. Already 7% of our graduates are working in these fields and these are nearly all recent graduates.

Salaries

Table 6 analyses salaries by year of graduation and gives lower quartiles, medians and upper quartiles. The median salary is such that half the sample earn more than this amount and the upper quartile such that a quarter earn more.

TABLE 6

Year of Graduation	Lower Quartile	Median	Upper Quartile
1948	2980	3460	4100
1949	2997	4000	5542
1950	3080	3500	5100
1951	2950	3305	4200
1952	2780	3050	4600
1953	2650	3007	3800
1954	2400	3915	3800
1955	2280	2640	2800
1956	2150	2600	3468
1957	2250	2855	3343
1958	2231	2500	3000
1959	1920	2200	2712
1960	1750	2192	2750
1961	1720	2000	2500
1962	1609	2100	2250
1963	1500	1782	2100
1964	1340	1550	1837
1965	1140	1359	1500
1966	1050	1251	1383
1967	900	1000	1150

We also compared our figures with the Ministry of Technology Survey and found that Cambridge graduates are much better paid than average as table 7 shows.

TABLE 7

	Cambridge Graduates			All graduates in Mintech survey		
Age	L.Q.	Median	U.Q.	L.Q.	Median	U.Q.
Under 25	1000	1200	1414	981	1102	1229
25–29	1550	1850	2250	1299	1476	1692
30–34	2155	2500	3000	1710	1938	2241
35–39	2700	3250	4200	2069	2382	2798
40–45	2980	3550	4900	2347	2822	3644

The Mintech figures have been increased by 8% to allow for inflation.

To see how salaries have changed over time we looked at the average salaries of graduates over the last twenty years for each group graduating in the same year. Because of inflation it is meaningless to compare salaries in different years directly and so the salaries were all converted into 1967 equivalents using the Consumers Price Index taken from the Central Statistical Office production "National Income and Expenditure". The results are given in Table 8.

The table does not include salaries in the first two years because of the huge variation due to some graduates having to do national service and others taking graduate courses.

A regression analysis was performed on these figures and we estimate that the average salary increases by £180 for each year since graduation, but that the average salary of comparable groups, that is groups who have the same number of years experience, has increased by only £9 per year. Our graduates are scarcely better paid now than they were twenty years ago, and as the overall standard of living has risen in this period we can conclude that our graduates are relatively much worse off than they used to be.

Finally we looked at the relationship between qualifications and salaries and found that Ph.D's tend to earn rather more than their contemporaries. Table 9 compares the average salaries of graduates with different degree classes and shows that there is no clear relationship between salary and class of degree. The extra salary earned by those with firsts can be accounted for by a very few people in the United States who are earning very high salaries indeed.

TABLE 8

Average Salary by Year of Graduation

Year	1948	1949	1950	1951	1952	1953	1954	1955	1956	1957	1958	1959	1960	1961	1962	1963	1964	1965
1950	881																	
1951	959	1224																
1952	1039	1347	1256															
1953	1122	1635	1350	1394														
1954	1298	1766	1520	1484	1115													
1955	1573	1932	1717	1637	1441	872												
1956	1636	2084	1828	1747	1619	1007	953											
1957	1857	2326	1941	1865	1825	1289	998	1029										
1958	2066	2590	2084	2040	2031	1489	1115	1106	1280									
1959	2307	2923	2302	2134	2285	1799	1315	1360	1379	1253								
1960	2564	3255	2568	2207	2526	2015	1542	1490	1601	1421	1111							
1961	2781	3427	2877	2245	2650	2201	1751	1616	1782	1520	1260	1185						
1962	2980	3565	3176	2467	2775	2344	1959	1759	1803	1673	1480	1381	1221					
1963	3284	3773	3502	2751	3002	2548	2314	1996	2251	1858	1761	1650	1357	1218				
1964	3504	3545	3750	3030	3246	2716	2467	2153	266υ	2003	1949	1766	1626	1356	1224			
1965	3587	3765	4229	3278	3359	2817	2533	2099	2758	2248	2024	1776	1760	1570	1439	1395		
1966	3702	3924	4697	3619	3473	2897	2607	2488	2956	2499	2252	2198	1918	1837	1722	1398	1287	
1967	3818	4326	5262	3968	3724	3086	2836	2747	3328	2860	2447	2537	2299	2079	2022	1619	1574	1180

TABLE 9

Class of Degree	Average Salary (all graduates)
I	2930
II	2588
III	2608

Class of Degree	Average Salary (all graduates since 1959)
I	2004
II (i)	1596
II (ii)	1973
III	1663

The second class was undivided until 1959.

References

The Brain Drain: Report of the Working Group on Migration. Cmnd 3417.
The Flow into Employment of Scientists, Engineers and Technologists: Report of the Working Group on Manpower for Scientific Growth. Cmnd 3760.
The Survey of Professional Engineers 1966: Ministry of Technology H.M.S.O.

PART V

18
A New Entry to the Civil Service

J. A. Rowntree
Civil Service Department, London

Introduction

This paper presents a statistical study of the feasibility of introducing a new
level of entry into the United Kingdom Civil Service. This work was fairly
straightforward and has been superseded by work arising from subsequent
policy decisions, but it is hoped that this paper will serve both to illustrate
the type of work which is now in hand in the Statistics Division of the Civil
Service Department and also to indicate the type of difficulties which can arise.

Background

The current levels of entry to the non-specialist, non-industrial Civil Service
have been traditionally related to the levels of output from the educational
system. In particular, one of the qualities sought in direct entrants to the
Administrative Class has been very high academic ability. Hitherto the two
highest levels of recruitment direct from the educational system have been: —

Executive Officer (General Certificate of Education (Advanced level))
at age 18 or so[†]

Assistant Principal (top-quality university graduate) at age 22 or so.

These levels of entry have remained unchanged for many years, during which
the context of recruitment has changed considerably. In particular, the number
of young people attending universities has risen markedly (from 93,000 in
1955/56 to 180 000 in 1965/66). This has made it likely that a higher proportion
of the better quality people with General Certificate of Education Advanced
level (GCE 'A' level) qualifications who would formerly have left school at
18 to seek employment are now staying within the educational system until
they have obtained a university degree or a qualification of similar standing.
Two further features make the problem more acute. The first is that the labour
market has become increasingly competitive compared with the situation before

* The views expressed in this paper are those of the author and in no way represent
the official views of the Civil Service Department.

† A few graduates enter the Civil Service as Executive Officers but they are not
typical of this type of entry.

1939. The other is the increasingly sophisticated nature of our society which leads to a growing demand for the more highly qualified at the expense of the less qualified.

Apparent Gap

The existence of the situation described above has become increasingly apparent but the impetus to meet it was stimulated by the report of the Fulton Committee.* Although this report did not specifically recommend a wider entry, its recommendations concerning salary of entrants, training, etc clearly implied that they anticipated a wider entry (Fulton Report Volume 1, Recommendations 30, 36 & 37). Some of the evidence given by the Treasury (Fulton Report, Volume 5, Memo No. 1) pointed out the need for more graduate entrants. Another feature of interest has been the marked increase in the number of graduates entering the Executive class. These numbers increased from 57 in 1964 to 217 in 1968. This increase in graduate entrants in itself suggested a lack of correspondence between the educational system and the strategy of recruitment to the Civil Service, even though many of the graduates who were thus entering the Executive class were of lower academic achievement than envisaged for the proposed new entry.

Method of Approach

Clearly, the problems involved in assessing the need for hypothetical new entrants are considerable. In order to introduce some form of structure into the investigation a number of fairly arbitrary assumptions had to be made for working purposes. The approach used was a two-pronged one. A statistical exercise was launched to investigate the current career patterns of staff in the relevant area and to derive a likely pattern for what was essentially an intermediate new entry. The results of part of this exercise were used to give guidance to the second approach, which was an inquiry to Departments asking them to assess the proportion of their middle management jobs (the Principal/ Chief Executive Officer level was taken) which were really suitable for the envisaged new entry and also to assess the potential of their Executive Officer entrants in recent years to fill these positions adequately.

It is on the statistical investigation that this paper concentrates.

The Administrative/Executive Model

The first step was to analyse the current pattern of careers in the relevant areas. The area in which interest centred included the Administrative Class (particularly the lower grades up to and including Assistant Secretary) and the General Service Executive class. Certain of the Departmental Executive classes (those in the Department of Employment & Productivity and Customs & Excise) were included, but the others were excluded. Departmental classes are found in particular departments where they perform functions similar to those of the General Executive class but with a long-recognised degree of specialisation particular to their department. The inclusion of the Department of Employment &

* "The Civil Service" Report of the Committee 1966–68 Chairman: Lord Fulton: London HMSO Cmnd 3638.

Productivity and Customs & Excise classes in this statistical exercise was without prejudice to their possible treatment when the merging of General Service and Departmental classes is considered.

Within this area, attention was concentrated on three groups of entrants: those graduates entering as Assistant Principals, those coming in direct to the Principal grade, usually in their 30s and 40s, and the Executive Officer (i.e. mainly school-leaver) entrants. The main flows in these recruitment grades are illustrated in Figure 1, which also indicates salary scales as from 1 July 1969. The numbers in the Administrative and Executive classes classified by grade of entry at the starting date of the projection (1.1.68) were as shown in Table 1.

As already pointed out, it is with the Principal, Assistant Principal and Executive Officer entry streams that we are mainly concerned. Although the Clerical Officer entrants have made a considerable numerical contribution to the middle management posts, they are not considered further in this exercise, it being implicitly assumed that their contribution will not change greatly. Similarly the "others" stream of entrants (which is very varied) has also been left out of explicit account.

Basic Data

The first stage was to examine the current wastage and promotion experience of the existing types of entrant. Particular attention was paid to the Assistant

Table 1. *Staff in Post at* 1.1.68, *Showing Grade of Entry*

Present Grade	Grade of Entry					
	Principal	Assistant Principal	Executive Officer	Clerical Officer	Others	Total
Under Secretary & above	41	225	11	13	79	369
Assistant Secretary	70	373	60	94	196	793
Senior Chief Executive Officer*	—	1	128	154	194	477
Principal	236	342	115	160	184	1037
Chief Executive Officer	—	—	239	677	480	1396
Senior Executive Officer	—	—	701	1494	1459	3654
Higher Executive Officer	—	—	1686	5427	4171	11284
Assistant Principal	—	268	12	4	17	301
Executive Officer	—	5	5600	15401	9205	30211
TOTAL	347	1214	8552	23424	15985	49522

* includes Principal Executive Officers and higher posts in the Executive Class.

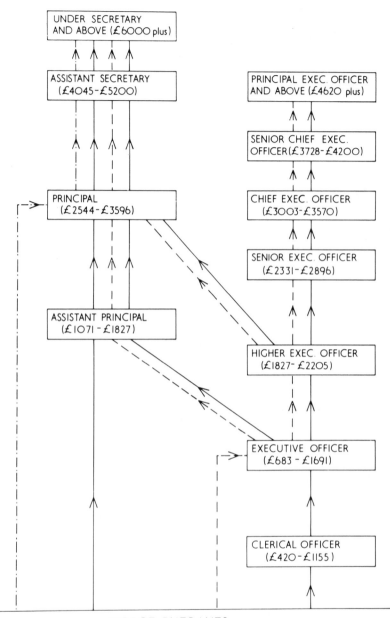

Figure 1. Model for Management Group — Outline

Principal and Executive Officer entries, since the proposed new type of entrant
would be intermediate between these two, both as regards academic achievement
and career prospects.

available only for movements during 1967. This was a drawback. Data from
a single year must always be of limited value since it cannot provide any guide
as to the direction in which changes are taking place. The enforced use of
1967 was a further handicap because during that year the size of the Civil
Service was growing (the total strength increased from 430 thousand at
1 April 1966 to 454 thousand at 1 April 1967 and 476 thousand at 1 April 1968 —
these figures include casual staff). This meant that the promotion experience
of 1967 must be of limited value as a guide to the longer term prospects of the
group with which we were concerned.

Wastage

The assumptions on wastage were based on experience during 1967. The wastage
rates used were age specific (which in the Civil Service is closely correlated
with duration of service) and can be summarised in the following table. These
rates were "smoothed" to remove the minor irregularities which are inherent in
the experience of a single year.

Table 2. *Wastage Rates during* 1967 *by Age & Grade of Entry*

A P Entrants		Principal Entrants		E O Entrants		C O Entrants	
Age	Rate %	Age	Rate %	Age	Rate %	Age	Rate %
Under 28	5			20 & under	14	20 & under	14
28–37	2	28–32	3	21–25	10	21–25	10
38–49	1	33–50	2	26–30	6	26–30	6
50–57	2	51–57	2	31–35	2	31–35	2
58	4	58	4	36–40	1	36–40	1
59	40	59	40	41–45	1	41–45	1
60	35	60	35	46–50	1	46–50	1
61–63	20	61–63	20	51–55	1	51–55	1
64	40	64	40	56–59	2	56–59	2
65 & over	100	65 & over	100	60–65	20	60–65	50
				66–69	56	66–69	75
				70 & over	100	70 & over	100

It is possible to see from the above data the fairly familiar pattern of wastage
declining with increasing age until it reaches a basic minimum of 1 or 2
per cent a year and then rising as the minimum retirement age (60 for the
Civil Service) is reached. Separate rates specific for current grade were not

computed; there is no evidence to suggest that current grade has a marked differential effect.

Promotion

As already indicated promotion rates were based on 1967 experience and again the actual rates were smoothed to remove small irregular fluctuations. The amount of such arbitrary adjustments was larger for promotions than for wastage. The rates used are shown in Table 3 below.

Table 3. *Promotion Rates Assumed in Administrative/Executive Model*

ADMINISTRATIVE CLASS			EXECUTIVE CLASS		
Grade	Age	Rate (per cent a year)	Grade	Age	Rate (per cent a year)
AP ENTRANTS:			CEO—SCEO & above	45—51	6
Ass. Sec to Under Sec.	42—43	5	SEO—CEO	36—41	2
	44—47	20		42—47	15
	48—51	12.5		48—51	10
Principal to Asst. Sec.	33—35	2.5	HEO—SEO	32—33	5
	36—41	30		34—40	15
	42—43	75		41—44	5
	44—50	30		45—55	1
Asst. Principal to Principal	25—26	5	EO—HEO	23—26	5
	27—28	40		27—31	10
	29—30	50		32—35	30
	31 & over	100		36—38	15
PRINCIPAL ENTRANTS:				39—55	3
Asst. Sec to Under Sec. & above	48—55	15			
Principal to Asst. Sec	39—53	9			

Career prospects of Middle Quality Graduates

Since they were expected to form an intermediate level of entry, it seemed reasonable to assume initially that the new middle quality graduate entrants would have career prospects intermediate between those of Assistant Principal entrants and Executive Officer entrants. Thus, whereas a direct entrant Executive Officer might reasonably expect to reach Senior Executive Officer (i.e. have 2 promotions — see Figure 1) and an Assistant Principal might similarly expect to reach Assistant Secretary, the "career grade" of a middle quality graduate entrant could reasonably be taken as Chief Executive Officer or Principal. Within this broad constraint, and assuming that the new type of entrant would pass through grades analogous to the present Senior Executive Officer and Higher Executive Officer grades, a set of assumptions were derived which were sufficient to determine the likely career pattern of middle quality graduate entrants in some detail. The first assumptions made were as follows:—

a. Annual intake was assumed to be 100 indefinitely

272

b. The age distribution on entry would be similar to that of APs and would be as follows :—

Age 21	15%
22	33%
23	35%
24	12%
25	5%

c. Annual wastage rates were assumed to correspond to the average of those obtaining for AP and EO

First 5 years after entry	5% or 7%
6–10 years after entry	5%
11–15 years after entry	3%
From then on up to age 59	1%
Age 60–65	30%
Over 65	100%

Alternative rates have been chosen for the first 5 years after entry because, although the annual wastage rate for Assistant Principals is about 5%, the rate for Executive Officers of the same age is about 10%. The lower wastage rate in these early years (i.e. 5%) results in an eventual stock that is 7½% larger than would result if the higher wastage rate of 7% were used.

d. The promotion path was at this stage assumed to be, in terms of current grades :—

EO – HEO – SEO – CEO/Principal – SCEO – Assistant Secretary

e. The rates of promotion to HEO and SEO would correspond closely to the age distribution on entry since it was thought that in the first two promotions seniority would be an important factor, i.e. promotion to HEO would probably begin after roughly 3 years' service had been completed and promotion to SEO would normally be expected to start about six years or so after that. The pattern produced by these assumptions was : —

EO to HEO All survivors promoted not later than 6 years after entry with a proportional distribution of promotions as follows :—

3 years after entry	20%
4 years after entry	30%
5 years after entry	35%
6 years after entry	15%
	100%

HEO to SEO All survivors promoted with a proportional distribution of promotions as follows :—

6 years after becoming HEO	10%
7 years after becoming HEO	15%
8 years after becoming HEO	30%
9 years after becoming HEO	30%
10 years after becoming HEO	15%
	100%

SEO to CEO/ 85% of those surviving to SEO promoted to CEO with the
Principal   following distribution of promotions:

8 years after becoming SEO	10%
9 years after becoming SEO	10%
10 years after becoming SEO	20%
11 years after becoming SEO	15%
12 years after becoming SEO	15%
13–22 years after becoming SEO	1½% at each year
	85%

CEO to SCEO *60 per cent* of those reaching CEO would be promoted between 7 and 19 years after reaching the CEO grade. These promotions to be spread evenly at about 5 per cent each year.

SCEO to Asst. *70 per cent* of those reaching SCEO would be promoted
Secretary   between 3 and 12 years after reaching SCEO. These promotions to be spread evenly at 7 per cent each year.

These above assumptions were sufficient to enable us to construct not only the steady state population, based on 100 such recruits a year, but also to calculate the intermediate stages between the initial entry and attainment of the steady state. This involved a considerable amount of tedious arithmetic, parts of which we were able to reduce by the use of a computer. It is, of course, this intermediate transition situation which is of greatest interest at present. This is because the steady state is essentially hypothetical and also because interest must inevitably centre on staff already in the Civil Service who naturally have their own career expectations. Such expectations could be markedly affected by the introduction of a new group of entrants who could be expected to progress more rapidly than some staff already within the Civil Service.

The resulting steady state is shown in Table 4 and the build-up towards it in Table 5.

Steady State Projections of Existing Entries

In order to estimate the possible long term effect of the new type of entrant it was decided to compute the steady state stationary population which would result from the indefinite continuation of the wastage and promotion flows of 1967. In order to simplify the computation the promotion rates were modified from those shown in Table 4 by assuming that all promotion took place at a single age rather than during the range of ages which were in fact covered.

Table 4. *"Steady State" Structure produced by Middle Quality Graduate Entry of 100 a Year*

Grade (in current terms)	Numbers
Executive Officer	381
Higher Executive Officer	397
Senior Executive Officer	612
Chief Executive Officer/Principal	611
Senior Chief Executive Officer	170
Assistant Secretary	100
TOTAL	2271

Table 5. *Structure produced by Middle Quality Graduate Entry of 100 a Year after 5, 10, 15, 20, 30 & 40 years*

Grade (in current terms)	Structure after specified number of years					
	5	10	15	20	30	40
Executive Officer	372	381	381	381	381	381
Higher Executive Officer	57	362	396	396	396	396
Senior Executive Officer		23	276	441	548	605
Chief Executive Officer/ Principal				104	433	596
Senior Chief Executive Officer					53	160
Assistant Secretary					10	87
TOTAL	429	766	1053	1322	1821	2225

The assumptions used for Assistant Principal entrants were as follows:—

All entered at 22 and experience wastage at 5 per cent a year.

All promoted to Principal at 28, wastage then falling to 2 per cent a year.

All promoted to Assistant Secretary at 38, wastage remaining at 2 per cent a year.

Half promoted to Under Secretary at 46, the rest remaining Assistant Secretaries. For both groups wastage rises to 3 per cent a year until all retire at age 60.

The transition flows for those entering as Executive Officers can be set out in a similar way:—

All enter at 18, are subject to 14% annual wastage up to 20, to 10% annual wastage up to the age of 25 and then 6%.

All promoted to Higher Executive Officer at 31, wastage then falling to 2 per cent a year until age 35 when it falls further to 1 per cent a year.

At age 38, 75% of Higher Executive Officers promoted to Senior Executive Officer, wastage remains at 1 per cent a year for both grades.

At age 45, 75% of Senior Executive Officers promoted to Chief Executive Officer; wastage still 1 per cent a year for all grades.

At age 48, 33.3% of Chief Executive Officers promoted to higher grade; wastage remains at 1 per cent a year until age 56 when it rises to 2 per cent, where it remains until age 60 when all retire (in contrast to the actual experience in 1967 when a lot of people retired at ages over 60).

The stationary population supported by a continuing intake subject to these two sets of transitions can be represented diagramatically as shown in Figure 2.

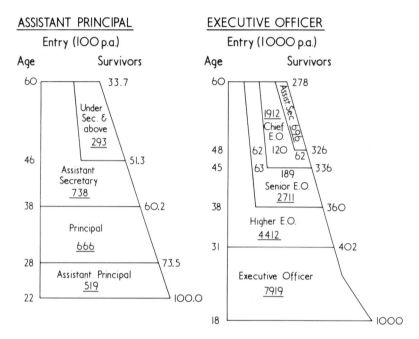

Figure 2. *Note*: Figures underlined (eg 4412) are areas and represent strength

Given the above assumptions, the strengths supported by a continuous annual intake of 100 APs, 100 Middle Quality Graduates and 1000 EOs are shown in Table 6.

Having obtained these estimates of the structure of the various types of entrant in which we were interested (it being assumed for the purpose of this exercise that the entry at Principal level ceases) it is then necessary to try and relate these to an estimate of demand for such staff. To obtain good demand estimates would be a major exercise in its own right and work in this area is proceeding, on an experimental basis, in the Civil Service Department. For the purposes of this paper it has been deemed sufficient to make one or two very arbitrary estimates of demand purely for the purposes of illustrating the sort of approach needed.

It is of some interest to look first at the situation at 1.1.68 as shown in Table 1. The figures from Table 1 were restricted to those entries with which we were mainly concerned — the Principal, Assistant Principal and Executive Officer levels of entry — and to simplify the figures slightly by combining a

Table 6. *"Steady State" Structure of Different Grades of Entry*

Grade (in current terms)	Grade of Entry and Number of Entrants			
	Assistant Principal (100)	Middle Quality Graduate (100)	Executive Officer (1000)	Total
Executive Officer/ Assistant Principal	519	381	7919	8819
Higher Executive Officer	–	397	4412	4809
Senior Executive Officer	–	612	2711	3323
Principal/Chief Executive Officer	666	611	1912	3189
Assistant Secretary	738	170	696	1604
Under Secretary +	293	100	–	393
TOTAL	2216	2271	17 650	22 137

few of the grades. Thus, in the figures in Table 7 below, the Principal and Chief Executive Officer grades were combined, as were those of Assistant Principal and Executive Officer, while the Senior Chief Executive Officer and higher posts in the Executive class were all combined with the Assistant Secretaries. On this basis the figures were as shown below: –

Table 7. 1.1.68 *Situation – Estimated Demand* (derived from Table 1)

Grade (in current terms)	Grade of Entry			
	Principal	Assistant Principal	Executive Officer	Total
Executive Officer/ Assistant Principal		273	5612	5885
Higher Executive Officer			1686	1686
Senior Executive Officer			701	701
Principal/Chief Executive Officer	236	342	354	932
Assistant Secretary	70	374	188	632
Under Secretary +	41	225	11	277
TOTAL	347	1214	8552	10 113

The comparison could be made more easily if the supply was scaled down to give the same total as that in Table 7: this produced the figures shown in Table 8.

A comparison of Tables 7 and 8 immediately shows a basic problem with the EO entrants. For this group the steady state produced by current wastage and promotion rates differs markedly from the current structure, on which Table 9 is based. In the current structure about $\frac{2}{3}$ of the posts filled by EO entrants are at EO level. In the steady state this proportion falls to 45%. This problem with the EO entry, which numerically dominates this area, would seem to imply that fairly drastic changes in either structure or promotion experience are likely.

Table 8. 1.1.68 *situation — Structure of different grades of entry, assuming "Steady State" career pattern*

Grade (in current terms)	Grade of Entry and Number of Entrants			
	Assistant Principal (46)	Middle Quality Graduate (46)	Executive Officer (457)	Total
Executive Officer/ Assistant Principal	237	173	3518	4028
Higher Executive Officer	–	181	2016	2197
Senior Executive	–	280	1238	1518
Chief Executive Officer/Principal	304	279	874	1457
Assistant Secretary	337	78	318	733
Under Secretary +	134	46	–	180
TOTAL	1012	1037	8064	10113

For the AP entrants, on the other hand, the present structure and the steady state are fairly close, the main difference being that the proportion of the total strength at Under Secretary level and above drops from 19% in the present structure to 13% in the steady state.

In the absence of such drastic changes the sizes of the suggested intakes might remain at the 1 : 1 : 10 ratio suggested above but with the career progression of the Executive Officer intake (which numerically dominates the lower grades) adjusted in order to obtain numbers in each grade which balance the supply and the demand. One possible adjustment along these lines is shown in Table 9 below.

Table 9. 1.1.68 *situation: Adjusted supply (entry ratio 1 AP: 1 MQG: 10 EO)*

Grade	Grade of Entry and Number of Entrants			
	Assistant Principal (46)	Middle Quality Graduate (46)	Executive Officer (457)	Total
Executive Officer/ Assistant Principal	237	173	5695	6105
Higher Executive Officer	–	181	1649	1830
Senior Executive Officer	–	280	519	799
Principal/Chief Executive Officer	304	279	190	773
Assistant Secretary	337	78	3	418
Under Secretary +	134	46	8	188
TOTAL	1012	1037	8064	10113

Although the figures for each grade were then much closer than in Tables 7 and 8, differences remained which, in the higher grades at least, were proportionately large; thus for example the supply on the above bases produced only 188 staff at Under Secretary and higher level compared with a demand of 277.

This imbalance could be modified by increasing the Assistant Principal entry to 75 a year and making a corresponding reduction in the Executive Officer entry. The effect of making these changes is shown in Table 10. Comparison of the totals in this table with those in Table 7 show that match between the supply numbers and the demand numbers for each grade was then quite close.

Table 10. 1.1.68 *situation: Supply modified to balance demand*

| Current Grade | Grade of Entry and Number of Entrants | | | |
	Assistant Principal (75)	Middle Quality Graduate (46)	Executive Officer (421)	Total
Executive Officer/ Assistant Principal	387	173	5240	5800
Higher Executive Officer		181	1518	1699
Senior Executive Officer		280	478	758
Principal/Chief Executive Officer	498	279	175	952
Assistant Secretary	551	78	3	632
Under Secretary +	219	46	7	272
TOTAL	1655	1037	7421	10113

It is perhaps worth looking at one other demand estimate and this is shown in Table 11. This is an extract from a forecast made for other purposes based on the assumption that posts in those grades which now form part of the Administrative class would increase at a rate of 0.7 per cent a year and that posts in the current Executive class would grow at the rate of 1.5 per cent a year. It should be emphasised that these particular assumptions were used for purposes of illustration only. Applying such rates of growth to the numbers shown in Table 1, the position shown in Table 11 would be reached after a period of 15 years (i.e. from a base date of 1.1.68 this position would be reached 1.1.83.)

Assuming the same drastically modified career prospects for Executive Officer entrants as were used for the estimates in Tables 9 and 10 and retaining the adjusted ratio of entrant streams as in Table 10 would allow the assumed demand at 1.1.83 to be met by a supply as shown in Table 12.

Because of the differential growth rates assumed for the different types of post now labelled administrative and executive, the balance of entry streams in Table 10 was not wholly satisfactory for the 1.1.83 situation and hence two adjustments were made. The first was to reduce the Assistant Principal entry from 92 a year to 83 a year and the second to cut the Middle Quality Graduate entry from 56 a year to 50 a year. The resulting figures are shown in Table 13.

One feature which could become of increasing importance is the size of the possible contribution of the new level of entry to the middle reaches of management. Thus Table 10 shows an annual entry of 46 Middle Quality Graduate entrants would eventually support nearly 30 per cent of the Principal/Chief Executive Officer posts hitherto filled from Principal, Assistant Principal and

Table 11. 1.1.83 *situation*: *Estimated demand*

Current Grade	Grade of Entry and Number of Entrants			
	Principal	Assistant Principal	Executive Officer	Total
Executive Officer/ Assistant Principal		298	7015	7313
Higher Executive Officer			2108	2108
Senior Executive Officer			876	876
Principal/Chief Executive Officer	262	380	427	1069
Assistant Secretary	78	414	227	719
Under Secretary +	46	250	12	308
TOTAL	386	1342	10665	12393

Table 12. 1.1.83 *situation*: *Estimated Supply*

Grade	Grade of Entry and Number of Entrants			
	Assistant Principal (92)	Middle Quality Graduate (56)	Executive Officer (516)	Total
Executive Officer/ Assistant Principal	476	212	6420	7108
Higher Executive Officer		222	1860	2082
Senior Executive Officer		343	586	929
Principal/Chief Executive Officer	610	342	215	1167
Assistant Secretary	674	96	4	774
Under Secretary +	268	56	9	333
TOTAL	2028	1271	9094	12393

Table 13. 1.1.83 *situation*: *Estimated Supply with adjusted entry*

Grade	Grade of Entry and Number of Entrants			
	Assistant Principal (83)	Middle Quality Graduate (50)	Executive Officer (535)	Total
Executive Officer/ Assistant Principal	432	189	6651	7272
Higher Executive Officer		198	1927	2125
Senior Executive Officer		307	607	914
Principal/Chief Executive Officer	553	305	222	1080
Assistant Secretary	611	86	4	701
Under Secretary +	243	50	9	302
TOTAL	1838	1135	9420	12393

Executive Officer entrants. If the number of posts grows to the level assumed in Table 13, a slightly augmented entry of Middle Quality Graduate entrants would fill nearly as great a proportion (305 out of 1080) of the Principal/Chief Executive Officers. However, it must be remembered that only a portion of the total number of posts at this level are under consideration here; as Table 1 shows there were at 1.1.1968 some 2400 posts at this level, of which only 942 were filled by Principal, Assistant Principal and Executive Officer entrants, the remainder then being filled by entrants from other sources whose supply may well be diminished in years to come. These figures underline the considerable impact which can be made on higher posts by an entry of modest size at the recruitment level whose progress is accelerated in comparison with the bulk of recruits. In these circumstances the relative impact of the new entrants will be dependent on the total size of the higher grades. Since this impact will not be felt fully for some 15 or 20 years it is very difficult to forecast the strength of this impact at this juncture.

In the supply estimates shown above it has been necessary to adjust the career progression of the Executive Officer entrants markedly from the level implied by the promotion rates etc experienced during the base period of this exercise. In order to produce the structure used in Table 10 and in a slightly modified form in later tables it has been necessary to allow the average age of promotion from Executive Officer to Higher Executive Officer to rise to 45. In terms of current career expectations this may seem unrealistic, though if the better of the present Executive Officer entrants were to be diverted into the new entry stream those remaining could well be of poorer quality. Since the demand estimates were produced quite artificially there is perhaps no need for more than a warning note to be sounded at present.

In order to produce reasonably steady state career progression for the Executive Officer entrants, it would be necessary to modify the demand structure by reducing markedly the proportion of Executive Officer posts, that is to move towards the steady state situation on the supply side. In practice the lack of long term correspondence between the very favourable promotion experience of 1967 and the actual structure at 1.1.68 is likely to change over time. Already it can be seen that the exceptional experience in 1967 is not being maintained.

On the whole, it looked as though the introduction of the Middle Quality Graduate entry was unlikely to have a critical effect on career prospects in the areas examined above, which are dominated numerically by the posts filled by Executive Officer entrants. In the light of this, perhaps the most positive conclusion that can be drawn is that there appear to be no strong manpower planning reasons for not introducing a Middle Quality Graduate entry for which there are good arguments from the changing pattern of education etc.

19

The Use of a Steady State Model to Obtain the Recruitment, Retirement and Promotion Policies of an Expanding Organisation

R. W. Morgan

University of Cambridge

Introduction

This work arose out of an attempt to define the optimal recruitment and promotion policies for certain groups of employees within the British Civil Service.[*] For each group our starting point was a table giving the number of employees by age and by grade at a particular point in time, together with supplementary data about wastage patterns, plans for expansion and so on. Our analysis is partly descriptive — what for example will be the consequences of present policies on the future promotion prospects of employees, and partly prescriptive — for example what should be done to prevent promotion blockages from occurring. The former problem has normally been solved either by making deterministic assumptions and then moving people around according to the defined rules or by an application of the theory of stochastic processes. The prescriptive problem has been solved by decision models, in particular by linear programming. The present paper presents the beginnings of a computationally much simpler procedure using a steady state model.

Steady state or hypothetical models

Let us consider one particular grade in the organisation. An employee concerned about his career prospects will want to know what his chances are of reaching this grade and, if he does reach the grade, at what stage in his career the promotion is likely to occur. For this grade we call the proportion of employees who ever reach the grade q, and the average age at which promotion occurs A. If q is low or A is high compared with the employees' expectations then the organisation is said to suffer from a promotion blockage at this grade.

A promotion blockage may be caused by there not being enough posts available at this grade to satisfy the employees. In this case the only solution is to permanently increase the number of such posts. Alternatively a promotion blockage can be caused by an irregular age structure. If for example an organisation at some point employs largely young men the age of promotion to senior posts will

---

[*] Based on data supplied by the Civil Service Department for research and development purposes. The opinions expressed are those of the author.

be quite low, If subsequently no one leaves and the organisation does not expand then there will be no further vacancies to senior posts and in ten years time the promotion prospects of a new employee will be quite different from that of a new employee of the same ability ten years earlier. Such a promotion blockage would only be temporary but its effects could well be permanent.

Our approach to the problem of a particular organisation is to imagine another organisation which has many factors in common with the real organisation except that its age structure does not cause promotion blockages. We call this organisation a 'hypothetical organisation', and of course the real and hypothetical organisations will have quite different age structures. Our objective is to eliminate promotion blockages in the real organisation as quickly as possible, and we do this by gradually changing the age structure of the real organisation into that of the hypothetical one.

It is worth enumerating the factors to be held in common between the two organisations.

1. The total number of employees in each grade.
2. The long term rate of expansion (or decrease).
3. Wastage rates.
4. Retirement policy.
5. The distribution of the ages of recruits is the same for the hypothetical organisation as would be ideal for the real organisation. This need not be the same as the present recruiting policy.

An example

To illustrate we give a simple example of the construction of such a hypothetical organisation. Suppose that the real organisation would like all its recruits to be age 20 and all its employees to retire at 60. Suppose too that there is no wastage and that the number of employees is expected to remain constant over time. At present the numbers of employees age 20, 21, ..., 59 are n_{20}, n_{21}, ... n_{59}. The organisation has two grades, the proportion of employees in these grades being p for the upper grade and $(1 - p)$ for the lower grade.

The corresponding hypothetical organisation will also have two grades with proportions p and $(1 - p)$, recruit at age 20 and retire everyone at 60, and there will be no wastage or rate of expansion. However the number of employees for each age will be the same, say n, so that the promotion prospects will not vary with time. The diagram shows the age structure for the two organisations.

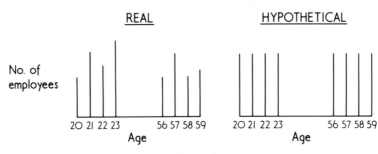

Figure 1

The basic difference between the two organisations is in the age distribution. Because of this the promotion prospects in the real organisation will fluctuate over time, but they will remain constant for the hypothetical organisation. We can now use this hypothetical model to say something of practical value about recruitment and promotion in the real situation.

Recruiting

The objective in recruiting must be to turn the age distribution of the real organisation into that of the hypothetical organisation as quickly as possible. Each year because of retirement and possibly because of wastage we can set an overall recruitment target. These recruits would normally all be aged 20 but in the coming year it may be possible to recruit men of various ages without conflicting with other aims of the organisation. It may also be possible to have some redundancies. Ideally the policy will be to recruit $(n - n_i)$ men aged i if n_i is less than n and to make $(n_i - n)$ redundant if n_i is greater than n. Typically other circumstances will prevent us from reaching these targets but the targets represent the direction in which our recruiting policy must take us if we are to ever realise the objective of avoiding a promotion blockage.

Promotion

The second problem is to say something about the age at which employees can expect to be promoted from the lower grade to the upper grade in this two grade organisation. Of course for the real organisation this typical age of promotion will fluctuage over time, the degree of fluctuation depending on the success of our recruiting policy in changing its age structure into something more like that of the hypothetical one. However the hypothetical organisation will have no such problem since it has been chosen so that the promotion prospects will not vary.

We calculate the average age of promotion for the hypothetical organisation. A small calculation (see the Appendix) shows that

$$A = 60 - 40p/q$$

where p is the proportion of employees in the top grade and q is the proportion of those entering who will reach the top grade before retirement. This equation tells us whether the proportion of top grade posts in the organisation is a satsifactory one. If there are no values of a and A which both satisfy the equation and represent reasonable prospects from the employees' point of view, then the value of p must be changed or the organisation will head for difficulties. For fixed q the typical age of promotion for the real organisation will fluctuate about A and it may well be that the value of A given by the equation is much higher than the typical age of promotion being currently experienced. This would be a reflection of a favourable age structure making promotion easy at present, but the high value of A would be a danger signal indicating that there is a period ahead during which promotion will be very difficult.

A model for the Scientific Officer Class of the Civil Service

We now show how the hypothetical organisation was built up for the Scientific Officer Class. The same model was also used for other groups though possibly with less justification.

The model can be divided into three parts corresponding to the age ranges 21–32, 32–60, and 60–65. The final age structure for the hypothetical organisation is shown in the diagram.

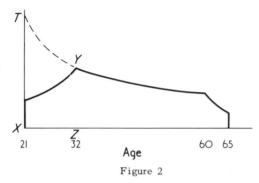

Figure 2

We consider first the age range 21–32 where there is a large amount of wastage and all the recruitment occurs. Any model we might choose would give rise to some line joining the points X and Y in the diagram – the line XZY would correspond to the case where all recruits are aged 32 and the line XTY to the case where all recruits are aged 21. We decided to adopt the simplest model which would both allow us to vary the average age of recruits and also correspond well with what happens in practice. This was to assume that the hypothetical organisation would have numbers at ages 21, 22,..., 32 which were in geometric progression. A high value for the ratio between employees aged $i + 1$ to employees aged i would then correspond to a high average age of recruits. The only justification for using this model in these circumstances is that it fits the data, and of course in other circumstances a more complicated recruitment model might well be needed.

In the middle age group it is observable that there is a negligible amount of wastage and ideally there would be hardly any recruitment. It seems that once employees reach the age of 32 they are extremely likely to remain with the organisation until they retire, so that this middle age group behaves very like the organisation in the example of the previous section, the only difference being that in constructing the hypothetical organisation we must allow for expansion. The rate of expansion determines the slope of the line in the middle section of the diagram. The exact form of the line required to maintain constant promotion prospects is considered in the appendix.

The model assumed for retirement is that a fixed percentage γ of those aged 60 or over retire each year except that those aged 65 all retire. Thus $\gamma = 0$ corresponds to the case where everyone retires at 65 and $\gamma = 100$ corresponds to the case where all retire at 60. By varying γ we can feed into the model different retirement policies. This model corresponds well with what is happening at present with γ equal to about 40.

Morgan

To summarize we have shown how to construct a hypothetical organisation which can be varied according to the choice of the following four parameters;

1. The age (so far we have assumed this to be 32) at which employees can be expected to remain with the organisation until they retire.

2. The ratio of the number of those aged $i + 1$ to those aged i amongst the young employees (i.e. those under the age defined by 1.).

3. The retirement rate γ.

4. The rate of expansion of the organisation.

The second of these parameters is not one which can be easily specified but it can be directly calculated once any one of the following three requirements are known.

(i) The average age of recruits.

(ii) The proportion of recruits aged over 27 — this corresponds roughly to those recruited to the second rather than the lowest grade.

(iii) The proportion of men under the age of 32 in the organisation as a whole.

For different choices of the four parameters we can calculate the recruitment targets and the promotion prospects for the real organisation in much the same way as we outlined in the example of the previous section.

Recruitment

We begin with a table giving the number of employees for each age between 21 and 65 at the beginning of the current year and for a suitable choice of the parameters we can calculate a table giving the number of employees for each age at the end of the current year for the hypothetical organisation. If n_i is the number of employees of age i in the real organisation, w_i is the proportion of employees of age i who will leave during the current year and h_{i+1} is the number of employees of age $i + 1$ in the hypothetical organisation in one year's time when the recruiting target for the coming year for this age group should be

$$h_{i+1} - n_i w_i .$$

The wastage rates w_i for the current year are of course unknown at the time the estimates for recruiting are required and so must be estimated from previous years. We could simply calculate the wastage rates for the previous years and assume that they will be the same again for each age, but we preferred to smooth out the data by fitting it to a simple wastage model. The curve we used was

$$w_i = \frac{1}{1 + e^{\alpha + \beta i}}$$

where α and β are parameters to be estimated. If of the n_i aged i, r_i leave during the year and we think of w_i as a probability rather than as a proportion, then the likelihood of the data L is

$$\prod_i \binom{n_i}{r_i} w_i^{r_i} (1 - w_i)^{n_i - r_i}$$

If we substitute for w_i and maximise L with respect to α and β we obtain the following equations for α and β.

$$\sum_i \frac{n_i}{1 + e^{\alpha+\beta i}} = \sum_i r_i$$

$$\sum_i \frac{i n_i}{1 + e^{\alpha+\beta i}} = \sum_i i r_i.$$

It is now a simple matter to find solutions for α and β using iterative methods, and in practice four figure accuracy can be obtained after four or five iterations. This wastage model provided a good fit to the various sets of data on which it was tested.

It seems wrong to estimate α and β only from data for one previous year and so we decided to combine data from earlier years where this was available. We begin the calculation with the wastage figures (that is r_i and n_i) for the year just completed and the estimates of α and β which we had used the year before. From these estimates of α and β we calculate the wastage figures we would have expected during the year just completed by $\hat{r}_i = w_i \times n_i$. We then replaced r_i by a weighted average of r_i and $\hat{r}_i$ in the equations above to obtain estimates of α and β for the coming year.

Promotion

We concerned ourselves only with those grades to which promotion will normally occur during the age range 32–60. For the hypothetical organisation we can calculate the average age at which promotion occurs in much the same way as we did in the example of the previous section. The revised formula is now

$$A = 60 - \frac{\log\{1 + (p/q)(r^{28} - 1)\}}{\log r}$$

where p is the proportion of those aged over 32 who are in the grade concerned or in some grade above, and q is the proportion of those who are in the organisation at age 32 who will reach the grade concerned before retirement. The figure 28 in the formula arises as the difference between the earliest retirement age (60) and the age at which employees almost all remain with the organisation for life (assumed to be 32). In different circumstances we might use a different figure than 28; r is the expansion parameter. If the organisation expands at a rate of 2% then $r = 1.02$, if at 4%, $r = 1.04$, and so on. The calculation of the formula is given in the appendix.

Computer output

A revised version of the computer output is given as follows with comments. The data used is actual data from one particular class of employees; but the assumptions are hypothetical and are used only to illustrate difficulties which can arise.

Output: Rate of expansion   –1%
        Retirement rate   40%
        Average age of recruits   28
        Age after which employees rarely leave   32

Comment:

This is a set of values for the parameters which must be read in as data. Typically the program would run with a variety of sets of values for these parameters and the results compared. A single run for one set of parameters used about six seconds of computer time

Output: Recruitment

    –66. 3. 4. –4. –18. –10. –24. –16. –2. 11. 6. 0. –7. 10.
    –1. –2. –6. 5. 6. 8. 16. 11. 12. 11. 17. 16. 13. 7.
    15. 9. 8. 5. 8. 3. 1. 1. 4. 3. –1. 1.

Comment:

These 40 numbers give the recruiting targets for the coming year for the age groups 60 and over, 59, 58, ..., 21. Negative numbers represent redundancy targets if the real organisation is to become like the hypothetical one in one year.

Output:

Age	Over 50	40–49	33–39	27–32	21–26
Target	–117	28	87	48	9

Comment:

The 40 numbers above are now condensed into a simple table. To create an ideal age structure in one year we would need to make 117 redundancies in the over 50 age group during the coming year and recruit heavily in the other age groups. There are few organisations in which this policy would be countenanced, and so we must instead adopt a policy which will put the age structure right as quickly as possible while avoiding redundancies. It is not difficult to see from the figures what this policy should be.

The figure –117 means that during the next 10–15 years 117 more men will retire than would occur if the age structure was ideal. These extra 117 must be replaced by recruits and they must be recruited to the right age groups, that is to the next oldest age groups which have a shortage. The shortage of 115 in the age group 33–49 almost balances the surplus in the over 50 group so that the appropriate policy is to aim to recruit 117 men from those who are now aged 33–49. This recruitment would be spread out over the next 10–15 years and so a suitable target for the coming year would be 10 men. This would make a sensible recruiting target for the coming year to be as follows:

Age	Over 50	40–49	33–39	27–32	21–26
Target	None	2	8	46	9

If this policy is followed then in 10–15 years time the age structure will be ideal and during this period the situation will improve steadily.

The use of a steady state model   289

Output:

	Proportion promoted before retirement	Eventual average age of promotion	Average age in next 10 years	
			max.	min.
To senior grade	54	51.0	55.1	50.5
	93	56.0	59.0	55.8
	100	56.5	59.2	56.2

Comment:

This information is given for the other grades as well. Using the formula calculated in the text the proportion who will be promoted to the grade concerned before retirement is calculated for three different ages, in this case 51.0, 56.0, and 56.5. The second of these ages is always the current average age after promotion and the other ages are given to show the effect on promotion prospects of changing the age of promotion. These figures are based on the assumption that the hypothetical structure can be reached at once. The figures in the last two columns show the fluctuations that will occur in the next ten years if all the recruiting is to be to younger age groups — that is if nothing is done to improve the age structure.

The figures shown give considerable cause for concern. It is desirable that a substantial proportion of the class should reach this grade but as things are this can only be achieved by making the typical age of promotion very high. During the near future this promotion age will be higher still because of the unfavourable age structure. In such a case one might wish to consider the possibility of creating more senior posts in the class as a whole.

Appendix

Suppose that each employee enters the organization at the same age and remains for K years of service. Let p be the proportion of employees in the top grade and q be the proportion of those entering who reach the top grade before retirement.

Let the number of years of service at which a person is promoted be a random variable X with p.d.f. $f(x)$ and c.d.f. $F(x)$. Let the number of completed years of service of a random member of the organization be a random variable with p.d.f. $g(x)$ and c.d.f. $G(x)$. Then the probability that a person of years of service x has been promoted is $qF(x)$, and hence the probability that any member of the organization has been promoted is

$$p = \int_0^k qF(x)g(x)dx.$$

Integrating by parts we obtain

$$\frac{p}{q} = \left[[F(x)G(x)] \right]_0^k - \int_0^k G(x)f(x)dx$$

$$= 1 - E[G(X)] \tag{1}$$

We now consider the two cases discussed in the text.

1. Suppose that the age of the employees is uniformly distributed. Then

$$G(X) = \frac{X}{K}$$

and applying equation (1) we get

$$\frac{p}{q} = 1 - \frac{A}{K}$$

where A is the average age of promotion.

2. Suppose that $G(x)$ does not change with time but the organisation increases at a rate $100(r - 1)\%$ per annum. Then we must have

$$r^s = G(k - s) + r^s G(s) \quad \text{for all } s$$

and hence

$$G(x) = \frac{r^{k-x} - r^k}{1 - r^k}.$$

Applying (1) we get

$$\frac{p}{q} = 1 - \frac{r^k \left\{ E\left(\frac{1}{r^x}\right) - 1 \right\}}{1 - r^k}$$

We can write

$$\frac{1}{r^x} = \frac{1}{r^A} - (X - A)\frac{\log r}{r^A} + \frac{(X - A)^2}{2}\frac{(\log r)^2}{r^A} \dots$$

and since r is very close to 1 we have to a close approximation

$$E\left(\frac{1}{r^x}\right) = \frac{1}{r^A}$$

and hence

$$A = k - \frac{\log\left\{ 1 + \frac{p}{q}(r^k - 1)\right\}}{\log r}$$

The use of a steady state model

291

20

'Rolling Up' A Number of Civil Service Classes

R. W. Drinkwater, O. P. Kane

Civil Service Department, London

Introduction

We are not describing in detail in this paper the nature of the pay structure of the UK Civil Service, but briefly it is multi-class (there are over 1400 grades split according to the type of work between 200 distinct classes, or pay structures), "open" (all salaries are published) and "age and service" based. Our problem is to rationalise this system by rolling together a number of classes into a single class and to determine the position of the grades in this new class so that the transfer cost is a minimum.

Figures 1a and 1b show diagramatically the main features of a single class and of one of the grades in the class.

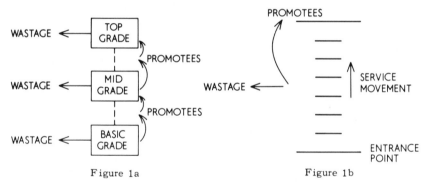

Figure 1a   Figure 1b

An entrant to any grade receives an annual increment and if unsuitable for early promotion (and does not leave the Civil Service) he climbs to the grade maximum on which he must mark-time until he is either eventually promoted or retires. In this early work we have made a number of simplifying assumptions: —

a. All entrants to a grade come in at the lowest salary level in the grade.

b. The steady state condition holds; that is, the number of entrants, and the promotion and wastage rates from each level of each grade remain the same from year to year. Thus the number of employees on each level remains constant as shown in Figure 2.

We are not concerned in this paper with the whole range of considerations which would bear on decisions to roll up a number of separate class structures.

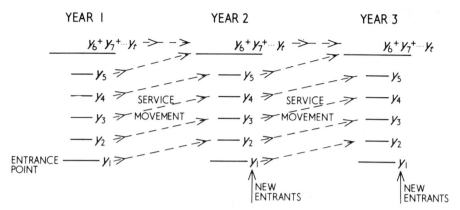

Figure 2. The Steady State. Here y_i is the number of employees who have spent i years in the grade and $1 \leqslant i \leqslant t$, where t is the maximum number of years which anyone spends in the grade.

Rather we have proceeded by postulating a number of simple rules so that we may be able to throw light on some of the difficulties which will arise; and it must be emphasised here that this example is given for illustrative purposes only and has no necessary implications for Civil Service Department policy.

Transferring One Grade to a New Structure

Firstly let us consider the transfer of staff from a single grade into a new grade which has a different salary structure, where, for illustrative purposes, the transfer rules are defined in the most beneficial possible way to the staff, i.e. so that no employee can suffer either in the long or the short term. That is,

    a. the maximum salary level of the new grade must not be less than that of his present grade;

    b. the salary level of the new grade to which an employee transfers must not be less than that in the present grade;

    c. the salary level in the new grade which an employee reaches after t years must not be less than he would have reached after t years in the present grade.

    d. the proportion of new entrants to the grade promoted after time t must be equal for both the present and the new grade.

In this analysis we shall assume that the new scale has been constructed so that there is one-to-one correspondence between salary levels on the present grade and the new grade. This gives two further transfer rules;

    e. staff from adjacent levels on the present scale do not transfer to the same level on the new scale.

    f. there is no occasion on which one of the new levels receives no transferred staff.

We are not able to make these last two assumptions when considering the rolling up of many classes as in the next section; however only a simple, but laborious, modification in the analysis is necessary. We add to these the simplifying assumptions that the proportion who leave after t years is the same for both present and new grades and that the number of promotees to the new grade remains the same throughout the time period considered.

Figure 3, below, shows diagramatically the two pay structures, and Figure 4 shows the distribution of staff on the new grade for t years.

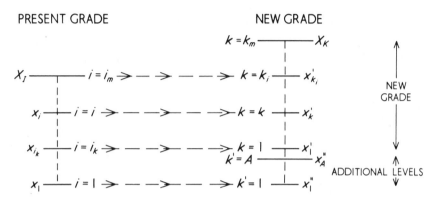

Figure 3. Immediate transfer

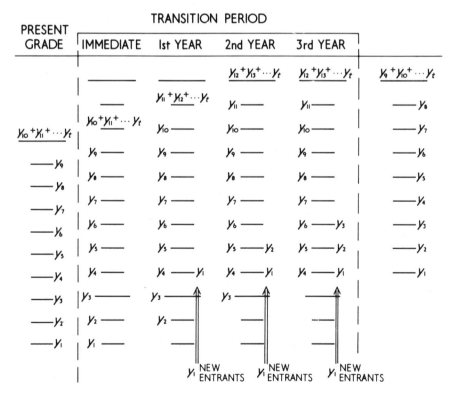

Figure 4

Here we are transferring staff from their present grade of i_m salary levels, ranging from x_1 to x_{i_m} $(= X_I)$, over to a new grade of k_m salary levels, ranging from x'_1 to x'_{k_m} $(= X_K)$; where the first transfer rule has constrained X_K to be greater than X_I. In this example we have taken $x'_1 \geqslant x_1$, the most complex case, even though this is not dictated by the transfer rules. A simple modification in the following analysis would take account of the situation where new entrants to the grade after the transfer had taken place were penalised by having a lower entrance point i.e. $x'_1 < x_1$.

The transfer rules define two boundaries which will be useful in the analysis;

a. staff on the maximum of the present grade transfer to the k_i th level of the new grade where,

$$x'_{k_i} - x_{i_m} \text{ has minimum positive value;}$$

b. staff who transfer to the 1st level of the new grade come from level i_k of the present grade where,

$$x'_1 - x_{i_k} \text{ has minimum positive value.}$$

In general, staff on the ith level of the present grade, where $i_m \leqslant i \leqslant i_k$ transfer to the nth level of the new grade where, $x'_k - x_i$ has minimum positive value.

Now, rather than allow all staff on levels 1 to $(i_k - 1)$ of the present grade to transfer straight to the 1st level of the new grade we construct a temporary scale of A additional levels, ranging from x''_1 to x''_A, below the new grade minimum — in our example of the rolling up of many classes this "temporary scale" will in fact be the top salary levels of the new grades below.

Then staff from the ith level of the present grade, where $i_k > i \geqslant 1$ transfer to the k' level of this temporary scale where, $x''_k - x_i$ has minimum positive value.

Let the number of staff who have been i years in the present grade be y_i where $i \leqslant i_m$, the total time anyone can spend in the grade. Then the cost of the present grade is simply,

$$C_p = \sum_{i=1}^{i_m - 1} y_i \cdot x_i + x_{i_m} \sum_{i=i_m}^{i_m} y_i. \tag{1}$$

The cost immediately after transfer can be considered in three parts;

a. those who transferred over to one of the additional levels below the new grade minimum.

b. those who transferred over to the new grade, excluding those who were on the present grade maximum.

c. those who transferred over to the new grade from the present grade maximum.

The cost immediately after transfer is,

$$C_{o,N} = \sum_{i=1}^{i_k - 1} y_i \cdot x''_i + \sum_{i=1}^{k_i - 1} y_{i+i_k-1} \cdot x'_i + x'_{k_i} \sum_{i=i_m}^{i_m} y_i \tag{2}$$

Drinkwater, Kane

To determine the cost of the new structure in the 1st year after transfer we note that,

a. there are now no staff on the lowest additional level ($k' = 1$) since of the y_1 originally there, y_2 have moved up to $k' = 2$ while the remainder have either left the Service or have been promoted to the grade above the new grade;

b. of the y_{i_k-1} staff on the highest additional level ($k' = A = i_k - 1$), y_{i_k} have moved up to $k = 1$ while the remainder have either left the Service or have been promoted to the grade above the new grade;

c. y_1 new entrants have entered at the lowest level of the new grade;

d. the staff who transferred from the old grade maximum have now started to "unwind" i.e. there are now y_{i_m} staff at level $k = k_i$ (they came from level $k_i - 1$) and $\displaystyle\sum_{i=i_m+1}^{t_m} y_i$ staff at level $k = k_i + 1$.

Then the cost of the new structure in the first year after transfer is,

$$C_{1,N} = \sum_{i=2}^{i_k-1} y_i \cdot x_i'' + \sum_{i=1}^{k_i} y_{i+i_k-1} \cdot x_i' + x_{k_2+1}' \sum_{i=i_m+1}^{t_m} y_i + y_1 \cdot x_1' \tag{3}$$

Before writing down the expression for the cost in the tth year after transfer we can simplify the relation considerably by considering that the maximum salary level of the new grade consists of a large number of salary levels $x_{k_m}', x_{k_m+1}', \ldots x_{t_m}'$ where $x_{k_m}' = x_{k_m+1}' = x_{k_m+2}' = \ldots x_{t_m}'$.
Then the cost in the tth year after transfer is,

$$C_{t,N} = A + B + C + D \tag{4}$$

where
$$A = \sum_{i=t+1}^{i_k-1} y_i \cdot x_i'' \qquad \text{for } t < i_k - 1$$

$$= 0 \qquad \text{for } t \geq i_k - 1$$

$$B + C = \sum_{i=1}^{k_i+t-1} y_{i+i_k-1} \cdot x_i' + x_{k_2+t}' \sum_{i=i_m+t}^{t_m} y_i \qquad \text{for } t \leq i_k - 1 \tag{5}$$

$$= \sum_{i=t-(i_k-1)}^{k_i+t-1} y_{i+i_k-1} \cdot x_i' + x_{k_i+t}' \sum_{i=i_m+t}^{t_m} y_i \qquad \text{for } t > i_k - 1$$

$$D = \sum_{i=1}^{t} y_i \cdot x_i'$$

It can further be shown that after $k_m + i_k - 2$ years, the new grade has reached the steady state, i.e. the number who have spent i years in the grade remains constant. The cost of the new structure for $t \geq k_m + i_k - 2$ is simply.

$$C_{t,N} = \sum_{i=1}^{t_m} y_i \cdot x_i' \tag{6}$$

Clearly management is more concerned with increases in salary costs in the near rather than the distant future and so to determine the difference in cost between the new grade and the present grade, had it been allowed to continue in existence, we must introduce a suitable discounting factor. Then comparing the two systems from zero to infinity we have that the difference in salary cost is,

$$\sum_{t=0}^{\infty} (C_{t,N} - C_p) \cdot \frac{1}{(1 + \alpha)^t} \tag{7}$$

While one could question the use of this discounting factor when considering only one possible new grade structure, in the following work on rolling up many classes it will be seen to be of importance when comparing many possible new structures.

Rolling up the Classes

As an example of the use of the preceding analysis we consider the problem of devising a new single structure suitable to contain the staff from a number of present classes. While one could "optimise" the shape of this structure using any number of criteria we have chosen an analysis which produces a new structure under minimum cost conditions — with again the provision of transfer rules to safeguard the interests of employees.

We firstly define that the new salary levels between the entry point of the lowest grade and the maximum of the highest grade are of the form of a geometric progression where the rate of increase is 4%. A scale of this type was chosen mainly because of the ease with which it can be handled — a much greater flexibility in the choice of increment size all through the pay scale will be needed in a more realistic model. The 4% was chosen because it represents roughly the mean increment size throughout the Civil Service. Our problem is then to determine, for a given number of grades, where the grade maxima should be located to give minimum cost.

Preliminary analysis showed that the task could be immediately simplified, since for a minimum cost solution the new grade maxima must be selected from a population consisting of salary levels defined by the grade maxima and entrance points contained in the present grades under consideration. This can easily be seen if we try to locate a new grade barrier between any two adjacent present grade barriers; say grades A and B with maximum salary levels at £a and £b where $a > b$. If we do not choose £a as the position of our new barrier but choose *any* point lower, then grade A staff cannot be contained by this new barrier and must seek the next higher new barrier (somewhere above £a). Since we cannot contain grade A staff with any new barrier below £a it must then be cheaper for management to bring the new barrier right down to £b and thus prevent grade B staff being given unnecessarily a new maximum salary level higher than they have at present. Similar reasoning applies if one tries to locate a new barrier between say any two entrance points or between an entrance point and a grade maximum salary level. Further simplification was also possible by associating many of the entrance points with the highest level of the grade below in the same class of the present structure. Even with this reduction it is still not feasible to evaluate all possible solutions and so a

Drinkwater, Kane

dynamic programming solution was devised (by E.M.L. Beale of SCS Ltd.) to reduce the amount of computation required.

Briefly, the method starts with every possible barrier position fixed on the new scale and the cost of the structure calculated — any difference in cost must result entirely from non-alignment of salary levels between the new structure and the present grades since with all possible barriers in position any one present grade will be transferring to a new grade with the same entrance point and the same grade maximum.

We then calculate all possible terms a_{ij} where this is the additional cost of removing all barriers from $i \to j - 1$. We assume that these a_{ij}'s are strictly additive; for example, if there were 10 possible barrier positions and we wished to know the cost of the structure with barriers 2, 3, 4 and 8, 9 missing, we could, if we had already calculated them, merely add $a_{2,5}$ and $a_{8,10}$. Although this condition does not hold in all cases it can quite easily be allowed for in obtaining a final solution — a "tree search" procedure has in fact been devised to overcome this difficulty and to produce the true minimum cost once the DP solution has been obtained. The "state" which we use for this DP is that in which all barriers from j to N are occupied and with only k barriers optimally located in the remaining $j - 1$ possible positions. If we let $C_k(j)$ be the cost of this structure, then the recursive relationship is

$$C_k(j) = \min_{1 \le i \le j-1} [C_{k-1}(j) + a_{i+1,j}]$$

Table 1. Data

Years spent in Grade	Grade 1		Grade 2	
	Salary Levels	Number in ith Year	Salary Levels	Number in ith Year
1	£2771	93	£3745	35
2	£2880	89	£3905	32
3	£2988	84	£4095	29
4	£3125	79	£4280	27
5	£3260	74	£4280	24
6	£3260	69	£4280	22
7	£3260	64	£4280	20
8	£3260	59	£4280	17
9	£3260	54	£4280	15
10	£3260	49	£4280	12
11	£3260	44	£4280	10
12	£3260	39	£4280	7
13	£3260	35	£4280	5
14	£3260	30	£4280	2
15	£3260	25	£4280	
16	£3260	20		
17	£3260	15		
18	£3260	10		
19	£3260	5		

Since $C_0(j)$ is merely $a_0(j)$, $C_1(j)$ to $C_N(j)$ can be obtained from the above relationship and the position of the N required new grade maxima optimally located and the cost determined.

For this example we considered the rolling up of 14 Classes, consisting of 50 grades and totalling 182 500 Civil Servants; and Table 1 below gives a sample of the type of data used. At this early stage we have made no attempt to determine the exact staff distributions but have merely concocted figures which in many cases follow a straightforward linear decrease with length of time in a grade.

Figure 5 shows one of a set of results obtained, that is the variation in the difference in cost between the present and the new structures for different numbers of grades in the new structure. A number of interesting features are immediately apparent:

a. The difference in cost decreases as the number of grades in the new structure increases – this is to be expected because the more barrier points there are, the more likely one of the present grades will transfer to a new grade with either exactly the same grade maximum or one which is only slightly above its own.

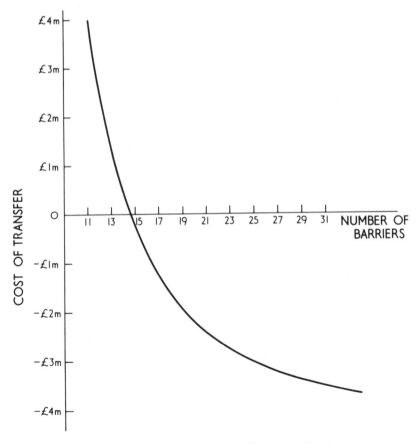

Figure 5. Cost of Transfer vs Number of Barriers

Drinkwater, Kane

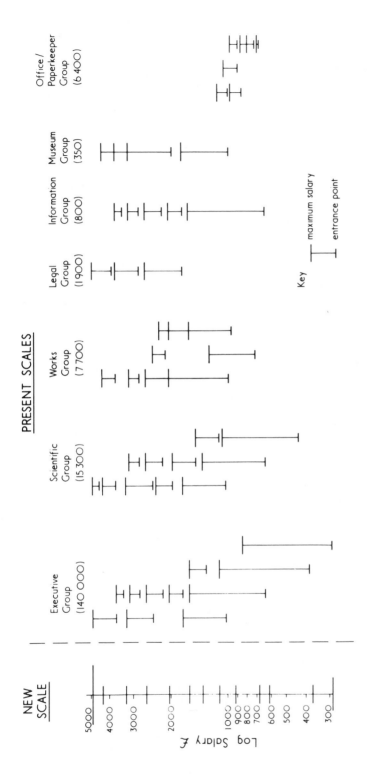

Figure 6. Position of Barriers on New Scale (Note: The number in brackets above each "group" structure is only a rough guide to the actual number. For this example we excluded grades above £5000)

b. The difference in cost can be negative. This highlights the f act that by a suitable definition of rules, even though they are beneficial to existing employees, one can produce a new structure which costs either the same or less than the present structure. In our example the negative cost results from giving less favourable terms to new entrants to one of the lower grades who have at present an annual increment of much greater than 4%.

Figure 6 shows the positions of the grade barriers for the case when twelve grades were optimally located on the new structure. Also shown are the the positions of the present grades with their maximum salary levels rounded up to the nearest level on the new 4% increment scale.

Further examination of the distribution of staff on the new structure revealed a number of difficulties which we are currently considering.

a. At least one of the present grades now stretches over two new grades. We are examining the effect that a split in this grade would have on the promotion prospects of those staff who enter the grade after the transfer has taken place, in terms of promotion probabilities and total numbers required in each of the two new grades.

b. Some of the grades which exist at the moment have been completely "swallowed" in the new structure and clearly when we are dealing with grades with either a very small salary range or very small numbers special consideration must be given.

Conclusion

Even accepting the various refinements needed in the optimising model to overcome the difficulties described, it is unlikely that our objective function, to minimise transfer costs, would be accepted by any organisation as the only criterion. Management would most probably wish to make use of job evaluation and other techniques to find the approximate positions of the new grades. However there seems to be no reason why our model cannot be adapted to include other criteria, i.e. to produce a final solution which meets the desire to produce a structure which satisfies overall career management considerations and does so at minimum cost.

Acknowledgements

The tree search and dynamic programming approach to the optimisation of the barrier positions was devised and implemented by E.M.L. Beale, Mrs D. Bubley and B. Hall of Scientific Control Systems Limited, to whom we offer our thanks.

References

E.M.L. Beale and J.P. Ultt. "Selecting Sub-sets by Dynamic Programming" — 7th *Mathematical Programming Symposium*, Sept. 1970.

Drinkwater, Kane

21
Planning in the U.K. Government Statistical Service

David Harris*

Central Statistical Office, U.K.

1.   The improvement of Government statistics is a continuing process. But over the last decade the need and demand for statistics by Government, industry and, indeed, every one else, has increased remarkably. The greater emphasis on detailed planning and on a quantitative basis for decision making have enlarged the appetite for statistics. At the same time, the techniques for satisfying this new appetite have vastly improved so that statisticians – all over the world and not just in Britain – have entered a new era. The phrase "computer revolution" has been used so freely that it has lost some of its force but in the field of large scale statistical work it is apt enough. Government statisticians thus face a quite unprecedented demand for their wares and also possess equally unprecedented technical tools for producing them. All this is fine but it has brought problems as well as potentialities. Resources are limited (perhaps more so in terms of skilled manpower than in money and computers), and there seems no question of being able to meet all the demands, all the time, with all the speed everyone wants. This is the background to the problems and developments described in this paper.

2.   The United Kingdom Government service is organised on a decentralised basis in which individual ministries have their own statistics divisions. The Government Statistical Service is formed by the statistics divisions of 20 or so ministries, and a relatively small Central Statistical Office which controls and co-ordinates the overall statistical effort. Each of the divisions is financed and directly controlled by its own ministry. Total employment is upwards of 5000 of whom rather less than 300 are in the Central Office. About 250 – including some 50 recent graduates – are professional statisticians and there are about an equal number of other specialists. By and large the rest of the staff are departmental civil servants on a tour of duty in one or other of the statistics divisions. Traditionally, the calibre of recruits to the professional class has been set

---

* The author is a Government statistician employed by the Central Statistical Office but the ideas and account given in the paper are his alone and do not in any way represent the views of the Department or anyone else in the Government Service.

high — equal to the highest civil service standard, and this has enabled statisticians to make a real contribution in policy making. In many ways, it is the number of statisticians — who are in very short supply — which forms the main constraint to the amount of work which may be undertaken.

3. There is something to be said for the view that the only satisfactory way of achieving an efficient statistical system is through complete centralization where all the statistics are produced by a single office. This is the system in Canada, Australia, Holland, Sweden, Norway, Germany and many other countries. A single organization facilitates the task of keeping up with the increasing demand for statistics and of taking an unbiased view of priorities. There are economies of scale in data collection and processing and in computer services and so on, so that a centralized form of organization offers great possibilities for the efficient production of statistics.

4. As against this, a decentralized system also has advantages — and one of these is crucial — it provides a greater opportunity for statisticians to participate in policy making. All data contain errors, estimates and assumptions so that there is always a critical requirement for complete objectivity and integrity in handling them. A close working relationship between statisticians and policy makers should therefore help towards better policies and decisions. The link between policy makers and statisticians at senior levels which the United Kingdom system offers is not therefore something to be lightly discarded.

5. The adequacy of official statistics has been a matter for debate in recent years and in 1966/67 was considered by a Committee of the House of Commons which pinpointed a number of defects. The recommendations in the report of the Committee (4th Report from the Estimates Committee, session 1966 to 1967) included a much stronger central co-ordinating role for the Central Statistical Office. As a result of the coming report new co-ordinating and planning units were set up to deal with standards, classifications, computers and data systems and with integration and overall planning. The unit concerned with planning was charged with working out overall programmes and priorities and with moving towards a comprehensive phased programme of statistical work for some years ahead. It is rather less than twelve months since the first steps towards systematic planning were taken and the planning activity is still on a modest scale with the staff now engaged amounting to four people and not all full time. The Unit works to a small group of directors of statistics from various ministries which meets under the Chairmanship of the Director of the Central Statistical Office who is also the Head of the Government Statistical Service.

6. Essentially the task is to provide the advantages of central management and co-ordination while retaining the benefits which the decentralized service offers. Much statistical work comprises the regular collection and processing of data through clerical or executive sections or by computers and it is in this area where economies of scale are mostly to be achieved. At much the same time as the planning unit was set up, a start was made in concentrating the collection and processing of data from busines establishments in a single large office and there has been a similar development in concentrating the collection of social data from households and individuals. When complete, these changes should

secure some of the more important advantages of scale enjoyed by centralized statistical systems and enable managerial and technical staffs to be used with much greater flexibility than hitherto.

7.   Meanwhile however and particularly in the area of priority determination, the extent to which the Central Office is able to influence statistical work done by the largely autonomous statistical divisions within the Ministries – though considerable – is not at all complete. The Central Office derives considerable advantage from being situated in the Cabinet Office and responsible to the Prime Minister. But the lack of direct control over statistical work as a whole means that programming and planning necessarily depend to a greater extent than in most organizations on the achievement of a concensus, often between conflicting interests. In other respects too, the organizational climate is perhaps not ideal for a planning operation. There is, for example, no co-ordinated budget for the Statistical Service as such and very little detail about statistical expenditure in the budgets of the various ministries. A first task therefore was to put together a comprehensive account of current statistical work and the resources involved in it, as a basis for the consideration of future intentions and possibilities. The second major task was to collect and collate an account of the plans and forward thinking in the various parts of the Service and their implications for resources. It might be mentioned in passing that the range of statistical work is as wide as the interests and activities of Government itself, so that the planning exercise is in some respects similar to corporate planning in a wide ranging, loosely-knit conglomerate.

8.   In other respects, and particularly in the assessment of the utility of output as a guide in the determination of priorities, it is, however, quite different from much commercial planning. The benefits which flow from improvement in statistics are the improvements in the quality of decision making which result from the better information and all too often these are difficult, if not impossible, to quantify. And there are some statistical tasks which stem from political decisions, sometimes taken quickly, and not always easy to evaluate except in political terms. In this regard, the decentralized system itself has some advantages in that the divisional directors of statistics who are all senior professionals act as a sieve, so that work without strong political or technical justification is unlikely to be put in hand, and within the various ministries only the more important projects receive priority. The main shortcoming which has to be dealt with centrally is that more important work in some departments might be delayed while less important work in others was tackled. In some instances the comparative costs of the projects will be a guide and in others the costs of faulty decision-taking. However in general wholly satisfactory criteria for comparing the relative importance of work in different areas have yet to be developed.

9.   Planning in the United Kingdom – and indeed in most other government statistical services – has been mainly regarded as having to do with optimization in the allocation of limited resources (money or machines or manpower) between competing demands. This is a proper short term reaction to an unexpected spurt in demand but it is also a function of management to anticipate all reasonable demands and to plan for their timely satisfaction. That is to say to work towards increasing supply in appropriate circumstances as well as on curtailing demand. Though our

arrangements for systematic planning are still in their infancy it became clear at a very early stage that because large scale statistical work is still very labour intensive, anything other than very short term planning would have a great deal to do with labour force or manpower planning. In our general planning work, we expect, therefore, to give a great deal more emphasis to these aspects and to moving through manpower planning towards a relaxation of the constraints imposed by the shortage of suitable professional staff. It has been our experience that it takes around six years after graduation for the new professional recruit to become sufficiently experienced to meet most of the demands likely to be made of him, and that as the profession expands, a need for more specialization is becoming apparent. Manpower planning therefore is likely to have to do with such topics as patterns of recruitment and their effectiveness, development of specialist skills and experience, education and training, as well as studies of the output of universities and of the scope for dilution and delegation. Much of this, of course, is already in being and well established so that it is an increase in the scale of effort that the planning exercise has suggested rather than something completely new. But the detailed forward look has provided new information in the form of an indication of the type of specialist skills and the number at different levels which we shall be looking for over the next few years.

10. Finally, experience in launching this particular planning activity has served to dispel any doubts that those engaged in it may have had about the more or less uniform opinion of the planning experts that new planning mechanisms are likely to take upwards of two years to develop to the point of pay-off; and that the whole business can be most frustrating over this period for those engaged in it.

References

Statistical News No. 1 May 1968. HMSO
Fourth Report from the Estimates Committee Session 1966/67 HC 246

22
The Career Assignment Program

D. Morley
Public Service Commission Ottawa

Introduction

The Canadian federal public service has approximately 220 000 permanently engaged employees. Of this group, some 50 000 are in the "officer" category. The most senior level – the executive group – consists of some 600 executive officers responsible for the first three levels of management.

One particular feature of the Canadian public service is that it must be responsive to the needs of both the English and French elements of the Canadian society. The Royal Commission on Bilingualism and Biculturalism has recently pointed out that if the language and culture of French-speaking Canada are weakly expressed in the federal government or the public service, government cannot even begin to execute its duties towards all Canadians – Francophones as well as Anglophones.[1] For this reason, the career planning and manpower development processes described in this paper place particular emphasis on the need for developing a more bilingual and biculturally aware public service.

In the past, several major reports on Canadian government organization and personnel administration stressed the need for the public service to pay more attention to its executive development problems. The 1962 Glasco Royal Commission on Government Organization pointed out that the demands on senior managers resulting from advances in technology and the changing structure of society require an increasing degree of professionalism in management as well as a broad understanding of the economic, social and political and cultural environment in which the public service operates. Education, training and career planning and mobility programs must be developed to ensure those moving to the top have proven ability to cope with these changes.[2]

In the Canadian public service the executive replacement problem will become particularly acute in the next ten years. The low birthrate during the depression and early war years has created a serious shortage of manpower in the critical age group of 35 to 45 from which prime executive material must be drawn to offset anticipated retirements, organizational growth factors and the loss of executives to the private sector.[3]

Realizing that more must be done to develop public service manpower resources, the Career Assignment Program (CAP) was started in September 1968 to identify and develop high potential personnel at an early stage in their careers. The objective of this program which was developed in co-operation with the Treasury Board Secretariat, is to develop a pool of experienced senior managers who will be ready to move into executive level positions when vacancies occur.

The purpose of this paper is to describe the main features of CAP which include: a specially designed management course; a far reaching psychological testing and research program; and a unique work assignment and career planning process which includes interchanges between the public and private sectors, provincial governments and universities.

Program description

In 1967, a study of Executive Career Paths [4] was undertaken to determine what factors influenced progression into the executive levels of the public service. Among other things, this study revealed that those at this level had, on the average, 11 years' experience in the private sector. Of this group, 15% had entered the public service directly at the executive level. More importantly, however, there was found to be a direct correlation between rate of progress and mobility. Those who had moved between organizations four or more times during their careers advanced the fastest. Conversely, those who remained in one organization up to the time they entered the executive level, progressed the slowest as measured from the time they left high school or graduated from university to the time they entered the executive level. On the basis of this information and other non-empirical observations, it was concluded that any development program should provide those participating in it with the opportunity to broaden their experience through interoccupational and interorganizational movement. Through this process, the capabilities of those in the program would be developed and tested to the fullest extent possible. CAP was, therefore, structured to include five major elements:

- selection by government departments of officers judged to have senior executive potential
- evaluation of their developmental needs through review of their past experience and career aspirations
- taking of a psychological test battery as part of a research program to evaluate their personal characteristics and capabilities
- attendance at a three month in-residence management course prior to moving into the assignment system
- assignment of participants to positions for one to three year periods inside and outside the public service to prepare them for assuming more senior positions, if they meet their assignment objectives.

CAP is a high risk, no guarantee program. No one is told they will become a senior executive. Whether participants succeed depends, to a large extent, on themselves. If individual objectives are not met at any time during an assignment, the participants may be returned to the organizations which selected them for CAP. On the other hand, if they perform effectively, promotion will be accelerated and the chances of reaching the executive level at an early stage of their career is increased.

The program is co-ordinated through the Career Assignment Office (CAO) which is part of the Executive Staffing Program of the Public Service Commision.

Selection for CAP

Thirty-five participants are selected three times a year for CAP. Selection is made by each department from individuals who have either been nominated by their supervisor or who have indicated that they want to be considered for CAP. Selection criteria are based on:

- age/salary profiles (i.e. under 35 years of age and earning over $13000)
- excellence of past performance and assessment of future potential
- work experience of not less than
  - six years if not a university graduate, of which two must have been with the federal government;
  - four years from successful completion of bachelor's degree or its professional equivalent, of which two must have been with the federal government;
  - two years with the federal government from successful completion of a Master's or Ph.D. degree
- willingness to accept inter-occupational, inter-organizational and inter-regional assignments
- acceptance of the need to become proficient in both French and English[5]

Selection is also based on: first, the assumption that participants will move into a one to three year assignment outside the "home" organization after which they will return to a more senior position in their "home" organization; second, that the "home" organization will accept the return of a participant if an assignment to another organization (outside assignment) cannot be arranged or a participant fails to meet his or her performance objectives while on an outside assignment. This first provision encourages departments to select their high performers knowing they will normally get them back. The second feature ensures a quality control factor is built into the selection process, as the CAO does not have a veto on a selection made by a department.

Career planning and evaluation of developmental needs

Since selection of CAP participants is based on the assumption thay they will return to their home organization after their first outside assignment, effective career planning is an essential element of the program. Once a participant is selected, the CAO discusses with a personnel officer of the organization concerned and the participant's supervisor:

- performance strengths and weaknesses
- the position or area of work to which he or she will return after the outside assignment
- developmental needs and career aspirations as identified by the supervisor through discussion with the participant.

As each group of 35 is brought into CAP, an induction briefing session is arranged for participants to meet each other, as well as to make sure that they are aware of the objectives, commitments and operational aspects of the program. At this stage, if participants are not proficient in both French and English and are not already taking language training, they will be phased into a second language program. They are expected to continue with this training until they have reached the desired level of proficiency.

After the induction briefing, an officer of the CAO meets individually with participants for a detailed discussion of developmental needs and career aspirations. These may vary from the perception the home organization has of them. Any significant differences are, of course, resolved through further discussion with the participant and the home organization. Once agreement is reached, participants prepare career resumés outlining their previous experience and assignment objectives. These are included in a booklet which is widely circulated inside and outside the government to organizations interested in having CAP participants assigned to them. However, before this booklet is prepared, each participant takes the psychological test battery. The interpretation of this battery may be used, at the participants' discretion, to help them reach a better understanding of themselves and their developmental needs.

The psychological testing program

The testing program associated with CAP has three major purposes:

(1) to provide, through the use of paper-and-pencil and situational tests, much needed research on styles of management and administrative skills;

(2) to ascertain, through an evaluation process, whether CAP as a whole is achieving its objectives;

(3) to provide feedback of information to participants.

Within the next year or so, a new phase of the testing program will be introduced. An assessment centre will be established to help departmental managers in the selection of CAP participants.

A problem sometimes encountered with psychological testing programs is the fear that a negative interpretation of the tests may be used to make administrative decisions. As the testing program associated with CAP is essentially for research purposes, the following assurances are given to each participant:

(1) the tests are an integral part of the program as they form part of a research project.

(2) participants may choose whether they wish the results to be interpreted to them. All test results are confidential and will be used only with the participant's written consent.

(3) test results will not be used as a final authoritative comment on participants nor will they constitute a complete description of a participant. The Personnel Assessment and Research Division of the Public Service Commission which administers the tests is fully aware of both the value and the deficiencies of psychological tests and of when and how they should be used.

At first, the two-day testing program was given during the management course. As many participants have found interpretation of the tests to be useful in helping them reach a better understanding of themselves and their developmental and assignment needs, the tests are now administered four months before the start of each course. The Personnel Assessment and Research Group indicates that after interpretation of the tests each participant is in a better position to evaluate:

(1) ability, strengths and weaknesses and their relationships to jobs in which they could succeed and to jobs which would make excessive demands on them which could not be met;

(2) need patterns and the possibilities for satisfaction in assignments;

(3) interest patterns and their relationships to persons employed in various occupational groups;

(4) psychological characteristics and personality dynamics;

(5) attitudes and value systems relative to the work environment;

(6) styles of management and administrative skills;

(7) appreciation of line/staff differences;

(8) psychological distance and capacity of adjustment in assignments other than in their present fields;

(9) a past look at employment history in relation to future career aspirations.

Information on the above-mentioned areas is gathered by using tests which measure general intelligence, creativity, interests and values, personality, motivation, style and leadership qualities and administrative judgement.[6] Appendix A indicates the coverage of the psychological assessment battery given to CAP participants. Appendix B is a summary of reports which have been or are in the process of being prepared to interpret the test results.

The management course

Participants are phased into one of the CAP 3-month in-residence management courses starting in January, April and September. The course, which is an integral part of the program, provides an educational input in the development process and is intended:

(1) to create an understanding of the aims and objectives of the Canadian Government; its political, sociological and economic setting, form of organization; methods of management; and relationship to current management theory and practice;

(2) to increase each participant's ability to analyze, think through and resolve management problems;

(3) to provide insight into the characteristics required for effective leadership and motivation of people as related to the management function;

(4) to foster values and attitudes essential for identification with and commitment to, the goals of the public service.

For most, it offers an opportunity for re-vitalization and re-thinking of existing values and a chance to exchange ideas with thirty-four participants drawn from other departments and occupational backgrounds.

Participation from the non-governmental sector will add to the value of this learning experience. In brief, the content of the course is focussed on *Decision-making* for the *Manager* of the *Public Service* in his *Environment*.

Unit A. Preview and Preliminaries

This introduces the course and the staff to the participants as well as outlining teaching methods and course objectives.

The next three units consider the foundations and framework for making decisions.

Unit B. Man in His Culture

This unit is concerned with the concept of culture, the man-made environment of man, its reality and power, and its importance in decision-making for managers in the Canadian public service.

Unit C. Prerequisites for Decision

Focus of attention is on the prerequisites for decision-making; practical logic or formal reasoning, ethical constraints and ends, and insights about man as the decision maker, in part sub-rational but capable of learning.

Unit D. Format for Decision

In this unit a systematic and disciplined process for analyzing situations to reach a managerial decision is reviewed and tried.

The following three units emphasize three inter-related but distinguishable approaches to the work of managing.

Unit E. The Work of a Manager

This unit emphasizes the distinctive work of a manager, under such headings as planning, organizing, integrating and measuring.

Unit F. The Art of Managing

The theme of integrating the needs of individuals, the behaviour of groups within the objectives of the organization is developed in this section.

Unit G. The Science of Managing

Three weeks are spent emphasizing measurement as the core of the scientific approach to management, stressing its importance in the information and decision system linking the public service.

The next three units focus on the public service manager in his department, or central agency, functioning within the machinery of government, operating in our political society.

Unit H. The Machinery of Government

This unit will give an overview of the institutional structure.

Unit I. The Environment

Through returning to the opening theme of man in his man-made environment, the emphasis this time is on the economic, social and political aspects of our developing world with an eye to the Year 2000 A.D.

Unit J. Syndicate Presentations

The last two days are spent in presenting syndicate solutions to a major current policy problem to a panel of deputy ministers.* [7]

One important feature of the management course is the contribution which it will be making to the development of bilingualism and biculturalism within the public service. Starting in September 1970, it is planned that alternate courses will be carried on in a completely bilingual atmosphere. To achieve this, all participants will have to be sufficiently bilingual to comprehend both French and English. There will also be a sufficient number of participants whose mother tongue is French to ensure bilingual discussion and exchange of points of view, based on differences in cultural backgrounds.

The assignment program

By far the most important part of CAP is the opportunity for participants to broaden their experience through a diversity of work assignments both inside and outside the federal public service. Each assignment is undertaken to achieve set objectives which will determine whether a participant will remain in the program. While participating in CAP, individuals remain associated with their home organizations as long as this arrangement is mutually satisfactory. Depending on the level of the participant on entry into CAP, the first, and at least one other assignment, will be outside the "home" department. It is hoped that one assignment will also be outside the federal public service.

To avoid the danger of talent poaching, good faith on the part of the participating organizations is an essential element, as is the accuracy of their judgement of the participant's motivation for undertaking an assignment. Persons continuing to meet fully the high performance standard set for them can expect, under normal circumstances, to be promoted on each re-assignment, or about every two years.

As mentioned earlier, organizations receiving the career resumé booklet will indicate to the CAO which participants they wish to interview. The CAO screens each request to make sure it meets the participant's assignment objectives and developmental needs and arranges the interview. Those in CAP essentially compete in an open market situation. While the CAO will assist participants in finding assignments, in the final analysis they must sell themselves to prospective employers. The number of requests for interviews that each participant receives has some relationship to his or her saleability as a high potential product. If any participant does not receive sufficient requests for interview, the CAO will actively open up doors. In doing so, however, it will be objective in telling a prospective employer about the particular participant's strengths and weaknesses. Experience has shown that no difficulty has been encountered in finding most participants interesting and challenging assignments. The problem they face is often in deciding which of a number of offers they should accept.

* A deputy minister is the senior departmental public servant.

One important feature of CAP is that no special treatment is given to participants. All assignments are subject to regulations and other conditions of service governing employment in the public service.

Of the 115* who have participated in CAP so far, 8 have returned to their home organizations because assignments could not be found for them in other organizations or because they failed to meet assignment objectives. A certain "rejection" factor was expected and indicates the high level of performance expected of CAP participants.

Separation of a participant from CAP may occur for a number of reasons:

- voluntary withdrawal by a participant
- inability to find a participant an assignment
- refusal to accept the commitments imposed by the program
- failure to meet performance objectives while on assignment
- satisfactory completion of the first assignment after promotion to one grade below the executive level or on appointment as an executive officer
- decision by the "home" department that the participant will no longer benefit from further assignments.

The interchange program

While the program was being developed, value was seen in interchanging CAP participants with personnel from industry, provincial and foreign governments, international organizations, unions and universities. The Canadian Chamber of Commerce was invaluable in publicizing the program to industry and early in 1970, representatives from twenty-two major companies who had indicated an interest in CAP, attended a two-day seminar to discuss the program. The seminar concluded that CAP would provide an opportunity for both the public and private sectors for

- a long rather than short term investment in management development
- retaining an individual who might otherwise leave the organization for lack of immediate developmental opportunities
- testing and proving potential of a manager in a new environment
- developing new dimensions to the professional expertise of a manager
- creating awareness of all facets of the social, economic, political, business and technological structure of the Canadian environment
- sharing experience among future leaders of both the public and private sectors
- companies to tap a new source of manpower without the obligation of having to make reciprocal arrangements
- providing industry managers with an understanding and knowledge of government and the decision-making process, as it affects industry

* During the first few courses, some senior officers attended the CAP course without participating in the assignment program. This accounts for the difference between 115 and 175, the course loading for the first five groups. From the sixth group on, most of those in CAP will participate in the full program.

- keeping government managers aware of the views and needs of the private sector and developing a better understanding of business management and of work in the business environment
- outside input into CAP (participants and resource persons) to enrich the course experience.

The seminar has been followed up by visits to a further seventeen companies, as well as all ten provinces and twenty-two universities. The interchange program has been well received. One assignment of a CAP participant has already been arranged to a private company, as well as two to international organizations. In the group starting in January, 1971, it is expected that industry and provincial representatives will participate.

No major administrative problems have been encountered in arranging interchanges. It has been generally agreed that each participant would remain on the payroll of the "home" organization with the amount of reimbursement of salary and fringe benefits by the "employing" organization being subject to negotiation. Relocation expenses will be paid according to the "home" organization's policy with payment being split on a 50/50 basis.

Publicity

One reason CAP has been well received is because of the attention that has been paid to explaining and publicizing the program both inside and outside the public service. When CAP was launched, briefings were given to all deputy ministers and their senior management groups, as well as to departmental personnel in all the major centres across Canada. A brochure was prepared and distributed to all public servants. The press has been kept informed of the program's development and has run a number of articles on it. The CAO keeps in constant touch with its departmental and outside contacts to make sure that CAP is meeting their needs. News bulletins are issued periodically and meetings are held on a continuous basis with departments to ensure that CAP is responsive to and meeting their needs.

Obviously the best form of advertising comes from satisfied participants and managers who are pleased with their performance. As the program expands more managers are being made aware of CAP and the quality of most of its participants. However, commitment of senior management to the program is essential to its success. A continuing effort has to be made to keep this commitment, as development of personnel is too often considered a luxury rather than a necessity.

Evaluation of CAP

The sixth group entered CAP in April, 1970, and it is now possible to arrive at some general conclusions as to the degree to which the program's original objectives have been met.

Objective: To gain senior managerial support and acceptance of CAP.

All government departments, as well as a number of crown corporations have placed participants on CAP, as well as taking them on assignment.

Objective: To arrange interdepartmental and inter-occupational assignments to develop participants' capabilities and broaden their experience.

102 of the 115 participants in the first five groups have taken on assignments outside their "home" organization; 75 of these have resulted in assignment to a position with a different occupational classification.

Objective: To obtain a balanced representation of both language groups and sexes.

As of Novermber, 1969, 4430 officers met the basic age/salary selection criteria. Of this group, 7.8% have as their mother tongue French and 5.0% are women. In the first five groups, 7.8% of the participants' mother tongue was French and 2% have been women. To redress a historical inbalance in the representation of these two groups at the senior managerial level, special steps will have to be taken to ensure an increased participation of both groups.

Objective: To develop a pool of senior managers capable of moving into senior executive positions.

8 of the 115 participants have been assigned into executive level positions, with 3 having been promoted into the executive group.

Objective: To ensure high selection standards are maintained.

As already mentioned, 8 participants have returned to their "home" organization because assignments could not be arranged or as they failed to meet performance objectives while on outside assignment. Certainly, it was not originally anticipated that all participants would be "flyers". Rejection of some who do not meet the program's standards is, therefore, understandable. At this stage, it is difficult to evaluate whether this rejection rate is reasonable.

Objective: To establish a psychological assessment and research program.

Under the direction of the Personnel Assessment and Testing Services, this has been accomplished. Initial interpretation of the tests indicate that this research program will contribute significantly to the understanding of the personal characteristics, needs and management styles of this high potential group. It is too early, however, to determine exactly how this information can be used to structure training and development programs, or to facilitate a better understanding of organizational development needs or to aid in the selection of senior executives.

Objective: To establish a management course that meets the educational need of CAP participants.

Data would indicate that the management course established by the Bureau of Staff Training and Development is providing a valuable educational input. Assessment of its impact on participants most probably can only be carried out in conjunction with an evaluation of the benefit of experience gained while on assignment. A program to evaluate changes in performance and attitudes is being developed.

Objective: To extend participation in CAP to include interchanges with industry, provincial governments and universities.

Three assignments outside the federal government have already been arranged. By January, 1971, it will be possible to evaluate the success of the program in expanding the number of outside assignments and in attracting outside participation in CAP. Present indications are that this objective will be achieved.

Operating costs

The cost of operating the CAO and the management course, including accommodation, salaries and course administrative expense, but not including participants' salaries is $685 000 or $3900 per participant.

The cost per participant is approximately equal to one quarter of the average annual salary of those so far participating in CAP. It may appear to be high, but if the program continues to meet its objectives, it is a relatively small investment towards ensuring the future effectiveness and efficiency of the public service.

Conclusion

Possibly, the unique aspect of CAP is that no individual or department has been forced into participating. On this basis alone, it is presumably meeting the users' needs by providing another dimension to departmental career development programs. However, the process of re-evaluation of objectives and program operations must continue. Much has still to be done in terms of improving selection and assignment processes, career planning before and after assignments, in obtaining continued senior manager support and commitment, and in extending the program outside the federal public service. More empirical data and additional studies will have to be developed to confirm its viability. Apart from the visible benefits that have been described, possibly the most valuable and immeasurable pay-off is the extent to which CAP has stimulated a greater awareness of the need for effective career development and manpower planning. Every time a person is selected for CAP and his future is discussed with his supervisor, or a participant moves into a new assignment, this awareness is increased. This may well be the most important contribution that CAP has made to the public service of Canada.

Appendix "A"

Coverage of the Psychological Assessment Battery
for Career Assignment Program Participants

General Intelligence is assessed by a general mental ability test to determine capacity to think rationally and to deal with the environment.

Creativity Battery determines how much creativity, initiative, originality and mental flexibility an individual has.

Interests and Values are assessed through the questionnaire technique which compares an individual's likes and dislikes with other persons in a wide variety of occupations.

Personality is assessed through a questionnaire technique which determines an individual's relative degree of strength in an extended list of personality traits and characteristics.

Motivation is assessed by examining those attitudes and needs that are deemed essential for effective managers.

Management Style and Leadership Qualities are assessed to identify the assumptions an individual makes about human nature in the world of work and his attitudes towards various management practices and the human side of enterprise.

Administrative Judgement is tested by using techniques to assess an individual's capacity to solve problems framed in the administrative context and to assess certain administrative skills.

Dimensions of Managerial Work are assessed with departmental co-operation using an executive position description questionnaire, revealing common characteristics among positions and providing a measure of the degree to which each characteristic is a part of the position, also, revealing to management unrecognized differences among positions as well as similarities.

Appendix "B"

Summary of Reports Prepared by the Personnel Assessment and
Research Group, Public Service Commission, Ottawa 4,
Resulting from CAP Psychological Testing Program

Reports Written

1. Biographical Information on Participants for CAP #1, #2 and #3 — by S.W. Watt and L.W. Slivinski

2. Attitudes of Managers in the Canadian Public Service — by L.W. Slivinski

3. Interests of Managers in the Canadian Public Service — by L.W. Slivinski

4. The Relative Importance of Certain Aspects of Executive Ability as seen by Members on CAP — by W. Noe

5. Investigations Into the Work of Some Managers in the Public Service — by L.W. Slivinski

Reports to be Written

1. Managerial Job Functions and Job Profiles in the Canadian Public Service — by L.W. Slivinski and B. Desbiens

2. The Relationship Between Managerial Functions and Managerial Characteristics Needed to Perform these Functions — by L.W. Slivinski

3. The Relationship Between Managerial Skills as Found in Managers in Industry, a Graduating MBA Class and Managers in the Canadian Public Service — by L.W. Slivinski

4. Creativity and Various Levels of Management in the Canadian Public Service — by L.W. Slivinski

5. Personality and Various Levels of Management in the Canadian Public Service — by L.W. Slivinski

6. Prediction of Managerial Success in the Canadian Public Service — by L.W. Slivinski

7. Trends of CAP Selection as Examined by Biographical Information — by S. Watt and L.W. Slivinski.

References

1 *Report of the Royal Commission on Bilingualism and Biculturalism* Ottawa: The Queen's Printer, 1969, Book III, p. 90.

2 *The Royal Commission on Government Organization*: Ottawa: The Queen's Printer, 1962, Report #3 Personnel Management.

3 D. Morley, 1968: "A Co-ordinated Approach to Management Development", UN Interregional Seminar on the Development of Senior Administrators in the Public Service of Developing Countries.

4 P. Chartrand and K. Pond, 1969: "Executive Career Paths in the Public Service", *The Canadian Personnel and Industrial Relations Journal*; Vol. 16, No.3, May 1969.

5 *The Career Assignment Program*, 1968: Brochure prepared by the Public Service Commission and Treasury Board Secretariat Ottawa: The Queen's Printer, Cat. No. SC3–3463.

6 L. Slivinski, "Personnel Assessment Service to CAP Participants", March 1970.

7 CAP, Management Course Daily Plans 70–2, pp. 2–3.

23
'Data Stream':
A Manpower Data Bank

G. R. D'Avignon
G. Guruprasad
Public Service Commission Ottawa

Summary

DATA STREAM is an acronym for DATA System for Training, Research,
Employment, and Appraisal of Manpower. The system holds 63 000 personnel
information records relating to Administrative, Foreign Service, Professional,
Scientific and Technical employees of the Public Service of Canada. It also
holds the records of prospective entrants to these cadres from the private
sector. Each record contains information relating to basic characteristics
(tombstone data), education, skills and aspirations. The data files are held
on-line on disk files, and can be interactively interrogated on a real-time basis
by staffing and planning officers from remote consoles distributed across
Canada. Actions which occur in the personnel area are monitored by the system
for update information: As a by-product, statistical files are maintained. The
first section of the paper describes the concepts underlying Data Stream.
Properly, the system is more an information management system, than one of
the popular systems such as Total Information Systems, Integrated Data Systems
or Management Information Systems. The second part of the paper describes the
advantages and disadvantages of possible routes to implementation and highlights the criteria that determined in the case of Data Stream, a total package
approach to the development of systems and programs.

The Canadian Economy and the Public Service

The pace of economic growth, the resultant structural changes, and the impact
of technology upon economic development have caused, in recent years, a
shortfall of supply over demand for technical, professional and competent
managerial personnel. Possibly, this is a universal trend. The Bureau of
Labour Statistics (USA) projections indicate that in 1970 the net shortfall of
supply of Engineers and Scientists over demand is in the order 236 000, and
that by 1975 this gap is likely to widen to 339 000.[1] Available information
in Canada points to an identical trend.[2] This applies also to types of
professional manpower other than scientists and engineers.[3]

These analyses say little about the characteristics of the labour force. In current years, advances in education, and the availability of higher and extramural educational facilities has tended to increase the proportion of multi-specialty personnel: personnel who can be moved easily through a series or compatible range of occupations. This substitutability means, an opportunity to optimize manpower utilization.[4] Given scarcity and competition between the Public and Private Sectors of the economy for the same pool of labour, resources will tend to shift to that sector which tends to achieve optimality.

The situation regarding other types of labour (classified in the Public Service as Operational and Administrative Support categories) is quite different. The impact of technology on the North American economy will create problems in finding suitable jobs for the semi-skilled annual additions* to the labour force.[5]

The economic backdrop to the operations of the Public Service Commission can, therefore, be described in terms of shortfalls of supply over demand of scarce personnel, and changing economic structural relationships. In addition, the Canadian economy is a growing economy, with the impetus for growth emanating from an efficient private sector.

The Federal Public Service is approximately 215 000 strong, and broken up for administrative (i.e. collective bargaining and placement) purposes into six occupational categories: Operational; Administrative Support; Technical; Scientific & Professional; Administrative & Foreign Service; and Executive categories. The latter four categories, which make up the bulk of the scarce manpower categories number 63 000 employees in their ranks. The Public Service Commission is responsible to Parliament in all aspects of personnel management relating to placement and recruitment of Public Service employees and its operational arm is the Staffing Branch. The Staffing Branch, although it has Ottawa as its Headquarters, discharges its functions through six regional offices throughout Canada and where possible by delegating authority to departmental personnel offices.

The wide geographical and organizational dispersal of actions, the economic background, the competitive nature of the staffing function, and the legal accountability to Parliament for all actions within the Public Service Employment Act, create a variety of information requirements in a variety of centres. The purpose of information is to provide an efficient response capability. Problems relating to information needs are basically related to the means of obtaining the information required, on time. This, of course, does not mean that the problems of data capture, manipulation, and storage are any less important.

The Search for a Solution

The need for a central manpower information system was first forecast by by Mr. Ron Packman of the Public Service Commission in 1961. His attempts at solving the problems were based on a batch file processing system, based

---

* The OECD estimate of this type of addition to the labour force is 2.8 million per annum. The committee on Technology and the American Economy in its report to the President estimated that by the end of the century the proportion of the labour force employed in manufacturing would drop to 20%.

partly on punch cards and partly on magnetic tape files. In the final analysis these attempts resulted in Basic Employee Data files and Job Classification History files. The problems of common and unique keys to data records, the controls required for maintaining the files, also became apparent. Nevertheless, the basic employee data files provided a nucleus for the development of a rudimentary skills inventory. In December 1966 formally, a study was commenced to develop a sophisticated information system. While the system that developed out of this study,[6] Data Stream, is (necessarily) unique to the Public Service Commission of Canada, the Analysis of the solution models and the implementation approaches are of general applicability to the design and implementation of DATA BANKS.

Concepts underlying Data Stream

DATA BANK implies the arrangement of data so as to provide practicable access for the largest possible number of users at the minimum cost. This definition necessarily relates to 'recognized' users, as opposed to 'possible' users.[7] It is applicable equally to batch as to real-time users, for that matter to non-computer environments. The key to design therefore is the organization. In an analytical context, the problem reduces to defining an organization model.

The Organization Model

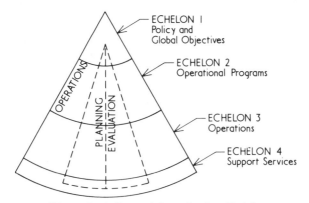

Figure 1. A General Organization Model

Figure 1, illustrates a general organization model. The emphasis is not on portraying the various functions (such as finance, personnel, etc.) in the organization, but on highlighting the number of echelons in terms of command and control, and also on the need to distinguish between operations, planning and evaluation. It is assumed that because of the cohesive nature of the model, the necessary information flows between echelons (suitably filtered or amplified, as the cases warrant), and the necessary dialogues between planning and operations, operations and evaluation, and evaluation and planning take place. Given adequate participation of management both in the planning and evaluation process, the organization model is self-contained, except for shocks or disturbances from outside. Although the model displays a high degree of abstraction, in real-life, many single-product (or service) single location firms display the features of this model. Even in the case of the many-product (service) firm, as long as the degree of diversification is not severe, and as long as the firm's activities are not geographically dispersed, the model can be considered to be representative. The real problem is communications.

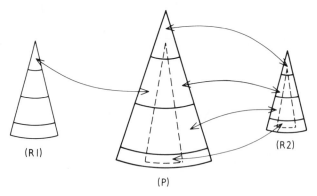

Figure 2. Decentralized Organization Model

Figure 2 illustrates a decentralized organization model: Two different kinds of decentralized relationships are shown. On the left hand side the regional office (or branch), R1, is mainly an operations unit responding to communications from, and accountable to, the operations management of the main firm (P). The operations management (2nd echelon) are themselves accountable to, and directed by, the policy echelon (or 1st echelon). The Branch itself does not carry out any planning or evaluation functions. This kind of relationship is often found in manufacturing companies who have branch sales offices or service plants. On the right hand side of the model, the regional office (or branch), R2, is not merely an operations unit but is also capable of modifying or adapting policies, and perform the necessary planning and evaluation activities to fulfil its objectives. The branch organization, however, is accountable at the policy level, and because of the dominance of the parent organization, has to maintain strong links between the respective echelons on a counterpart basis, if it is to be effective. An example of such decentralization is the case of multi-national companies.

The model displayed in Figure 3 is a variant of the model shown in Figure 2: an organization model with decentralization and delegation. It is perhaps rather unique to public service organizations. By historical tradition or as an act of national policy, an organization is given paramountcy over a certain facet of governmental operations. This represents the parent firm in the model (P). Because of regional demands and also because of geographical distances, regional offices (R), are established to effectively undertake the operation. If the organization exists to serve non-public service clients then decentralization can take any or all of the forms shown in Figure 2, according to considerations of efficiency and special circumstances. If, on the other hand, the parent organization serves other government organizations, in the absence of conclusive evidence of economy or efficiency, over a period of time, the pressure for autonomy (or self-help) will develop among the clients (D). At this point,

D'Avignon, Guruprasad

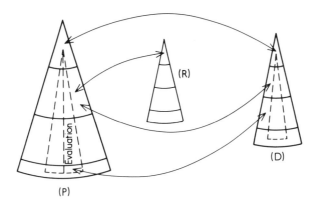

Figure 3. Organization Model with Decentralization and Delegation

if the main organization cannot cease to be accountable for that facet of operations it has been entrusted with, some means of delegating the authority to undertake the operations has to be developed. The links are then not at counterpart levels but at the policy levels, program management levels, and at the evaluation and operations levels of the parent and department organizations. Even this complicated relationship structure is an over-simplification: In real life, the problem is compounded by selective centralization of select services, and shared services between groups of clients, etc.

The Solution Determinants

The organization model shown in Figure 3 represents the Public Service staffing situation. The Public Service Commission is responsible to Parliament to ensure that staffing within the Public Service is based on the merit principle — the best qualified man for the job, subject to statutory preferences. Its operational staffing arm is the Staffing Branch. For the sake of efficiency, the Staffing Branch operates regional offices in Vancouver, Edmonton, Winnipeg, Toronto, Montreal and Halifax. Also, to speed up staffing operations, and to bring about a closer participation of line management in staffing operations, the authority to appoint is delegated to departments. This delegation, however, is subject to monitoring: this is the only way the Commission can be meaningfully accountable to Parliament.

Delegated and decentralized operations, in the absence of readily available information on a broad base, can also lead to a number of problems: In the case of in-service appointments, a tendency towards parochialism, and away from a service-wide outlook can develop in departments and regions; also, in the case of appointments from outside the service, cross bidding for scarce personnel can develop.

The problems range from the realm of policy through management practices to individual appointments. They all do have, nevertheless, a common solution determinant — information. Information serves as the countervailing force necessary to bind decentralized and delegated operations into one related set. The provision of information across such a wide range of activities, however, can be a difficult and expensive proposition unless it can be organized, systematized and managed.

Data Stream: *An information management system*

The data required to serve the needs of the three top echelons of the organization (Staffing Branch), and the hierarchical relationships between the data files are shown in Figure 4. At the lowest level are the Basic Data

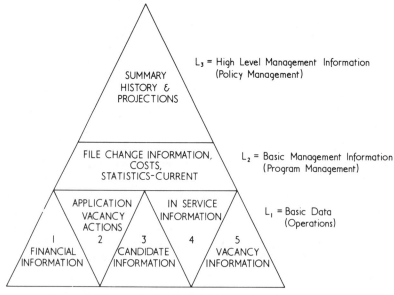

Figure 4. Hierarchical relationships within the Data Bank

files, that provide information necessary for operations, and conceivably can serve as "clarification" information to the higher echelons of the organization. These files are:

(1) Financial information – giving budgetary breakdowns, data relating to relative cost factors such as advertisements and responses, removal costs, etc., necessary for efficient staffing operations;

(2) A progress file on pending applications and vacancies actions – necessary for reducing duplication of work in a delegated context, and for reducing delays in a decentralized context;

(3) Candidate information – an inventory of skills available amongst prospective candidates to the Public Service, who cannot be placed immediately;

(4) In-service employee information – A skills bank of public service talents necessary for optimum utilization of manpower; and

(5) Vacancy information – Current as well as forecasted vacancies, the demand side of the manpower placement equation.

The information required for the efficient administration of operations is shown at the second level (L2). Given adequate integration of the files at level 1, the changes in the composition of the files, the movement of Data records between files, and the changes to the Data elements within records, themselves become statistics that throw light on the efficiency of the operations. In addition, descriptive statistics of the level 1 base can become useful planning information if measured and recorded periodically over time.

The level 3 base is a select summary of the level 2 base and, in addition, given policy constraints, contains projections for the immediate future.

Figure 4 shows only the relationships between the elements comprising the data base. The DATA BANK includes the necessary directories, and classification/query tables, file management and data manipulation programs necessary for the organization, manipulation and retrieval of data.

It is popular to characterize special purpose DATA BANKS as integrated systems, Management Information Systems, etc., depending on their purported uses (and perhaps on the buzzwords closest to the designer's hearts). Data Stream is *not* a total information system. In fact, it does not even take into account all the categories of Public Service employees. It does not concern itself with matters relating to Pay, and employee benefits, etc., which have some, perhaps indirect, bearing on optimum utilization of manpower. In fact, it is doubtful if total systems can be designed for any, except the most trivial, operations.

It *may* or *may not* be a Management Information System depending on the definition of MIS. One prevailing definition of MIS is "a completely integrated system of data gathering, data transmission, data processing, information storage and information retrieval, as concerning the entire enterprise".[8] With the qualification that there are degrees of completeness or entireties, and absolute completeness etc. is not attainable, this particular definition of MIS fits Data Stream. On the other hand, MIS can also be defined as "an information system which provides the manager with that information which he needs to make decisions".[9] A liberal interpretation of this definition would equate it to the one discussed earlier; the assumption is that the manager is interested in the organization in its entirety. A more narrow and rigid interpretation can be that a MIS provides the manager with information in the form of timely reports that eliminate the risks inherent in decision making.

For a number of reasons, such systems are difficult, if not impossible to design. The function of management is to respond to (and decide in the face of) uncertainty. Any system which can eliminate uncertainty can theoretically also eliminate managers! Such a system should also be able to forecast management requirements, and also anticipate changes in management styles, etc!

On the positive side, Data Stream is an Information Management System which provides information to the various echelons of the Staffing Branch to assist them to discharge their functions. It is a system that manages the information needs of the organization within given budgetary and technological constraints. It has an integrated data base and it can be queried interactively — in the form of dialogues. Actions on any one part of the System (or a file, etc.) can trigger chain reactions on other parts of the system without manual intervention and thus generate additional information, or alternately purge the system of redundant data. Such a system is not easy to develop unless the right implementation strategy is adopted.

Implementation Alternatives

Figure 5 is a schematic which describes the Data Stream System. It is basically a real-time on-line system. The System could also have been developed as a batch system. The justifications for real-time, on-line are:

(1) the need to bridge the geographic and departmental dispersal of action centres with a central information bank;

(2) the fact that on a detailed analysis, such communications links become cheaper than manual interfaces, given a high volume of transactions, and also;

(3) an interactive capability (with its many benefits) cannot be achieved in any other way. [10]

There are a number of interesting technical alternatives to be chosen in the implementation of such a system. One example is the choice between simulation models and evaluation bench marks, etc., during the hardware selection stage. Another choice is that between preco-ordinated index systems and faceted index systems, etc., as the basis for the classification and retrieval vocabulary. [11] The choice between the use of inverted lists as against the use of descriptor bit maps for structuring the file management algorithms can have significant impact on the efficiency of the overall system. Quite often, the best results may be obtained not by choosing one or the other of the alternatives, but by combining them and developing new hybrid techniques. [12] Notwithstanding these choices, the crucial determinants of success, in the case of personnel systems, are in the realm of inter-personal relations: the employee acceptance and co-operation is paramount to the creation of a viable data base; equally important is the participation of the ultimate users of the system during the development and implementation stages.

The Participatory Implementation Approach

User participation in the case of Data Stream was achieved by making the development of the detailed systems design (in terms of data definition, input formats, output data requirements, output formats, etc.) the responsibility of a task force of user representatives. The team varied in composition from Personnel experts, through Organization and Methods experts to Computer Analysts. In parallel, the vocabularies were developed by another task force consisting of user as well as employee representatives. In addition, through dialogues with staff associations, etc. employee participation was obtained.

An alternative to the task force approach would have been a system designed by technical experts, with user consultation and not participation: In view of the numerous trade-offs that occurred during the task force deliberations, in retrospect, a turn-key system implemented by experts would not have had the same acceptance by users. Similarly, an alternative to dialogues with employees, would have been direct imposition. Judging from the enormous apprehension initially generated by the announcement of the system, it is fair to say imposition would have been an invitation to disaster. Continued participation of the user in the maintenance of the system is ensured by

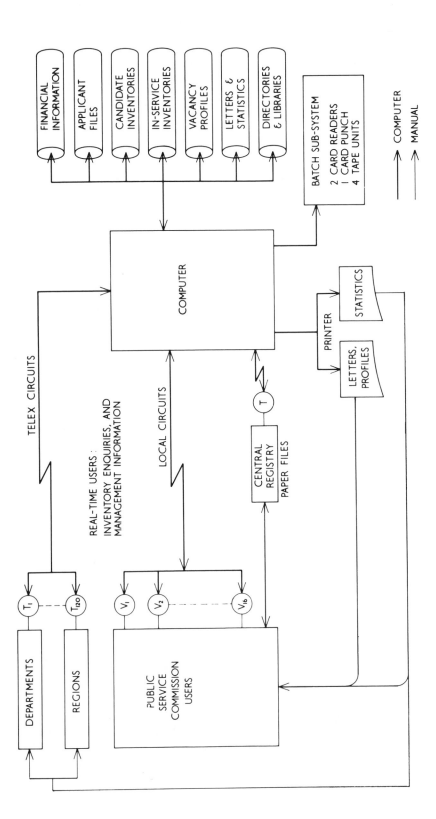

Figure 5. The Data Stream System

involving him in the operation of the system on the basis of man-machine interdependence. For example, when a staffing officer informs the system that he will call a set of candidates for interviews, the system will automatically generate letters, etc., for his signature. The basic philosophy is to provide the user with a reciprocal service from the system when he provides the system with an item of valued and required information to update the files. In the absence of such explicit design philosophies, the system will soon cease to represent the "current status". Similarly, the employees' participation is also enhanced by providing an open but secure system: The system is open in the sense that all the information held about an individual is open to his scrutiny and correction at any time. In addition, each time a significant action on the individual occurs (through the system), he is automatically informed. Given these freedoms, the onus is then on the employee to keep his system correct. The security of the system is maintained through "user" codes which regulate the access to data.

Once the concepts of any system have been defined and the feasibility established, the question arises whether the system should be designed and implemented as a total package or on an evolutionary basis, as a series of related sub-systems. Given a participatory implementation approach, this choice is purely theoretical. To be effective the system has to be designed as a total package and the programs developed as interrelated modules: This may be anathema to those who advocate the development of complex systems, through "evolution". Task forces consisting of experts drawn from line-operations cannot be re-convened for extended periods of time without ceasing to be representative, and without losing continuity. Also a system cannot be designed in bits and pieces by different groups designing different sub-systems without running into compatibility problems. Therefore, it is necessary for one group to design the system as a total package. This development should proceed up to the point where programming activities can commence with the full knowledge of all the interrelationships.

The proof of the success of the participatory approach is the fact that the system formally became operational on April 1, 1970, on target and within forecasted budgetary ceilings. Terminals consisting of keyboards and small visual displays are already in operation. Using these, staffing officers can retrieve information concerning employees in matters of seconds. Initial reaction to the system from users other than staffing officers, such as planners and researchers is also extremely promising. Based on these reactions, the Commission is rapidly going ahead with its plans for installing terminals all across Canada and Departments.

The data base was generated out of employee questionnaires. The return on questionnaires has been over 90%. Once the applicant files and candidate files are brought into operation (October 1, 1970) the value of the Data Bank will have increased sufficiently to permit the retrieval of meaningful statistics both for management planning and co-ordination as well as for manpower planning and optimum utilization of manpower.

Conclusions

In the area of Management Science, particularly manpower resource engineering, much has been written in a theoretical vein, about the techniques and possibilities of optimization of resource utilization. The main drawback has always been the paucity of meaningful data and knowledge about the skills of the population. In the Canadian Public Service context, even though Data Stream may not be the final solution, it will certainly advance the art of manpower management. It is also likely to throw more light on the capabilities and limitations to the programming of human resources in terms of "Manpower Plans". These are valuable questions that urgently require pragmatic answers in this age of rapid changes in technology and social structures.

References

1 National Science Foundation, 1963: N.S.F. Report 63–34; N.S.F., Washington, D.C.

2 OECD, 1966: *Manpower Policy and Programmes in Canada*, Page 12; OECD, Paris.

3 Harry G. Johnson, 1966: "The Social Sciences in the Age of Opulence", *Canadian Journal of Economics and Political Science*; XXXLL, 4 Novermber 1966.

4 OECD: Op.Cit. Page 146.

5 *The Committee on Technology and the American Economy*, 1966; Report to the President, Washington, D.C.

6 C. Guruprasad, 1967: *Management Information System – Data Stream*. Vol. 1; Bureau of Management Consulting Services, Ottawa.

7. C. Guruprasad and R.H. Taylor, 1967: *Design Problems of a Scientific and Technical Manpower Data Bank*, Proceedings of the International Symposium on Automation of Population Register Systems, Vol. 1; pages 75–83: Information Processing Association of Israel; Jerusalem.

8 Macdonald W. Anderson, 1969: *Management Information Systems*, Data Displays for Information Systems, Page 4, American Data Processing Inc., Detroit, U.S.A.

9 J.D. Aron, 1969: "Information Systems in Perspective", *Computing Surveys*, Vol. 1, No. 4, pages 213 and 214, ACM, New York, U.S.A.

10 C. Guruprasad, 1967: *Management Information System Data Stream*. Vol. 1, pages 142–174; Bureau of Management Consulting Services, Ottawa.

11 R.L. Swift, (University of Waterloo) 1969: *Description of an Information Retrieval Language for a Personnel Inventory System*: Information Management Centre, Staffing Branch, Public Service Commission, Ottawa.

12 Data Stream Task Force, 1970: *Data Stream Detailed Systems Reports*; Information Management Centre, Staffing Branch, Public Service Commission, Ottawa.

24

Manpower Planning in the United States: A State's View

Paul A. Weinstein

Executive Assistant to the Governor of Maryland

Introduction

Planning has different meanings depending upon how sophisticated the background may be. To some, planning means only establishing lines of communication between people ·in a relevant program area. To others, it implies the setting up of formal objective functions, targets and procedures for reaching target levels of output. This paper will attempt to outline the authorized roles of the relevant decision-makers in the United States and make explicit the rules of the game.

While the University community has developed the research dealing with manpower programs, little of this technique has been transferred to the operational end of the business. Theoretically, we are aware of the benefits to utilization of equimarginal principles for allocating public sector funds and know that there are problems inherent in the measurement of the relevant outputs.* But policy makers at all levels are faced with a number of parameters in their decision making process and have available to them the most meager data. It is unreasonable to develop more sophisticated analytical technique for the establishment of Paretian optimal solutions or generalized second-best solutions to manpower programs, when we are at a loss in developing minimally satisfactory procedures.

After reviewing existing planning and programming, the paper suggests a type of programming that would be useful to the decision-maker and of benefit, generally, in providing a stepping stone for more sophisticated levels of analysis and planning in the future.

1 - The current manpower planning system

The 1960's could be described in the United States as the Manpower period. The impetus from the programmatic side came from the recession of the late 1950's and early '60's, which was attributed to the increase in automation as well as

---

* Proceedings of a North American Conference May 14th & 15th, 1969 — Title, *Cost Benefit Analysis of Manpower Policies*, Editors G.G. Somers and W.D. Wood (Industrial Relations Center, Queen's University, Kingston, Ontario, 1969).

structural changes within society. It focused attention on pockets of unemployment geographically spread throughout the country and this gave rise to the first of the area redevelopment programs. Subsequent developments fostered programs dealing with displacement due to international trade, permanent shifts in demand, alterations in production functions and problems of special population subsets. All these programs emphasized investing in human beings and have been supply-oriented.

Research in theoretical and operational manpower was advancing at the same time. The developments in the United States are characterized by the works of Becker, Mincer, Weisbrod and a number of economists who blended capital theory with analysis of human problems. While the intellectual roots of the analysis lay in the capital theory, operational activities developed via cost benefit analysis and program planning budgeting systems. The drive in the United States eminated from the defense establishment and under the auspices and encouragement of Secretary of Defense, Robert McNamara, soon spread out from the areas such as military procurement to military analysis and from there to other levels of manpower analysis. One stumbling block to the infusion of the analytical systems was the inability to gain acceptance in the public sector's personnel system. This is essential in realising the obstacles in modernizing and making sophisticated the primitive employment systems.

To understand both the current planning system and the inability to establish manpower planning, we briefly analyze the various centers of decision making and the planning systems that revolve about them.

Substantially, the funds for all manpower programs come either completely or dominantly from the federal government. The historical accretion of the program set is important in understanding the ability to establish a comprehensive planning system. The programs derive from specific Congressional Acts and relate to programmatic additions historically developed. Congressmen annually put into effect specific programs that carry with them sizable blocks of funds. These specific Acts are the source of the program goals but leave the interpretation of these goals, that is the actual mission program, to the permanent bureaucracy. Neither the Congress nor the Bureau of the Budget has attempted to balance the allocation of funds to achieve any type of correspondence in the productivities of these programs. Line item budget-making by Congress is clearly one of the most rigid constraints for any type of manpower planning at the state and local level.

The bureaucratic procedure provides the next level of planning. For example, during the past decade manpower programs have been given for either planning or operational review or funding purposes to the Office of Economic Opportunity, Department of Labor; the Department of Health, Education and Welfare; the Department of Defense; the Department of Housing and Urban Development; the Veterans Administration and, more recently, the Department of Transportation. The federal departments fight against outside interference with programs over which each has legislative authorization and control. A corollary is that interdepartmental programs are likely to fail because the integration of independent operations and allocation of resources requires strong leadership.

To illustrate the problem of missing authority, I shall employ Job Corps experience. The Job Corps was originally designed as an experimental program under the Office of Economic Opportunity to deal with the younger disadvantaged person. Job Corps Centers were divided into rural or Conservation Centers whose input was individuals with low objective test scores, and Urban Centers, which were larger units and with a slightly more able group as measured by the same test. In Job Corps planning, the guidelines are relatively broad, and the broadness became a subject for continuing concern. The object of the program was to give training so that individuals could get jobs, and an obvious criterion was the rate of successful placement in jobs. This could be restricted to successful placement in the jobs for which the young people were trained. If the training was unrelated to the jobs, then the programmatic structure of Job Corps might be altered.

Altering attitudes is an alternative to the job activity as a goal. The argument can be made that in dealing with the disadvantages we face an inappropriate decision making process which, by its own logic, is irrational for the job market. Thus, the young men are so interested in immediate utility gratification that they aren't concerned about training, reliability, regularity or getting on with their co-workers. Output on this sort of scale becomes very difficult to determine. The result of this ambiguous mission was that crude estimates were taken of individuals who completed more than one month; who continued and passed the general education sequence; and lastly, who stayed and completed some training program and, independent of that, people who were positive terminations, i.e. entering the military, going on to other schools or getting a job, without respect to the content of the job.

The measurement of change in attitude is difficult in the short run. Certainly, the effect which is highly desired is that the attitude should be permanently altered. No reasonable surrogate for this is operationally available, and the result is that time spent in the program becomes the assigned measure of success. As a consequence, when poor job placement is uncovered, the defense is that emphasis was not upon job placement, but on changing attitudes and behaviour. In the City of Baltimore, the first experimental inner-city Job Corps Center in one year spent $3.1 on about twenty graduates, and not all of these got jobs. The contractors running the Center indicated that output was not their interest as they were carrying out an experimental operation. When asked what hypothesis they were testing in the experiment, they indicated that there was no formal hypothesis or, in fact, any informal hypothesis. There was no data system and they abjured talk about a controlled experimental situation because the problem of the unemployed youth of the City of Baltimore was intense and of immediate concern. I told the contractor that there was a conflict and, as a consequence, they had to choose either one or the other of two alternatives; but once they chose one, they would be evaluated on that basis. Evaluation is nullified if program goals are not carefully articulated.

Two years ago, the federal government formed the CAMPS System (Cooperative Area Manpower Planning System) as a device to rationalize the crazy quilt of programs required, to develop plans and to coordinate the various program elements coming from the Department of Labor and all federal agencies providing funds for the States. In addition to that comprehensive plan, there are other planning processes going on simultaneously; for example, vocational education for Health Education and Welfare and land use plans for the Department of Housing and Urban Development. As a consequence, we now have a proliferation of planning mechanisms *within* each State. Still absent is an overall comprehensive plan within a state that would encompass all the programs, and all the departments and agencies dealing with a prescribed program goal. This system was imposed by one level of government upon another and suffers from that sort of patronage.

Within the last six months, a program for evaluation has been developed. This requires quarterly evaluation, but the states are trying to move toward a six-monthly evaluation of the programs. What is meant by evaluation? The evaluation really consists of listing the various programs that are going on in the State without establishing any projected target to allow the development of evaluation mechanisms. We turn now to the analysis of the planning and evaluation programs.

2 – Criticisms of the current system

Criticisms of the current manpower planning and evaluation systems fall in two broad categories; theoretical and operational. The primary difficulty in planning and evaluation is the absence of a clearly defined objective function. In the first section it was shown that the objective function was set by the legislature and then developed at the operation level within departments.

Planning *should* effect decisions which allocate resources in the manpower area or alter the production process for accomplishing specific objectives. Evaluation is then part of a servomechanism indicating whether one is meeting the expected levels, productivity or output of the system. If the objectives are not being met the servomechanism should indicate, to a decision-maker or an automatic system, new instructions to make the system abide by the initial rule set. The current planning and evaluation system does not approximate either of these idealized functions. The system has no objective function. That is to say, it lacks a defined function permitting evaluation. The vagueness of missions precludes the establishment of a learning process to determine future goals or processes.

The constraints upon planning forbid application of any planning tools, such as an equimarginal principle. The level of expenditure is determined by a process totally separate from the manpower planning mechanism. There appears to be no linkage between the determination of need and the Congress or Bureau of the Budget at the national level, or state legislative mechanisms at the local level.

The mission of the Departments is set. There appears to be no feed-back from the surveys made by local planning organizations to mission control at a higher level. Programming decisions are a product of two separate systems. Agencies such as those dealing with welfare or education or rehabilitative services prepare their allocations to various geographical locations or parts of their own program according to rules which are established outside of the planning mechanism. In fact, the various administrative units do not care to report their own decisions or how their decisions are made to a central manpower planning body. Most of these allocations are mandated by state legislatures employing their own political process of decision-making, or by specific agencies according to their own rules. Hence, if the goal of planning is to achieve more efficient utilization of resources in order to optimise progress towards some pre-set goal, then planning as currently constituted is inadequately defined.

From the point of view of state and local government where the programs are brought ultimately into operation, there are a number of procedural problems which limit the effectiveness of the current state of manpower planning.

A – Exclusivity:

The planning and evaluation process designed by the federal government, compartmentalizes activities and makes it impossible to plan for the total use of resources in the manpower area. Also, it is not possible to examine the nature of the gross demand for services (public or private) and the varying needs of target populations. Two points may illustrate the difficulties. A recent decision by the administration has placed the major responsibility for dealing with manpower problems and the disadvantaged on the private sector. To accomplish their ends they have established the National Alliance for Business and what is commonly referred to as the "NAB–Jobs" Program. This program is set up within metropolitan areas and is intended to be the major thrust of administration manpower policy. However, planning for it and evaluating its effectiveness is totally outside the area of the state and local government planning system. We in state government are uncertain as to what the target population is, what resources will be used in meeting the aims of the NAB's Job Program, and what is the effectiveness of their activities. Our attempts have been only partially successful in trying to establish some relationship with this organization, but it is not feasible to have two separate planning and operating systems on the manpower field where one of them is supposed to be responsible for overall planning.

A second problem arises from the inability of the federal government to bring together all of the resources that are necessary to make appropriate manpower policy and plans. A particular problem lies in the transportation field. Our concern, and one which is shared by states across the country and by local groups, is the inability to move individuals from their homes to the locations of day care facilities, training, education services or employment. One of the largest stumbling blocks in the Work Incentive Program (WIN) is the difficulty of providing adequate transport to take children to day care centers. This failing will become even more pronounced if the program for welfare reform is passed by the U.S. Congress.

B – Resources available for planning:

There has been growing interest in planning but no corresponding increase in the amount of resources available for planning. A result of the failure to keep the resource level up to the requirement level is inevitably a short fall on requirements as viewed by the planners. The final planning document becomes less and less an instrument for decision making. Recently, the federal government put additional funds in the hands of states. It is now discussing placing responsibility in the hands of mayors of cities in order to reduce the problem.

The difficulty is that there is also an increase in the formalism of plans. It appears that the United States may be at a turning point in making more realistic the demands upon planners, and, at the same time, considering the funding for planning. There is obviously a marginal problem in the amount of resources that should be made available to be offset against the benefits that would be gained by increases in sophistication.

A difficult problem is the lack of clarity on data requirements for planning purposes and on the desired accuracy of this data. There appear to be discrepancies between the data gatherers' knowledge, their technical competence in the information processing system, the people who are establishing the rules and guidelines for planning and, lastly, the plan users. The failure to establish appropriate resources for planning emerges in the question of the appropriate timing of the plans.

C — Timing of the planning process:

The overall planning system is composed of separate plans each required by a separate funding authority. The Department of Employment Security has the labor market clearing function and its own plan of service, as does the Department of Vocational Rehabilitation, the Department of Social Services, etc. The planning cycles of these agencies are not coordinated and are not consistent one with another or with the planning mechanism of State Government. Thus, if consideration was given to linking plans, it would be possible to achieve a more efficient utilization of staff for planning among departments. The development of one planning format would allow the component subplans to link to an overall manpower plan in the state.

A deeper failure of the timing is that it is out of phase with the federal budget cycle, as well as the state planning budget cycles. The plan of service for a given fiscal year is between fourteen to twenty months behind the planning for the federal budget. If the first part of manpower plans* is to determine needs, then this should be an input into the federal budgetary process geared to Congressional decision making. There is no indication that even on a lagged system there is an attempt to link state plans to any national plan. In fact, it has even been asserted that the state plans are strictly state documents and not for national purposes. In that event then, the State CAMPS Planning, or manpower planning cycle, should be based upon the legislative needs of state governments, but this is not the case. Some states have biennial legislatures and a planning and budgeting process linked to the biennial calendar, while other States, such as my own, have an annual budget process. The federal calendar used is still inappropriate.

The result is that when these three procedural problems are added, the planning process is truncated.

D — The absence of the payoff:

At the state and local levels there is no clear indication that the effort put into planning leads to any tangible benefit.

* The Mandated Plan is in two parts. Part A is to determine needs and B to allocate appropriations.

The utilization of resources in planning, while justifiable on almost any grounds, becomes difficult to justify when it is simply an intrusion on operations and there is no benefit from the planning process. The failure of local governments to put more money into planning for their own purposes or to supplement the expenditures on the part of the federal government are indications of the current level of organizational sophistication in planning. We are asking too much from planning and giving back little in return. The first aim in developing planning should be education and, to this end, as we have experienced in tackling the problem of the disadvantaged, there must be clearly defined payoffs to those who are forced into the system. We now turn to the discussion of a planning system.

3 – A simple planning system

Any planning operation for manpower, or any other purpose, should have three main characteristics. It should state explicitly the goals of the plan; second, it should establish trade-off positions between goals – that is to say, in most cases, the goal will not be so obvious as to preclude alternatives. Thus, the decision-maker must be able to choose between these alternatives. Having established the choices in both quantitative and qualitative terms through a trade-off, the plan should provide a method of evaluating success in achieving these goals. The scheme outlined here has these characteristics. It also suggests the procedures necessary for the establishment of an acceptable manpower planning system.

Each agency should define carefully populations with which it is concerned. Frequently, we speak of a certain target population and design programs for it. In the United States, this has been interpreted in the terms of the "poor" or "disadvantaged". On the other hand, there are some programs that are for the aging, the veteran or the handicapped. "Poor", "aging," "handicapped" are words of imperfect descriptive meaning. These descriptions treat large blocks of people as homogeneous. The poor are not homogeneous. They range from people who are poor because of inherited or environmental factors, to poor in an income sense because of a possibly random series of events affecting their current income. The social policies which deal with these individuals must cater for their individuality. Thus, the first mission is for each agency and program planning unit to divide its target population into more clearly defined groups. The cells should be clearly defined and as homogeneous internally as possible, although there may be explicit exceptions for some people. One good way of defining the groups is in terms of the unit costs of completing specific activities for each group. Activities are defined as training, education, medical care, job placement, job development, job retention. All of the activities with which we are concerned in the manpower or social services field have unit costs for achieving a desired level of activity dependent upon the target population. Therefore, the unit costs of discharging a defined responsibility for that population should be established.

The analysis should go one step further and establish, mathematically, the expected cost and return for each program and each group. We know that in dealing with the disadvantaged, problems fall into two program groups. People of low literacy may also have a history of criminal offenses. The time taken to complete a given program may be significantly longer for these people than for those with a higher education. The probability of achieving some defined level of activity varies directly with the quality of the input to the program. The program's basis or cost should then reflect the true prospects of completion. Thus, if the cost is $100 with a probability of 0.1 of completing the program, then the expected cost per unit of the population would be $1000.

Having established basic costs for each population, the next step would be to define a series of "production" sets relating to department's programs and individual target groups. For example, each department could indicate the output for a dollar expenditure on each population for each program. Thus, from the initial cost estimates, one could compare pay-offs to each program relating to a specific population. This process would establish a production frontier relating the level of productivity to expenditures. Simultaneously, one would establish any minimal constraints on programs or populations. The analogue is the returns to scale in the normal production process. Frequently, in the area of manpower planning, we are faced with absence of any criteria of the critical mass that may be required for a specific program. I suggest that it is essential to establish whether there is some critical mass for programs. This would give some boundaries for the opportunity space.

This categorization by population and program would indicate to the principle decision-maker the possibilities in payoff terms of a dollar expenditure in each area. This would establish a means of assessing the size of the budget which would be allocated between target populations as well as programs. We could then face squarely the programmatic implications of scarce resources. A specific question is whether one should "cream" a population or not? Should the funds for training go into training the marginally disadvantaged who need only a small advance, or the hard core disadvantaged who need the most benefits? One could apply something approximating an equimarginal principle to dealing with populations, and various programs outputs. This principle would relate to a welfare function established by political means as well as by the judgement of the decision-maker. It is unreasonable to believe that we could either solve all the problems for one part of the population or do everything possible within one specific program or department. This underscores the notion that convexity conditions are certain to occur on the programmatic side and indicates that trade-off be made at the highest level of decision-making.

Once a decision has been made on the size of the budget and the allocation made explicit both in terms of programs and population, then each agency has allocated to it not only funds but a target level of output. The target level, in fact, goes back to the primary cost conditions that are established by the historic track record of the department. Therefore, on a regularized basis one can examine how the output of each specific department compares with the budgeted level of output. As a result of such a system for evaluation, one could alter the production process within a program or have a basis for re-allocating funds among programs.

This system is nothing more than the application of a program budget mechanism to the manpower area. The application of this in the manpower area is not so difficult to achieve, at least conceptually. Cost estimates, while not readily available in many of the program fields and by defined population, can be established from an appropriate data-based system. In establishing data systems, one should look for information which would emerge in any event from the types of data collected by civil servants. In addition, the system should be designed to be relatively man error free and simple. Basically, not much data is required. What is necessary is the provision of good quality data to satisfy management needs. Too frequently, the data we obtain from Social Services and other departments seem largely designed for some future fishing expedition by fellow researchers and not necessarily geared to the managerial problems faced by public and private decision makers.

An important task that needs to be accomplished if this program (or any planning system) is to work is missionary activity to the people in the manpower business. The stress should be on the usefulness of such a system at the operational level. The decision-maker at the state, local and even national level, will be able to define more clearly the output of a tax dollar. It must be accepted that the decision-maker needs this material because it gives him a better opportunity to assess payoffs to the community.

A problem emerges, at the operational level in the setting down of a production standard. While this production standard, I readily admit, is not easy to prepare, it is necessary for the establishment of performance criteria. The system offers greater choice for the decision-maker, as well as the operating professions.

The outstanding question is who should take decisions ... whether a social worker, for example, should decide that he should only deal with, say, two people or whether some level of management should, in fact, decide what his work-load should be. I believe that it is in this area that conflict will arise but it is the perogative of the chief decision-maker in consultation with the professional, to ultimately make the choice.

Conclusion

The scheme presented allows levels of government to define more clearly what they need to accomplish and the efficiency of their production system. Efficiency is an important criterion because it establishes what part of the population will be aided and what part will not be aided by any and all social plans. This is based on appropriate data systems. The amount of quantitative work required is not excessive, yet a number of conceptual questions are still open. The study of the various target populations, the definition of handicaps and the need to ascribe payoffs and costs are activities already under way within parts of the system, but these need development before we can have an adequate planning system. At the heart of this is the establishment of an appropriate data mechanism which will allow decision-makers to make choices at all levels. Faced with vast numbers of disadvantages and the need to create programs which will have some payoff in a relatively short period, it is essential that there should be a sharp policy thrust to research. If we did not have the imminent prospect of some grave dislocations, it would be easier to take the longer view. I think that we are now at a point where we must trade-off the long term goods against what are, essentially, the necessities of continuing the system.

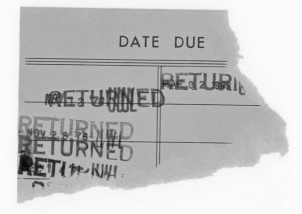